HISTORY OF OUR NATION
1865 to the Present

by
Wayne E. King
and
John L. Napp

AGS Publishing
Circle Pines, Minnesota 55014-1796
800-328-2560

About the Authors

Wayne E. King is the Academic Dean at the Baltimore School for the Arts. He received his Bachelor of Science and Master of Science degrees from The Johns Hopkins University. He has taught American History and social studies at all educational levels. Mr. King has served as a consultant to schools, museums, and federal agencies and has lectured at national and international conferences on the teaching of American history and culture.

John L. Napp taught history for 30 years in both public and private schools. He also taught other social studies subjects, including political science, economics, and geography. He has been recognized for his excellence in teaching.

Photo credits for this textbook can be found on page 485.

The publisher wishes to thank the following educators for their helpful comments during the review process for *History of Our Nation: 1865 to the Present*. Their assistance has been invaluable.

Nelson Acevedo, Alternative Schools and Programs, Jamaica, NY; **Mary Ames**, Central Hardin High School, Cecilia, KY; **Ellen August**, City of Angels, Los Angeles, CA; **Phyllis Berman**, Scott School Assistance Center, Toledo Public Schools, Toledo, OH; **Gayle Boroughs**, Oak Ridge High School, Oak Ridge, TN; **Dr. Virginia Bryg**, Reading Consultant, Omaha Public Schools, Omaha, NE; **Sherryl Duff-Conrad**, Penn Hills Senior High School, Pittsburgh, PA; **Judy Faught**, Bowling Green High School, Bowling Green, KY; **Gustav Mark Gedatus**, Consulting Editor, Minneapolis, MN; **Jan Gleason**, Omaha Public Schools, Omaha, NE; **Gay Nita Grimm**, Emporia High School, Emporia, KS; **Debora J. Hartzell**, Lead Teacher, Special Education, East DeKalb Campus, Stone Mountain, GA; **Michael P. Hawkins**, SED Teacher, Brandon High School, Brandon, FL; **Dawn Holley**, Social Studies Teacher, Camden High School, Camden, NJ; **Craig Hughes**, Middle School Teacher, Gregory Portland ISD, Portland, TX; **Janice Jones**, Curriculum Specialist/Special Education, Toledo Public Schools, Toledo, OH; **James John Kelly Jr.**, Social Studies Teacher, Camden High School, Camden, NJ; **Desi Kovacs**, Department Chair, Education Specialist, Canyon High School, Canyon Country, CA; **Gary Lussier**, Intern Assistant Principal, Barton Open Middle School, Minneapolis, MN; **Virginia Malling**, Oak Ridge High School, Oak Ridge, TN; **Laurence R. Manchester**, St. Paul School District, St. Paul, MN; **Anne Mandeville**, Santana High School, Rowland Heights, CA; **John Andrew O'Connor**, Accotink Academy, Springfield, VA; **Diane Odegard**, School District of Kansas City, Missouri, Kansas City, MO; **Debbie Persky**, City of Angels, Los Angeles, CA; **Lynn Pritchett**, Colquitt County High School, Moultrie, GA; **John W. Reiners**, Social Studies Teacher, Camden High School Camden, NJ; **Alice C. Richardson**, Central High School, Detroit, MI; **Christina Rivett**, Special Education Teacher, East Jackson High School, Coldwater, MI; **Dr. Clifford Watson**, Principal, Malcolm X Academy, Detroit, MI; **Cheryl Weglewski**, Wilmington High School, Wilmington, IL

Publisher's Project Staff

Vice President of Curriculum and Publisher: Sari Follansbee, Ed.D.; Director of Curriculum: Teri Mathews; Managing Editor: Patrick Keithahn; Assistant Editor: Stephanie Hasselmann; Development Assistant: Bev Johnson; Director of Creative Services: Nancy Condon; Senior Designer: Diane McCarty; Production Artist: Peggy Vlahos; Production Artist: Carol Bowling; Purchasing Agent: Mary Kaye Kuzma; Product Manager: Brian Holl

© 2005 AGS Publishing
4201 Woodland Road
Circle Pines, MN 55014-1796
800-328-2560 • www.agsnet.com

AGS Publishing is a trademark and trade name of American Guidance Service, Inc.

Printed in the United States of America
ISBN 0-7854-4014-3
Product Number 94050
A 0 9 8 7 6 5 4 3 2 1

Contents

Biography

History in Your Life

Document-Based Reading

Civics Connection

Focus on Economics

Technology Connection

Unit Skill Builder

Map Study

Appendixes

How to Use This Book: A Study Guide

Welcome to the study of *History of Our Nation: 1865 to the Present*. You may be asking yourself, "Why do I need to know about people, places, and events that happened a long time before I was even born?" When we study the past, we can have a better understanding of why some things happened the way they did. We can learn from the mistakes and the successes of the past.

This book is a story about the United States from Reconstruction through the 2004 election. As you read the units, chapters and lessons of this book, you will learn about the important people and events that shaped U.S. history.

Before you start to read this book, it is important that you understand how to use it. It is also important that you know how to be successful in this course. Information in this first section can help you achieve these things.

How to Study

These tips can help you study more effectively:

◆ Plan a regular time to study.

◆ Choose a desk or table in a quiet place where you will not be distracted. Find a spot that has good lighting.

◆ Gather all the books, pencils, paper, and other equipment you will need to complete your assignments.

◆ Decide on a goal. For example: "I will finish reading and taking notes on Chapter 1, Lesson 1, by 8:00."

◆ Take a five- to ten-minute break every hour to keep alert.

◆ If you start to feel sleepy, take a break and get some fresh air.

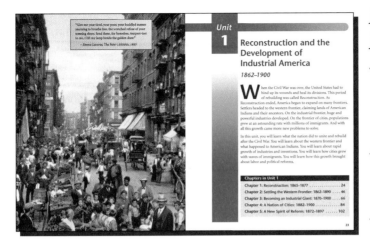

Before Beginning Each Unit

◆ Read the unit title and study the photograph. Do you recognize anything in the photo?

◆ Read the quotation. Try to connect the ideas to the picture.

◆ Read the opening paragraphs.

◆ Read the titles of the chapters in the unit.

◆ Read the Chapter Summary and Unit Summary to help you identify key ideas.

Before Beginning Each Chapter

◆ Read the chapter title and dates.

◆ Read the opening paragraphs.

◆ Study the Goals for Learning. The Chapter Review and tests will ask questions related to these goals.

◆ Study the timeline. Timelines help you see the order in which key events occurred. The timeline covers the years in the chapter title.

◆ Read the Chapter Summaries to help you identify key issues.

◆ Look at the Chapter Review. The questions cover the most important information in the chapter.

Note These Features

You can find complete listings of these features in this textbook's table of contents.

Biography
Highlights people who have made contributions to America

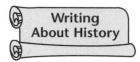

Writing About History
Provides history topics to write about in each chapter

History in Your Life
Relates history to the modern world

Focus on Economics
Shows the impact of economics in history

Civics Connection
Shows how civics relates to the study of history

Technology Connection
Highlights inventions at the time that made life better or easier

Document-Based Reading
Presents primary- and secondary-source documents related to each chapter

Then and Now
Compares and contrasts something existing now to how it existed in the past

Unit Skill Builder
Focuses on social studies skills

Before Beginning Each Lesson

Read the lesson title and restate it in the form of a question. For example, write: *How did Reconstruction begin?*

Look over the entire lesson, noting the following:

◆ bold words

◆ text organization

◆ photos

◆ maps

◆ graphs and charts

◆ Lesson Review questions

As You Read the Lesson

◆ Read the major headings.

◆ Read the subheads and paragraphs that follow.

◆ Study the maps, graphs, and charts.

◆ Before moving on to the next lesson, see if you understand the concepts you read. If you do not, reread the lesson. If you are still unsure, ask for help.

◆ Practice what you have learned by completing the Lesson Reviews.

Using the Bold Words

Bold type

Words seen for the first time will appear in bold type

Glossary

Words listed in this column are also found in the Glossary

Knowing the meaning of all the boxed words in the left column will help you understand what you read.

These words appear in **bold type** the first time they appear in the text and are often defined in the paragraph.

Voters took an **oath** to support the Union.

All of the words in the left column are also defined in the **Glossary**.

Oath (ōth) A pledge that promises loyalty to a government or other cause (p. 25)

Word Study Tips

◆ Start a vocabulary file with index cards to use for review.

◆ Write one term on the front of each card. Write the chapter number, lesson number, and definition on the back.

◆ You can use these cards as flash cards by yourself or with a study partner to test your knowledge.

Oath

Chapter 1, Lesson 1

A pledge that promises loyalty to a government or other cause

Taking Notes in Class

◆ Outline each lesson using the subheads as the main points.

◆ Always write the main ideas and supporting details.

◆ Keep your notes brief.

◆ Write down important information only.

◆ Use your own words.

◆ Do not be concerned about writing in complete sentences. Use phrases.

◆ Do not try to write everything the teacher says.

◆ Use the same method all the time. Then when you study for a test, you will know where to go to find the information you need to review.

◆ Review your notes to fill in possible gaps as soon as you can after class.

Using the Summaries

◆ Read each Chapter Summary to be sure you understand the chapter's main ideas.

◆ Review your notes and test yourself on vocabulary words and key ideas.

◆ Practice writing about some of the main events from the chapter.

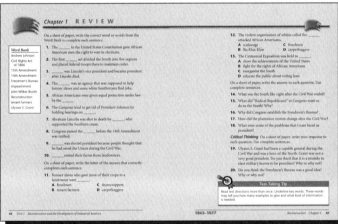

Using the Reviews

◆ Answer the questions in the Lesson Reviews.

◆ In the Chapter Reviews, answer each fill-in-the-blank, multiple choice, and short-answer question.

◆ Review the Test-Taking Tips.

Preparing for Tests

◆ Complete the Lesson Reviews and Chapter Reviews. Make up similar questions to practice what you have learned. You may want to do this with a classmate and share your questions.

◆ Review your answers to Lesson Reviews and Chapter Reviews.

◆ Reread the Chapter Summaries.

◆ Test yourself on vocabulary words and key ideas.

History of Our Nation: 1865 to the Present explores United States history from the start of Reconstruction through the 2004 presidential election. As you know, there are many important events that happened in the United States before 1865. This section includes a timeline that will help you better understand the early history of the United States. Take a moment to look at these pages. Notice the colors on the timeline. The different colors will help you keep track of the dates when events took place. Also notice the vocabulary boxes at the left side of each page. Important vocabulary words are boldfaced in the text and defined in the vocabulary boxes.

In this section, you will read about the first Americans and European explorers. You will also learn about the American colonists and how they fought for independence from Great Britain. The timeline will guide you through the writing of the Constitution and the creation of our democracy. As you continue, you will read about how the United States gained land and expanded west. At the end of this section, you will read how slavery and the Civil War divided the nation. After reading this section, you will be ready to begin your study of *History of Our Nation: 1865 to the Present*.

The First Americans

Culture

The values, attitudes, and customs of a group

Civilization

A high level of cultural development

Settlement

A place or region newly settled

20,000 B.C. — Hunters who crossed a land bridge from Siberia to North America may have been the earliest Americans. Scientists have learned about these ancient **cultures** from remains they have dug up.

4500 B.C. — **Civilization**, a high level of cultural development, began in the Mississippi River Valley. These people were among the first known to have used plants. Farming became central to their culture around A.D. 800. The Mississippians became the most advanced civilization in eastern North America.

1200 B.C. — The Olmec civilization settled in Mexico around this time. They carved enormous pillars and altars from jade and stone.

700 B.C. — The Adena people lived in the Ohio River Valley in the present-day United States. They built elaborate burial mounds in animal shapes. The Hopewell descended from the Adena and existed until A.D. 300. Their lifestyle influenced people in **settlements** from the Great Lakes to the South.

300 B.C. — The Hohokam began their civilization in what is now Arizona. They were farmers and also built irrigation systems to water crops as their civilization developed.

250 B.C. The Plains Indians began to develop villages. Until then, they had moved around from place to place. They did not farm but grew needed food, fished, and hunted.

200 B.C. The Mogollon built communities on high ground in the southwest area of the present-day United States. The Mogollon were skilled farmers and were the first southwestern people to make pottery.

100 B.C. The Anasazi civilization began. These people were called "Cliff Dwellers" because they built houses into cliffs. They grew corn and hunted. The Anasazi civilizations lasted until about A.D. 1300.

A.D. 250 The Mayan civilization in Central America developed arithmetic, astronomy, architecture, and an advanced form of writing.

A.D. 400 The Pacific Northwest civilizations developed. They depended on the sea for food and trade. The Tlingit, Haida, Tsimshian, Kwakiutl, Nootka, and Eskimo, or Inuit, are among the northwestern cultures.

A.D. 900 The Toltecs in the Mexican highlands developed a strong civilization. They worshiped the god Quetzacoatl, a great feathered serpent. Experts believe the Toltecs were taken over by **nomads** and went on to form the Aztec civilization. Nomads are people who move from place to place.

1200 The Aztecs had strong government and **military** forces. They built elaborate structures including their main city of Tenochitlán, which is now Mexico City. They also built roads, bridges, and **canals.**

The Incas started their **empire,** or kingdom, in the area now known as Peru, in South America. The Incas were lawmakers, builders, warriors, and astronomers.

1300 The Pueblo and Navajo civilizations developed in the southwest area of the present-day United States after the Anasazi civilizations declined.

The Anasazi built dwellings in cliffs.

Exploring the Americas

1477

For many years, Arab traders sold jewels, silks, and spices to Italian **merchants.** A merchant is a buyer and seller of goods. Soon, Europeans wanted to find their own way to the Far East.

Marco Polo **published,** or printed, a book describing the Far East. The book excited the people of Europe and encouraged exploration.

1492

Christopher Columbus made his first **voyage** in search of the Far East. Queen Isabella of Spain paid for the voyage. She gave Columbus three ships, the Niña, the Pinta, and the Santa María for his voyage. Columbus did not know there was land between the **continents** of Europe and Asia. The land he explored is now called the West Indies.

1497

John Cabot explored North America. He claimed much of northeastern North America for England.

1499

Amerigo Vespucci of Italy made his first of many voyages to South America. He was the first to describe what he had found as new land. Later, the continent he explored was named "America" after him.

1513

Juan Ponce de León of Spain searched for gold and the Fountain of Youth. He named the land he explored "Florida."

Spanish explorer Vasco Núñez de Balboa led a voyage in search of gold and silver. He and his crew were the first Europeans to see the Pacific Ocean from North America.

Queen Isabella of Spain agreed to pay for Columbus's voyage. He explained his plan to Isabella and her Royal Court before she agreed.

Conquer

A gain something by force; defeat

Slavery

Forcing a person or group to work without pay or rights

Expedition

A journey made by a person or group for a certain purpose

Colony

A group of people living in a new area under rule of their native land

Charter

A written agreement granting power in the name of a state or country

Religious

Relating to a belief in a higher being

Political

Relating to government or the way it runs

1519 — Ferdinand Magellan from Portugal led a voyage around the world. He sailed around the tip of South America and found the water route around the New World. Magellan was killed in the Philippines, and only one of his five ships completed the trip. However, Magellan's voyage proved that the Earth is round.

1521 — Spanish explorer Hernando Cortés **conquered** the Aztecs.

1524 — Giovanni da Verrazano of France searched for the Northwest Passage, a northern water route to Asia. He later reached what is now North Carolina and Newfoundland.

1533 — Francisco Pizzaro conquered, or defeated, the Incas and forced them into **slavery.**

1534 — Jacques Cartier also searched for the Northwest Passage. He explored the St. Lawrence River in Canada for the French.

1577 — Sir Frances Drake of England led the second **expedition,** or journey, around the world. The voyage was completed in 1580.

1584 — Sir Walter Raleigh of England led the first of three expeditions to the New World. Under Raleigh, John White formed a **colony** in Roanoke, North Carolina. A colony is a group of people living in a new area under rule of their native land. White left for England in 1587 to get more supplies. When he returned in 1590, the colony had disappeared.

Early 1600s — Samuel de Champlain started the first French colony on the St. Lawrence River. The settlement was called Quebec.

1606 — King James I of England granted **charters** for land in the New World. The people who went to live in these faraway lands wanted **religious** and **political** freedom.

1607 — The Virginia Company settled a colony in Jamestown, Virginia. Captain John Smith was the first leader of the new colony.

Colonial Times

General assembly
A group that makes laws for a larger group

Governor
A person chosen to lead a group of people within a given area, such as a colony or a state

Representative
A person who is given the power to act for others; a government with officials elected by the people

Majority
A number greater than half of the total

Equality
Having the same rights as others

1619 — The Virginia Company gave Jamestown settlers permission to form a **general assembly.** This group was known as the House of Burgesses. It met with the **governor,** Lord Delaware, to make laws for the colony. Settlers also chose their own **representatives** to serve in the House of Burgesses.

1620 — After leaving England for religious reasons, the Pilgrims reached the shore of what is now Cape Cod. The group elected John Carver as its first leader. William Bradford led the Pilgrims for 30 years after Carver died. The Pilgrims also wrote the Mayflower Compact. It stated that they agreed to a democratic government and to obey laws created by the majority. They later formed a settlement at Plymouth.

1630 — The Puritans landed in Boston and formed the Massachusetts Bay Colony. John Winthrop became governor of the new settlement. Within a few years, nearly 10,000 people came to live in the colony.

1634 — Lord Calvert established a colony in what is now St. Mary's City, Maryland, on the shores of the Chesapeake Bay. Calvert allowed religious freedom in this new colony.

1636 — Roger Williams settled Providence, Rhode Island.

Thomas Hooker started a settlement in Connecticut.

1649 — The Toleration Act established an **equality** of rights for people of all religions.

1663 — English nobles, under a charter from King Charles II, settled Carolina. The colony was divided into North Carolina and South Carolina in 1729.

1664 — The English took over the Dutch colony of New Netherland. They renamed it New York in honor of the Duke of York.

1679 — New Hampshire, which had been part of Massachusetts, was sold to the king of England. The king made it a royal colony. He selected the governor, and there was no elected government.

1681 — William Penn was granted a charter to create a colony between New York and Maryland. He called this colony Pennsylvania.

Enforce

To make sure something is done according to a law; to see that laws are obeyed

Frontier

A region with little population

Alliance

An agreement that joins groups of people or countries together

Stronghold

A place, such as a military base, that is well protected from attack

Treaty

An agreement to end fighting

George Washington

1700s	Trading between the West Indies, Africa, and New England formed what is known as triangular trade. Africans and American Indians suffered from this trading practice.
	Great Britain began **enforcing** the Navigation Acts that were passed in 1660 and 1663. They tried to to direct trade between the colonies and other countries. Most American merchants paid little attention to these laws.
1702	The regions of East Jersey and West Jersey united into the colony of New Jersey.
1704	The area of Pennsylvania called the "Three Lower Counties" became the colony of Delaware.
1733	James Oglethorpe settled a colony in what is now Savannah, Georgia. This land was granted by King George. It was a place where the poor and unfortunate could settle after being released from prison.
	The 13 original colonies had been settled. The society in these colonies was made up of a wealthy class, a middle class, and a lower class. The colonies included three regions—the northern or New England colonies, the southern colonies, and the middle colonies.
	Settlers were moving westward, developing the **frontier.**
1749	Problems developed between Great Britain and France over land claims in the Ohio Valley.
1754	George Washington was sent to the Ohio Valley to drive the French away from Fort Duquesne. Shots were fired and Washington was forced to retreat.
1755	This fighting became known as the French and Indian War. It is also sometimes called the Seven Years' War. The American Indians and the French formed an **alliance** and defeated General Braddock's army at Fort Duquesne.
1758	King George appointed William Pitt as prime minister and secretary of state of Great Britain. Pitt sent troops to the colonies and formed an army of 50,000.
	The British captured Fort Duquesne. They captured the **stronghold** of Quebec in 1759.
1760	France surrendered to Great Britain to end the French and Indian War.
1763	Great Britain and France signed the **Treaty** of Paris. Great Britain gained the most land from this agreement.

The American Revolution

Legal

Having to do with the law

Repeal

To remove something, especially a law

Boycott

To refuse to have dealings with a person, country, or group

Congress

The body of government that makes laws; the House of Representatives and the Senate

Convention

A formal meeting called for a special purpose

Delegate

A person elected to serve in government; a representative of a group

Minutemen

A group of men trained to be soldiers and who agreed to gather at a minute's notice

Revolution

The act of overthrowing and replacing a government

Interfere

To enter into or take part in other people's business

Commander

A person who controls an army or some other group

1763 King George of England signed the Proclamation of 1763. Settlers were to leave the Ohio Valley. The king said there could be no new settlements west of the Appalachians.

1764 The British Parliament agreed that it had the right to tax the colonies in exchange for protection against all enemies. The colonists disagreed with this policy.

1765 The British passed the Stamp Act. This allowed the British government to tax all **legal** business papers and other items used in America. The colonists protested the Stamp Act. Parliament **repealed** the tax in 1766.

1767 The British passed the Townshend Acts, which reduced the colonists' freedom to govern themselves. The acts included new taxes on many items important to the colonists, including glass, paper, and tea. The colonists agreed to **boycott** British goods.

1770 A crowd of colonists threw stones and snowballs at a group of British soldiers. The soldiers shot into the crowd, killing and wounding several colonists. Crispus Attucks, an African, was the first person killed. This event was called the Boston Massacre.

1773 A group of colonists dressed as Mohawks threw 90,000 pounds of tea into Boston Harbor. This became known as the Boston Tea Party. The colonists made it clear that they would not accept a tax imposed without their consent.

1774 The Intolerable Acts allowed Great Britain to close the port of Boston to all trade. The British also banned all town meetings and began housing troops in people's homes.

The first Continental **Congress** met at a **convention** in Philadelphia. The **delegates** wrote the Declaration of Rights. The Congress agreed to meet in 1775 if Great Britain rejected the declaration.

1775 On April 18, the British fought a small group of American **minutemen** at Lexington and Concord. This battle would eventually lead to the **Revolutionary** War.

On May 10, the Second Continental Congress met in Philadelphia. John Hancock was chosen as its president. Congress decided that it could declare war and that it would not **interfere** in the private matters of the colonies. Congress chose George Washington as **commander** in chief of the American army.

Invade

To attack or take over something

Loyalist

An American who supported the king of Great Britain

Independence

The ability to take care of oneself

Isolate

To set apart from others

Traitor

Someone who turns against his or her own country

1775

■ On June 17, British warships in Boston Harbor attacked Breed's Hill and Bunker Hill. The British won this battle, known as the Battle of Bunker Hill. The next spring, American victories forced the British to leave Boston to the Americans. Congress was afraid the British would **invade** New York from the north.

■ American General Richard Montgomery captured Montreal in Canada. Then he led his troops to Quebec. The British defeated the Americans, and General Montgomery was killed.

1776

■ In February, Americans defeated British **loyalists** at Moore's Creek, North Carolina.

■ Thomas Jefferson wrote the Declaration of **Independence** and presented it to Congress. On July 4, 1776, the 13 colonies considered themselves to be free states.

■ Also in July, the British drove the American army from New York.

■ In December, General Washington guided his troops across the Delaware River. They defeated British soldiers in a surprise attack on Trenton, New Jersey.

1777

■ British General Howe planned an attack to **isolate** New England and defeat the Americans all at once. The plan failed, and the Americans defeated the British at Saratoga. France then came to help the United States.

1779

■ Benedict Arnold was found to be a **traitor.** He had turned against America and helped the British.

1781

■ After being pushed back by the Americans, British general Lord Cornwallis surrendered on October 19. The Americans had won their independence.

Conditions were difficult for the American army at Valley Forge.

Creating a New Government

Boundary

A real or imaginary marker that shows what land a person owns or an outline of a country; a line that sets a limit

Pioneer

One of the first to settle in a territory

Rebellion

A group fighting another group that is in power; an uprising against authority

Compromise

A settlement of differences in which each side gives up some of its demands

Federal government

A government that is shared between central and state governments

Executive

The branch of government that works to enforce laws

Legislative

The branch of government that makes laws

Judicial

The branch of government that interprets laws

Interpret

To explain or tell the meaning of something

1781 ■ The states adopted the Articles of Confederation. The articles set up a government with limited power over each state.

1783 ■ Great Britain signed the Treaty of Paris. The treaty established new **boundaries** for the United States—Canada on the north, the Mississippi River on the west, and Florida on the south. Great Britain also was forced to return Florida to Spain.

1784 ■ By this time, many **pioneers** were settling in western lands. Thomas Jefferson developed a plan for a short-term government of this area.

1786 ■ The government under the Articles of Confederation was out of control. Delegates met in Annapolis, Maryland, to work out some of the problems of the Articles of Confederation. The convention was a failure because only five states sent delegates.

■ Daniel Shays led a **rebellion** to protest low farm prices and high state taxes. The rebellion, called Shays's Rebellion, lasted for several months.

1787 ■ Delegates met at the Constitutional Convention in Philadelphia to create a plan for a stronger central government. George Washington was chosen to lead the convention.

■ On July 16, the delegates agreed to the "Great **Compromise**." In the new government, the Senate would have two representatives from each state, no matter the size of the states. The number of members of the House of Representatives would be based on the population of each state.

■ The Three-Fifths Compromise stated that three out of every five slaves would be counted for population and taxes in the South.

■ Congress passed the Northwest Ordinance. The area east of the Mississippi River and north of the Ohio River would become three to five new states as soon as the population became large enough.

■ Delegates signed the Constitution on September 17. The Constitution set up three branches of the **federal government** —the **executive, legislative,** and **judicial.** In this new government, the legislative branch would make laws. The executive branch would enforce laws, and the judicial branch would **interpret** laws.

Supreme
To the highest degree

Ratify
To approve something

Cabinet
A group of advisers to the president

Permanent
Lasting a long time or forever

Appoint
To name or choose a person to do something

Financial
Having to do with money

Organize
To put together in some kind of order

Political party
A group that represents a certain political belief

Amendment
A change

1788
■ The Constitution became the **supreme** law of the land on June 21. At this time, 9 of the 13 states had **ratified** the Constitution.

1789
■ George Washington was elected the first president of the United States. John Adams was elected vice president.

■ Congress created four **Cabinet** departments that became a **permanent** part of the United States government. President Washington **appointed** Alexander Hamilton, Thomas Jefferson, Henry Knox, and Edmund Randolph as his advisers.

■ Alexander Hamilton created a **financial** plan to get the country out of debt. He **organized** the first Bank of the United States. He also helped to create the first mint, or place to coin money.

■ Hamilton's financial plan helped form **political parties.** Those who supported his plan formed the Federalist party. The Democratic-Republican party thought states should have more power to run their own day-to-day business.

1791
■ Congress added the Bill of Rights to the Constitution. These first 10 **amendments** protect individual rights.

The delegates signed the Constitution in 1787. George Washington, leader of the convention, is standing by the flags.

The Government's Progress

Neutral
Not siding with any particular person or group

Candidate
A person who has been selected to run for a political office

Alien
Someone who lives in one country but is a citizen of another

Immigrant
A person who comes to live in a new country

Resolution
An expression of opinion or intent voted on by a group

Electoral college
A group of people chosen to elect the president and vice president

Negotiate
To work out a deal

Territory
Land

Resource
A thing of value, often found in nature, that can be used to do or make something

1793 ■ France declared war against Great Britain. France asked the United States to help fight the war, but President Washington kept the country **neutral.**

1797 ■ John Adams became the second president of the United States. The **candidate** who ran against Adams was Thomas Jefferson.

■ Several countries were at war with France. France seized American ships carrying supplies to the British. President Adams wanted to avoid war, so he tried to work out a deal with France. France's agents, called X, Y, and Z, refused unless they were paid. This became known as the XYZ Affair.

1798 ■ Congress passed the **Alien** and Sedition acts. The Alien Act stated that **immigrants** must live in the United States for 14 years before becoming citizens. The Sedition Act made it a crime to speak out, write about, or print articles against the government.

1799 ■ Thomas Jefferson and James Madison wrote the Kentucky and Virginia **resolutions.** These resolutions stated that the Alien and Sedition acts did not follow the Constitution.

1800 ■ The **electoral college** vote resulted in a tie between Thomas Jefferson and Aaron Burr. The House of Representatives decided to make Jefferson president and Burr vice president.

1803 ■ After much **negotiation,** the United States purchased the Louisiana **Territory** from France for $15 million. This gave the United States access to New Orleans and doubled the size of the country. The Louisiana Purchase cost the United States about four cents per acre of land. The United States gained valuable **resources** in this fertile land.

1804

Congress passed the 12th Amendment. This change would prevent a tie in a presidential election from happening as it had in 1800. The amendment stated that **electors** must vote separately for a president and a vice president.

President Jefferson sent Meriwether Lewis and William Clark to explore the Louisiana Territory. They explored from St. Louis to the Pacific Ocean in Oregon Country.

1805

Zebulon Pike explored the northern area of the Louisiana Purchase and discovered the source of the Mississippi River. In 1806, Pike led an expedition to the Southwest.

1807

Congress passed the Embargo Act on December 22. Under this act, no American ships could trade with foreign nations. President Jefferson tried to show the world that war was not always necessary. American trade suffered because of the Embargo Act. Jefferson repealed the act in 1809.

Sacajawea with Lewis and Clark

The War of 1812

Policy

A set of rules or an action plan of a person or group

Conflict

A fight, battle, or war

1809 ■ James Madison became the fourth president of the United States.

1810 ■ President Madison began a new trade **policy** with France and Great Britain. The policy said if either country stopped its trade restrictions against the United States, America would refuse to trade with the other country.

■ The population of the United States reached seven million. Industry was rapidly developing in the North. In the South, states were producing valuable cash crops. Slavery also was increasing.

1811 ■ The 12th Congress met. Many members wanted to settle the American Indian **conflict** and wanted freedom on the seas. These Congress members were called "War Hawks."

■ The British continued to seize American ships. Two War Hawks, Henry Clay and John C. Calhoun, tried to persuade the public that war with Britain was necessary.

■ The United States military was not prepared for war. Even so, the War Hawks thought British-owned Canada was a good target and could be easily defeated.

1812 ■ The United States Congress declared war on Britain on June 19. Congress was unaware that Britain had decided to reopen trade with the United States. This war became known as the War of 1812.

■ President Madison was re-elected to a second term with help from the War Hawks.

■ The war turned out to be more difficult than the Americans had thought. Three attempts to invade Canada failed.

The American warship Constitution *defeated the British warship* Guerrière *in 1812. After this battle,* Constitution *was nicknamed "Old Ironsides."*

Anthem *A song or hymn of praise or gladness*	

1813
- Americans won battles at Lake Erie and the Thames. American Indian leader Tecumseh was killed. Tecumseh's death put an end to the cooperation between the American Indians and the British.

1814
- Americans won the battle at Horseshoe Bend. After their defeat American Indians were forced to sign a treaty. The treaty opened up Georgia and present-day Alabama to American settlers.

- The American army held off the British as they invaded New York.

- The British attacked Washington, D.C. They burned the Capitol and the White House before moving on to attack Baltimore, Maryland.

- Francis Scott Key, a Washington lawyer, was captured and held on a British ship in Baltimore's harbor. From the ship, he watched the fighting at Fort McHenry. Key wrote a poem called "The Star-Spangled Banner," which later became the American national **anthem.** An anthem is a song or hymn of praise or gladness.

- In December, the Americans and the British signed the Treaty of Ghent to end the war. However, the news had not reached New Orleans, and one final battle was fought in 1815. The United States benefited from the war because it won the respect of other countries.

The British attacked Washington, D.C., in 1814. They burned the capitol building and the White House.

The Country Expands West and Industry Grows

1817 ▪ President Monroe took office. His election finished the Federalists as a political party.

1818 ▪ The Cumberland Road leading from Maryland to Virginia was completed. This route allowed settlers to travel west.

1819 ▪ The Adams-Onís Treaty gave Florida to the United States. The United States gave up Spanish Texas.

▪ Slavery became an issue when Missouri tried to enter the Union as a **slave state.** This would have upset the balance of **free states** and slave states in Congress. People in the North had different views about slavery than did people in the South. The antislavery **movement** concerned southern **plantation** owners who used slave labor to complete work.

1820 ▪ The population of the United States increased to 10 million. By this time, the country also had gained nine new states. Much of the population increase was on the frontier.

▪ The Missouri Compromise attempted to solve the slavery problem. It allowed Maine to enter the Union as a free state and Missouri as a slave state. The compromise also said that no new state north of 36 degrees 30 minutes north latitude in the Louisiana Territory could allow slavery.

▪ With the help of the cotton gin, cotton production in the South increased to 400,000 bales per year. Cotton became known as "King Cotton," or white gold. Before the cotton gin was invented, cotton was not **profitable** because of the labor involved to remove the seeds.

▪ President Monroe was re-elected. His two terms as president were known as the "Era of Good Feelings."

Cotton plantations such as this one thrived in the South.

Execute

To put to death

Revolt

A rebellion

Doctrine

A statement of a certain government policy

Western Hemisphere

The land and oceans around North and South America

Capable

Having the ability for a task

Tariff

A tax on goods leaving or entering a place

Campaign

A group of activities connected to getting elected to office

Spoils system

The practice of giving government jobs to loyal supporters

Mass-produce

To make great amounts of a product very fast

Melting pot

A nation where several groups of people belonging to different races or cultures live together

---

1822
■ Denmark Vesey, a freed African, and others were **executed** in South Carolina for planning a slave **revolt.**

1823
■ The Monroe **Doctrine** stated that any attempt by a European power to extend its influence in any part of the **Western Hemisphere** would be considered a threat to the peace and safety of the United States.

1824
■ John Quincy Adams became president. The House of Representatives chose him because none of the candidates received a majority vote. Adams was **capable** and experienced in government, but he was not a popular president. He did not consider the differences between the various parts of the country in his decisions.

1825
■ The completion of the Erie Canal created additional routes to the West.

1828
■ The **Tariff** of 1828 imposed a tax on imported goods. Northern industrialists favored the tax, but farmers in the South thought the tax hurt them.

■ Andrew Jackson was elected president. He was a popular president because he was a "common person" and defended states' rights. This election **campaign** created the Democratic Party and the National Republican Party.

1829
■ When President Jackson took office, he gave jobs to many of his friends and political supporters. This became known as the **spoils system.**

1830s
■ Cyrus McCormick invented the reaper, and John Deere invented the steel plow. Both of these machines had major effects on farming. These inventions, along with others, made **mass production** of goods possible.

■ The Cumberland Road now spread westward for nearly 600 miles, all the way into Illinois. Many wagons and stagecoaches traveled along this road.

■ The population of the United States reached 13 million.

■ Newer, faster ships made it easier and less expensive for people to come to America. Many immigrants came to the United States from Great Britain, Ireland, and Germany. The United States became known as the **melting pot** of the world. A melting pot is a nation where people belonging to different races or cultures live together.

Industry and Expansion Continue

Dictator
A person ruling a country with total control

Depression
A period of financial difficulties experienced by an entire country

Unemployment
The state of not having work

Homeland
Land that a person or group came from originally

1831 ■ Nat Turner, a slave from Virginia, led a revolt. He wanted to free all slaves in America. Many slaves and slave owners were killed in this revolt. Nat Turner was also killed. Turner became a hero among slaves because of his courage to fight.

1832 ■ The South Carolina Ordinance of Nullification showed an early sign of separation between southern states and the Union. It said that South Carolina would not obey tariff laws.

■ President Jackson was re-elected to a second term. His policy to break up the Bank of the United States helped him win re-election.

1836 ■ Many Americans began to settle in the Texas territory, which was owned by Mexico. The Mexican army attacked and killed Texans at the Alamo. Sam Houston defeated Santa Anna, the **dictator** of Mexico, at the Battle of San Jacinto. Texas became independent and called itself the Republic of Texas. Sam Houston was chosen as its first president.

1837 ■ Martin Van Buren became the president. He offered Americans the same approach to govern the country as Jackson had.

■ The Panic of 1837 caused the country to enter a **depression,** or period of financial difficulty. Many banks failed, prices fell, and **unemployment** spread. President Van Buren was unable to find a way to solve the problems the depression created.

■ As many as 300 steamboats carried passengers and cargo on the Mississippi River and rivers that joined it. In addition, thousands of miles of canals and rivers connected the Northeast.

■ Horace Mann helped to reform the education system in Massachusetts. He required all children to attend schools. These schools were paid for by state taxes. Mann stated that all schools in the state had to have the same program of studies. He also required training for teachers.

1838 ■ During his presidency, Andrew Jackson had asked Congress for help to decrease the fighting among settlers and American Indians. Land west of the Mississippi River was set aside for the American Indians. In 1838, the largest movement, known as the "Trail of Tears," forced them to give up their **homeland.** Many American Indians died along the way.

Telegraph

A device that uses coded signals to send communications over a wire

Communication

The act of sending and receiving information

Manifest Destiny

A belief that something is meant to happen, especially that America would own land from coast to coast

1840 ■ Railroads became another important means of transportation. By 1840, there were over 3,000 miles of railroad lines in the United States.

1841 ■ William Henry Harrison was elected president. When Harrison died after one month in office, his vice president, John Tyler, became president.

1842 ■ A dispute arose between Great Britain and the United States over the northern boundary of Maine. The Webster-Ashburton Treaty created a compromise that gave land to both countries.

1844 ■ Samuel F. B. Morse developed the **telegraph.** This was the first of many important improvements in **communication.**

■ During his campaign, James K. Polk suggested the idea of **Manifest Destiny.** He believed the United States was meant to control the land and people from the Atlantic coast to the Pacific coast. President Polk took office in 1845.

1846 ■ A compromise set the boundary of Oregon Country at 49 degrees north latitude. Great Britain received the northern part, and the United States received the southern part.

■ Texas had become a state in 1845. However, there were questions about the border between Mexico and Texas. Mexico refused to sell the land to the United States. In April, Mexico attacked American troops near the Rio Grande. Soon after the attack, the United States declared war on Mexico.

1848 ■ The Treaty of Guadalupe Hidalgo ended the Mexican War and gave the United States the California territory.

■ The United States now stretched from coast to coast. President Polk had accomplished Manifest Destiny. He also had added more than one million square miles of land to the United States during his presidency.

■ Slavery was a major issue in the election of 1848. Zachary Taylor was elected president.

■ Gold was discovered in California on land owned by John Sutter.

The Slavery Issue Grows

Abolish

To get rid of something

Fugitive

One who is fleeing from danger or from being kept against one's will

Tension

Uncomfortable feelings toward another person or group

1849
- The California gold rush caused the population of California to increase by over 10 times.

1850
- President Taylor died in office. Vice President Millard Fillmore became the new president.

- The Compromise of 1850 allowed California to enter the Union as a free state. The compromise set rules for the addition of future free and slave states. It also **abolished** slavery in the District of Columbia.

- The **Fugitive** Slave Law was established by the Compromise of 1850. The law stated that northerners had to return runaway slaves to their southern owners. Those caught helping slaves would be fined.

- The Underground Railroad was a secret escape route for slaves seeking freedom. The routes ran northward to Canada. Frederick Douglass, Sojourner Truth, and Harriet Tubman were among those who helped slaves escape.

1852
- Harriet Beecher Stowe wrote a book called *Uncle Tom's Cabin.* The book described the terrible conditions in which slaves lived. It added to the movement to abolish slavery. William Lloyd Garrison and Frederick Douglass also published newspapers that added to the movement.

1853
- Franklin Pierce became president.

- The Gadsden Purchase added the final piece of land to the United States. America purchased the strip of land, which is now New Mexico and Arizona, for $10 million.

1854
- The country needed to establish a railroad route from the east coast to the west coast. To do this, it had to organize the territories of Kansas and Nebraska. This caused new problems between free and slave states.

- The Kansas-Nebraska Act allowed voters in the territories to decide if they would be admitted to the United States as a free state or a slave state. At this time, **tension** between slave states and free states was high.

- The Republican Party formed as a new political party. Members of this party did not like it that existing parties had no clear stand on slavery.

1856
- James Buchanan became president. At this time, the country was becoming more separated by the issue of slavery.

Ruling

The decision of a court case

Arsenal

A place used to make or store military weapons

Ammunition

Bullets, gunpowder, and other things used with guns or other weapons

1857 ■ The Supreme Court made an important **ruling,** or decision, in the Dred Scott case. Scott was a slave who said he should be free because he had lived in a free state. He was living in Missouri, a slave state, when his master died. The court said that slaves were property and could be taken anywhere. Many people in the North thought the decision meant that slavery could expand into all states.

1858 ■ Cyrus Field laid a telegraph cable on the floor of the Atlantic Ocean. Although it took a few years for the cable to work properly, the United States and Europe were now connected.

■ The Lincoln-Douglas Senate debates showed that Abraham Lincoln had great wisdom and leadership. Lincoln lost the Senate election, but his popularity grew.

1859 ■ Abolitionist John Brown attacked an army **arsenal** at Harpers Ferry, Virginia. Brown wanted to take guns and **ammunition.** He then wanted to arm African slaves and lead them in a revolt. He was captured and hanged. This increased tensions between the North and the South even more.

1860 ■ The pony express carried mail from St. Joseph, Missouri, to Sacramento, California. This postal system ended 18 months later when the telegraph came to California.

■ By the 1860s, many books had been written. Tales of adventure and bravery became popular. Writers including Washington Irving, Edgar Allan Poe, Emily Dickinson, and Nathaniel Hawthorne were important to American literature.

■ Abraham Lincoln ran for president as a Republican and won. He opposed slavery and said that no state could leave the Union.

Dred Scott

The Civil War Years

Confederacy

A group that has formed an alliance for some purpose; the Confederate States of America

Civil war

A war between two groups within the same country

Blockade

To prevent goods or people from entering or leaving

1861

■ Soon after Lincoln won the election, several southern states voted to leave the Union. South Carolina, Mississippi, Florida, Alabama, Georgia, Texas, and Louisiana formed the Confederate States of America.

■ Jefferson Davis was chosen to serve as president of the **Confederacy.** The Confederate States created a new constitution. It said that each state was independent, slavery would be protected, and the states would pay no federal tariffs.

■ When Lincoln took office in March, he hoped to unite the country and avoid a **civil war.**

■ The Confederacy captured Fort Sumter, a Union fort in South Carolina, in April. Shortly afterwards, Virginia, North Carolina, Arkansas, and Tennessee joined the Confederacy.

■ The Union established a **blockade** to prevent the South from selling cotton to Europe. The Union did not want the South to have money to buy military supplies.

■ On July 21, 1861, the South defeated the North in the battle of Bull Run. The South continued to win major battles during the early part of the war.

1862

■ The Confederate ship, the *Merrimac (Virginia),* and the Union ship, the *Monitor,* battled in March. Neither side won the battle, but the Confederates stopped the Union from approaching Richmond, Virginia.

■ The Union lost many battles, including the Seven Days' Battles, a second battle at Bull Run, and Fredricksburg. Confederate General Robert E. Lee became the commanding general, while the Union used many different commanding generals. The Battle of Antietam, where the Confederates were forced to retreat, was the bloodiest single day of the war.

Reconstruction and the Development of Industrial America

1862–1900

When the Civil War was over, the United States had to bind up its wounds and heal its divisions. This period of rebuilding was called Reconstruction. As Reconstruction ended, America began to expand on many frontiers. Settlers headed to the western frontier, claiming lands of American Indians and their ancestors. On the industrial frontier, huge and powerful industries developed. On the frontier of cities, populations grew at an astounding rate with millions of immigrants. And with all this growth came more new problems to solve.

In this unit, you will learn what the nation did to unite and rebuild after the Civil War. You will learn about the western frontier and what happened to American Indians. You will learn about rapid growth of industries and inventions. You will learn how cities grew with waves of immigrants. You will learn how this growth brought about labor and political reforms.

1 Reconstruction
1865–1877

The bloody war between the North and South had ended. Slavery was over once and for all. The nation needed to heal its wounds. Both the North and the South had changed during the war. The South lay in ruin and had to be rebuilt. The period of Reconstruction, or rebuilding, was a time of political unrest. Some members of Congress tried to punish the South. Former slaves fought to keep their freedom. They became voters and landholders. By the end of Reconstruction, however, much of their freedom became limited. In this chapter, you will learn about Reconstruction in the South.

Goals for Learning

◆ To describe the assassination of Abraham Lincoln, problems in the South after the Civil War, and the 13th Amendment

◆ To explain the 14th Amendment, Andrew Johnson's conflicts with Congress and his impeachment, and the effects of Reconstruction on the American Indians

◆ To explain social and economic changes in the South, and changes in the status of women

◆ To explain the 15th Amendment, the problems in Grant's administration, and the end of Reconstruction

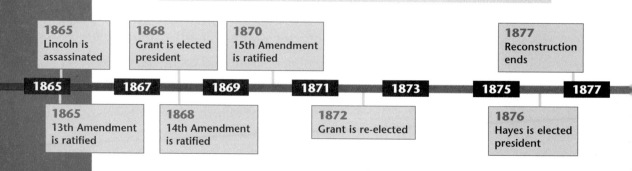

1865 Lincoln is assassinated

1868 Grant is elected president

1870 15th Amendment is ratified

1877 Reconstruction ends

1865   **1867**   **1869**   **1871**   **1873**   **1875**   **1877**

1865 13th Amendment is ratified

1868 14th Amendment is ratified

1872 Grant is re-elected

1876 Hayes is elected president

Inaugural address

A speech a president gives to accept the presidency

Oath

A pledge that promises loyalty to a government or other cause

Amnesty

A pardon granted by the government

Assassination

The killing of a politically important person

Abraham Lincoln began his second term as president as the war was ending. In his **inaugural address,** Lincoln expressed his hopes for rebuilding the Union. He wanted all Americans to forget the war as soon as possible. He put together a plan to rebuild the nation.

The president's plan said a state could rejoin the Union when 10 percent of its voters took an **oath,** or promised, to support the Union. He offered **amnesty,** or forgiveness, to Southerners. This would allow the states to rejoin the Union as quickly as possible. New state governments could be formed, but they would have to obey the ban on slavery. Lincoln knew that many in Congress did not agree with his plan. However, Lincoln felt that he had the power to proceed even if Congress did not accept the plan.

On the evening of April 14, 1865, Lincoln attended a play at Ford's Theater in Washington, D.C. John Wilkes Booth went to the box where Lincoln was sitting and shot the president in the back of the head. Booth had supported the Southern cause. Lincoln died the next morning. A few days after the **assassination,** soldiers killed Booth. President Lincoln did not live to see his plans carried out. His death delayed rebuilding in the South.

John Wilkes Booth assassinated President Lincoln at Ford's Theater.

What Were the Problems in the South?

In the South, the damage from the war had been great. Countless farms and large plantations were ruined. Confederate money was worthless. As a result, many formerly wealthy people had no funds. They could not rebuild. Most banks, also victims of the failed Confederate cause, had closed. Roads throughout many Southern states had become blocked with rubble from the war. Many bridges had been destroyed. Even the railroad tracks had been damaged during efforts to slow down shipments of troops and supplies.

The South had few police, no judges, and no courts. Some groups of desperate people tried to take the law into their own hands. None of the Southern states had an established government to help people during the hard times that lay ahead.

Richmond, Virginia, was one of many areas in the South ruined by the Civil War.

Among the homeless and the unemployed were the former slaves, who had to find a way to support themselves.

What Was Reconstruction?

Reconstruction—the rebuilding of the South—was now in the hands of the new president, Andrew Johnson. Although he had served as vice president to Lincoln, Johnson was not well liked by many members of Congress. Johnson was a Democrat, former governor of Tennessee, and representative in Congress. He had been a senator at the outbreak of the war. He had remained loyal to the Union even though he had strong ties to the South.

President Johnson tried to follow Lincoln's Reconstruction plan. He forgave most Southerners who took an oath. He appointed temporary governors in many states to help them change their governments and elect new representatives to Congress.

Black Codes

Laws that prevented African Americans from owning certain land, voting, and working certain skilled jobs

Freedmen

Former slaves

Within a few months, most of these states had reorganized and ratified the 13th Amendment, which abolished slavery. By the end of 1865, Johnson announced that all of the Southern states but Texas were readmitted to the Union. Congress did not agree.

Congress met in December 1865. Members of Congress called the "Radical Republicans" opposed the Reconstruction plan. The Radical Republicans wanted to punish the former Confederate States for the trouble they caused the nation. The Radicals refused to recognize the newly formed Southern governments or the recently elected representatives from them. They did not accept the states back into the Union.

Some newly established state governments in the South had adopted **"Black Codes."** These laws only applied to African Americans. Under the Black Codes, former slaves, now called **freedmen,** were restricted from voting, owning certain kinds of land, and working certain skilled jobs. Many members of Congress felt that the Black Codes proved that the Southern states did not intend to end slavery.

Lesson 1 Review Write the answers to these questions on a sheet of paper. Use complete sentences.

1. Under Lincoln's plan, how could states come back into the Union?
2. Who assassinated Abraham Lincoln?
3. What was the South like after the Civil War?
4. What was the importance of the 13th Amendment?
5. What was the name of the group that was against Reconstruction?

What do you think?

Do you think African Americans were really free in the South? Explain your answer.

Veto

The power given to the president to turn down a bill

Lawsuit

A case brought before a court of law

Due process

The formal process of justice carried out in a court of law

Agency

An organization set up by the federal government

In readmitting states to the Union, Johnson allowed voting rights to white men in the South. He made no effort to give such rights to the freedmen. Southern whites, who blamed Republicans for the war, were strongly Democratic. The freedmen, on the other hand, were pro-Republican, because President Lincoln had helped them gain their freedom. Republicans in Congress were eager to win the votes of African Americans. Northern business leaders were happily back into successful business deals. They did not want a Democratic South to start lowering tariffs again.

Congress began to put its own Reconstruction plan into effect by passing the Civil Rights Act of 1866. Put into effect over President Johnson's **veto,** this act was intended to reverse the Black Codes. Under this law, African Americans were allowed to own property, to bring **lawsuits,** and to marry legally. A lawsuit is a case brought before a court of law. Shortly afterward, Congress proposed the 14th Amendment. The amendment made the Bill of Rights cover all Americans, including whites and African Americans. It said that no state shall "deprive any person of life, liberty, or property without **due process** of law; nor deny to any person . . . equal protection of the laws." Due process is the formal process of justice carried out in a court of law. The 14th Amendment did not apply to American Indians.

Tennessee was the only Southern state that accepted the 14th Amendment and was readmitted to the Union. The other Confederate States rejected the amendment and were not readmitted.

What Was the Freedmen's Bureau?

Congress had started the Freedmen's Bureau in 1865 as a temporary **agency** to help former slaves and some white Southerners. One of the first programs of the Freedmen's Bureau was to establish hospitals to aid Southern African Americans injured in the war.

Civil rights

Basic human rights belonging to all people

Geography Note

Secretary of State William Seward learned that Russia wanted to sell its Alaska territory. He planned to buy this land. Most Americans laughed at the idea. They called Alaska "Seward's Icebox" because it was so cold. On March 30, 1867, Seward signed a treaty that gave Alaska to the United States. The purchase price was $7.2 million, which is about two cents an acre!

In 1866, with the Freedmen's Bureau Bill, Congress enlarged the agency. It was extended to give freedmen food, clothing, and shelter until they found jobs. Freedmen and their children were given opportunities to go to school. Agents of the Freedmen's Bureau tried to help protect the **civil rights** of the African Americans. Civil rights are basic human rights belonging to all people.

What Was the Second Great Indian Removal?

In the 1830s, the United States government had forcibly removed Indians from the Southeast to an area in present-day Oklahoma. When the Civil War began, many of these Indians supported the Confederacy. With the defeat of the Confederacy, the Reconstruction Treaties of 1866 forced these tribes to give up the western part of their Indian Territory. They were also forced to allow railroads to cross their land. The federal government used the western half of this territory to resettle Indians from other areas. The government moved eastern tribes such as the Delaware and Shawnee to this area. Tribes were also relocated from Kansas. Plains Indians were forced onto reservations, too, even though they put up strong resistance. This relocation of Americans Indians is known as the "Second Great Removal."

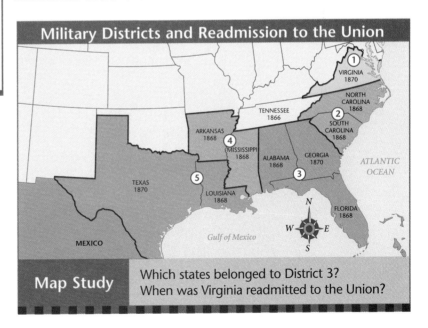

Military Districts and Readmission to the Union

VIRGINIA 1870 ①

NORTH CAROLINA 1868

TENNESSEE 1866

SOUTH CAROLINA 1868 ②

ARKANSAS 1868 ④

MISSISSIPPI 1868

ALABAMA 1868

GEORGIA 1870

ATLANTIC OCEAN

TEXAS 1870 ⑤

LOUISIANA 1868 ③

FLORIDA 1868

MEXICO

Gulf of Mexico

Map Study Which states belonged to District 3? When was Virginia readmitted to the Union?

What Was the Reconstruction Act of 1867?

Constitutional

Following the ideas set forth in the Constitution

Radical

Extreme

Override

To reject or not accept

In March 1867, Congress passed the first of four Reconstruction acts over the veto of the president. The first act stated that the 10 states that had not returned to the Union would be put under military rule by the federal government. The South was then divided into five sections. In order to be readmitted to the Union, states had to hold **constitutional** conventions with delegates elected by all men—white and African American. Congress had to approve a state's constitution and the state had to accept the 14th Amendment before it could rejoin the Union. By 1870, all 10 Southern states were readmitted to the Union.

Why Did Congress Try to Impeach Johnson?

Johnson tried to veto a number of bills passed by **Radicals** in Congress. Congress was able to **override** his veto. In 1867, Congress passed the Tenure of Office Act. This act required approval from the Senate before the president could fire an appointee. Believing that the act limited the president, Johnson vetoed it. Congress overrode the veto.

THIS LITTLE BOY WOULD PERSIST IN HANDLING BOOKS ABOVE
HIS CAPACITY.

AND THIS WAS THE DISASTROUS RESULT.

This cartoon from 1868 makes fun of President Andrew Johnson. It shows what happened to Johnson—the "Little Boy"—when he broke a law.

Impeach

To charge a public official with misconduct

Misconduct

Wrongdoing by someone holding a political or business position

Writing About History

Write a song about this time period. The song could focus on a certain event covered in the chapter or on a feeling people had at that time. Write the song in your notebook.

President Johnson then fired one of his Cabinet members, Edwin Stanton. Stanton disagreed with Johnson's Reconstruction policy. Some powerful senators were very upset. They wanted to **impeach** Johnson, which means that he would be charged with **misconduct.** The House of Representatives did impeach Johnson. The Senate then had to decide if he should be removed from office.

A trial was held in the Senate. In order to reach a decision, two-thirds, or 36, of the senators had to agree. The vote was 35 for impeachment and 19 against. The Radical Republicans failed to remove President Johnson by only one vote.

Unfortunately, Johnson had lost much support during these problems. For the remainder of his presidency he was unable to do anything further to promote the Reconstruction efforts he favored.

Civics Connection

Impeachment

The Constitution gives Congress the right to remove high government officials from office for wrongdoing. First, Congress must find the official guilty of "treason, bribery, or other high crimes and misdemeanors." The House of Representatives and the Senate each have a role in impeachment. The House charges an official with wrongdoing. This is called impeachment. Then the Senate holds a trial. If two-thirds of the Senate agrees that the official is guilty, the official is removed from office.

The Constitution says that the three branches of government are separate and independent. Impeachment gives Congress power over the president. The writers of the Constitution wanted a way to remove a guilty official from office. However, they did not want impeachment to be easy. They did not want Congress to remove someone for political reasons.

Congress has never removed a president from office. In 1867, Congress tried to impeach President Johnson. Charges also were brought against President Richard Nixon in 1974. Nixon resigned before the House voted on the charges. In 1999, the Senate found President Bill Clinton not guilty at his impeachment trial.

1. Do you think the meaning of "high crimes and misdemeanors" should be made clearer? Explain your answer.

2. Do you think the impeachment process seems fair? Explain your answer.

Who Won the Election of 1868?

In 1868, the Republicans chose General Ulysses S. Grant to be their candidate. Grant had no political experience, yet he was well known for leading the Union army in the Civil War. The Democrats chose former New York Governor Horatio Seymour as their candidate. Many felt that Grant had saved the Union, so now he would save the country. Grant won the election in a very close popular vote. About 450,000 African Americans had voted for Grant. Political parties became aware that African Americans were important to the outcome of an election.

Lesson 2 Review On a sheet of paper, write the correct word or words from the Word Bank to complete each sentence.

Word Bank

Andrew Johnson

Democrats

14th Amendment

Radical
   Republicans

Ulysses S. Grant

1. The House of Representatives voted to impeach _____.

2. The _____ said that African Americans had "equal protection of the laws."

3. Most of the Southern whites were _____.

4. _____ created their own Reconstruction plan.

5. _____ was elected president in 1868.

What do you think?

What sorts of things would a president have to do for you to vote for impeachment?

Technology Connection

Dynamite

As the nation grew, builders sometimes had to remove rock or tear down buildings. For example, to tunnel through a mountain, workers had to remove many tons of rock. Drilling and digging by hand took a lot of time. An explosive could remove the rock more quickly, but explosives were dangerous. Some, like nitroglycerine, could explode without warning. Alfred Nobel, a Swedish inventor, worked to make nitroglycerine safe to use.

In the 1860s, Nobel found that nitroglycerine could be mixed with silica. He could handle the resulting substance safely. He shaped it into rods. Workers could place the rods into drilled holes. Then they used a blasting cap to explode the mixture at the right time. Nobel called his invention dynamite. It made construction work easier and much less costly. It allowed for faster growth and change than ever before.

Scalawag

A white Southerner who controlled the new politicians who had little government knowledge

Corruption

Using wrong or unlawful ways for financial gain

Carpetbagger

A Northerner elected to political office in the South who took advantage of people; carried belongings in carpetbags

The Reconstruction acts provided for political reorganization of the South. Under the acts, the right to hold office was taken away from men who had been political leaders of the Confederacy. Other Southerners, however, were allowed to be legislators. During the 13 years that followed, a total of 16 African Americans served in Congress.

Who Were the Scalawags and Carpetbaggers?

In some states, such as South Carolina, white Southerners put African Americans in state offices. In general, former slaves had little knowledge of government. They did what they were told to do. White Southerners who controlled the new politicians were called **scalawags.**

Some Northerners traveled to the Southern states looking for jobs. Others from the North wanted to help the cause of the freedmen, as either teachers or school administrators. Still other Northerners were elected to political office in the South. Some took advantage of the people and made money through **corruption.** Many of these Northerners carried their belongings in bags made from carpet material. They became known as **carpetbaggers.**

THE MAN WITH THE (CARPET) BAGS.
The bag in front of him, filled with others' faults, he always sees. The one behind him, filled with his own faults, he never sees.

Some carpetbaggers took advantage of people and carried belongings in bags made of carpet material.

What Happened to the Plantations?

The Civil War brought many changes to the South, particularly to the old plantation system. Plantations could no longer use slave labor. Large plantation owners now paid wages to their former slaves. Even though the wages were low, they decreased the profits of the plantation owners.

Tenant farmer

A farmer who pays rent to a landowner for use of the land

Sharecropper

A farmer who pays some of his or her crop to a landowner as rent

Many of the large plantations were divided into smaller pieces of land for **tenant farmers.** In this situation, landowners rented their land to owners of small farms. Usually, the tenant farmer paid a set amount of rent. They sold their crops to pay the landowner. Sometimes they might use crops to pay their rent. No matter how they paid it, the farmers ended up with less than the landowner.

Some large landowners let former slaves have land to farm. In return, the owner would get a large share of the crop. The owner provided the seed, tools, food, and general supplies to the farmer. The crop was payment for the supplies the farmer had received. These farmers were known as **sharecroppers.** Slavery had ended, but sharecropping was not much better. The owner sold the crops at a high price and paid the sharecropper a lower price. The sharecropper never stopped owing money. The sharecropper's debt got bigger and bigger. A new form of slavery had begun.

In sharecropping and tenant farming, the freedmen had a place to live and a chance to do the work they knew. Neither practice was good for the farmer. Even though they worked hard, the farmer and the farmer's family remained poor.

History in Your Life

The Works of Mark Twain

"Mark Twain" was a humorous author and lecturer in the late 1800s. Born Samuel Clemens, he found his pen name while working as a Mississippi riverboat pilot. The call "Mark twain!" meant the water was two fathoms deep and thus safe to travel on. Twain's first notable tale was "The Celebrated Jumping Frog of Calaveras County." He wrote many other short stories and novels. His most famous novels are *The Adventures of Tom Sawyer* (1876) and *The Adventures of Huckleberry Finn* (1884). Twain created memorable characters in American literature and realistic portraits of life in the 1800s. Twain's later works are gloomier than his early works. His writing sometimes reflected the prejudice of his time. As a result, many people today are uncomfortable with his work. Nonetheless, his books have been loved for their colorful pictures of childhood and humorous insight into human folly.

Tobacco

A plant that some people smoke or chew

Industry

Business and manufacturing

Suffrage

The right to vote

Cotton remained a major crop throughout the South, as did **tobacco** and rice. After the war, pecans, peanuts, corn, wheat, fruits, and vegetables were planted. This gave the South several different kinds of crops. They no longer had to depend on just cotton, tobacco, and rice.

How Did the Civil War Change the Status of Women?

The roles of women changed a great deal during and after the Civil War. The role of the traditional European woman began to fade as women of the frontier encountered the hardships of pioneer living. Strong women emerged. They demanded rights that had been denied to them since colonial times.

During the war, some women worked as nurses, taking care of the sick and wounded. Some women joined the fighting. Some even disguised themselves as men and fought along with the other soldiers. In both the North and the South, women formed aid societies. The women in these groups collected food and supplies for the soldiers. Sometimes they sewed clothing and blankets.

The rapid expansion of **industries** in the North during and after the Civil War encouraged women to seek employment. Greater financial independence and the **suffrage** movement added to the importance of women in the workplace and in politics.

Focus on Economics

Southern plantation owners no longer had free labor. Much of the South lay in ruins, and the economy had been destroyed. Farmers did not have money to buy farm equipment such as reapers. Sharecropping did not help renters or landowners. Sharecroppers rarely got out of debt. Landowners lost their lands because they could not pay debts or taxes. Landowners insisted on planting cotton although the demand for it had dropped. The Southern economy would not recover for many decades.

What Were Other Changes in the South?

People discovered iron ore, coal, and limestone in various parts of the South. This led to the creation of a strong iron and steel industry. Birmingham, Alabama, became a major steel-producing center. In other cities, lumber mills provided a good deal of the nation's building material. Mills to make cotton cloth were built. Railroads, roads, and new industries spread throughout the South. Towns and cities got larger. Progress was beginning to shape the once-rural South.

Before the war, the South had paid little attention to public education. Those who could afford it sent their children to private schools. During Reconstruction, states began to require public education for children. Schools were **segregated,** which meant white and African American children attended separate schools. This practice of segregation continued for many years.

Biography

P. B. S. Pinchback: c. 1837–1921

Captain Pinckney B. S. Pinchback fought for the Union in the Civil War. He served as a member of General Richard Butler's Corps d'Afrique. During Reconstruction, he became lieutenant governor of Louisiana. Governor Henry C. Warmouth was impeached in 1872. Pinchback thus became the first African American governor. He served only one month in that position. Within the next year, he was elected as both a Republican representative and senator to Congress. However, opposing Democrats feared his outspoken fight for African American rights. Some claimed he broke laws to become elected. As a result, Pinchback was never seated as a representative or senator. In the years that followed, he published a weekly newspaper. He also kept fighting to end segregation and violence against African Americans.

Lesson 3 Review On a sheet of paper, write the answers to the following questions. Use complete sentences.

1. What was the purpose of the Reconstruction acts?

2. Who were the scalawags?

3. What did carpetbaggers do?

4. What was the difference between a tenant farmer and a sharecropper?

5. How did public schools in the South become segregated?

What do you think?

Would you choose to be a tenant farmer or a sharecropper? Explain your answer.

It Happened in History

African Americans Leave the South

The Civil War left many African Americans poor and without a home or an education. There were few opportunities for African Americans, and some states would not allow them to own land. Many whites were uneasy with African Americans who were no longer slaves. Between 1870 and 1880, thousands of African Americans left the South, convinced that this was the only way they could gain true freedom. A few set sail for Africa. Many moved west hoping to start a new life. During this time, thousands of African Americans, called Exodusters, looked for a better life in northern and western parts of the United States.

Kansas became a popular western destination. By about 1880, thousands of former slaves had settled there. They were able to own their own land in Kansas. Some became cowhands and others worked as prairie farmers. Some settled in cities, and some worked in mines. Gradually they became more successful. They had the right to vote and hold political office.

Grandfather clause

A clause that stated that any adult African American male could vote if his grandfather was a registered voter on January 1, 1867

In February 1870, the 15th Amendment gave African American men the right to vote. Regardless of race, color, or previous slavery, every male citizen could vote. Suffrage, or the right to vote, had been given to all citizens except women. Southerners opposed the new amendment. They were concerned that African Americans could decide the outcome of an election. Most Northerners were not concerned because the African American population was small.

Some Southern states prevented African Americans from voting. African Americans were told that they could not vote because they could not read or did not understand the Constitution. Voting laws were passed that contained a **grandfather clause.** Any adult male could vote if his grandfather was a registered voter on January 1, 1867. Because no African American was allowed to vote before that date, all freedmen were prevented from voting. By the end of the 1800s, most African Americans had lost the right to vote in the ex-Confederate Southern states.

The 15th Amendment gave African American men the right to vote for the first time in history.

African Americans faced other problems. Whites organized secret groups such as the **Ku Klux Klan.** The Klan wanted to keep African Americans from voting, to punish the scalawags, and to make the carpetbaggers leave the South. They used **violence** to scare their victims. Sometimes the violence led to murder. African Americans were most often the target of their attacks.

What Problems Did Grant Have?

President Grant had very little training in political matters. He found that being president was very different from serving as a general. He appointed his friends to government jobs and trusted that they would be honest. Although Grant was an honest man, many of his friends were not.

These Ku Klux Klan members were captured during an uprising in 1868.

His **administration** was hurt by several **scandals.** Grant's friends tried to get rich by using the power of their government offices. In 1872, Grant was elected for a second term.

Ku Klux Klan

A secret group against people who were not white

Violence

A severe or harmful act

Administration

The period of time a president is in office

Scandal

A disgraceful event

Depression

A period of financial difficulty experienced by a country

Shortly after President Grant began his second term, the country went into a **depression.** Businesses and factories began to shut down. Thousands of workers lost their jobs. Many families had no money to buy food. This depression lasted for more than five years. During this time the Republicans lost many seats in Congress. President Grant was a Republican. The country's problems were getting worse, and people blamed the Republicans.

How Did Reconstruction End?

Northerners had grown tired of high taxes. They wondered how much longer Reconstruction could go on. Ten years had passed. Many Northerners had lost interest in the problems of the South. They felt it was time to forget about the war. Grant's two terms had been full of scandal. The election of 1876 called for a president who could restore the people's trust in the government.

The Republicans chose Rutherford B. Hayes, the governor of Ohio, as their candidate. He was an honest man. The Democrats chose Samuel J. Tilden, the governor of New York, as their candidate. Tilden won the popular vote, but neither candidate won a majority of electoral votes. An Electoral Commission decided the election. Twenty electoral votes were in dispute.

Hayes made a political deal. He told Southern Democratic leaders that he would end Reconstruction if they would support him. This deal was called the Compromise of 1877. With Southern support, the House of Representatives agreed with the Electoral Commission's decision to make Hayes president. Hayes took office in March 1877. Within a few months all federal troops left the Southern states. Reconstruction had come to an end.

The country celebrated its **centennial** in 1876. A centennial is a 100th year celebration. A Centennial Exposition was held in Philadelphia to show the achievements of the young nation. Americans were becoming masters of science and industrial development. A great nation had risen from the wilderness. It was strong and ready to face the next 100 years.

Then and Now

Think what a subway ride was like in 1870 when Alfred Beach built America's first subway. It ran under Broadway in New York City and extended only 312 feet. The luxurious car held about 20 passengers and was "shot" through a tunnel like a cannonball. The tunnel was decorated with wall paintings. This was intended only as a demonstration subway. When Beach was unable to get city approval to expand the system, it failed.

Have you ridden on today's subways? Many large cities have them. New York City's subway is about 230 miles long—the second longest system after London's. Opened in 1904, New York's subway is powered by electricity. About 3.5 million people ride the New York subway every day.

The country still had social and political problems. Sometimes white Americans and African Americans did not get along. Freedmen continued to fight for the rights they felt they deserved. African American voters helped elect two African American senators and 15 African American representatives between 1865 and 1877. Both senators were from Mississippi. Those members of Congress proved to be good politicians.

After Reconstruction, Southern state governments began denying African Americans social equality and the right to vote. The gains achieved during Reconstruction quickly vanished. In some states, conditions for African Americans were not much better than they had been before the Civil War.

Lesson 4 Review Choose the word or words in parentheses that best complete each sentence. Write your answers on a sheet of paper.

1. A secret society called the (Ku Klux Klan, Scalawags, Radical Republicans) used violence to prevent African Americans from voting.

2. The presidency of (Hayes, Grant, Tilden) was marked by corruption.

3. After Reconstruction, most African Americans (lost, gave up, gained) most of their rights.

4. The United States celebrated its centennial in (1865, 1867, 1876).

5. When federal (leaders, carpetbaggers, troops) left the South, Reconstruction ended.

What do you think?

Grant chose friends to fill important government posts. If you were president, how would you choose people to fill posts?

Advice to African American Students

W. E. B. Du Bois lived from 1868 to 1963. He argued that African Americans need good schools and a good education. In a letter, he once advised a student not to leave school.

There are in the United States today tens of thousands of [young African-American women] who would be happy beyond measure to have the chance of educating themselves that you are neglecting. If you train yourself as you easily can, there are wonderful chances of usefulness before you: you can join the ranks of 15,000 Negro women teachers, of hundreds of nurses and physicians, of the growing number of clerks and stenographers, and above all the host of homemakers.

Ignorance is a cure for nothing. Get the very best training possible and the doors of opportunity will fly open before you as they are flying before thousands of your fellows.

On the other hand every time a colored person neglects an opportunity, it makes it more difficult for others of the race to get such an opportunity. Do you want to cut off the chances of the boys and girls of tomorrow?

Document-Based Questions

1. Why does Du Bois urge the student to stay in school?

2. What does Du Bois say happens to African Americans who neglect to get a good education?

3. What do you think Du Bois meant when he said that "ignorance is a cure for nothing?" Do you agree? Why?

4. Du Bois warned the student about neglecting the opportunity for education. He said that neglecting the opportunity would "cut off the chances of the boys and girls of tomorrow." What do you think he meant by that?

5. Du Bois named some careers that were open to African American women at that time. How do you think careers have opened up for all women since then?

Source: Herbert Aptheker, A Documentary History of the Negro People in the United States, *1989.*

Chapter 1 SUMMARY

- John Wilkes Booth assassinated Abraham Lincoln on April 14, 1865, at Ford's Theater in Washington, D.C. Andrew Johnson became president.

- The war ruined the former Confederate States. Plantations, roads, bridges, and railways were destroyed. President Johnson appointed temporary governors in many Southern states to help them form new governments.

- Some Northerners punished the former Confederate States by refusing to recognize newly elected officials.

- Congress set up the Freedmen's Bureau in 1865 to help former slaves and some white Southerners find jobs and to provide medical help, clothing, food, and shelter.

- Some Southern governments adopted "Black Codes" that prevented freedmen from owning certain kinds of land, voting, and working certain skilled jobs. The Civil Rights Act of 1866 allowed freedmen to own property, marry, and bring lawsuits.

- The 14th Amendment to the Constitution, which gave African Americans equal protection under the law, was ratified in 1868. The 15th Amendment, ratified in 1870, gave African American men the right to vote.

- In 1867, Congress passed the first of four such Reconstruction acts. It divided the South into five sections and put them under military rule. It also required the Southern states to create new constitutions that had to be approved by Congress.

- Because of a dispute over the powers of the president, Congress impeached Andrew Johnson but failed to remove him from office.

- Scalawags were white Southerners who controlled new politicians, particularly African American politicians. Carpetbaggers were Northerners who traveled to the South and sometimes took advantage of people.

- Most Southern plantations were divided into smaller pieces of land. Landowners farmed their land using tenant farmers and sharecroppers.

- Ulysses S. Grant was elected president in 1868. His two terms as president were marked with corruption and problems.

- Rutherford B. Hayes became president in 1877. Hayes made a deal with Southern congressmen that he would end Reconstruction and remove federal troops from the South.

Chapter 1 REVIEW

On a sheet of paper, write the correct word or words from the Word Bank to complete each sentence.

Word Bank

Andrew Johnson

Civil Rights Act
  of 1866

15th Amendment

14th Amendment

Freedmen's Bureau

impeachment

John Wilkes Booth

Reconstruction

tenant farmers

Ulysses S. Grant

1. The _____ to the United States Constitution gave African American men the right to vote in elections.

2. The first _____ act divided the South into five regions and placed federal troops there to maintain order.

3. _____ was Lincoln's vice president and became president after Lincoln died.

4. The _____ was an agency that was supposed to help former slaves and some white Southerners find jobs.

5. African Americans were given equal protection under law by the _____.

6. The Congress tried to get rid of President Johnson by holding hearings on _____.

7. Abraham Lincoln was shot to death by _____, who supported the Southern cause.

8. Congress passed the _____ before the 14th Amendment was ratified.

9. _____ was elected president because people thought that he had saved the Union during the Civil War.

10. _____ rented their farms from landowners.

On a sheet of paper, write the letter of the answer that correctly completes each sentence.

11. Former slaves who gave most of their crops to a landowner were _____.

    A freedmen   **C** sharecroppers
    B tenant farmers   **D** carpetbaggers

12. The violent organization of whites called the _____ attacked African Americans.

   A scalawags   **C** freedmen

   B Ku Klux Klan   **D** carpetbaggers

13. The Centennial Exposition was held to _____.

   A show the achievements of the United States

   B fight for the rights of African Americans

   C reorganize the South

   D educate the public about voting laws

On a sheet of paper, write the answer to each question. Use complete sentences.

14. What was the South like right after the Civil War ended?

15. What did "Radical Republicans" in Congress want to do to the South? Why?

16. Why did Congress establish the Freedmen's Bureau?

17. How did the plantation system change after the Civil War?

18. What were some of the problems that Grant faced as president?

Critical Thinking On a sheet of paper, write your response to each question. Use complete sentences.

19. Ulysses S. Grant had been a capable general during the Civil War and was a hero of the North. Grant was not a very good president. Do you think that it is a mistake to elect military heroes to be president? Why or why not?

20. Do you think the Freedmen's Bureau was a good idea? Why or why not?

Test-Taking Tip

Read test directions more than once. Underline key words. These words may tell you how many examples to give and what kind of information is needed.

2 Settling the Western Frontier

1862–1890

The end of the Civil War turned more attention toward the West. The "last frontier," as it was called, was a land of freedom and adventure. It was a place where pioneers could find an opportunity for a better life. From 1862 to 1890, settlers took up the challenge to tame the nation's last frontier. In this chapter, you will learn how the United States expanded westward.

Goals for Learning

◆ To explain how pioneers traveled in the West and how the transcontinental railroad was built

◆ To describe what kinds of people lived on the frontier and what life was like for them

◆ To explain how the westward movement affected the American Indians in the West

◆ To describe the help that Congress gave the Indians and the end of the frontier

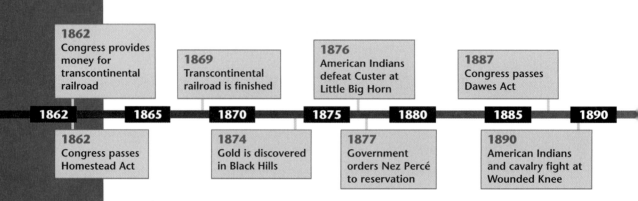

1862 Congress provides money for transcontinental railroad

1869 Transcontinental railroad is finished

1876 American Indians defeat Custer at Little Big Horn

1887 Congress passes Dawes Act

| 1862 | 1865 | 1870 | 1875 | 1880 | 1885 | 1890 |

1862 Congress passes Homestead Act

1874 Gold is discovered in Black Hills

1877 Government orders Nez Percé to reservation

1890 American Indians and cavalry fight at Wounded Knee

Stagecoach

A horse-drawn coach that was used for transporting people or mail

Wagon train

A large number of wagons traveling together

Transcontinental

Extending across a continent

The Great Plains is a vast stretch of land between the Missouri River and the Rocky Mountains. During the 1840s and 1850s, European settlers passed up this area on their way to the rich lands of Oregon and the gold in California. The flat, dry Great Plains seemed useless to them.

Beginning in 1858, many Americans traveled westward by **stagecoach** from St. Louis, Missouri. A stagecoach is a horse-drawn coach that was used for transporting people or mail. St. Louis was the western end of the railroad at that time. The three-week journey over mountains and deserts was a difficult one. Travelers were under constant danger of attack by robbers or American Indians. The Indians often saw the settlers as invaders. At the same time, most shipments of supplies from the East traveled by long, ox-drawn **wagon trains.** A wagon train is a large number of wagons traveling together. Communication improved in 1861, with the completion of the telegraph. The appeal of the western frontier grew stronger to many Americans in the East.

How Was the Transcontinental Railroad Built?

European and Chinese immigrants were hired to help build the transcontinental railroad.

In 1862, Congress provided money for the construction of the **transcontinental** railroad. The time had come to link the far western parts of the country to the East. Two companies were chosen to build the railroad. The Central Pacific Railroad started in the West at Sacramento, California, and was built eastward. The Union Pacific Railroad started at Omaha, Nebraska, and was built westward.

Work on the railroad increased after the Civil War ended in 1865. The Union Pacific Railroad hired thousands of war veterans, many of whom were Irish.

Early American explorers called the Great Plains the "Great American Desert." Senator Daniel Webster said, "To what use could we ever hope to put [them] . . . ?" Such descriptions kept white settlers away from the area for years. Not until the 1840s could settlers see that the area might be farmed successfully.

The work was hard and dangerous. Many workers were killed in accidents and American Indian raids. Because of difficult working conditions and the loss of workers, only a few miles of track were laid each day.

Chinese immigrants on the West Coast worked for the Central Pacific Railroad. They worked very hard, but progress was very slow because the land was so mountainous. The workers had to blast tunnels. Sometimes it took all day to go just a few feet.

In May 1869, the two railroads met at Promontory Point, Utah. The Central Pacific Railroad had laid about 700 miles of track. The Union Pacific had laid more than 1,000 miles of track. A golden spike was driven into the final link of the track. The news of the completed transcontinental railroad went out on the telegraph to the country. Now, settling the Great Plains was more appealing to many Americans.

This poster announces the opening of the Union Pacific Railroad in 1869.

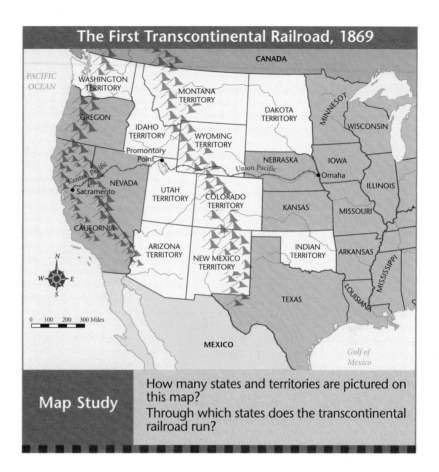

The First Transcontinental Railroad, 1869

Map Study
How many states and territories are pictured on this map?
Through which states does the transcontinental railroad run?

Word Bank

Central Pacific

Great Plains

St. Louis

Union Pacific

Utah

What do you think?

Why do you think many immigrants were willing to work on the railroad?

Lesson 1 Review On a sheet of paper, write the correct word or words from the Word Bank to complete each sentence.

1. The _____ was land between the Missouri River and the Rocky Mountains.

2. The _____ Railroad started at Omaha, Nebraska, and was built westward.

3. The _____ Railroad started in the West at Sacramento, California, and was built eastward.

4. The Union Pacific and Central Pacific railroads met at Promontory Point, _____.

5. The western end of the railroad in 1858 was _____.

Cowhand

A person who tends cattle

Prospector

A person who searches an area for gold, silver, or other minerals

Miners, farmers, and people who tended cattle, called **cowhands,** were important in settling the western frontier. They were made up of a variety of different ethnic and racial groups and were both men and women. Chinese and Irish miners, African American and Hispanic cowboys, and German farmers all looked to the western frontier as a place of opportunity. Each sought to enhance their lives as they searched for gold, ran cattle ranches, or farmed the land.

There were other opportunities for women too. The first major step toward universal suffrage was taken in Wyoming in 1869. That was when women at least 21 years old and living in Wyoming Territory were given the right to vote. Colorado, Utah, and Idaho had granted women suffrage by 1896. By 1914, women's suffrage had been granted in 11 states. The effort of women in World War I advanced the campaign for universal suffrage for women. Finally, in 1919, the 19th Amendment was ratified by a narrow margin. It went into effect in 1920. This amendment granted voting rights to all women. Very early successes in the western states were important to the passage of this amendment.

How Did Mining Start in the West?

Gold was discovered near Pikes Peak, Colorado, just before the start of the Civil War. Silver and gold were found in Nevada. Miners and **prospectors** traveled many miles to these places. A prospector is a person who searches an area for gold, silver, or other minerals. During the 1860s, gold was also discovered in Montana, Idaho, and Wyoming. The mining boom throughout this Rocky Mountain region was the same in many ways to the California gold rush of 1849.

Most miners never became rich. Individual prospectors could not do as much as large mining companies that brought special equipment to the mountains. These machines were faster than the pick, pan, and shovel methods that individual miners used.

Many of those who had traveled westward in search of gold settled down as farmers or ranchers. Others became loggers, taking advantage of the rich timber resources.

The lack of law and order in many mountain areas during this gold rush was similar to that in California in 1849. Many former miners grouped together to form city governments. They elected sheriffs to help provide them and their families with some law and order. As their lives became more civilized, the settlers in cities on the former frontier developed some pride in their new homes.

What Was Cattle Country?

Settlers in Texas discovered that large herds of longhorn cattle were running wild. This kind of cattle had been brought to America many years earlier by Spanish settlers. The Texans rounded up the cattle and raised the animals for beef, hides, and other goods. Texas became an important ranching area. Cattle were easy to raise in the grasslands of the Great Plains.

Ranchers wanted to bring their cattle to Chicago, Illinois, and many eastern cities. They could make more money if the cattle were sold in these areas. The ranchers' main problem was a lack of transportation. However, this problem was solved with the development of the railroad system. The railroads linked the grasslands to America's major cities.

Cowhands like these spent as many as 18 hours per day in the saddle during cattle drives.

Cowhands guided cattle to the holding pens near railroads. Before moving the cattle, every calf was branded with the special mark of its owner. Some cattle were moved over 1,000 miles. The Chisholm Trail was a widely used route. This trail stretched from San Antonio in southern Texas to Abilene in east central Kansas.

The herd traveled 10 to 15 miles a day. A cattle drive took more than two months. During that time, cowhands usually spent as many as 18 hours a day in the saddle. The cowhands' main jobs were to prevent a **stampede** and to protect the cattle from thieves. A stampede is a wild rush of animals.

Cow towns were a welcome sight to tired cowhands. Cow towns had many **saloons** and gambling houses. A saloon was a public building where people gathered to drink or gamble. The only law in cow towns was provided by U.S. marshals such as Wild Bill Hickock. It was a difficult job, for a marshal had to cover a large territory. Law and order developed as the frontier became more settled.

 History in Your Life

Barbed Wire

After the Civil War, pioneers moved rapidly into the West. Farmers claimed land and raised crops. Cowhands drove huge herds of cattle onto open range to graze. Farmers soon found that they needed practical fencing to keep cattle from trampling their crops. In 1867, Lucien Smith patented an artificial thorn hedge. This was wire with short metal spikes, or barbs, twisted onto it and stretched between posts. In 1868, a twisted double-strand wire was invented to hold the barbs. In 1874, an improved production process locked the barbs into place. At first, the barbed wire did not prevent all problems. Sometimes cowhands cut farmers' fences so cattle could graze freely or blocked cattle trails so other herds could not use them. However, the fences did keep cattle off railroad tracks. The fences made expansions of railroads to the West easier.

What Was the Homestead Act?

In 1862, Congress passed the Homestead Act. This act made it very easy for pioneers to own land. Settlers were given 160 acres of land provided they agreed to live on it for five years. This offer brought many farmers, factory workers, and immigrants to the Great Plains.

 Focus on Economics

In 1862, Congress passed the Homestead Act, which gave land to settlers. The same year, Congress also passed another important act called the Morrill Act. The Morrill Act was the first time the federal government provided money for higher education. It gave every state in the Union 30,000 acres of land for each member of Congress. The smallest amount of land a state could receive was 90,000 acres. States were supposed to sell the land and use the money to create colleges that focused on agriculture, engineering, and military science. Over 70 "land grant" colleges were established under the Morrill Act.

What Problems Did Plains Farmers Face?

Pioneers who owned land under the Homestead Act were called **homesteaders.** These people faced difficulties that were unknown to the farmers east of the Mississippi River. Eastern farmers were used to good land, plentiful water, and good supplies of wood. The plains farmers found the ground hard to plow, and there was little rain. In many areas, trees for building materials and fuel could be found only on the riverbanks.

Farmers soon learned that **sod,** which is thickly matted grass and roots, could be used in place of wood as building material. Brick-like chunks of sod were cut from the ground. They were piled one on top of the other to build the walls of a house. Trees from riverbanks formed the roof, which was then covered with sod. A sod house kept a farm family cool in the summer and warm in the winter.

Windmill

A wind-powered device used to pump water from a well

What do you think?

Do you think being a cowhand was really like it seems on television and in books? Explain.

There was enough water on the plains for farming, but it was underground. New inventions made it possible to drill deep wells into the earth. Farmers then pumped water to the surface by using wind-powered devices called **windmills.** Farmers also used a dry farming method. Part of the land remained unplanted each year so that the area could absorb rainwater.

Lesson 2 Review On a sheet of paper, write the answers to the following questions. Use complete sentences.

1. What did many of the people who set out to search for gold end up doing?

2. Why did ranchers want to bring their cattle to Chicago and eastern cities?

3. What were cow towns like?

4. What was the Homestead Act?

5. How did farmers build their houses?

Then and Now

Early colonists used horse-drawn wood plows to turn the soil for planting. This was hard work and took a long time. Farmers could plant and harvest only a small field. In 1797, the first cast-iron plow received a patent. This made plowing faster and easier. After 1830, farmers wanted to settle the Great Plains, but the heavy roots prevented even iron plow blades from working.

In 1837, the first steel plows, called "grasshopper plows," were introduced. These plows easily sliced and turned the tough grasses, opening the plains to widespread farming. By 1850, farmers needed about 80 hours of labor to produce 100 bushels of corn in a field. Now farmers use huge, modern tractors to pull giant plows. They need less than 3 hours of labor to produce 100 bushels of corn.

The Cheyenne, Comanche, Blackfeet, and the tribes of the Sioux Nation lived on the open plains. They were called the Plains Indians. Their way of life depended on the buffalo. The Plains Indians were hunters and nomads. They followed the constantly moving buffalo herds. They ate the meat, used the hides for clothing and shelter, and made the bones into tools.

How Were American Indian Ways Destroyed?

Some army and government officials wanted to kill all the buffalo. That way the American Indians could no longer follow the herds and would settle in one place. Farmers and ranchers wanted the buffalo out of their way. Others killed the buffalo so that they could sell the hides. Between 1865 and 1875, millions of buffalo were killed. William F. Cody got the name "Buffalo Bill" after he killed more than 4,000 buffalo in 18 months.

Buffalo hides were very valuable for making high-quality leather products. Buffalo robes were popular in winter. By 1889, only 541 buffalo survived in the United States. As the buffalo herds disappeared, the Plains Indians lost their independence. They were forced to find another way to live.

Lacrosse, similar to soccer, came from American Indian ways. Indians like this group of Sioux played the game.

Why Were American Indians Moved to Reservations?

The settlers and the U.S. government thought that the American Indians were in the path of progress. Government officials had little understanding of the Indians. They thought that the tribes should settle in one place.

Reservation

Land set aside by the government for the American Indians

The government signed treaties with the Indians. According to these treaties, the Indians would stay within certain boundaries. The remaining land would be used for the European settlers and railroads. In return, the government would teach the Indians to become farmers. Most Indian nations, feeling that they had little choice, moved to a government **reservation.** A reservation is land set aside by the government for the Indians. Some Indians, however, chose to fight.

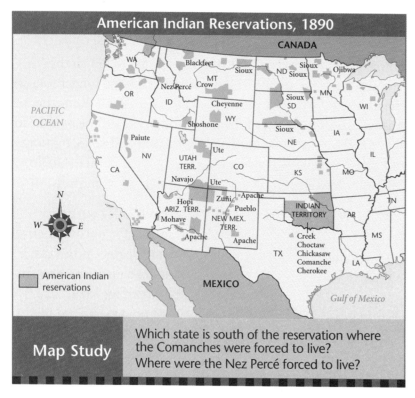

American Indian Reservations, 1890

CANADA

WA · Blackfeet · Sioux · ND Sioux · Ojibwa · MN
MT · Crow · Sioux · WI
Nez Percé · OR · ID · Cheyenne · WY · Sioux · SD
PACIFIC OCEAN · Shoshone · Sioux · NE · IA · IL
Paiute · NV · UTAH TERR. · Ute · CO · KS · MO
CA · Navajo · Ute · TN
Hopi · Zuni · Apache · INDIAN TERRITORY · AR
ARIZ. TERR. · Pueblo · NEW MEX. TERR. · MS
Mohave · Apache · Apache · Creek Choctaw Chickasaw Comanche Cherokee · LA · TX

MEXICO

Gulf of Mexico

☐ American Indian reservations

N W E S

Map Study

Which state is south of the reservation where the Comanches were forced to live?
Where were the Nez Percé forced to live?

By the mid-1870s, after many battles and much bloodshed, most American Indians agreed to live on a reservation. These reservations were in New Mexico, Arizona, and the territories of Dakota and Wyoming. By 1890, there were reservations in many more states, as shown on this map. The government told the Indians that their way of life would be protected.

What Happened When Gold Was Discovered?

The government's reservation policy was tested in 1874. That is when gold was discovered in the Black Hills of what is now South Dakota. This land was holy to the Sioux. They believed the Great Spirit was present in these hills. The United States government had promised that the Black Hills would belong to the Sioux forever.

Government troops tried to protect these hills for the American Indians. But the number of prospectors who wanted gold was too great. It was clear that the government could not keep its word. Chiefs Sitting Bull and Crazy Horse gathered more than 2,000 Sioux and Cheyenne warriors together. They decided to defend their lands.

Colonel George Armstrong Custer and his Seventh Cavalry met this force. It happened at the Little Big Horn River in Montana on June 25, 1876. Custer and about 210 of his troops were killed. The only person or animal that lived was an officer's horse named Comanche.

The defeat of Custer shocked the country. The American Indians had won a great victory. However, Custer's Last Stand, as it was called, would be the last big victory for the Plains Indians. They eventually surrendered to government troops because of lack of food and ammunition.

Chief Joseph

In response to Custer's defeat, the government decided to move all American Indians onto reservations. In the summer of 1877, the government ordered the Nez Percé to a small reservation in Idaho. Settlers took their horses when the Nez Percé were leaving their homes. Angry warriors raided European settlers. The Nez Percé tried to escape to Canada to avoid any more bloodshed.

About 750 Nez Percé fled. Chief Joseph led them. They traveled 1,500 miles in 75 days. The weather was cold, and they did not have blankets. Little food was available. Many died along the way.

The Nez Perce were about 30 miles from the Canadian border when Chief Joseph urged his people to surrender. He told them he was tired of fighting. "Hear me, my chiefs," he said. "I am tired; my heart is sick and sad. From where the sun now stands I will fight no more forever."

Misunderstanding

Failure to understand

What Did Chief Red Cloud Do?

In 1870, Chief Red Cloud of the Oglala Sioux wanted to inform the government officials of the problems of the Plains Indians. He spoke at a meeting in Washington, D.C. He told the audience about broken treaties, dishonest government agents, fear, and **misunderstanding.** Red Cloud wanted the president of the United States, whom he called the Great Father, to understand that he wanted peace.

What do you think?

What do you think Chief Joseph meant when he said, "I will fight no more forever"?

Lesson 3 Review Choose the word or name in parentheses that best completes each sentence. Write your answers on a sheet of paper.

1. (Colonel Custer, Buffalo Bill, Red Cloud) was defeated at Little Big Horn.

2. The Nez Percé were led by Chief (Sitting Bull, Joseph, Red Cloud).

3. In 1877, the U.S. government ordered the (Cheyenne, Sioux, Nez Percé) to a reservation.

4. Chief (Crazy Horse, Joseph, Red Cloud) spoke at a meeting in Washington, D.C.

5. Gold was discovered in (the Black Hills, Montana, Canada) in 1874.

Biography

Cochise: 1815–1874
A chief of the friendly Chiricahua Apaches, Cochise was falsely accused of seizing a rancher's child in 1861. Cochise declared he was innocent, but the U.S. Army arrested him. He escaped, and fighting followed. Thus the Apache Wars began. Cochise led his band of Apaches on raids against American troops and European settlers. The raids nearly drove the settlers from Arizona. In 1871, General George Crook forced Cochise to surrender. With a peace treaty in 1872, Cochise agreed to live peaceably on a reservation. He lived on the reservation along Apache Pass until his death in 1874.

(Cochise's picture was never taken for religious reasons. Therefore, no picture appears with his biography.)

Writing About History

Imagine that you are an American Indian Chief. Write a speech in your notebook to your people. Talk about a problem your people face, such as being forced to live on a reservation or losing the buffalo herd.

The American people became aware of what had happened to the American Indians living on the western frontier. In 1881, Helen Hunt Jackson published *A Century of Dishonor*, a detailed history of how the Indians were mistreated. Her book was sent to every member of Congress.

Why Was the Dawes Severalty Act Passed?

Congress passed the Dawes Severalty Act in 1887. *Severalty* means separateness. The purpose of the law was to turn the American Indians into independent farmers. Their lands were divided into family-size farms. Any Indians who accepted land would be made citizens of the United States. They could not sell their land for 25 years. The Dawes Act attempted to protect the Indians from being cheated. In many cases, however, the Indians were cheated by land-hungry European settlers. In some cases, even government agents took advantage of them. It was not until 1924 that all Indians were made citizens.

What Happened at Wounded Knee?

In the late 1800s, some American Indian tribes practiced a religion called the Ghost Dance. The Indians wore special clothing during the dance. They believed this clothing would protect them from soldiers' bullets. They also hoped to bring back the buffalo herds, remove settlers from their lands, and bring back their old way of life.

The Seventh Cavalry killed hundreds of Sioux on this site at Wounded Knee, South Dakota.

The Ghost Dance frightened the settlers. They thought it might be a war dance. An army was sent to prevent violence. The Seventh Cavalry arrived to arrest and disarm several hundred Ghost Dance followers at Wounded Knee, South Dakota, on December 28, 1890.

The next day, the cavalry tried to disarm the Ghost Dance followers. Someone fired a shot. It is not known who fired. The soldiers turned their guns on the Indians and killed or wounded about 290 men, women, and children. Twenty-five soldiers were also killed. This massacre at Wounded Knee ended the fighting between the United States government and the American Indians of the western plains.

It Happened in History

George Catlin, Painter of American Indians

Much of what we know about different American Indian cultures during this time comes from the work of George Catlin. George Catlin was a painter who spent many years painting pictures of American Indians. Beginning in 1830, he lived among them and learned their languages. Catlin made more than 500 paintings of people from 50 different tribes. He continued to paint and write almost until his death in 1872. His paintings and the books he wrote about his experiences recorded many sides of the daily lives of the Indians. Today, most of his paintings are in a special wing of the National Museum of American Art in Washington, D.C.

George Catlin

This George Catlin painting shows a Mandan Bull Dance.

Western States Admitted to the Union, 1864–1912			
1864	Nevada	1890	Idaho
1867	Nebraska	1890	Wyoming
1876	Colorado	1896	Utah
1889	North Dakota	1907	Oklahoma
1889	South Dakota	1912	New Mexico
1889	Montana	1912	Arizona
1889	Washington		

Which Western Lands Became States?

Settlers had moved into most areas of the western frontier. By 1890, for the first time in American history, there was no frontier line. The frontier had been conquered. Between 1864 and 1912, the United States created 13 states from these western lands.

Word Bank

American Indians

citizens

farmers

ghost dance

13

Lesson 4 Review Choose the word or words from the Word Bank that best complete each sentence. Write your answer on a sheet of paper.

1. Helen Hunt Jackson's book *A Century of Dishonor* described how _____ were mistreated.

2. The purpose of the Dawes Severalty Act was to make American Indians into independent _____.

3. Beside granting them farmland, the Dawes Severalty Act made Indians who accepted the farmland _____.

4. In 1890, the cavalry killed 290 American Indians who were attending a _____ at Wounded Knee.

5. The western lands were made into _____ states between 1864 and 1912.

What do you think?

Why do you think the Ghost Dance was important to American Indian people?

"The Laws"

In the late 1800s, thousands immigrated to America from Europe and Asia. Chinese-American writer Maxine Hong Kingston has examined immigrants' right to belong in America. In her book China Men, *Kingston included laws against Chinese immigration.*

The United States . . . and . . . China . . . recognize the . . . right of man to change his home and allegiance, and . . . the advantage of free . . . emigration of their citizens . . . from the one country to the other. . . . Article V of the Burlingame Treaty, signed in Washington, D.C., July 28, 1868. . . .

1868: . . . the year 40,000 miners of Chinese ancestry were Driven Out. The Fourteenth Amendment, adopted in that same year, said that naturalized Americans have the same rights as native-born Americans, but in 1870 the Nationality Act specified that only 'free white' and 'African aliens' were allowed to apply for naturalization. Chinese were not white. . . .

1878: California . . . prohibited Chinese from entering. . . . New state laws empowered cities . . . to confine them . . . or to throw them out. Shipowners . . . were to be fined for . . . transporting them. . . . [Chinese] were barred from attending public schools. The only California fishermen forced to pay fishing and shellfish taxes were the Chinese . . . they were prohibited from owning . . . real estate. They could not apply for business licenses.

Employers could be fined . . . for hiring them. No Chinese could be hired by . . . governments. . . . No Chinese . . . could testify in court 'either for or against a white man'. . . . Federal courts declared some of the state and city laws unconstitutional. . . . The . . . laws were reenacted in another form.

1880: The Burlingame Treaty was modified. . . . the immigration of Chinese laborers to the United States would be 'reasonably limited.' In return . . . the American government promised to protect Chinese from lynchings.

1881: The Burlingame Treaty was suspended for . . . twenty years. . . . In protest . . . China ordered scholars studying in the United States to return home. . . .

Document-Based Questions

1. What did the Nationality Act of 1870 say?

2. How did the U.S. government offer to protect the Chinese?

3. The Burlingame Treaty was suspended for 20 years. How did the Chinese respond?

4. How did the United States never really abide by the original Burlingame Treaty?

5. Which do you think was the most unreasonable law or event in the passage? Why?

Source: China Men *by Maxine Hong Kingston, 1980.*

- The Great Plains stretched between the Missouri River and the Rocky Mountains.

- In 1862, Congress provided money for the transcontinental railroad. The railroad was finished in 1869. It was built by two companies—the Union Pacific Railroad and the Central Pacific Railroad.

- Miners, farmers, and cowhands were the first Europeans to settle the West. Miners were drawn to gold discoveries in Nevada, Montana, Idaho, Wyoming, and Colorado. Cowhands and cattle ranchers raised cattle for beef, hides, and other goods. The Homestead Act of 1862 encouraged farmers and homesteaders to settle land in the West.

- The Plains Indians were nomads. Their way of life was changed forever when farmers, ranchers, and others killed off the buffalo herds. Many American Indians were moved to reservations. The U.S. government promised the Indians that their way of life would be protected.

- When gold was discovered in 1874 in the Black Hills of South Dakota, the government's policy to protect the American Indians was tested. Gold prospectors wanted to make claims on the land, a holy land for the Sioux.

- Government troops tried but could not protect the Black Hills region for the American Indians. In the end, the Indians chose to protect their land. Colonel Custer and about 210 members of the U.S. Cavalry fought and lost a battle against the Sioux and the Cheyenne at Little Big Horn in 1876.

- Congress passed the Dawes Severalty Act in 1887. This act tried to protect American Indians. However, settlers still cheated the Indians.

- In 1890, the Seventh Cavalry was sent to prevent violence between settlers and American Indians because of the Ghost Dance. The soldiers ended up killing or wounding about 290 men, women, and children at Wounded Knee.

- Between 1864 and 1912, 13 states were added to the United States.

Chapter 2   R E V I E W

On a sheet of paper, write the correct word or words from the Word Bank to complete each sentence.

1. The _____ Railroad laid over 1,000 miles of railroad track.

2. Chinese immigrants worked for the _____ Railroad.

3. Gold discovered in the _____ region tested the government's reservation policy.

4. The _____ was land between the Missouri River and the Rocky Mountains.

5. The _____ was passed to turn the American Indians into farmers.

6. A _____ is a person who searches for gold, silver, or other minerals.

7. The _____ made it easier for pioneers to settle land.

8. Some American Indians believed in a religious movement known as the _____.

9. _____ was defeated at Little Big Horn.

10. U.S. soldiers killed or wounded about 290 men, women, and children at _____.

On a sheet of paper, write the letter of the answer that correctly completes each sentence.

11. The transcontinental railroad was completed in 1869 at _____.

A Sacramento, California   **C** Promontory Point, Utah
B Omaha, Nebraska   **D** St. Louis, Missouri

12. A problem for ranchers that the railroad helped solve was _____.

A lack of transportation   **C** lack of law and order
B herding cattle   **D** Indian attacks

13. _____ led the Nez Percé to the Canada border before surrendering.

A Red Cloud   **C** Crazy Horse

B Sitting Bull   **D** Chief Joseph

On a sheet of paper, write the answers to the following questions. Use complete sentences.

14. Where in the West did pioneers travel? How did they get there?

15. Why was the transcontinental railroad built?

16. What three kinds of people lived on the frontier? What did each do?

17. How was the Plains Indians' way of life destroyed?

18. During what time period did many western states enter the Union? How many western states entered the Union during this time?

Critical Thinking On a sheet of paper, write your response to each question. Use complete sentences.

19. What do you think would be a good title for a book describing what happened to the Plains Indians? Why?

20. Do you think you would have liked living on the frontier? Why or why not?

Test-Taking Tip

Studying together in small groups and asking questions of one another is one way to review material for tests.

Becoming an Industrial Giant
1870–1900

In the early 1800s, most Americans were farmers or shop owners. Manufacturing in small factories was done mostly in areas of the Northeast. During the Civil War, the need for war supplies, farm equipment, and machines of all types increased. Following the completion of the railroads after the war, the transportation of people and materials between the two coasts made manufacturing in all parts of the country easier. Tariffs on imports made products from other countries more expensive. Americans wanted products that had been made in America. As the population continued to grow, so did the demand for more and better products. Industry became common. In this chapter, you will learn more about how industry increased in the United States.

Goals for Learning

◆ To describe the development of the steel industry

◆ To describe the development of the petroleum industry and the new ways in which businesses were organized

◆ To list new industries and inventions that changed the world

1870
John D. Rockefeller starts Standard Oil Company of Ohio

1876
Thomas Edison starts lab in Menlo Park

1877
Thomas Edison invents phonograph

1870   1872   1874   1876   1878   1880   1882   1900

1873
Andrew Carnegie enters steel industry

1876
Alexander Graham Bell invents telephone

1883
Brooklyn Bridge opens

Petroleum

A liquid that can be made into fuel

Entrepreneur

A person who starts and organizes a business

Purify

To make something pure

Flexible

Able to move or twist easily

Method

A way of doing something

People all over America began discovering and using the country's many natural resources—coal, iron, lumber, and **petroleum**. Petroleum is a liquid that can be made into fuel. As ways of doing things were improved and machines were invented, new industries were formed. A large flow of immigrants gave these industries an eager labor force.

Strong business leaders helped American industries grow. Andrew Carnegie and John D. Rockefeller were **entrepreneurs**. An entrepreneur is a person who starts and organizes a business. They used the opportunities of this new industrial age. These men played an important part in starting the nation's steel and oil industries.

How Did Andrew Carnegie Develop the Steel Industry?

Andrew Carnegie realized that most bridges in the country were made from wood. One day he saw men building a bridge out of iron instead of wood. He soon organized the Keystone Bridge Company to build iron bridges for railroad companies.

Carnegie began to realize that iron was not the best product with which to build bridges. Iron would rust, and it was not very strong. It cracked and broke when bent. He needed to find another material to make bridges. He knew steel, which is **purified** iron, was very strong and **flexible**. However, steel was expensive to produce in large amounts.

Andrew Carnegie

Back in the 1850s, two men had developed an inexpensive way of making large amounts of steel. William Kelly, an American, discovered a **method** of making iron into steel. Meanwhile, in England, Henry Bessemer had developed a similar method. They had both discovered that the impurities in iron could be "burned off" by blowing cold air through heated iron.

Suspension bridge

A large bridge supported by wires or chains attached to tall towers

Engineering

Using science and math to design and construct buildings or other objects

Skyscraper

A tall building

While visiting England, Carnegie learned about how this method worked. He returned to America and entered the new steel industry in 1873. Carnegie's company made steel for railroad tracks that cost half as much as iron tracks and were much stronger.

How Did Steel Become an Important Building Material?

Inexpensive steel rapidly changed America. The longest **suspension bridge** in the world at the time, the Brooklyn Bridge in New York, was opened in 1883. A suspension bridge is a large bridge supported by wires or chains attached to tall towers. It was a wonderful example of modern **engineering.** Tall buildings built on steel supports began to appear. They rose 10 to 20 stories high. This height seemed so great that people called them **skyscrapers.** Soon steel was used to make such things as pins, nails, washtubs, and barbed wire for fences.

Agricultural and Industrial Workers

3.75 million | 2.3 million
1840

6.7 million | 5 million
1870

9.5 million | 13.75 million
1890

■ Agricultural workers
□ Industrial workers

By how much did the number of industrial workers increase between 1840 and 1890? How many agricultural workers were there in 1870?

Carnegie's steel company produced most of the steel in the United States. He retired a very rich man in 1901. He was generous with his money. Carnegie funded libraries, colleges, medical research, and many other projects. He gave away more than $350 million in his lifetime.

History in Your Life

The Brooklyn Bridge
Until the 1880s, New Yorkers used a ferry to cross the East River from Manhattan to Brooklyn. In 1867, a bridge was designed and a company was hired to build it. John A. Roebling, a pioneer in suspension bridge design, created the Brooklyn Bridge plan. He died before the bridge was built. Roebling's son, Washington, supervised construction, which began in 1869. In 1872, Washington Roebling became ill and could not leave his bed. His wife, Emily, managed the rest of the construction.

When the bridge opened on May 24, 1883, it was hailed as the "eighth wonder of the world." With a main span of 1,595 feet, it was the world's longest bridge. It also was the first suspension bridge to use steel wire cables. Four main cables nearly 16 inches thick are hung from two massive 275-foot granite towers. Foundations 78 feet below water level support the towers. The bridge cost $15 million. In 1964, the Brooklyn Bridge was declared a national historic site. Its six traffic lanes and its sidewalks make crossing the East River easy.

New York's Brooklyn Bridge opened in 1883. The bridge is a national historic site today.

Technology Connection

The Mail-Order Catalog

In 1870, the majority of Americans lived on farms. They had to go to town to buy goods. Usually, this meant a long trip. Once the farmer arrived in town, the store might have only a few goods that the farmer needed.

In 1872, A. Montgomery Ward helped change how farmers bought goods. He set up a mail-order company in Chicago, Illinois. It sold many kinds of goods to farmers. The idea caught on quickly. Soon, many farmers were ordering from catalogs.

In the 1880s, Richard W. Sears began selling watches by mail. Before long, he and a partner set up a mail-order company for general goods. They sold tools, clothes, and things for the home. They published their first catalog in 1888. By 1900, Sears and his partner were selling about $10 million in merchandise per year.

Farm families could now order products in the latest styles and models. The prices were lower than those at local stores. The buyer did not have to pay delivery charges for the goods. Mail order greatly improved the lives of American farmers.

Word Bank

Andrew Carnegie

Brooklyn

entrepreneur

skyscraper

William Kelly

Lesson 1 Review On a sheet of paper, write the correct word or words from the Word Bank to complete each sentence.

1. A(n) _____ is a person who starts a business.

2. The longest suspension bridge in the world at the time it opened was the _____ Bridge.

3. A(n) _____ is a tall building.

4. _____ built the first steel plant in the country.

5. _____ discovered a way to make iron into steel.

What do you think?

How is steel still important today?

Refinery

A place where a good is made pure or made into other products

Geography Note

Oil fields dot the United States. When people think of oil, they often think of Oklahoma. Oklahoma's oil reserves are among the largest in the United States. Oil wells and their towers appear all around the state. Today, visitors can view oil pumps on the dusty plains. The pumps duck up and down, like giant insects sucking their black riches from the ground.

A stream called Oil Creek flowed through the village of Titusville, about 100 miles north of Pittsburgh, Pennsylvania. It was called Oil Creek because of the black, sticky oil that came up to the surface from below the ground. Most people believed that oil was not very valuable. Then, in 1855, a scientist reported that half of the petroleum or "rock oil" could be made into a product that could be burned in lamps.

This report caught the attention of Edwin Drake, who traveled to the small village of Titusville, Pennsylvania. After one unsuccessful attempt, Drake drilled a hole in the ground using pipes to keep the sides from falling in. From 69 feet in the earth, oil began running through the pipe. This happened in August 1859. This first oil well turned out to be the beginning of America's giant oil industry.

Soon, Titusville was filled with "oil prospectors" in search of "black gold." Oil wells appeared all along Oil Creek and areas of southwestern New York. Railroad tank cars and large pipes called pipelines were built to carry the oil to **refineries**. Oil was made into different products at these refineries. Titusville became a place where fortunes could be made overnight.

Edwin Drake (right front) built this oil well in Titusville, Pennsylvania.

What Business Did Rockefeller Start?

John D. Rockefeller traveled from Cleveland, Ohio, to Titusville to see how he and his partners could make money from the new oil business. Rockefeller decided that he was not interested in drilling for oil because it was too risky. He believed that he could make more money refining it.

Rockefeller organized and became the president of a new company, the Standard Oil Company of Ohio, in 1870. Within 10 years, the company became the most powerful company in its field. The company controlled the production and price of oil throughout the country.

In the early years, most oil was refined into a fuel called **kerosene** that was used for lamps. The need for these lamps ended about 1900, after the electric light was invented. However, the widespread popularity of the motor car in the 1900s created a new use for an oil product—gasoline.

How Did Business Change?

Before the Civil War, most businesses were owned by one person or a group of partners. These businesses usually employed a few workers. They sold their goods to local customers. This simple organization worked well for small businesses. After the Civil War, as businesses grew larger, many organized into **corporations.** These are large companies owned by shareholders.

John D. Rockefeller

Andrew Carnegie, John D. Rockefeller, and other business leaders were **criticized** for forming large companies. The critics believed that big businesses were too powerful. They felt it was impossible for smaller businesses to compete with them. Large corporations that have little competition are called **monopolies**. Without competition from other companies selling the same product, a monopoly can charge higher prices for poorer quality products. The buyer, with no other company to turn to, has little choice but to pay that price or do without the product.

Kerosene

A fuel used in lamps

Corporation

A large, organized company owned by stockholders

Criticize

To show disapproval

Monopoly

A corporation that has little competition

How Were Corporations Important to Business Growth?

Corporations are usually a safe form of business organization. Individuals invest, or deposit, money into corporations. They are protected if the corporation fails. A person who invests in a corporation has limited risk, or **liability,** for the company's debts.

Money used for investment is called **capital**. A corporation allows thousands of people to invest in a business by buying shares of stock. People who own stock can make money on their investment if the company is profitable. Corporations like Carnegie Steel and Standard Oil raised millions of dollars by selling stock.

How Did Companies Become Larger?

Business leaders searched for new ways to organize their companies. Andrew Carnegie did not want to depend on other companies to produce his product. He relied on mining and railroad companies. He found a new, simple solution. He bought

Ore
Coke
Coal
Manganese

Ships
Railroads

Furnace
Mills
Products

Freight
for
Export

Carnegie Steel Company

mining and transportation companies and combined them into one large company. This allowed Andrew Carnegie to control each step in making steel. This type of new business organization became known as **vertical combination.**

John D. Rockefeller was also concerned with control. He decided to get rid of competition by buying other oil refining companies. This type of organization is known as **horizontal combination**. Standard Oil Corporation became more powerful each time Rockefeller bought a new refinery.

Vertical combination allowed Carnegie to control each step in steel production.

Raw Materials	Area of Combination	Sales

Drilling
Mining

Refinery

Standard Oil

Oil • Gas • Tar
Kerosene

Horizontal combination allowed Rockefeller to eliminate competition.

Trust company

A large, powerful company that often is a monopoly

What do you think?

How is oil still important today?

Each of these types of businesses took away competition. Carnegie Steel and Standard Oil became monopolies. They were called **trust companies**. Many kinds of trust companies developed. A trust company became a popular tool for businesses to increase their wealth. Sugar, copper, railroad, and tobacco companies were all controlled by monopolies or trusts. Trust companies could employ thousands of workers. They became giant industries that were very powerful. This changed America into an industrial nation.

Lesson 2 Review Choose the best word or name in parentheses to complete each sentence. Write your answers on a sheet of paper.

1. The first oil well was built in (New York, Pennsylvania, Ohio).

2. (Andrew Carnegie, John D. Rockefeller, Edwin Drake) organized Standard Oil Company.

3. A (monopoly, liability, refinery) is a company that has little competition.

4. A kind of business organization that controls each step in making something is called a (trust company, horizontal combination, vertical combination).

5. A large, powerful company that often is a monopoly is called a (trust company, vertical combination, liability).

As the railroads were built across the nation, they helped provide the key to the success of cattle ranching. The ranchers shipped their cattle to large midwestern cities such as Chicago. In these cities, the meatpacking industry, as developed by Philip Armour, Gustavus Swift, and Nelson Morris, began to do well in the late 1890s. Cattle and hogs were **slaughtered** for meats and meat **by-products**. These products were transported to all parts of the country in refrigerated railroad cars.

Cornelius Vanderbilt

Leaders in the construction of new railroad lines in the late 1800s included Cornelius Vanderbilt and James J. Hill. Vanderbilt linked a number of short railroads in the Northeast, creating America's first great railroad system—the New York Central. His system was the first to use steel rails, steel bridges, and double tracks. James J. Hill, who became known as "The Empire Builder," developed the Great Northern Railway System to the Northwest. He encouraged immigrants to settle in that region by teaching them the newest farming methods. He founded schools and helped to start businesses that could provide different types of employment and services.

How Did Inventions Change American Society?

Americans have always been proud of their ability to invent new machines and tools. This sense of pride was never higher than after the Civil War. These were exciting years for American inventors. Some of the most important inventions used in America today were produced during this time. Many were made by Thomas Alva Edison.

Edison was known as "The Wizard of Menlo Park." A wizard is someone who is supposed to have magical powers. Edison, who never claimed to have any special powers, said his success was due to hard work.

Thomas Edison invented the phonograph.

In 1876, Edison started a research laboratory in Menlo Park, New Jersey. He brought scientists, engineers, machinists, and even clock makers together in this one place. He organized them into a team to produce things that businesses and the public could use. Edison said that his "invention factory" could turn out a minor invention every 10 days and a major one every six months.

The indoor electric lightbulb was one of Edison's finest inventions. For several years, outdoor electric lights had been used in a few cities. Up until Edison's time, however, oil and gas lamps provided the only indoor lighting. After searching for two years, Edison found the solution for safe indoor electric lighting.

Reproduce

To copy or duplicate

Phonograph

A machine used to reproduce sound

The first words **reproduced** by a machine were "Mary had a little lamb." Edison spoke this line from a children's poem into his **phonograph** in 1877. Phonographs were used to reproduce sound. His improvements to Alexander Graham Bell's telephone allowed people to speak naturally instead of shouting, as was necessary with Bell's early telephone. Edison invented a successful motion picture machine. He later added sound by joining it with his phonograph.

It Happened in History

George Washington Carver

The work of an African American scientist, George Washington Carver, changed farming in the South. Carver was born near the end of the Civil War. His family was enslaved. He graduated from Iowa State Agricultural College in 1894. Booker T. Washington, an African American leader, asked Carver to join the Tuskegee Institute in Alabama two years later. At Tuskegee, Carver taught and did research. He developed many new products from pecans, peanuts, and sweet potatoes. Because of his work, southern farmers had other cash crops to grow besides cotton.

What Were Other Important Inventions?

Typesetting

The methods used to prepare type to be printed

Many important inventions came out of the 1870s and 1880s. Bell invented the telephone in 1876. George Eastman simplified the Kodak camera in 1880 so that more people could take photographs. Ottmar Mergenthaler invented a machine in 1884 that would make **typesetting** much easier for newspaper and book publishers all over the country. Typesetting is the method used to prepare type to be printed. Elisha Otis invented the elevator, which made the construction of skyscrapers more appealing. The first electric elevator was installed in 1889.

Other inventors followed. Henry Ford experimented with gasoline-powered automobile engines. He developed an assembly line method for building cars cheaply. Shortly into the next century, Ford would make it possible for the average American to own an automobile.

Each of these inventors did more than create a new machine. Each invention created a new industry. These industries created new jobs for the American worker and a brighter future for the country.

Alexander Graham Bell made the first long-distance call with his telephone in 1892.

Environmental

Having to do with the surroundings that affect the growth and development of living things

Pollution

Anything added to the environment that is harmful to living things

Conservation

The act of protecting or limiting the use of natural resources

Natural resources

Raw materials from nature, such as water and soil

How Did Industrial Development Affect the Environment?

Industrial development created new industries, new jobs, and new wealth. But it changed the nation in another way too. There was an **environmental** cost to this development. The air near factories grew more **polluted.** Waste products from factories and mines caused water pollution.

Starting in the 1890s, concern about the environment gradually became more common. Laws were passed to help protect forests, rivers, and wildlife. National parks were created, such as California's Yosemite National Park in 1890. The Sierra Club started in 1892, one of many groups and clubs that came together to promote **conservation** of **natural resources**. Theodore Roosevelt, who would become president in 1901, started many important conservation programs.

Writing About History

Research an invention that was developed between 1870 and 1900. Then write a paragraph in your notebook describing what it is used for and how it works.

Then and Now

How do you think the Wright brothers' airplane compares with a modern jet? It was the Wrights who completed the first successful flight in 1903. Look at this table to compare the two planes.

Description	Wright's Flyer	A Boeing 747
Materials	Wood and cloth	Metal
Weight	750 pounds	775,000 pounds
Wing span	40.5 feet	196 feet
Length	21 feet	231 feet
Flight distance	120 feet	6,000 miles
Time in flight	12 seconds	15 hours
Altitude	40 feet	40,000 feet
Passengers held	1 person	400 people
Speed capacity	30 mph	600+ mph
Power source	Two propellers	Turbojet engine
Fuel storage	Less than 1 gallon	47,000 gallons

Lesson 3 Review On a sheet of paper, write the answers to the following questions. Use complete sentences.

1. How were railroads the key to success for cattle ranchers?

2. Why is James J. Hill called "The Empire Builder"?

3. What are some of the inventions that Thomas Edison and his team at Menlo Park produced?

4. What contribution did Alexander Graham Bell make?

5. How did Henry Ford make automobiles cheap and affordable?

What do you think?

Which of the inventions mentioned in this lesson do you think had the most impact on society today? Why?

Biography

Horatio Alger: 1834–1899
Horatio Alger wrote more than 100 books about poor young boys who became rich and successful through honesty and hard work. His popular "rags-to-riches" stories were meant to inspire and teach young people. He also wanted to educate adults about the horrible conditions in which some children lived. An activist, Alger helped to inspire new laws against child labor. Alger disappointed his father—a Unitarian minister—when he abandoned a career as a minister and became a writer. Alger moved to New York City, where he befriended many homeless orphan children. The children had come to the city after the Civil War. He often based characters in his books on children he knew.

Queen Liliuokalani's Statement on Hawaii

With the help of U.S. Marines, American business leaders attempted to take over the government of Hawaii in 1891. Queen Liliuokalani of Hawaii was unwilling to surrender the government. Still, she did not want to see any battle. She issued this statement to American authorities on January 17, 1893.

I Liliuokalani, by the Grace of God and under the Constitution of the Hawaiian Kingdom, Queen, do hereby solemnly protest against any and all acts done against myself and the Constitutional Government of the Hawaiian Kingdom by certain persons claiming to have established a Provisional Government of and for this Kingdom.

That I yield to the superior force of the United States of America, whose minister... His Excellency John L. Stevens, has caused the United States troops to be landed at Honolulu and declared that he would support the Provisional Government.

Now to avoid any collision of armed forces, and perhaps the loss of life, I do this under protest and impelled by said force yield my authority until such time as the Government of the United States shall, upon the facts being presented to it, undo the action of its representatives and reinstate me in the authority which I claim as the Constitutional Sovereign of the Hawaiian Islands.

Document-Based Questions

1. What did Queen Liliuokalani say the business leaders had established?

2. What did John L. Stevens do and say about the Hawaiian situation?

3. Why was Queen Liliuokalani giving up control of Hawaii?

4. For how long was she giving up control of Hawaii?

5. Do you think that Queen Liliuokalani's response was a wise one? Why or why not?

Source: History of the Later Years of the Hawaiian Monarchy *by W. D. Alexander, 1896.*

Chapter 3   S U M M A R Y

- In the second half of the 1800s, the United States began to develop new industries. Before this time, most Americans were farmers or shopkeepers.

- Andrew Carnegie began a business that built iron bridges. Carnegie's factories used an inexpensive method of converting iron into steel.

- Carnegie dominated the steel industry. He became a very wealthy man and contributed to many charities.

- Edwin Drake drilled the first oil well near Titusville, Pennsylvania. "Black gold" brought many people to Titusville to search for their fortunes.

- John D. Rockefeller formed a corporation, the Standard Oil Company of Ohio, to refine crude petroleum into usable oil. Rockefeller's company became the most powerful in the oil business.

- Early oil companies refined kerosene for lamps. Later they produced gasoline to be used in cars.

- After the Civil War, companies became much larger. Large companies called corporations were started. They were owned by many investors who bought stock in the corporation and earned money from their investments.

- Carnegie bought mining and railroad companies and combined them into one large corporation. Rockefeller tried to eliminate competition by buying other oil refining companies. These large companies were monopolies, since they had little competition.

- Cornelius Vanderbilt and James J. Hill made fortunes by constructing and running railroad systems. Railroads were important for the meatpacking industry.

- Many inventions changed peoples' lives during this period. The inventions included Thomas Edison's indoor electric lightbulb and phonograph, Alexander Graham Bell's telephone, George Eastman's Kodak camera, and Henry Ford's assembly line.

Chapter 3 REVIEW

On a sheet of paper, write the correct word or name from the Word Bank to complete each sentence.

Word Bank

Andrew Carnegie

"The Empire Builder"

engine

George Eastman

meatpacking

monopoly

natural resources

phonograph

railroads

Standard Oil Company

1. James J. Hill built the Great Northern Railway System and was known as _____.

2. _____ gave millions of dollars to fund libraries, colleges, and medical research.

3. Rockefeller's _____ refined crude petroleum into oil and kerosene.

4. A large company or corporation that has little or no competition is called a(n) _____.

5. Railroads helped people like Philip Armour and Gustavus Swift develop the _____ industry.

6. Thomas Edison recited "Mary had a little lamb" on the _____, one of his inventions.

7. _____ simplified the Kodak camera, making it possible for thousands of people to take photographs.

8. Henry Ford helped develop a gasoline powered _____ that would later be used in automobiles.

9. Cornelius Vanderbilt made his fortune building _____.

10. _____ such as coal, iron, and petroleum helped the United States to become an industrial giant.

On a sheet of paper, write the letter of the answer that correctly completes each sentence.

11. The manufacture of _____ made it possible to build strong railroad tracks, skyscrapers, and bridges.

   A automobiles   **C** telephones
   B steel   **D** electricity

12. To control their markets, business owners bought competing companies. This strategy is called _____.

    A horizontal combination   **C** capital growth
    B vertical combination   **D** shares of stock

13. Indoor electric lighting was invented by _____.

    A Alexander Graham Bell   **C** Cornelius Vanderbilt
    B Elisha Otis   **D** Thomas Edison

On a sheet of paper, write the answers to the following questions. Use complete sentences.

14. How did Andrew Carnegie's steel company become so successful?

15. How did James J. Hill bring people to the Northwest?

16. How is a corporation organized?

17. What was Rockefeller's contribution to the oil industry?

18. How did Edison create so many inventions at his Menlo Park laboratory?

Critical Thinking On a sheet of paper, write your response to each question. Use complete sentences.

19. What are some of the problems with becoming an industrial society?

20. Oil is one of the most highly used natural resources today. How do you think the world would be a different place today without oil?

Test-Taking Tip

When studying for a test, practice writing or saying the material out loud. Have a partner listen to check if you are right.

4 A Nation of Cities
1882–1900

As industry grew in the United States, so did the nation's cities. Immigrant groups and other people began to live in cities because they wanted to be close to factories. Though city life had much to offer, people living in cities faced tough working and living conditions. Many people faced discrimination. In this chapter, you will learn what it was like to live in the nation's cities.

Goals for Learning

◆ To identify reasons for the growth of cities

◆ To describe working conditions in factories

◆ To explain the reasons for different immigrant groups coming to the United States

◆ To explain how immigrants and African Americans faced discrimination

◆ To describe some of the developments that made city living interesting

◆ To explain why cities had social problems

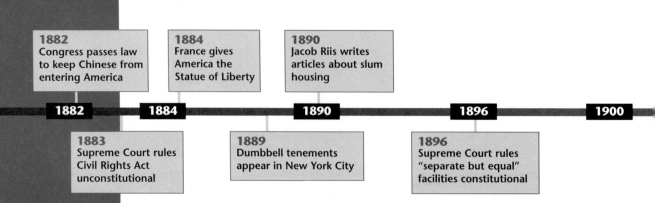

1882
Congress passes law to keep Chinese from entering America

1884
France gives America the Statue of Liberty

1890
Jacob Riis writes articles about slum housing

1882   **1884**   **1890**   **1896**   **1900**

1883
Supreme Court rules Civil Rights Act unconstitutional

1889
Dumbbell tenements appear in New York City

1896
Supreme Court rules "separate but equal" facilities constitutional

Dweller

A person who lives in a place

Specialize

To make and sell goods or services in one or two areas of business

Urban

Related to the city

By 1850, more than 23 million people lived in the United States. Twenty million of them lived on farms, in towns, and in areas smaller than towns called villages. Three and a half million (or 15 percent) of the American people lived in cities. By 1900, this percentage of city **dwellers** had increased to 40 percent.

People were drawn to cities for many reasons. Cities had exciting events. Cities had many different things to do and places to go. The main reason people moved to cities was because they could find jobs. American industry grew as more and more factories were opened in or near cities. Factories were usually built near railroad lines or a good seaport. Large factories needed many workers.

American cities usually **specialized** in one or two industries. Pittsburgh, Pennsylvania, became the nation's center for making steel. Cleveland, Ohio, became an important oil-refining city.

Chicago, Illinois, grew because of the meatpacking business. Other cities like Salt Lake City, Utah; Kansas City, Missouri; and San Francisco, California, grew with the arrival of the railroad.

Railroads were a good way to move products and people from one end of the country to the other. Cities were no longer isolated from one another. Raw materials and products in one city could be shipped easily and cheaply to other cities around the nation.

Growth of Urban Population 1870–1900

Rural   Urban

Year	1870	1880	1890	1900
Rural	72%	72%	68%	60%
Urban	28%	28%	32%	40%

Population in Millions

Employer

A person or company that pays workers for their services

Geography Note

Immigrants moved to cities because that's where the factories were. Factories meant jobs. They were usually built near seaports and rivers that made moving products easier, because boats and barges could be used. Sometimes factories and mills used waterwheels, which used energy from flowing water in rivers.

How Were American Workers Treated?

America's new industries needed workers. Large factories and industrial plants employed hundreds or even thousands of workers. Mass production lowered the cost of products. The success of one industry usually led to new, similar industries. Each new industry created more jobs.

Competition for these jobs was great. **Employers** did not have to pay high salaries because so many workers were available. Many workers earned less than $10.00 for a 60-hour workweek, including only one day off.

Poor working conditions were also a problem. Powerful machines were dangerous. Most employers believed that it was the workers' duty to protect themselves from dangerous or unsafe working conditions. Workers who were hurt on the job received no help from the employer. Many children also worked in the factories.

Workers like these often worked long hours in poor working conditions.

If you were a child in the 1800s, you might have had to work. No laws restricted child labor at that time. Some poor children did not go to school and instead went to work. Children as young as seven or eight years old helped to make cloth in textile mills. They started by sweeping floors. Later they removed lint or mended broken thread. Barefoot boys under age 10 climbed onto running machines. They removed empty bobbins of thread and replaced them with filled bobbins. Child laborers worked 12 to 15 hours per day every day but Sunday. They made only a few cents per day.

Today, U.S. laws prevent employers from hiring children under 16 years old. However, child labor still exists in some

developing countries. American children are required to attend school until they are 16 years old. If you have a job, your working conditions are a lot different from those in the 1800s.

Lesson 1 Review On a sheet of paper, write the correct word from the Word Bank to complete each sentence.

Word Bank

dwellers

employers

jobs

steel

wages

1. By 1900, city _____ made up 40 percent of the American people.

2. People moved to the cities mainly because they could find _____.

3. Pittsburgh, Pennsylvania, was a city that specialized in making _____.

4. Many workers took factory jobs that paid low _____.

5. Workers who were hurt on the job did not get help from their _____.

What do you think?

Many children were forced to work in factories. Why was this unfair?

Steerage

A part of a ship for passengers paying the lowest fare

The Statue of Liberty, an 1884 gift to the United States from France, stands in the harbor of New York City. The huge copper lady holds a golden torch high above her head. She provided a first look at America for millions of immigrants. They had come to America seeking liberty, jobs, and an opportunity for a better life. Ellis Island is also in New York Harbor. There the immigrants faced medical inspections and questions about legal status. Some were turned away. The main building is now a museum.

Getting to the United States was very difficult for most immigrants. A ticket on a steamship often cost an immigrant family all of their savings. Most immigrants bought a ticket in **steerage.** Steerage had the lowest fare. Its passengers had to ride in the dirtiest and noisiest part of the ship in the lowest decks near the engines. The conditions were unhealthy in steerage. The air was stale, and the area was crowded. There was little food, and people often became ill. Immigrants were willing to put up with the conditions to get to America.

Most of the immigrants before the 1880s came from England, Ireland, Germany, Sweden, and Norway. These people were known as "old immigrants." During the 1880s, more than 500,000 "new immigrants" came from Italy, Russia, Poland, and Greece.

The first thing many immigrants to America saw was the Statue of Liberty.

Immigrants came to the United States for many reasons. Many were farmers. Others came to America to escape laws that were unfair. Some came for religious freedom. Almost half of the people who came from Poland and Russia were Jewish.

The Homestead Act of 1862 offered cheap, fertile land to immigrants. American railroad companies **advertised** in Europe to attract immigrants to the American West. However, by the time most immigrants arrived in America, the best land had already been taken. Unable to move on to the western farmlands, most immigrants stayed in America's eastern and midwestern cities.

More than 12 million immigrants passed through Ellis Island between 1892 and 1954.

What Problems Did Immigrants Face?

Few immigrants could speak English. Many were very poor. They had to work hard jobs. Men paved or cleaned streets. Many helped build new skyscrapers. Women found work in clothing factories. Many of these immigrants experienced **discrimination.** Discrimination is treating people unfairly because of their race, sex, religion, or age.

Immigrants from Asia had settled on the west coast, yet many were denied jobs. Much of the hard work on the transcontinental railroad had been done by the Chinese. In 1882, Congress passed a law saying that no more Chinese could come to the United States.

The largest group of new immigrants came from Italy. Most of the immigrants were men. They planned to work in America for only a few years. They hoped to save their money and then return home to Italy and their families. Jewish immigrants from eastern Europe were the next largest group. Many left Europe to escape religious **prejudice**. Prejudice is a belief or action against someone because of race, sex, religion, or age. Unlike the Italians, Jewish immigrants from Russia and Poland did not plan to return to their homeland. Entire families of Jewish people had moved to America.

Some Americans did not like the new immigrants. They feared that immigrants might take jobs that Americans could have, or work at a lower wage. They disliked dealing with people who were not comfortable speaking the English language. Unfortunately, too many people had forgotten that many of their American ancestors had come to the United States as immigrants too.

What Other Groups Faced Discrimination?

Immigrants were not the only people to experience discrimination at this time. The Civil Rights Act of 1875 had made segregation in public places against the law. However, in 1883, the Supreme Court said the Civil Rights Act was unconstitutional. This cleared the way for more laws against African Americans.

The **Jim Crow Laws** were passed in the 1880s and 1890s. These laws separated African Americans and whites in public places. Signs saying "White Ladies Only" and drinking containers marked "White Water" and "Colored Water" began to appear in restaurants, theaters, and railroad cars. The goal of segregation was to develop "separate but equal" African American and white communities. The laws achieved the goal of separating the races. However, African Americans were never treated as equal to whites.

The only hope of ending Jim Crow Laws was the United States Supreme Court. The 14th Amendment, adopted in 1868, said the Bill of Rights applied to African Americans as well as whites. However, the court ruled that this Amendment applied only to state government and not to individuals. Therefore, store owners, railroad companies, and other private businesses could discriminate against African Americans or anyone else. Following this ruling, segregation in the South became even greater. This continued until segregation in the South was again outlawed after World War II.

Civics Connection

From Immigrants to Citizens

Immigrants came to the United States for a better life. They wanted to become citizens. They also wanted to become part of the American culture. This was not an easy task.

After 1860, many immigrants entered the country. Some Americans became uneasy. They feared that these newcomers threatened the nation's unity. Most Americans had ancestors who had come to the United States from other countries, yet they did not like the new immigrants. These newcomers did not look like them or share their culture.

The government put limits on immigration. People mostly from northern Europe were allowed to come to the United States. Jewish, Catholic, Italian, and Asian immigrants faced prejudice. For a time, the law said some ethnic groups, such as the Chinese, could not settle in America.

Yet all of the immigrants helped make America strong. They contributed to the economy and culture.

Today, to become a citizen, an immigrant must:

- live in the United States for 5 years;
- be at least 18 years old;
- be able to read, write, and speak English;
- show an understanding of American history and government;
- take an examination for citizenship;
- make an oath, or promise, of loyalty to the United States in court and in front of a judge.

1. Do you think the government should limit immigration? Explain.

2. Which requirement for citizenship do you think is most important? Explain.

Writing About History

Write a dialogue between an immigrant to the United States and an American-born citizen. Express each person's worries and hopes for the future. Include each person's feelings about immigration.

What Was *Plessy v. Ferguson?*

Louisiana passed a law in 1890 requiring railroad companies to provide "separate but equal facilities" for African American and white passengers. Homer Plessy tested this law in 1892. This African American refused to move from the "white only" car in which he was riding. Plessy's purpose was to challenge the "separate but equal" law. He was arrested and brought before a judge named Ferguson. Plessy was found guilty.

Plessy appealed his case to the United States Supreme Court. He argued that the Louisiana law was unconstitutional. He said the 14th Amendment forbids state laws that discriminate against African Americans. The Supreme Court disagreed. In 1896, the Supreme Court upheld the Louisiana law and wrote that "separate but equal" facilities were constitutional. This was a major setback for African Americans and their struggle for equal treatment before the law. This law stood until the Supreme Court overturned the Plessy ruling in 1954. That is when segregation in public schools was determined to be unconstitutional.

Lesson 2 Review Choose the correct word in parentheses to complete each sentence. Write your answers on a sheet of paper.

1. The Statue of Liberty was a gift from (Sweden, France, Ireland).

2. Immigrants after the 1880s were called (old immigrants, new immigrants, late immigrants).

3. The largest group of new immigrants came from (Italy, Ireland, Germany).

4. Jim Crow Laws segregated (African Americans, immigrants, American Indians) from white people.

5. (Discrimination, Steerage, Prejudice) is treating people unfairly because of their race, sex, religion, or age.

What do you think?

How do you think most African Americans felt about segregation?

Most cities provided **leisure** and entertainment. Theaters, roller skating rinks, and dance and music halls became popular. **Retail** areas included convenient stores, restaurants, and service shops. Public libraries offered all people the opportunity to escape their cares and read.

What Forms of Transportation Improved City Life?

People traveled around the city by foot or in private coaches until horse-drawn **trolleys** were invented. The trolleys carried 10 to 15 people. Horses pulled the trolleys along steel rails set into the street. These early "buses" were first used in Europe. Americans called them **streetcars**.

Transportation improved when Thomas Edison invented a system for sending electricity in the early 1880s. The electric motor made the electric streetcar possible. Electric streetcars carried about 45 people. They received electricity from overhead wires. Electric streetcars were faster than trolleys.

Streetcar routes affected the way a city grew. Streetcar routes fanned out from the center of the city like the spokes of a wheel. Housing and businesses developed along these routes. Streetcars ran on a time schedule and were inexpensive to ride. Workers could live several miles from where they worked. Streetcars allowed people to travel easily around the city.

Leisure

Something that is done for amusement

Retail

Relating to the buying and selling of goods

Trolley

A carriage that rides on rails and is used for transportation

Streetcar

A horse-drawn or electric carriage that rides on rails and is used for transportation

In the late 1800s, streetcars helped people get around the city. The streetcars ran on rails and were pulled by horses.

Fixed price

A set cost for a product or service

Income

Money earned

Spectator

One who watches an event

How Did Department Stores Begin?

At first, stores were small and specialized in a few products. Shoppers went from one store to another. Business owners later thought of putting all of these small stores into one building. It was called a department store. The new department store had hundreds of goods in one large building. Department stores became very popular. Soon every major American city had at least one department store.

F. W. Woolworth created a department store that sold many different products for a **fixed price.** A fixed price is a set price for a product or service. Most of the products sold in his store cost no more than 5 or 10 cents. Woolworth's "5 and 10 Cents" store became very popular with people who had a limited **income.** He eventually built the Woolworth Building in New York City. It was the tallest building in the world for a time.

What Other Leisure Activities Were Popular?

Cities became centers for the arts. Communities in Pittsburgh, Philadelphia, Chicago, and New York built opera houses and started symphony orchestras. New museums collected paintings and sculptures. Americans could listen to the music of the great composers and see works of art from around the world.

Sporting events also became popular. Professional sports teams developed. Baseball became the nation's first **spectator** sport. The National League was organized in 1876. However, baseball was a summer sport. In 1891, James Naismith of Springfield, Massachusetts, created a new indoor winter sport known as "basketball."

 What do you think?

Why do you think spectator sports were and still are important for American cities?

Lesson 3 Review On a sheet of paper, write the answers to the following questions. Use complete sentences.

1. What forms of transportation were used in cities?
2. What was the purpose of department stores?
3. What is a fixed price?
4. What kinds of places promoted the arts in cities?
5. Which spectator sports were started at this time?

Sanitation

The act of disposing of waste and keeping areas clean

Tenement

A cheaply made building divided into apartments

Slum

A run-down urban area often without electricity or indoor plumbing

Although America's growing cities were exciting places to live, they did have many problems. Most cities had grown rapidly. Housing and **sanitation** were not very good. Living conditions became worse as more people moved into the cities.

In an attempt to create more housing, landlords in Philadelphia, New York, and Boston, Massachusetts, built special kinds of housing. They were called **tenements.** Tenements were cheaply made buildings divided into apartments. Many people lived in the small apartments in these buildings.

By 1889, dumbbell tenements appeared in New York City. As many as 32 families lived in one of these five- or six-story brick buildings that were shaped like dumbbells. Dumbbells are narrow in the middle and larger at both ends. They were miserable places to live. People began to call these and other poor areas **slums.**

Immigrant families like this often lived in tenements. Tenements were crowded and noisy.

In the late 1870s, Jacob Riis, a New York newspaper reporter, began to write articles about the lives of people living in "slum housing." His book, *How the Other Half Lives,* told the story of the lives of new immigrant families. He described buildings with dark halls that served as playgrounds for children in winter. Many tenements did not have good **ventilation.** The air was stale in the winter and very hot in the summer. Because of the large numbers of people living so close together, the buildings were very noisy. Worst of all, many of these buildings had no fire escapes. This made them dangerous places to live.

How Were Cities Governed?

City governments were not prepared to deal with the problems of slums. Before the Civil War, people living in cities needed few services from the government. They got their water from a city spring or private well. Volunteer fire companies provided fire protection. People disposed of their own garbage. However, in the larger cities a different kind of organization was needed. City governments needed a lot of practice to successfully manage these large communities.

City, or urban, problems increased during the 1880s. City officials did not know how to deal with them. Little was known about the people who lived in slums. People believed that those living in slums were poor because they had no skills or they were lazy. Religious leaders began to question this belief. They knew that something had to be done to improve the living conditions. Many religious groups were set up to help the urban poor. Examples are the Salvation Army, the Young Men's Christian Association (YMCA), and Young Women's Christian Association (YWCA).

Word Bank

city officials

slums

tenement

urban

YMCA

Lesson 4 Review On a sheet of paper, write the word or words from the Word Bank to complete each sentence.

1. A(n) _____ is a five- or six-story building that houses 8 to 10 families.

2. The _____ was set up to help the urban poor.

3. Areas with poor living conditions were called _____.

4. If something is related to the city or city life, it is _____.

5. _____ did not know how to solve city problems in the 1880s.

What do you think?

Many city dwellers did not have good places to live. How can this cause problems for people?

Biography

Elizabeth Jane Cochrane (Nellie Bly): c. 1864–1922

In 1885, young Elizabeth Jane Cochrane answered an article in the *Pittsburgh Dispatch*. A newspaper writer had said that women belonged at home. They should not be a part of the workforce. Cochrane was angry. She described women who had little money and needed jobs. Her letter landed her a job at the newspaper, where she took the pen name Nellie Bly.

Soon Bly became a reporter for the *New York World*. She wrote about young women who worked in factories. She wrote about people who had difficult lives. She even went undercover in a hospital. There she learned how people with mental illnesses were treated.

In 1889, Bly traveled around the world. She hoped to beat the time of the fictional hero in *Around the World in Eighty Days*. Bly made the trip in 72 days. Because of this, she became famous. She captured people's attention as she told about wrongdoings in America and around the world.

Blanche Bruce's Speech to the Senate

Born into an enslaved family in Virginia, Blanche Bruce received his early education from his owner's son. During the Civil War, he left his master and opened a school for African Americans in Missouri. In the early years of Reconstruction, he held various Mississippi state offices. He was elected to the U.S. Senate in 1874. He held many other political appointments into the late 1800s. The passage below is from a speech Bruce made to the Senate in 1876.

We want peace and good order at the South; but it can only come by the fullest resignation of the rights of all classes. The opposition must concede the necessity of change, not only in the temper but in the philosophy of their party organization and management. The sober American judgment must obtain in the South as elsewhere in the republic, that the only distinctions upon which parties can be safely organized and in harmony with our institutions are differences of opinions relative to principles and policies of government, and that differences of religion, nationality, or race can neither with safety nor propriety be permitted for a moment to enter into the party contests of the day.

The unanimity with which the colored voters act with a party is not referable to [caused by] any race prejudice on their part. On the contrary, they invite the political cooperation of their white brethren, and vote as a unit because proscribed [limited] as such. They deprecate [criticize] the establishment of the color line by the opposition, not only because the act is unwise and wrong in principle but because it isolates them from the white men of the South, and forces them, in sheer self-protection and against their inclination, to act seemingly upon the basis of a race prejudice that they neither respect nor entertain. . . .

When we can entertain opinions and select party affiliations without proscriptions, and cast our ballots as other citizens and without jeopardy to person or privilege, we can safely afford to be governed by the considerations that ordinarily determine the political action of American citizens.

Document-Based Questions

1. According to Senator Bruce, what things should determine a person's political party affiliation?

2. In the second paragraph, Senator Bruce refers to a color line established by the "opposition." Who were the opposition?

3. Why did Bruce say African Americans disapproved of the color line?

4. Senator Bruce suggests that African Americans were being encouraged to show prejudice. How?

5. Do you think Senator Bruce was speaking more to African Americans or to European Americans? Explain your reason.

Source: Blanche Bruce, Speech to the Senate, 1876.

- Between 1850 and 1900, the population in cities grew from 15 percent to 40 percent.

- Many people moved to cities to find work in industry and manufacturing.

- Working conditions in most factories were poor. Workers were paid low wages for long hours of work. Employers showed little respect for the safety of their workers.

- In 1884, France gave the Statue of Liberty as a gift to the United States. It was placed in New York's harbor, where it welcomed millions of immigrants.

- In the second half of the 1800s, a majority of the immigrants came from Italy, Russia, Poland, and Greece.

- Some immigrants came to seek their fortunes. Others, such as Jewish immigrants from eastern Europe, came to find religious freedom.

- Many immigrants faced prejudice because they had different customs, languages, and religious values.

- As cities grew, new developments helped people live better lives. Public transportation systems helped people get around. Department stores offered many different items in one location. Museums, concert halls, and sporting events provided leisure activities.

- Because cities grew so rapidly, there was not enough housing. Lack of sanitation became a major problem.

- Most city governments were not able to deal with the problems, so religious organizations such as the YMCA, YWCA, and Salvation Army were set up to help the poor.

Chapter 4   R E V I E W

On a sheet of paper, write the correct word or words from the Word Bank to complete each sentence.

Word Bank

department stores

mass production

oil-refining

safety

sanitation

spectator

steerage

streetcars

wages

working
  conditions

1. _____ in most factories were very bad because of long hours, poor air quality, and dangerous machines.

2. F. W. Woolworth founded one of the first _____ in the country.

3. Cities had poor _____, which caused health problems for everyone.

4. Workers would receive as little as $6.00 in _____ for a 60-hour week of back-breaking work.

5. Public transportation often took the form of _____ pulled by horses and later powered by electricity.

6. Many employers were not concerned with _____, because they believed it was the workers' problem.

7. Cleveland, Ohio, became known as a center for the _____ industry.

8. Baseball was the nation's first _____ sport.

9. Large quantities of items were made in factories using a process known as _____.

10. Immigrant families traveled to the United States in the _____ section of steamships.

On a sheet of paper, write the letter of the answer that correctly completes each sentence.

11. Most immigrants to the United States settled in eastern and midwestern cities because _____.

  A the best lands of the West were taken

  B the best jobs were there

  C they preferred city life

  D there was less prejudice there

12. The Jim Crow Laws of the 1880s and 1890s attempted to _____.

   A destroy big-business monopolies

   B separate African Americans and whites

   C discriminate against immigrants

   D increase immigration

13. The *Plessy v. Ferguson* case caused a setback for _____.

   A Asian immigrants in the West

   B workers' rights

   C African American civil rights

   D Jewish immigrants in the East

On a sheet of paper, write the answers to the following questions. Use complete sentences.

14. What are two reasons immigrants came to the United States?

15. What problems did African Americans face?

16. Why were city governments unable to deal with the problems that population growth created?

17. Why were tenement buildings needed?

18. What was the advantage of shopping at a department store?

Critical Thinking On a sheet of paper, write your response to each question. Use complete sentences.

19. If you had been living in Europe in the late 1800s, would you have immigrated to the United States? Why or why not?

20. Compare life in cities today with life in cities in the 1890s. How is it the same? How is it different?

Test-Taking Tip

An essay question may ask you to compare and contrast things. Be sure to tell how the things are alike and how they are different.

5 A New Spirit of Reform
1872–1897

During the late 1800s, the United States was a modern nation filled with opportunity. The changes at this time improved the lives of many Americans. As communication, transportation, industry, and science advanced, so did American citizens. But problems remained. There was still political corruption. Working conditions remained poor. Beginning in the 1870s, people began to do something about these problems. In this chapter, you will learn how the nation worked on these reforms.

Goals for Learning

◆ To explain why reforms were needed
◆ To describe the major reforms that occurred during the period
◆ To explain how labor unions helped workers
◆ To explain the purpose of the Sherman Antitrust Act
◆ To describe the Populist movement

1881 President Garfield takes office

1881 President Arthur takes office

1889 President Harrison takes office

1897 President McKinley takes office

1872   1877   1882   1887   1892   1897

1877 President Hayes takes office

1881 Charles Guiteau assassinates President Garfield

1885 President Cleveland takes office

1892 Populist Party forms

Gilded

Covered with a thin coating of gold

Reform

A change intended to make something better

Contract

A work agreement between at least two groups

Author Mark Twain called the 1870s the "**Gilded** Age." He thought that American society was like a gilded piece of metal. Something that is gilded is covered with a thin coating of gold. Gilding covers up the original object. Twain thought many poor and powerless Americans were hidden under the control of the nation's wealthy few.

Many average American workers, certain that industrial America was hurting them, wanted change. A new spirit of **reform** began. Reform is a change intended to make something better. The people leading reform movements thought that many industrial leaders had corrupted the national and local governments for their own gain. They were becoming rich while common people suffered.

What Was the Crédit Mobilier Scandal?

The *New York Sun* newspaper published an article about the Union Pacific Railroad in 1872. The Union Pacific was one of the companies that helped build the transcontinental railroad. The article accused Union Pacific officials of making money illegally from the government through a construction company called Crédit Mobilier of America. Union Pacific had purchased the Crédit Mobilier Company. Then it gave the company **contracts** to lay railroad tracks for the federal government. Union Pacific overpaid Crédit Mobilier $50 million for laying the tracks. This way the company's records looked successful and the stock became very valuable.

RESIGNATION UNDER TRYING CIRCUMSTANCES.

President Ulysses S. Grant thinks how it would be if all the corrupt people quit at once.

1872–1897

People began to question the relationship between Union Pacific and Crédit Mobilier. The head of the company, Oakes Ames, was also a congressman. He gave company stock to members of Congress to try to prevent them from **investigating.** However, Congress still investigated and found that many politicians took part in the scandal. Even Schuyler Colfax, the vice president of the United States, was part of it. A congressional committee suggested that Ames be removed from the House of Representatives. However, he remained.

President Grant's administration was full of corruption in addition to the Crédit Mobilier Scandal. Secretary of War William Belknap made money by cheating American Indians living on reservations. Members of the Treasury Department had received illegal payments from the whiskey companies who wanted to avoid paying tax. Even President Grant's personal secretary was in on this Whiskey Ring Scandal, as it was called. The president, without knowing it, allowed people to make millions off the government.

Lesson 1 Review On a sheet of paper, write the answers to the following questions. Use complete sentences.

1. What is reform?

2. What was Crédit Mobilier?

3. How did Crédit Mobilier make its money illegally?

4. What government officials were part of the Crédit Mobilier Scandal?

5. How was William Belknap corrupt?

What do you think?

How do you think people feel when they learn about government scandals? Explain.

It Happened in History

General Grant won many battles during the Civil War and faced tough struggles while he was president. His most courageous battle came nine years after he left the White House. Grant was financially ruined in 1884 by a business partner who mismanaged their company. Though seriously ill, Grant wanted to give his wife financial security before he died. He worked for a year to write *Personal Memoirs of U. S. Grant*. Soon after he had finished it, Grant died. The 1,231-page book sold more than 300,000 copies and earned $500,000. Ulysses S. Grant had won the last battle of his life.

Political boss

A professional politician who controls a party or a political machine

Bribe

A payment to someone to make a person act in a certain way

Mugwump

A reform group that wanted to replace the spoils system with civil service

Civil service

A system in which people are appointed rather than elected to government jobs

Corruption was not limited to the federal government. **Political bosses** affected many city governments. These men pretended to befriend immigrants. They offered help to poor city neighborhoods. They provided clothing, heating fuel, and food. Often they would set up social events to become known and liked among city neighborhoods. In return, they expected the people to vote for the candidates they supported.

Who Was Boss Tweed?

William Marcy Tweed was a powerful boss in New York City. Boss Tweed, as he was called, controlled a Democratic political organization known as Tammany Hall. Tweed and his friends stole millions of dollars from the city. For example, the city of New York paid one of Tweed's friends $179,729 for 30 to 40 chairs and three or four tables.

This kind of behavior made reformers angry. Newspaper stories criticized the corruption. Tweed was not concerned about the stories. He thought his supporters could not read. Tweed overlooked the power of newspaper cartoons that Thomas Nast drew. Nast pictured Tweed as a crook. Nast's cartoons eventually frightened Tweed. The public's opinion of Tweed was changing. Tweed offered Nast $500,000 to leave the country for Europe. Nast refused the **bribe.** Boss Tweed was arrested for political corruption in 1871 and convicted in 1873. He died in jail in New York City.

Who Were the Mugwumps?

Reformers in the Republican party criticized the spoils system, under which friends of politicians were given government positions. These reformers were called **Mugwumps.** The name came from an American Indian word meaning "chief." Mugwumps wanted to replace the spoils systems with **civil service.** Under civil service, people are hired for government jobs according to their qualifications.

Writing About History

Think about living in New York City in the 1880s. Write a letter to a newspaper editor about political bosses. Tell what you think should be done to fix the problem.

Rutherford B. Hayes was elected president in 1876. The Mugwumps were disappointed that Hayes won. President Hayes surprised the reformers by investigating corruption when he took office in 1877. He found that hundreds of federal workers were being paid without doing any work. He fired the people responsible and saved the country over $1 million a year.

How Did the Spoils System End?

Four years later in 1881, James Garfield became president. The new president found himself in the middle of a political fight between two Republican groups. Each group wanted Garfield to give its members government jobs. Charles Guiteau was angry because he did not get a government job. He shot President Garfield at a train station. Garfield died several weeks later from the gunshot wound.

Vice President Chester A. Arthur became president after Garfield's death. President Arthur convinced Congress to pass civil service laws. The laws made sure government jobs went to qualified people. They also prevented government workers from being fired for political reasons.

Charles Guiteau (left) killed President Garfield in 1881.

What Happened in the Election of 1884?

Nominate
To choose someone to do something, such as run for office

The Republican Party did not **nominate** Chester A. Arthur for a second term as president. President Arthur had made many political enemies because he promoted civil service laws. The Republicans nominated James G. Blaine instead. He was the leader of a group who wanted the president to appoint friends to government jobs. The Democrats nominated New York governor Grover Cleveland. He ran an honest campaign and would not make deals with political bosses.

The campaign was rough. The Mugwumps and the Republican reformers worked to get Cleveland elected president. He won the election by about 25,000 votes. Cleveland took office in 1885.

What Happened During President Cleveland's Term?

Like the former president, Cleveland faced difficulties dealing with people who believed in the spoils system. He agreed with the Mugwumps that people should be appointed to government positions based on their skills. His appointments angered many former supporters who had expected jobs in his administration.

During Cleveland's term in office, many in the federal government tried to change the way the nation's powerful railroad companies did business. These companies did not want the government to regulate their business. However, in 1887, Congress passed the Interstate Commerce Act. This law forced the railroads crossing state lines to charge customers the same fees for the same services.

In the election of 1888, President Cleveland lost to the Republican candidate, Benjamin Harrison. Harrison took office in 1889. Grover Cleveland was elected again in 1892.

Word Bank

Boss Tweed

civil service

Grover Cleveland

Mugwumps

political boss

Lesson 2 Review On a sheet of paper, write the correct word or words from the Word Bank to complete each sentence.

1. A reform group that wanted to replace the spoils system with civil service was called the _____.

2. A _____ is a professional politician who controls a party or a political machine.

3. _____ was arrested in 1873 for political corruption.

4. Mugwumps wanted to start _____.

5. _____ did not believe in the spoils system.

What do you think?

Do you think civil service is fair? Why or why not?

Then and Now

Your bicycle in 1876 would have been the Ordinary.

You probably would have ridden the Safety bicycle in the late 1880s.

Maybe your bicycle today is one of the popular mountain bikes.

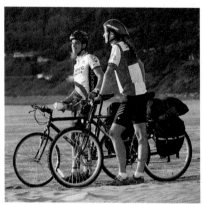

Strike

The act of stopping work to get better pay and working conditions

The need for reform spread beyond ridding the government of corruption. The treatment of American workers had become a growing concern. Labor leaders attempted to organize workers into labor unions as powerful as the big business corporations.

How Did Labor Unions Grow?

In 1869, Uriah Stevens formed the Noble Order of the Knights of Labor. This secret organization remained small until 1878, when Terrence V. Powderly became its leader. Powderly ended the secrecy and opened the union to all workers who wanted to join. Under Powderly, the union grew rapidly. Within seven years, the number of members increased from fewer than 50,000 to more than 700,000.

Samuel Gompers

A second labor union, the American Federation of Labor (AFL), began in 1886. Under the leadership of Samuel Gompers, this union wanted to organize groups of skilled workers. Each different trade such as carpentry or bricklaying would have its own small union within the larger AFL.

The two organizations had similar goals but were different in several ways. The AFL was considered to be more conservative than the Knights of Labor. Its members thought that peaceful bargaining was better than **strikes.** To strike a company means that union workers refuse to work until their demands are met. The AFL would not accept workers that were not white. The Knights of Labor, on the other hand, favored strikes and boycotts as bargaining tools. It welcomed women and blacks.

Strikebreaker

A worker used to replace a striking union worker

Anarchist

A person or group against all forms of government

How Did Labor Unions Use Strikes?

Without its workers, a company would lose money. Successful strikes were not easy at first. Companies fought back. Sometimes they would not allow striking workers to return to work after the strike. The company hired workers who did not belong to unions to replace striking workers. These workers were called **strikebreakers.** Often fights broke out between the strikers and strikebreakers. Police were often called to stop fights.

In May 1886, a violent strike in Chicago destroyed the Knights of Labor. Seeking an eight-hour workday, almost 80,000 workers went on strike. When fights broke out on the street, police tried to break them up. Police gunfire killed several workers. A group of **anarchists,** who were against all forms of government, met at Haymarket Square to protest the workers' deaths. Someone threw a bomb that killed several police officers and one civilian. The public blamed the deaths on the Knights of Labor. Membership for the Knights of Labor decreased after the bombing.

The Chicago police fired at workers during the Haymarket Square protest.

Jane Addams: 1860–1935
A social worker and reformer, Jane Addams was committed to the relief of poverty in cities. In 1889, she founded Hull House, a settlement house in Chicago. Hull House offered wide-ranging services and programs to meet the needs of poor immigrants of various backgrounds. It had about 40 clubs, a day nursery, a gym, a playground, and a place to give out medicine. It also had an art gallery, a theater, a music school, and classes in cooking and sewing. Addams pressured the government for various reforms. Among them were laws to protect working women, child-labor laws, and the first juvenile court. She was against war and led the fight to give women voting rights. In 1931, she was awarded the Nobel Peace Prize.

Lesson 3 Review Choose the word or name in parentheses that best completes each sentence. Write your answers on a sheet of paper.

1. A(n) (union, strike, anarchist) is a kind of protest in which union workers refuse to work until their demands are met.

2. The (American Federation of Labor, Knights of Labor) planned to give free land to farmers.

3. The (American Federation of Labor, Knights of Labor) worked mostly on labor problems.

4. (Uriah Stevens, Terrence V. Powderly, Samuel Gompers) led the American Federation of Labor.

5. A(n) (strike, anarchist, union) is a group against all forms of government.

What do you think?

What problems do you think strikers and businesses face during a strike?

Prosecute

To charge with a crime

Geography Note

In 1867 in the Midwest, farmers were concerned with the high cost of producing and shipping their crops. The Grange movement grew out of this concern. It was the first group of politically active farmers. They worked together and shared resources. They defined problems in terms of economics and campaigned for political candidates who would help them. In time, the Grange movement spread to other parts of the country. By the 1880s, farm alliances had taken over much of this work.

Reformers had become concerned about the power of giant industries. In many cases, large companies were forcing smaller ones out of business. Small businesses were organized into trust companies. Trust companies could take away competition. The trust company became a popular way for businesses to increase their wealth. They could charge higher prices if they did not have any competition. Trusts were established in the railroad, steel, copper, sugar, coal, and meatpacking industries.

A small group of businessmen controlled large industries. Reformers believed that giving so much power to a few business leaders harmed the country. They felt the average American could not fight these powerful businesses.

How Did Congress Try to Limit Trust Companies?

Congress passed laws to correct the problem of trust companies. The Interstate Commerce Commission (ICC) was created to regulate railroads. In 1890, President Benjamin Harrison signed the Sherman Antitrust Act into law. This law made it illegal for large companies to form monopolies. The laws were unsuccessful. The Sherman Antitrust Act was used more often to **prosecute** unions on strike than against businesses. To prosecute means to charge with a crime. This outcome was the opposite of what Congress had intended.

What Did the Populist Party Stand For?

In the late 1800s, farmers were hit hard by falling crop prices. To help improve their economic condition, farmers formed political organizations called farm alliances. Membership in farm alliances grew quickly, reaching more than 1.5 million members by 1890. African American farmers formed their own group called the Colored Farmers Alliance. This organization had more than one million members in 12 states. Farmers wanted an increase in the money supply, higher crop prices, and better regulation of the railroads that carried their crops to market.

Democracy

A form of government in which citizens take part

The farmers' spirit of reform created a new political party called the People's, or Populist, Party. This party, organized in 1892, represented the average farmer. The Populists thought that industrial workers would also join them to fight the powerful business interest. Populists believed that American **democracy** was in danger of being destroyed by a few powerful businesses.

In the presidential election of 1892, James Weaver, the Populist candidate, received more than one million votes. The Republican Party began to worry about the growing power of the Populists. To gain votes, the Democratic Party began to support some Populist proposals.

How Did the 1896 Election End the Populist Party?

During the 1896 presidential campaign, the Populist Party proposed many changes for the government, including the following:

- There would be a graduated income tax plan. Taxes would increase as a person's income increased.
- The public would own the railroad, telegraph, and telephone companies.
- Senators would be elected by the people, not chosen by state legislatures.
- The government would make more money available. It was hoped this would raise prices on farm products and help the economy.

The Populists thought the best way to increase the money supply was to make silver coins again. Most business owners felt only gold should be used as money. Businesses wanted to limit the supply of money to keep prices low and make it easier for big corporations to do business. President Cleveland agreed with the business owners.

In the 1896 presidential election, the Republicans nominated William McKinley. McKinley did not care about reforms. He supported the **gold standard**. The gold standard is a system that backs the nation's supply of money with gold. The Democratic Party was split. President Cleveland wanted the gold standard. Democrats from the West and the South wanted to use silver.

One cartoon of this time period called William Jennings Bryan the "Populist Paul Revere."

William Jennings Bryan, a Democrat from Nebraska, was asked to speak at his party's convention. Bryan felt that the gold standard helped only big business. It hurt American farmers, factory workers, and small business owners. Bryan said that the supporters of the gold standard could not win because "you shall not press down upon the brow of labor this crown of thorns; you shall not crucify mankind upon a cross of gold."

Popular Vote for 1896 Election

William Jennings Bryan 47%

William McKinley 51%

Other 2%

Bryan's "cross of gold" speech won him the Democratic nomination for president. The Populist Party nominated him too. The young man was running for president as the candidate of two political parties. He campaigned around the country. He traveled more than 18,000 miles and gave more than 600 speeches. No one before him had ever campaigned for president in this way.

McKinley, on the other hand, remained in his home state of Ohio and rarely gave speeches. Railroad companies and banks gave large amounts of money to his campaign. Campaign workers gave out buttons and posters. These efforts worked, because McKinley won the election. He took office in 1897.

The Populist movement ended with the defeat of Bryan, but the spirit of reform did not end. A new group of reformers, called the Progressives, were middle class, well-educated people from cities. Some were Democrats. Others were Republicans. They, too, wanted to make changes in American society.

What do you think?

Why do you think so many political parties come and go as the Populist Party did?

Lesson 4 Review On a sheet of paper, write the answers to the following questions. Use complete sentences.

1. How did trust companies control the country's wealth?

2. What was the Sherman Antitrust Act and why was it not successful?

3. What was the Populist Party?

4. Which presidential candidates in 1896 supported the gold standard? Why?

5. What happened to the Populist Party?

History in Your Life

The Works of Emily Dickinson
Emily Dickinson had a reputation in Amherst, Massachusetts, as being strange for years before she died in 1886. She rarely left her house. Some said she always dressed entirely in white. After her death, friends found hundreds of poems. Dickinson had written and neatly stitched the poems into little handmade booklets. Only seven of her 1,775 poems had been published during her lifetime. Her family allowed all of them to be published after she died. Dickinson came to be thought of as one of America's greatest poets. She had an unusual brief and symbolic style. Her poems were about such topics as death, love, and faith in God. While Dickinson traveled little, her imagination seemed to span the globe. Today millions of people have read her poems. Poets like William Carlos Williams and Adrienne Rich credited Dickinson with having a major influence on their work.

Declaration of Woman's Christian Temperance Union

A small group of Ohio women began the Woman's Christian Temperance Union (WCTU) in 1874. By 1890, membership had grown to 150,000 nationwide. The group's focus was the legal forbidding of alcoholic beverages. The word temperance *refers to people controlling their own actions. These people claimed alcohol was the root of many of America's problems at the turn of the century. This passage is taken from their Declaration of 1902.*

We therefore formulate [set down] and, for ourselves, adopt the following pledge, asking our sisters and brothers of a common danger and a common hope to make common cause with us in working its reasonable and helpful precepts into the practice of everyday life:

I hereby solemnly promise . . . to abstain from all distilled, fermented, and malt liquors, including wine, beer, and cider, and to employ all proper means to discourage the use of and traffic in the same.

To conform and enforce the rationale of this pledge, we declare our purpose to educate the young; to form a better public sentiment; to reform so far as possible, by religious, ethical, and scientific means, the drinking classes; to seek the transforming power of Divine Grace for ourselves and all for whom we work, that they and we may willfully transcend no law of pure and wholesome living; and finally we pledge ourselves to labor and to pray that all of these principles . . . may be worked out into the customs of society and the laws of the land.

Document-Based Questions

1. Women began the Woman's Christian Temperance Union. Who else besides women does the first paragraph ask for help in their cause?

2. What, if any, attempt is in this statement to make using alcohol illegal?

3. What was one purpose stated in the declaration?

4. The writers said in the last paragraph they would like to form a "better public sentiment." What do you think they meant?

5. How effective do you think the WCTU's methods were in convincing people not to drink alcohol?

Source: Woman's Christian Temperance Union Declaration of 1902.

Chapter 5   S U M M A R Y

- In 1872, the Union Pacific Railroad was found to be taking money from the government illegally. Many of the people who profited were members of Congress and business leaders. This was called the Crédit Mobilier Scandal.

- Corruption was found in federal, state, and city governments while Ulysses S. Grant was president.

- William Marcy Tweed, known as Boss Tweed, controlled an organization that stole millions of dollars from New York City's government. Thomas Nast drew political cartoons that exposed Boss Tweed. Nast's cartoons helped bring Tweed to justice.

- The Mugwumps were a group of reformers in the Republican Party. They wanted to replace the spoils system with civil service.

- Presidents Hayes, Garfield, and Arthur all worked to reform the way government jobs were performed. The civil service laws were finally passed while Arthur was president.

- During President Cleveland's first term, the government began to regulate major industries such as the railroads.

- The Interstate Commerce Act was passed in 1887. It regulated the way railroads could charge their customers.

- Labor unions changed the way workers were treated. Two of the first labor unions were the Noble Order of the Knights of Labor and the American Federation of Labor.

- The Knights of Labor pushed for higher wages and improved working conditions. The American Federation of Labor represented skilled trades and focused on labor relations.

- Unions used strikes as a way of improving working conditions. Many strikes turned violent.

- The Sherman Antitrust Act was signed in 1890. It was created to help control monopolies. The act was not successful. The outcome was the opposite of what Congress had intended.

- The Populist Party was formed to represent the average American instead of big business. The Populists proposed many changes in the government.

Chapter 5 R E V I E W

On a sheet of paper, write the correct word or words from the Word Bank to complete each sentence.

Word Bank

American
    Federation of
    Labor

Boss Tweed

Chester A. Arthur

civil service

Interstate
    Commerce Act

Mugwumps

Sherman
    Antitrust Act

Thomas Nast

Whiskey Ring

William Jennings
    Bryan

1. _____ and his people stole millions of dollars from New York City.

2. The _____ laws required that people be qualified before they could hold a government job.

3. Samuel Gompers was one of the early leaders of the _____.

4. The _____ was one of the first laws to limit or regulate big business in America.

5. The _____ was a law to limit large business monopolies.

6. The political cartoons of _____ helped put Boss Tweed in jail.

7. A group called the _____ believed that people should be given government positions because of their skills.

8. The _____ was a major scandal of President Grant's administration involving even Grant's secretary.

9. _____ was the presidential candidate of the Populists.

10. Politicians did not like President _____ because he tried to do away with the spoils system.

On a sheet of paper, write the letter of the answer that correctly completes each sentence.

11. The Crédit Mobilier scandal involved the Union Pacific Railroad, which cheated the government by _____.

    A illegally taking government money
    B buying civil service jobs
    C giving members of Congress free train rides
    D hiring strikebreakers

12. A powerful political boss who was convicted of corruption and died in prison was _____.

A Schuyler Colfax

B Mark Twain

C Chester A. Arthur

D William Marcy Tweed

13. Workers who were hired to work in place of striking workers were called _____.

A anarchists

B strikebreakers

C Mugwumps

D political bosses

On a sheet of paper, write the answer to each question. Use complete sentences.

14. Why did the Knights of Labor lose members after the Haymarket Square bombing?

15. What were the main ideas of the Populist party?

16. Why was the civil service system important?

17. What was the purpose of labor unions?

Critical Thinking On a sheet of paper, write your response to each question. Use complete sentences.

18. What is something that you would reform about the current government? Explain your answer.

19. If you could form a political party, what would be three of the things your party would stand for? Why?

20. Do you think that large companies need to be regulated by the federal government? Why or why not?

Test-Taking Tip

Look for specifics in questions or directions. These may tell you in what form to give your answer. For example, some questions say to use complete sentences.

Using Reference Materials

Reference materials are sources for finding different kinds of information. Here are some examples of reference materials and the kind of information you can find in them:

General information

almanac: Book of recent and historic facts and figures about many subjects, usually published once a year

Atlas: Book of maps of countries, states, and some cities

Encyclopedia: One book or a set of books with summaries and histories of many different subjects

Gazetteer: Dictionary of geographic place names and information

Newspaper: Daily or weekly publication with national, local, sports, and business news and regular features

Periodical index: Listing of magazine articles by subject and the publication in which they appear

Internet: Worldwide computer network with information on a wide variety of subjects. Includes online encyclopedias, newspapers, and periodicals

You could probably find the answers to all of these questions somewhere on the Internet. Name at least one other source listed above that you could use to answer these questions.

1. Where could you find the vice presidents who served between 1865 and 1900?

2. The Homestead Act of 1862 opened much western land to settlers. It did not, however, open land in Oklahoma, which was Indian Territory. On what date could settlers stake claims in Oklahoma?

3. In what year did Thomas Edison invent a safe indoor lightbulb?

4. What was the name of the first professional baseball team? In what year was the team formed?

5. There is a current dispute over fishing and hunting rights for an American Indian tribe in Minnesota. The Nelson Act of 1889 and 1890 took away rights originally granted in a treaty made in 1837. Where would you find the latest developments on this issue?

6. Where could you see a map of Montana with an enlargement of Great Falls?

7. Where would you find information about the Detroit River?

8. Where might you find an article about current methods of refining crude oil?

9. Where could you find last night's sports results for your local teams?

10. You do not remember where you recently read an article about public education in the 1870s. Where could you find the name and issue of the publication in which it appeared?

- President Lincoln was assassinated on April 14, 1865.

- Congress set up the Freedmen's Bureau in 1865.

- The 14th Amendment gave former slaves equal protection under the law. The 15th Amendment gave African American men voting rights.

- The Reconstruction Act of 1867 placed the South under military rule and required that new constitutions be written.

- Grant became president in 1868. Rutherford B. Hayes became president in 1877 and ended Reconstruction.

- The Union Pacific and Central Pacific railroads finished the transcontinental railroad in 1869.

- Miners, farmers, cowhands, and homesteaders settled the West.

- Many American Indians were moved to reservations. The government promised but was unable to protect their way of life.

- Between 1864 and 1912, the nation added 13 states.

- In the second half of the 1800s, new industries began to develop. Andrew Carnegie found a method of converting iron into steel. Edwin Drake drilled the first oil well. John D. Rockefeller's Standard Oil Company of Ohio refined crude petroleum into usable oil.

- Cornelius Vanderbilt and James J. Hill made fortunes with railroads.

- Many people moved to cities to find work in industry and manufacturing. Working conditions in most factories were poor.

- From 1850 to 1900, most immigrants came from Italy, Russia, Poland, and Greece. They sought their fortunes or religious freedom. Many faced prejudice because their ways were different.

- As cities grew, new developments made life better—transportation systems, department stores, museums, and concert halls.

- Corruption was found in federal, state, and city governments.

- Civil service laws were passed while Chester A. Arthur was president.

- The Interstate Commerce Act regulated the way railroads charged customers.

- Labor unions changed the way workers were treated.

- The Sherman Antitrust Act was signed in 1890 to control monopolies.

- The Populist Party represented the average American.

"Our country offers the most wonderful example of democratic government on a giant scale that the world has ever seen; and the peoples of the world are watching to see whether we succeed or fail."
~ *Teddy Roosevelt, September 27, 1910*

Unit

2

The Emergence of Modern America

1898–1929

Have you noticed as you get older that you have more and bigger responsibilities? As the United States grew and developed in the early 1900s, it took on more and bigger responsibilities. As its interests expanded, the country became concerned with the affairs of other nations. It also took responsibility for its own citizens and resources in good times and bad times.

In this unit, you will learn how America took on wider responsibilities in the world. You will learn about American involvement in smaller wars and in World War I. You will learn how America gave one-half of its citizens the right to vote. You will learn about America's economic crash after a period of great well-being.

6 America Becomes a World Power
1898–1913

Throughout the 1800s, the United States played a limited role in world affairs. Important European nations did not think of America as a world power. This changed late in the century. Confidence as a nation, new American leaders, and new world problems brought the United States into the world picture. In this chapter, you will learn how America became a world power.

Goals for Learning

◆ To identify the reasons for the Spanish-American War

◆ To explain the outcome of the Spanish-American War

◆ To describe how America expanded in the Pacific and became a stronger nation

◆ To explain President Theodore Roosevelt's reforms and the impact of the Progressive movement

◆ To describe other accomplishments of President Roosevelt

◆ To describe achievements of President Taft and the election of Woodrow Wilson

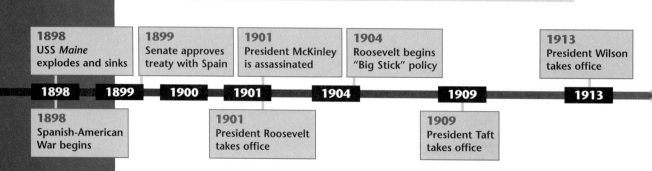

1898
USS *Maine* explodes and sinks

1899
Senate approves treaty with Spain

1901
President McKinley is assassinated

1904
Roosevelt begins "Big Stick" policy

1913
President Wilson takes office

1898　1899　1900　1901　1904　1909　1913

1898
Spanish-American War begins

1901
President Roosevelt takes office

1909
President Taft takes office

Compete

To try to win or gain something

Before the Civil War, the United States had been working on its goal of Manifest Destiny. Once it had extended its boundaries from the Atlantic Ocean to the Pacific Ocean, attention shifted to growth of industry and business. This put America in a better position to **compete** with the rest of the world. During this time, Americans became confident that they could compete with the nations of Europe.

Why Did America Go to War with Spain?

The only pieces of the former Spanish empire in North America were Cuba and nearby Puerto Rico in the West Indies. For many years, hundreds of thousands of people in Cuba had been victims of the unfair Spanish government there. Many Americans were living in Cuba, and many American businesses held important sugarcane industries there. These people felt that the United States should help Cubans become free of Spanish control.

Not eager to go to war with Spain, President McKinley offered to buy the island of Cuba. The Spanish refused. Then in January 1898, he sent the battleship USS *Maine* to Cuba to protect American lives and property. But the fighting inside Cuba continued.

The battleship *Maine* exploded on February 15, 1898, and sank into the harbor of Havana, Cuba. The explosion killed 260 American sailors. The sinking of the *Maine* shocked the nation. Newspapers blamed the Spanish government.

President McKinley demanded that Spain stop the fighting in Cuba. Meanwhile, Theodore Roosevelt, assistant secretary of the U.S. Navy, sent Admiral Dewey and a fleet of ships to the Philippine Islands in Asia. Spain controlled these islands. Roosevelt gave Admiral Dewey orders to attack the Philippines' main harbor if war broke out as a result of the *Maine* bombing.

The USS Maine exploded and sank in Havana Harbor in 1898.

On April 9, 1898, Spain promised that it would stop its fighting in Cuba. Spain wanted to avoid a war with the United States. Many Americans wanted to go to war. "Remember the *Maine*" was printed on posters and buttons.

President McKinley was criticized for not punishing Spain for the sailors who died on the *Maine*. On April 11, 1898, he asked Congress for permission to use the military to stop the war in Cuba. McKinley made it clear that the United States was interested in helping Cuba gain its independence, not in taking control of it. President McKinley ignored the fact that Spain, having already agreed to stop fighting, heard of McKinley's action. Spain declared war on the United States. Congress then declared war on Spain.

Word Bank

Cuba

Havana

Philippine

Puerto Rico

Spain

Lesson 1 Review On a sheet of paper, write the correct word or words from the Word Bank to complete each sentence.

1. The *Maine* was sunk in the harbor of _____, Cuba.

2. Spain controlled the _____ Islands.

3. American businesses held important sugarcane industries in _____.

4. Cuba and _____ were the last of the Spanish empire in North America.

5. _____ declared war on the United States.

What do you think?

Why do you think it was hard for Spain to maintain its empire?

Lesson 2 — The "Splendid Little War"

Armistice

A break in a war to talk peace

The Spanish-American War lasted four months. Admiral Dewey attacked and destroyed the Spanish navy in the Philippines. At the same time, a native Filipino group revolted on land. The Spanish quickly surrendered. Future control of the islands was left unsettled, but American troops were sent to set up bases.

The biggest battle took place in Cuba. Theodore Roosevelt left his government job to help with the war. He organized a group of soldiers called the "Rough Riders." With the help of other American groups, including the all-African American 10th Cavalry Regiment, the Rough Riders charged and captured San Juan Hill in Cuba. During this attack, the American navy under Admiral William Sampson sank all of the Spanish ships still guarding Santiago harbor.

Spain and the United States agreed to stop fighting on August 12, 1898. They discussed how to end the war. This is called an **armistice.** On December 10, 1898, Spain and the United States signed a treaty that ended the war.

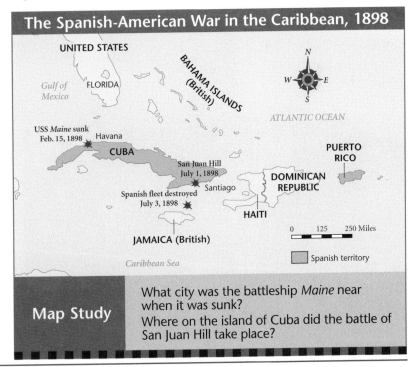

The Spanish-American War in the Caribbean, 1898

Map Study

What city was the battleship *Maine* near when it was sunk?

Where on the island of Cuba did the battle of San Juan Hill take place?

What Were the Results of the War?

Debate

An argument or discussion among persons or groups

The United States Senate had to ratify the treaty with Spain. Spain agreed to give Cuba its independence. The United States gained the island of Puerto Rico in the Caribbean Sea and the Pacific islands of Guam and the Philippines.

The treaty started a **debate** in the Senate. Some senators did not like the idea of the United States controlling foreign territories. Other senators argued the new land would make America a stronger nation. President McKinley agreed. The Senate approved the treaty in February 1899. The United States paid $20 million to Spain for the Philippine Islands.

The people of the Philippines did not want to belong to the United States. They declared their independence. The United States sent an army to the Philippines to stop the independence movement. The United States defeated the Filipino army after three years of fighting.

The Philippine Islands provided the United States with a valuable naval base in Asia. The United States had taken the first step toward becoming a world power. Secretary of State John Hay spoke for most Americans when he said that the Spanish-American War was a "splendid little war."

Theodore Roosevelt (center, with glasses) and his Rough Riders posed at the top of San Juan Hill in Cuba.

Agreement

An arrangement as to the course of action

Republic

A government in which citizens elect people to speak and act for them

Writing About History

What does it mean to be a world power? Write a short essay to explain your opinion. Describe the responsibilities and problems of a world power. Include in your essay the type of country you think usually is a world power.

What Happened to Cuba After the War?

To help the new government keep order, the United States forces remained in Cuba for four years. During this time, Cuba set up a modern educational system. New highways were built, and better sanitation was developed. Walter Reed, an American medical officer, rid the island of yellow fever, a disease that had caused problems there. In 1902, the United States withdrew from Cuba, having made an **agreement** with the Cuban **republic.** A republic is a government in which citizens elect people to speak and act for them. The agreement stated that America would be able to keep military bases there. It would also be able to step in if others threatened Cuba's independence.

Lesson 2 Review Choose the term in parentheses that best completes each sentence. Write your answer on a sheet of paper.

1. The Spanish-American War lasted four (weeks, months, years).

2. The biggest battle of the war took place in (the Caribbean, Cuba, the Philippines).

3. Spain and the United States called a halt to the war for peace talks. This is known as a(n) (armistice, treaty, ratification).

4. As a result of the war, (Cuba, the Philippines, Puerto Rico) received its independence.

5. After the war, an agreement with Cuba allowed the United States to (run schools, build highways, keep military bases) there.

What do you think?

When John Hay said that the Spanish-American War was a "splendid little war," what do you think he meant?

The United States continued to increase its power in the Pacific Ocean. In 1900, the Hawaiian Islands were made an American territory. The people became American citizens. These islands, in addition to the Philippines, gave America an even stronger ability to increase trade with the Far East.

America began to focus on China. China lost its independence in the 1800s. European countries took control of several Chinese cities, using them as trading centers. Great Britain, France, Russia, and Germany established their own government and courts in China. Japan also gained new land. America had been trading with China for years. However, now American merchants were concerned that China's trade might fall under the control of a few countries.

In 1899, Secretary of State John Hay offered a new trading policy for China. This was the Open Door Policy. Hay convinced the foreign nations in China to allow open and free trade for all countries.

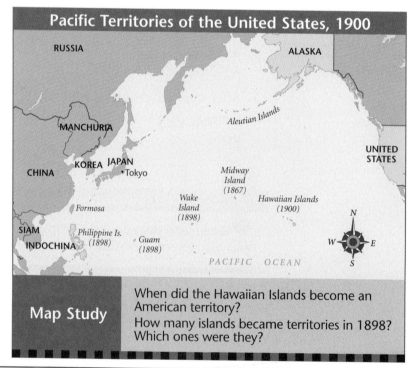

Pacific Territories of the United States, 1900

Map Study

When did the Hawaiian Islands become an American territory?

How many islands became territories in 1898? Which ones were they?

What Was the Boxer Rebellion?

Many Chinese were angry that parts of their country had been given to foreigners. They felt that something had to be done to stop what was happening. They formed political clubs and had secret meetings. Members discussed how to remove all foreigners from China. Each club had a different name, but they became known as "Boxers" because of the physical exercises many of them did.

The Boxers rebelled in the spring of 1900. European countries and Japan sent soldiers to stop the rebellion. The United States sent troops to protect its interests. The revolt of the Boxers threatened to destroy the Open Door Policy. The Boxer Rebellion, as it is called, did not last long. Foreign control of China was quickly brought back. Secretary of State Hay encouraged the countries to take no more Chinese territory. Instead, many countries imposed fines on the Chinese for damages done to their property and goods.

The United States returned a large part of this money to China. The money was used to allow Chinese students to attend American universities. This favor, along with other efforts by Americans to protect the land of native Chinese, helped bring friendly feelings between the two countries for many years to come.

What do you think?

Aside from improving trade with the Far East, why do you think making Hawaii a U.S. territory was important?

Lesson 3 Review Write the answers to the following questions on a sheet of paper. Use complete sentences.

1. What happened to Hawaiian people when the Hawaiian Islands became a United States territory?

2. Which countries established their own government and courts in China?

3. What was the Open Door Policy?

4. Why did the Boxer Rebellion start?

5. How did the United States gain friendly relations with China?

Imperialism

The practice of taking over land to become a stronger nation

Abroad

Throughout the world

William McKinley had become a popular president. During his administration, the United States had gained Puerto Rico. It had set up a system to protect Cuba. America was becoming an important power in Asia. The American navy had set up a base in the Philippine Islands. China had been opened to more American trade. European nations showed they respected the United States' new power. They knew America would help protect their interests in Asia.

What Happened in the Election of 1900?

McKinley had no problem winning a second term as president in 1900. For the second time, he easily defeated the Democratic candidate, William Jennings Bryan. Bryan had tried to make **imperialism** a campaign issue. Imperialism is the practice of taking over land to become a stronger nation. The Republicans avoided bringing up the issue as much as possible. McKinley chose Theodore Roosevelt as his vice president.

Less than one year after being re-elected, McKinley was assassinated. Theodore Roosevelt became the youngest president of the United States when he took office in 1901. He was 42 years old. He became a very powerful president. He believed in reforming America at home. He also wanted to strengthen the nation's power **abroad.** Roosevelt was a new, active leader for a new century.

What Reforms Did Roosevelt Support?

Roosevelt believed American society had many problems. He felt too many Americans were paid low wages. He thought that all Americans deserved equal opportunity to better their lives. American workers, said Roosevelt, should receive a "square deal."

Roosevelt wasted no time in showing that economic reforms were important to him. In 1902, Pennsylvania coal miners went on strike for higher pay. President Roosevelt agreed with their union, the United Mine Workers of America. He forced the owners to find a way to end the strike. This was the first time that the government had supported the rights of union workers.

President Roosevelt agreed that workers like these Pennsylvania coal miners deserved "a square deal."

What Political Reforms Did the Progressives Make?

Progressives believed that America should make progress by passing laws to correct the country's problems. In general, progressive economic reforms were more helpful to white workers than to African Americans. Roosevelt, however, had fought along with African American troops in Cuba. In 1903, he said that any African American who is "good enough to shed his blood for his country is good enough to be given a square deal." What a "square deal" meant for African Americans at this time was not clear. Some progressives did not support economic and social justice for African Americans.

Primary election

An election in which the people choose candidates

Reject

To refuse to accept

Referendum

The practice of giving voters the right to approve or not approve bills

Initiative

The power citizens have to suggest new laws

Recall

The act of voting someone who has performed poorly out of office

Muckraker

A person who wrote articles and books describing corruption and problems

In the same year, W. E. B. Du Bois published *The Souls of Black Folk*. A major African American leader, Du Bois argued that the "doors of opportunity" should not be closed for African Americans. In 1909, Du Bois, with other progressives, founded the National Association for the Advancement of Colored People (NAACP) to combat racial discrimination.

The Progressives believed that laws should be passed to correct America's social and political problems. Progressive reformers wanted the people to be able to choose political candidates in a **primary election.** At the time, political leaders picked the candidates. Progressives wanted to give the voters the right to approve or **reject** bills passed by state legislatures in a **referendum.** They thought that citizens should be able to suggest new laws in an **initiative.** They also believed that state and city government officials who performed poorly should be removed from office by the voters in a **recall.**

The Progressives informed the public of existing problems. Some Progressive writers, called **muckrakers,** wrote about political corruption and social problems in the early 1900s. For example, Lincoln Steffens wrote *The Shame of Cities,* describing political corruption. Upton Sinclair wrote *The Jungle,* about the terrible conditions in Chicago meatpacking plants. The *History of Standard Oil,* by Ida Tarbell, explained how John D. Rockefeller acted unfairly to create a monopoly in the oil business.

Progressives not only wrote about problems, they tried to solve them. How to help the new immigrants become part of American society became a major issue. The new immigrants came mostly from Eastern and Southern Europe. Few spoke English, and their cultural background was different from earlier immigrants. Those immigrants had come from Northern and Western Europe.

President Roosevelt said, "We must all of us be Americans, nothing but Americans." He, with many other Americans, believed that Americans could only be united by "one flag, one language, one set of national ideals." The Americanization movement promoted night school, where immigrants learned English. They could also learn about American democracy and citizenship.

Some reformers, such as Jane Addams, thought that it was more important to help the immigrants lead a better life than to try to change them. The Progressives were confident the nation was ready for reform. They had a president who believed as they did. Many business leaders feared Roosevelt.

How Did Roosevelt Control Big Business?

Although Roosevelt was in favor of **economic** growth, he did not want big businesses to harm society. He felt that to be fair in their business affairs, trusts should be broken into smaller companies. This would create competition and give less power to monopolies. He said that trust companies went against the Sherman Antitrust Act.

At first Congress did not respond to the president's desire to put controls on big business. However, when the president turned to the people for support, Congress started to listen. In time, many antitrust lawsuits were brought before the Supreme Court. The Department of Commerce and Labor was created to keep an eye on business dealings. People were pleased with the efforts of President Roosevelt, who came to be known as the "trustbuster."

What do you think?

Which do you think is most important to American citizens: referendums, recalls, or initiatives? Why?

Lesson 4 Review Choose the word or name in parentheses that best completes each sentence. Write your answers on a sheet of paper.

1. (William Jennings Bryan, William McKinley) won the election of 1900.

2. (Theodore Roosevelt, William Jennings Bryan) became president after McKinley was assassinated.

3. A (referendum, initiative, primary election) is the power citizens have to suggest new laws.

4. A (primary election, referendum, recall) is voting someone from office who has performed poorly.

5. A (trustbuster, monopoly, muckraker) was a person who wrote articles and books describing corruption and problems.

Foreign policy

The plan a government follows when dealing with other nations

Dispute

A quarrel between people or groups

During Roosevelt's administration, Congress passed many laws. They protected Americans from the sale of unhealthy meat and unsafe drugs. In 1906, Congress passed the Meat Inspection Act and the Food and Drugs Act. Government officials could inspect meatpacking plants to see if they were clean. Drug companies were required to prove their drugs were safe.

What Conservation Programs Were Started?

Before 1900, the nation's natural resources seemed unlimited. America had plenty of forestland, good soil, fresh water, coal, oil, and other minerals. President Roosevelt and others worried that America would run out of these resources. Conservation was needed to protect these resources.

President Roosevelt appointed Gifford Pinchot to head the United States Forest Service. Pinchot was committed to protecting the nation's natural resources. He convinced President Roosevelt to add 150 million acres to the country's forest reserve and to preserve valuable mineral-rich lands for future use. In 1902, Congress passed a law that gave the federal government the power to build dams and to establish irrigation projects. Land was developed for five national parks. In 1908, the president called state governors to a national conference to discuss steps they could take to preserve resources within their states. Soon after the conference, many state governments set up conservation groups of their own.

What Was Roosevelt's Foreign Policy?

The plan a government follows when dealing with other nations is called **foreign policy.** The United States had three foreign policy plans. The policies involved Europe, Asia, and Latin America.

The U.S. foreign policy toward Europe had been to stay neutral and isolated from European conflicts. The policy toward Asia had more to do with settling **disputes** and improving trade. The United States was also concerned about Japan's increasing use of military power. In 1894, Japan invaded and defeated China.

In 1905, Roosevelt helped negotiate a peace treaty to end a war between Japan and Russia. Two years later, he negotiated a "gentlemen's agreement" with Japan that discouraged Japanese workers from coming to the United States.

The United States' position on China trade was called the Open Door Policy. China was a weak nation. European nations and Japan had taken control of China's ports and natural resources. The Open Door Policy stated that every nation, including the United States, should have an equal opportunity to trade with China. To enforce American foreign policy, Roosevelt built a powerful navy. The navy protected America's interests in Asia and the Caribbean Sea.

The policy toward Latin America had to do with the Monroe Doctrine. The Monroe Doctrine had stated that European nations could not start any new colonies in North or South America. Santo Domingo, the Dominican Republic of today, ran into trouble with foreign debts. President Roosevelt then added the Roosevelt Corollary. Under this addition to the Monroe Doctrine, the United States would come to the aid of any Latin American country. The United States took over temporary control of Santo Domingo's finances and saw to it that its debts to Europe were taken care of peacefully.

Geography Note

The Panama Canal is considered one of the greatest achievements in American history. The workers faced many difficulties. All equipment and supplies had to be shipped from thousands of miles away. Thousands of workers died during construction, many from malaria or yellow fever passed on by mosquitoes. By 1906, mosquitoes were controlled, and years of construction began.

Why Was the Panama Canal Built?

The navy needed a fast way to move its warships from the Atlantic Ocean to the Pacific Ocean. Also, **commercial** shippers would benefit from having a direct route. To solve the problem, a canal needed to be built through Central America.

The shortest route for the canal was through Panama, a part of the Republic of Colombia. A group of Panamanians did not want the United States to build a canal, because they were afraid of losing control there. When the United States government offered the country $10 million for a strip of land through Panama, plus yearly rent, Colombia flatly refused.

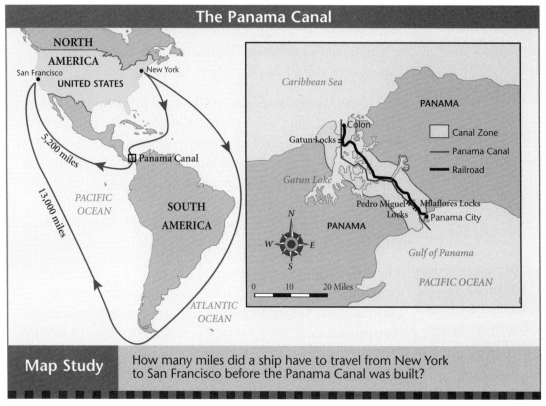

The Panama Canal

NORTH AMERICA

San Francisco

New York

UNITED STATES

5,200 miles

13,000 miles

PACIFIC OCEAN

Panama Canal

SOUTH AMERICA

ATLANTIC OCEAN

Caribbean Sea

PANAMA

Canal Zone
Panama Canal
Railroad

Colon

Gatun Locks

Gatun Lake

Pedro Miguel Locks

Miraflores Locks

Panama City

PANAMA

N W E S

Gulf of Panama

0   10   20 Miles

PACIFIC OCEAN

Map Study — How many miles did a ship have to travel from New York to San Francisco before the Panama Canal was built?

Panama revolted against Colombia in 1903. President Roosevelt sent American battleships to help Panama. The revolt was successful. That year Panama became an independent republic.

The United States paid the new Republic of Panama $10 million, plus yearly rent, for a strip of land 10 miles wide. The "Big Ditch," as the canal was called, was completed in 1914. It took 10 years to build. The canal was more than 50 miles long. It cut the distance for ships traveling from New York to San Francisco by more than 7,000 miles.

The Panama Canal was a huge building project. It took 10 years to finish.

What Was Roosevelt's "Big Stick" Policy?

Many countries in Latin America had political and economic problems in 1900. They borrowed money from European countries and had difficulty repaying the loans.

The United States feared that European nations would take control of the countries that owed them money. Britain, Germany, and Italy sent battleships to Venezuela in 1902. They wanted to force Venezuela to repay its loans. Venezuela asked the United States for help. President Roosevelt convinced the European nations to let the new Hague Tribunal, or World Court, settle the dispute. The World Court is in the Netherlands.

Foreign battleships in South America worried Roosevelt. In 1904, he **revised** the Monroe Doctrine. The United States would act as a "police" power in Latin America. The United States would try to solve any political or economic problem in a Latin American country. The United States could use the military to bring back order to a Latin American country. This was called the "Big Stick" policy. The policy was called that because Roosevelt often used an African saying, "Speak softly and carry a big stick. . . ."

Then and Now

If someone offers to sell you a medicine and claims it cures anything, will you buy it? Around 1900, newspapers were full of ads for "patent" medicines. The ads claimed the medicines could cure one or more illnesses or problems. Manufacturers never tested the medicines to prove their safety or the accuracy of the claims. The medicines were often 50 percent or more alcohol. People wanted to feel better, so they believed the claims and ordered the medicines. Sellers became rich, but the medicines did not help the buyers.

Today the Food and Drug Administration (FDA) regulates medicines. Researchers must do studies to prove a medicine does what it is supposed to do. No medicine can be on the market without FDA approval. Doctors must prescribe most medicines.

Lesson 5 Review On a sheet of paper, write the answers to the following questions. Use complete sentences.

1. Which laws were passed to protect Americans from unhealthy meat and unsafe drugs?

2. What steps were taken to protect America's natural resources?

3. Why did the United States want to build the Panama Canal?

4. How did the United States gain the right to build the Panama Canal?

5. What was the "Big Stick" policy?

What do you think?

Why do you think conservation of natural resources is important?

Biography

Matthew Henson: 1866–1955
Matthew Henson was a co-discoverer of the North Pole with Robert E. Peary in 1909. All the explorers on that journey received a Congressional medal in 1944. Henson was the first African American to reach the pole and the only American to accompany Peary on the last leg of his journey. Henson's association with Peary lasted more than 20 years. They made a surveying trip to Nicaragua and seven northern expeditions before they made their trek to the North Pole. Thirty-three years after his death, Matthew Henson was given a hero's burial in Arlington National Cemetery. In 2000, Henson was awarded the Hubbard Medal by the National Geographic Society.

Income tax

Tax placed on money people earn

Roosevelt enjoyed his two terms as president. He chose not to seek re-election. He said that he felt two terms as president were enough. The new president, he hoped, would continue his plan of strength abroad and reform at home. He convinced the Republican Party to nominate William Howard Taft.

What Did Taft Achieve as President?

Taft and the Republican Party had no trouble winning the presidency in 1908. The Democratic nominee, William Jennings Bryan, was defeated for the third time. President Taft took office in 1909. He did not enjoy being president. He had trouble working with Congress.

President Taft tried to fulfill promises that Roosevelt made. Taft ordered the breakup of the Standard Oil Trust. He demanded a restructuring of the American Tobacco Company, which had been operated much like a trust. While he was president, Congress passed the 16th Amendment to give the government power to collect **income taxes.** Income tax is tax placed on money people earn.

Before the amendment, it was unconstitutional to tax someone's personal income. Reformers wanted only wealthy Americans to pay taxes on their income. They thought the average worker's income was too low to tax.

Congress set up a separate Department of Labor in 1913. It also created a new Department of Commerce at this time. Laws were written to place communications companies under government control. Those who gave money to political candidates were forced to do so publicly. However, there were ongoing problems involving tariffs. At times, Taft was accused of trying to undo some of President Roosevelt's conservation plans.

What Happened in the Election of 1912?

Despite Taft's achievements, the Progressives felt he had not supported reform. They wanted Roosevelt to run against Taft for the Republican nomination in 1912. However, the Republican Party nominated Taft.

Theodore Roosevelt gestured with his hat to make a point during a campaign speech.

Roosevelt organized a new political party. The new Progressive Party nominated Roosevelt for president. Roosevelt was confident that the American people would re-elect him. People called this new political party the Bull Moose Party when Roosevelt said that he felt "as strong as a bull moose."

In 1912, the Democratic Party nominated Woodrow Wilson. The Democrats were in a good position to win, because the Republican Party was divided between Taft and Roosevelt. Wilson had a reform plan called the "New Freedom." He wanted to rid the country of all forms of trust companies, which he felt were bad for American democracy. He thought America would be a stronger nation if small companies could compete equally.

Roosevelt called his program the "New Nationalism." He believed the federal government should regulate big business. The government should be responsible for improving American society by limiting workday hours and setting a **minimum wage.** A minimum wage is the smallest amount a person can be paid to do a job. He felt that children, women, and the injured required special protection by law. Among his other wishes were an expanded conservation program and suffrage for women.

The Bull Moose Party and its candidate, Theodore Roosevelt, could not get enough support. The Democrats won the 1912 election. Woodrow Wilson took office as the 28th president in 1913.

1912 Presidential Election Results		
Candidate	Popular Votes	Electoral Votes
Woodrow Wilson	6,286,214	435
Theodore Roosevelt	4,126,020	88
William Taft	3,483,922	8

Word Bank

income tax

minimum wage

Taft

trust companies

William Jennings
Bryan

What do you think?

Even though Roosevelt was not elected president in 1912, how do you think his ideas affected the future of America?

Lesson 6 Review On a sheet of paper, write the correct word or words from the Word Bank to complete each sentence.

1. In the presidential election of 1908, _____ lost for the third time.

2. During Taft's presidency, Congress passed the 16th Amendment, giving government the power to collect _____.

3. During the election of 1912, the Republican Party was divided between _____ and Theodore Roosevelt.

4. Woodrow Wilson wanted to reform the country by getting rid of all forms of _____.

5. Theodore Roosevelt wanted to regulate big business by limiting workday hours and setting a(n) _____.

History in Your Life

Ragtime and the Music of Scott Joplin
Ragtime is a unique American style of jazz written chiefly for piano. Scott Joplin became known as "king of ragtime." The son of a former slave, Joplin left home at about age 14. For a time, he played piano in saloons and honky-tonks across Missouri. He settled in Sedalia, Missouri, playing piano at the Maple Leaf Club. In 1899 he published the "Maple Leaf Rag," and the sheet music sold over a million copies. Joplin wrote or helped write more than 60 pieces of music, including the Ragtime opera *Treemonisha* (1911). Joplin's music enjoyed a revival in the 1970s. *Treemonisha* won critical acclaim for its first full-scale production in 1975. The film *The Sting* (1973) used "The Entertainer" and other Joplin rags as its background music. The Advisory Board on the Pulitzer Prize awarded Joplin a special citation in 1976, 60 years after his death.

Speech of Booker T. Washington

Booker T. Washington was born in 1856. His mother was a slave. He became a teacher and a successful founder of schools for African Americans. Washington encouraged African Americans to become skilled laborers. Because of this, many rights activists of the time thought he was promoting further enslavement to white masters. In fact, Washington desired to create peace with white people. That desire also may have separated him from his African American peers. This passage is from a speech Washington made in 1895 to white business people in Atlanta.

As we have proved our loyalty to you in the past, by nursing your children, watching by the sickbed of your mothers and fathers, and often following them with tear-dimmed eyes to their graves, so in the future, in our humble way, we shall stand by you with a devotion that no foreigner can approach, ready to lay down our lives, if need be, in defense of yours; interlacing [joining] our industrial, commercial, civil, and religious life with yours in a way that shall make the interests of both races one. In all things that are purely social we can be as separate as the fingers, yet one as the hand in all things essential to mutual progress.

Document-Based Questions

1. What are two key words Washington used to describe an African American's relationship to his or her master?

2. Who did Washington say could not approach the kind of devotion African Americans had to white masters?

3. How did Washington see the lives of whites and African Americans "interlacing"?

4. In what ways did he see their lives being separate?

5. How do you feel about the attitude and tone of Washington's speech?

Source: Speech of Booker T. Washington, 1895.

- President McKinley wanted to help Cuba and Puerto Rico free themselves from Spanish rule and to expand American interests there.

- In 1898, the USS *Maine* was sent to Cuba to protect American interests. The ship exploded in Havana harbor in February and the Spanish were blamed.

- American Admiral Dewey's ships destroyed the Spanish fleet in the Philippines. Theodore Roosevelt led soldiers to capture San Juan Hill in Cuba. The United States and Spain signed a treaty in December. The treaty gave Puerto Rico, Guam, and the Philippines to America.

- In 1899, America established its Open Door Policy with China. It allowed China to have free trade.

- The Hawaiian Islands became an American territory in 1900, and its people became American citizens.

- In 1900, the Boxer Rebellion in China failed to rid the country of foreign control. The United States established good relations with the Chinese government.

- During the first year of his second term, William McKinley was assassinated. Theodore Roosevelt then became president. Roosevelt was a reformer and pushed for both social and political change. He served two terms as president.

- The Progressive Party established political reforms such as primary elections, referendums, initiatives, and voter recalls.

- Congress passed laws such as the Meat Inspection Act and the Food and Drugs Act to protect the American people.

- Roosevelt established policies for conservation and the better use of natural resources.

- Roosevelt built a strong navy to provide defense and to show other countries America's strength.

- America financed the building of the Panama Canal, which connected the Atlantic and the Pacific oceans.

- William Howard Taft became the next president. During his presidency, Congress passed the 16th Amendment, which established an income tax. Taft's administration helped create other reforms.

- After Taft's term, Roosevelt ran again as candidate of the Bull Moose Party, but lost to Woodrow Wilson.

Chapter 6 R E V I E W

On a sheet of paper, write the correct word or words from the Word Bank to complete each sentence.

Word Bank

Boxer Rebellion

conservation

Panama Canal

Progressive Party

"Remember the
  Maine"

Spain

"Splendid Little
  War"

"trustbuster"

William Howard
  Taft

William McKinley

1. _____ was the call to action for the Spanish-American War.

2. President _____ was assassinated during his second term.

3. The conflict with Spain was called the _____.

4. The "Big Ditch" is what some people called the _____.

5. Theodore Roosevelt encouraged wise use, or _____, of the country's natural resources.

6. _____ ordered a breakup of the Standard Oil Trust and set up the Department of Labor.

7. The _____ took place because the Chinese wanted to be rid of foreign control.

8. _____ controlled Puerto Rico, Cuba, and the Philippines before the Spanish-American War.

9. The _____ worked for political reform, especially the way voters could make choices.

10. Early in his presidency, Roosevelt became known as the _____.

On a sheet of paper, write the letter of the answer that correctly completes each sentence.

11. The United States increased its power in the Pacific Ocean by _____.

    A trading with the Philippines
    B stopping the Boxer Rebellion
    C adding Cuba as a territory
    D making Hawaii a territory

12. _____ was a president who sought reforms, began conserving resources, and held office for two terms.

    A William McKinley   **C** Howard Taft

    B Theodore Roosevelt   **D** Woodrow Wilson

13. Roosevelt used the saying "Walk softly and carry a big stick" to describe his policy about _____.

    A police power in Latin America

    B the "square deal" for workers

    C building the Panama Canal

    D breaking monopolies

On a sheet of paper, write the answers to the following questions. Use complete sentences.

14. What were two results of the Spanish-American War?

15. Who was Walter Reed and what did he do?

16. Why did some members of Congress want the United States to expand its interests in Asia?

17. What was the importance of the Panama Canal?

18. What is a primary election?

Critical Thinking On a sheet of paper, write your response to each question. Use complete sentences.

19. Theodore Roosevelt developed five national parks. Do you think national parks are important? Explain your answer.

20. Do you think it is important for the United States to have a strong foreign policy? Why or why not?

Test-Taking Tip

When you answer multiple-choice questions, read every choice. Cross out choices you know are wrong. Choose the best answer from the remaining choices.

7 World War I
1913–1920

The United States had done much to become a world power in the early part of the 20th century. As President Wilson took over the presidency, it was time for the nation to learn the consequences of having this power. Tensions in Europe were high at this time. Soon a war unlike one ever seen before—World War I—would affect the United States and most of Europe. In this chapter, you will learn what caused World War I and what resulted from it.

Goals for Learning

◆ To describe major successes in Wilson's presidency and explain the events that caused World War I

◆ To explain how America stayed neutral until 1917

◆ To describe American involvement in World War I

◆ To explain President Wilson's 14 Points and the problems with the Treaty of Versailles

1914 Archduke Francis Ferdinand is assassinated

1915 German U-boat sinks *Lusitania*

1919 World leaders meet at Paris Peace Conference

1919 Germany signs Treaty of Versailles

1913 1914 1915 1916 1917 1918 1919 1920

1914 World War I begins

1917 America declares war on Germany

1918 World War I ends

1919 Congress votes against Treaty of Versailles

Emperor

The male ruler of an empire

President Wilson had some political experience when he became president. He had been the governor of New Jersey. During that time he was successful in fighting political bosses in that state. President Wilson was very skillful in getting Congress to pass the reform laws he wanted. These reform laws brought major changes to American society. Early in Wilson's administration, a new national banking system called the Federal Reserve System was started. This change made it easier to put money into the economy when needed. The 17th Amendment was ratified in 1913. It provided for the direct election of senators by the people of their states.

President Wilson achieved a great deal in a short period of time. Many Progressive reformers were pleased with Wilson's actions.

How Did War Start in Europe?

For many years, the countries of Europe had been competing for trade markets. At times, they had tried to control the same colonies in different parts of the world. Some nations wanted to get back parts of their lands lost in earlier wars. Some small countries wanted to gain their independence from larger ruling nations. Each nation tried to build the strongest army. Two alliances had been formed. One included Austria-Hungary, Germany, and Italy. The other united Great Britain, France, and Russia. Neither group trusted the other.

Bosnia had been a part of the Austro-Hungarian Empire since 1908. However, many people in Bosnia did not want to be part of this empire. They wanted to be included in Serbia, a neighboring country. Talks of rebellion by Bosnian groups created tension within the empire. In June 1914, the **emperor** of Austria-Hungary sent his nephew, Archduke Francis Ferdinand, to Sarajevo. An emperor is the male ruler of an empire. Sarajevo was the capital of Bosnia. The emperor wanted to improve relations between Bosnia and the government of Austria-Hungary.

As a line of government cars passed through the streets of Sarajevo, a man threw a bomb at Archduke Ferdinand's car. The bomb missed its target and exploded when another car passed. This wounded several people. Hours later, the archduke went to visit the wounded people. His car slowed near a corner. Rebel Gavrilo Princip saw the archduke, raised a pistol, and shot the archduke and his wife. The archduke was killed immediately, and his wife died soon after.

The Austro-Hungarian emperor, Francis Joseph, blamed Serbia for the death of his nephew and his nephew's wife. Francis Joseph had no proof that Serbia was responsible. However, one month later, on July 28, 1914, Austria-Hungary declared war on Serbia.

Shortly after this photo was taken, Archduke Francis Ferdinand and Archduchess Sophie were shot in Sarajevo. The killing started World War I.

Why Did Other Countries Declare War?

Chain reaction

A series of events linked to one another

Central Powers

A group of allied nations that included Germany, Austria-Hungary, and later Turkey and Bulgaria

Allied Powers

A group of allied nations that included Great Britain, France, Serbia, Belgium, and Russia

When Austria-Hungary declared war on Serbia, it started a **chain reaction.** Russia decided to help Serbia defend itself against Austria-Hungary. Germany decided to help Austria-Hungary defend itself against Russia. France agreed to help Russia and made plans to attack Germany. Germany then declared war on France and marched its army through Belgium to attack the French. Committed to defending Belgium and France, Great Britain declared war on Germany.

By August 14, 1914, seven European nations were at war. The **Central Powers** included Germany and Austria-Hungary and, later, Turkey (also called the Ottoman Empire) and Bulgaria. The **Allied Powers** were Great Britain, France, Serbia, Belgium, and Russia. Japan supported the Allies in hope of gaining control of Germany's Pacific colonies after the war. Italy remained neutral in the early stages of the war. Later, it broke its former alliance with Germany and Austria-Hungary to join the Allied Powers.

The war spread into most of Europe and some parts of Africa and Asia. Even most smaller European countries took part in some way. Both sides had their defeats and victories. By 1917, the Central Powers had gained an advantage over the Allied nations.

Biography

Jim Thorpe: 1888–1953

A poll of sportswriters in 1950 declared Jim Thorpe the "greatest American athlete of the first half of this century." A native of Oklahoma, he was part Sauk and Fox Indian and part Irish. Thorpe was an outstanding college football player. Then he competed in the track and field events at the 1912 Olympic Games in Sweden. He won gold medals for both the pentathlon and decathlon—the first athlete in history to do so. Thorpe later played on seven professional football teams and three major league baseball teams. He was the first president of what is now the National Football League. After his death, Thorpe was elected to the Football Hall of Fame.

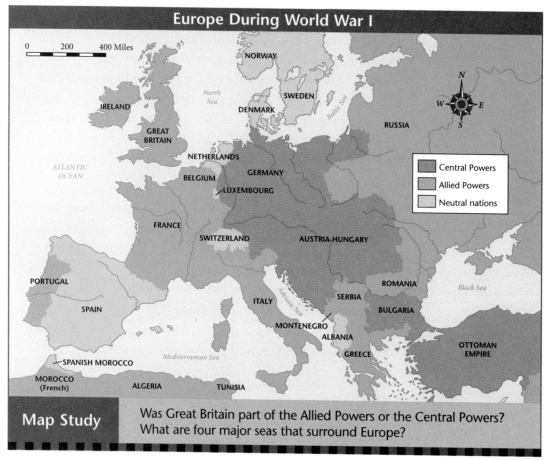

Europe During World War I

0   200   400 Miles

NORWAY

North Sea

SWEDEN

IRELAND

DENMARK

GREAT BRITAIN

RUSSIA

Baltic Sea

NETHERLANDS

ATLANTIC OCEAN

BELGIUM

GERMANY

LUXEMBOURG

FRANCE

SWITZERLAND

AUSTRIA-HUNGARY

Central Powers

Allied Powers

Neutral nations

PORTUGAL

ITALY

SERBIA

ROMANIA

Black Sea

SPAIN

Adriatic Sea

BULGARIA

MONTENEGRO

ALBANIA

OTTOMAN EMPIRE

SPANISH MOROCCO

Mediterranean Sea

GREECE

MOROCCO (French)

ALGERIA

TUNISIA

Map Study Was Great Britain part of the Allied Powers or the Central Powers? What are four major seas that surround Europe?

What do you think?

Why was it possible for one event to cause a war among so many countries?

Lesson 1 Review Choose the word in parentheses that best completes each sentence. Write your answers on a sheet of paper.

1. The (14th, 15th, 17th) Amendment was ratified in 1913.

2. The Federal Reserve System was a new way of (collecting taxes, banking, passing legislation).

3. Archduke (Francis Ferdinand, Gavrilo Princip, Francis Joseph) was assassinated in 1914.

4. Austria-Hungary declared war on (France, Serbia, Great Britain).

5. (Germany, Turkey, France) was part of the Allied Powers.

Submarine

A ship that can travel underwater

Torpedo

A self-powered bomb that is shot from a tube of a submarine or other ship

President Wilson said the United States would not take sides in the war. However, American companies could sell war supplies to fighting countries. Hundreds of ships from America crossed the Atlantic Ocean and carried war supplies to France and Great Britain. Germany accused the United States of not remaining neutral.

The British navy tried to prevent Americans from trading with Germany. They stopped American ships and set up "war zones" in the Atlantic Ocean. Ships from other countries were not allowed to enter the war zone. Germany also set up a war zone around the island of Great Britain. Germany thought that it could force the British out of the war by preventing them from receiving food and war supplies. Germany said that its **submarines,** called U-boats, would sink any ships found in their war zones. A submarine is a ship that can travel underwater. President Wilson felt that the war zones were illegal. He believed that all countries should be free to sail the oceans and seas of the world.

As the Central Powers appeared to be defeating the Allied nations, many Americans were concerned about Great Britain. The enemy at the time of the Revolutionary War had become a friend to them, largely because of shared democratic practices, language, and customs. France had been an ally at the time of the Revolution. Germany, on the other hand, had become cruel in the eyes of many Americans.

What Happened When the Germans Sank the *Lusitania?*

In 1915, the *Lusitania,* a large British passenger ship, was traveling from New York to England. Off the coast of Ireland, the captain of a German U-boat spotted the ship. The U-boat fired a **torpedo** that hit the *Lusitania.* A torpedo is a self-powered bomb that is shot from a tube of a submarine. The ship exploded and sank. Almost 1,200 people died; 128 were Americans.

The Lusitania *before its last voyage from New York's harbor. A German torpedo sank the ship near Ireland. Many Americans turned against Germany after the ship's sinking.*

Americans were shocked and upset. Some people, including Theodore Roosevelt, called on Congress to declare war on Germany. President Wilson sent a letter of protest to the German government. Germany said that the ship was carrying war supplies as well as passengers. Britain denied that any war materials were on the ship.

The sinking of the *Lusitania* turned the American public against Germany. It was becoming more difficult for the United States to remain neutral. Germany, fearing that America would enter the war, urged its U-boat captains to be more careful in selecting ships to attack. As a result, the German war zone around Britain became less **effective.** Some ships got through to Britain with goods to continue the war against Germany.

Woodrow Wilson ran for re-election in 1916 against Charles Evans Hughes. Wilson had been a good president. Democrats and many Republicans approved of his reform program.

Most Americans were pleased that the nation had stayed out of the war in Europe. The Democratic party used "He Kept Us Out of War" as Wilson's campaign slogan.

Wilson won the election. It was very close. His victory was important for the Democratic Party. Woodrow Wilson was the first Democrat to be re-elected to the presidency since Andrew Jackson in 1832.

What do you think?

Why do you think people other than soldiers are killed in wars?

Lesson 2 Review On a sheet of paper, write the answers to the following questions. Use complete sentences.

1. What policy did President Wilson support when war broke out in Europe?

2. What did Germany do to try to prevent goods from reaching Great Britain?

3. What did the United States have in common with Great Britain?

4. What happened to the *Lusitania?*

5. What did Wilson do to get re-elected in 1916?

History in Your Life

The Music of Irving Berlin
Songwriter Irving Berlin was a composer who never studied music. He could not read or write musical lines on paper. He was born in Russia in 1888. His family emigrated to New York in 1893. At 14, Berlin sang in New York's saloons and worked as a singing waiter.

Early on he discovered he had a talent for making music. He contributed words and some melodies to many ragtime songs. His first big hit was "Alexander's Ragtime Band" in 1911. Berlin's first complete musical score was *Watch Your Step* in 1914. By 1919, he had his own music publishing company. Among his most successful shows were *The Ziegfeld Follies* (1919) and *Annie Get Your Gun* (1946). Berlin produced more than 1,000 songs. Many of his most popular tunes are still sung today. One example is "There's No Business Like Show Business." Many Americans regard his "God Bless America" as the second national anthem.

Standstill

Something that is not changing or improving

President Wilson gave a speech on January 22, 1917, to "the people of the countries now at war." He wanted the war to end. He did not want a winner or loser. Wilson wanted "peace without victory."

At the time of the president's speech, the war in Europe had been at a **standstill** for months. Both sides were worn down by nearly three years of fighting. Then Germany announced that its U-boats would sink any ship without warning in the war zone around Britain. The Germans thought that this action would force Britain to stop fighting. Germany knew the United States would probably declare war. Germany thought the war would be over before the United States sent an army to Europe.

During February and March 1917, German U-boats torpedoed ships flying the American flag. Tension between the United States and Germany increased. Anti-war senators argued that it would be a mistake for the United States to go to war.

The United States government released to the newspapers a secret letter from Germany to Mexico. In this letter, known as the Zimmermann Note, Germany asked Mexico for help if Germany and the United States went to war. Germany told Mexico that if it helped to defeat the United States, Mexico would receive the states of Texas, New Mexico, and Arizona. Mexico had lost these lands to America in the 1800s.

How Did the United States Enter the War?

On April 2, 1917, Woodrow Wilson asked Congress to declare war on Germany. He said that America would fight for "peace and justice" and that "the world must be made safe for democracy." On April 6, Congress declared that the United States and Germany were at war. American neutrality had ended.

American factories stopped production of **consumer goods** to make war supplies. People started working longer hours to help increase the factory output. Many women joined the American workforce to replace men who had gone off to war. Other women joined the armed forces as nurses and office workers. Many others volunteered their time in other ways to support the war effort.

The war provided opportunities for African Americans as well. More than 400,000 became soldiers, although they fought in units separate from non-African Americans. Thousands of African Americans moved from the South to get jobs in northern steel mills, the meatpacking industry, and factories making war supplies. The increase in the African American population in northern cities such as Chicago, New York, and Philadelphia led to racial conflicts. Chicago's African American population increased by more than 70,000. By the end of the year, the nation experienced more than 25 race riots.

When American men went to fight in World War I, large numbers of American women joined the workforce. These women are making cannon shells.

Draft

The practice of selecting people to serve in the armed forces

The government increased taxes and sold bonds to raise money for the war. It asked Americans to limit their use of certain food products and fuels to conserve these items for military use. Farmers used more land for growing crops to increase food production. The United States Selective Service started to **draft** young men into the army. A draft is the selection of people to serve in the armed forces. The draft had not been used since the Civil War. In these ways, Americans were working to support their country in the Great War.

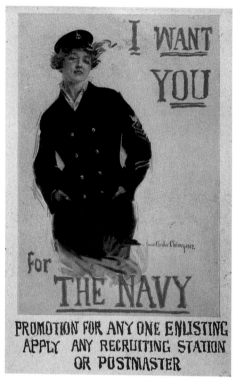

I WANT YOU for THE NAVY

PROMOTION FOR ANY ONE ENLISTING
APPLY ANY RECRUITING STATION
OR POSTMASTER

Posters like this encouraged people to join the armed forces.

American troops arrived in Europe faster than the Germans thought possible. The first American soldiers, called "doughboys," arrived in Europe by June 1917. Britain and France wanted American troops to join their military units. But American General John J. "Black Jack" Pershing argued that American soldiers should fight as a separate unit called the American Expeditionary Force (AEF). By July 1918, General Pershing commanded more than a million American troops in Europe.

American soldiers entered a war in which neither side was strong enough to defeat the other. On the Western front, both armies dug several hundred miles of trenches to protect their soldiers. The trenches were cold, wet, and unhealthy. Many soldiers died of diseases. Rapid-fire machine guns fired hundreds of bullets per minute. Huge artillery shells fired from miles away rained down deadly metal. Exploding shells released poison gas that would burn soldiers' lungs. For the first time, airplanes became weapons of war. Airplanes fought each other in the sky and dropped bombs on soldiers below.

Mine
A bomb that floats in water and explodes when touched

Aggressive
Forceful

World War I Statistics	
American soldiers killed	116,516
American soldiers wounded	204,002
Total deaths	8,528,154
Total wounded	21,189,154
Cost to the United States	$32.7 billion

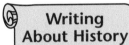

Writing About History

Find more information about American soldiers in World War I. Write in your notebook about what it was like to be an American soldier in the war.

Large groups of American ships began to blockade German ports. They positioned **mines** to destroy enemy ships. Mines are floating bombs that explode when touched. They torpedoed many of the **aggressive** German U-boats that had been causing so much damage in the Atlantic.

How Did the War End?

In several battles in Europe, more than two million American soldiers under General John Pershing upset the German stronghold. By the fall of 1918, the Germans realized they could not win the war. The government of Germany asked the Allies for an armistice. The fighting stopped while both sides prepared to discuss how to end the war.

The German army officers and the officers of the Allied forces met in a private railroad car in France. The Great War, which later became known as World War I, had lasted more than four years. The war ended on the morning of the 11th day, at the 11th hour, of the 11th month—November 11, 1918. In differing ways, the war had weakened the great powers of Europe. It had, however, increased the power of the United States.

Geography Note

To protect themselves, World War I soldiers dug a network of zigzagging trenches. These trenches cut France in half from north to south along the Western Front. Front-line trenches were about six feet deep. Two soldiers could pass each other in them. Support and communications trenches ran back from the front.

What do you think?

Do you think it is right for a country to use a draft to get soldiers to fight in wars? Explain your answer.

Lesson 3 Review On a sheet of paper, write the letter of the answer that best completes each sentence.

1. On April 2, 1917, President Wilson asked for _____.

   A a declaration of war from Congress

   B an end to the war

   C a temporary halt to the fighting

   D the United States to remain neutral

2. In the Zimmermann Note, Germany promised land to _____ if it helped defeat the United States.

   A Texas   **B** Mexico   **C** Britain   **D** Europe

3. To raise money for the war effort, the government increased taxes and _____.

   A drafted young men into the army

   B closed government offices

   C sold bonds

   D traded consumer goods

4. The use of _____ by the American navy destroyed many German ships.

   A U-boats   **B** torpedoes   **C** the draft   **D** mines

5. The Great War became known as _____.

   A the Civil War   **C** World War II

   B World War I   **D** the European War

Focus on Economics

World War I greatly affected the world economy. Germany was forced to pay huge war debts to other countries. This crushed the German economy. It also hurt other nations. Germany used goods and raw materials to pay for some damages. For example, Germany paid Great Britain with coal. This hurt Britain's own coal industry. After the war, the prices of goods in Britain more than doubled. The value of its money fell 258 percent.

Conference

A meeting among a large group of people

Wilson believed that if the world was to remain at peace, then the peace treaty had to be fair to all sides. In January 1918, he spoke of a plan for a lasting, or permanent, peace. This plan became known as Wilson's 14 Points.

Major Ideas of Wilson's 14 Points

- Secret treaties between nations would end.

- Any nation would be free to sail in any seas and oceans of the world.

- Nations would decrease the size of their armies and navies.

- Boundaries of nations would be changed so people with the same language and customs could live together.

- An organization called the League of Nations would be created to settle disputes between countries in a peaceful way.

What Happened at the Paris Peace Conference?

A **conference** was held in the Palace of Versailles near Paris, France, in January 1919. The purpose of the conference was to discuss and write a peace treaty that was acceptable to nations that fought in the war. President Wilson decided to go to the Paris Peace Conference. No president before Wilson had left the United States while in office. He wanted to make sure his League of Nations became a part of the treaty. Three other leaders who attended were David Lloyd George of Great Britain, Georges Clemenceau of France, and Vittorio Orlando of Italy. These political leaders became known as the "Big Four." Germany was not invited to attend until after the treaty was written.

The Treaty of Versailles changed the map of Europe. The Austro-Hungarian Empire was broken up into Austria and Hungary. Most of the rest of the empire was made into the new nations of Poland, Czechoslovakia, and Yugoslavia. Bosnia and Serbia became part of Yugoslavia.

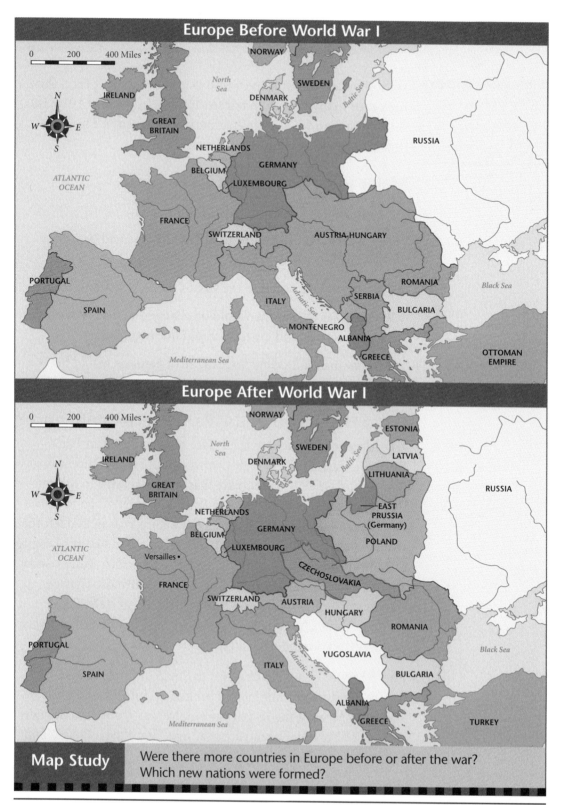

Europe Before World War I

0   200   400 Miles

NORWAY

North Sea

SWEDEN

IRELAND

DENMARK

Baltic Sea

GREAT BRITAIN

NETHERLANDS

RUSSIA

GERMANY

BELGIUM

LUXEMBOURG

ATLANTIC OCEAN

FRANCE

SWITZERLAND

AUSTRIA-HUNGARY

PORTUGAL

Adriatic Sea

ROMANIA

Black Sea

ITALY

SERBIA

SPAIN

BULGARIA

MONTENEGRO

ALBANIA

GREECE

OTTOMAN EMPIRE

Mediterranean Sea

Europe After World War I

0   200   400 Miles

NORWAY

ESTONIA

North Sea

SWEDEN

LATVIA

IRELAND

DENMARK

Baltic Sea

LITHUANIA

GREAT BRITAIN

NETHERLANDS

EAST PRUSSIA (Germany)

RUSSIA

GERMANY

BELGIUM

POLAND

LUXEMBOURG

ATLANTIC OCEAN

Versailles •

CZECHOSLOVAKIA

FRANCE

SWITZERLAND

AUSTRIA

HUNGARY

ROMANIA

PORTUGAL

Adriatic Sea

YUGOSLAVIA

Black Sea

ITALY

SPAIN

BULGARIA

ALBANIA

GREECE

TURKEY

Mediterranean Sea

Map Study

Were there more countries in Europe before or after the war?
Which new nations were formed?

President Wilson believed that the treaty did not provide the just peace he wanted. He agreed to the treaty in exchange for support of his League of Nations. Wilson thought that the league would correct the problems created by the treaty.

The treaty forced Germany to give land to France and Poland. It blamed Germany for starting the war and forced Germany to pay a huge sum of money for war damages. It took from Germany its colonies in Asia, Africa, and the North Pacific, and it demanded that the country not build a new army. The Germans were not pleased with the conditions of the treaty. However, having no other choice, Germany signed the Treaty of Versailles on July 28, 1919.

Why Didn't Congress Ratify the Treaty?

According to the Constitution, two-thirds of the Senate must approve all treaties between the United States and another nation. The Republican senators did not like the idea of a League of Nations. According to the treaty, members of the League of Nations agreed to protect the independence and territory of each member. Republican senators thought that the United States might get drawn into a number of foreign wars, perhaps without the approval of Congress. Some Republican senators were against the entire treaty, while others wanted parts of it rewritten. President Wilson would not make any major changes in the treaty.

In this cartoon, the League of Nations is trying to push the Constitution off the chair.

President Wilson toured the country to tell people about the League of Nations.

President Wilson decided to take the treaty to the American people. He set out by train to carry his message across the United States. The League of Nations, he said, was the first step in making the world safe from war. Crowds of people cheered Wilson wherever he spoke. However, the Republican senators did not change their opinion of the treaty.

Wilson became ill on September 25, 1919. He canceled the rest of the tour and returned to Washington, D.C. He had a stroke, which left him unable to move the left side of his body, but still allowed him to speak clearly. He never recovered. On November 19, 1919, the United States Senate voted on the Treaty of Versailles. The treaty did not pass. The Senate voted again in March 1920. The result was the same. It was the first time in United States history that the Senate had failed to ratify a peace treaty. The United States did not join the League of Nations. Without the United States as a member, the League of Nations was a weak organization. The Treaty of Versailles did not bring about a fair and just peace. The seeds for a second and more horrible world war had been planted. Within 20 years, the nations of the world would be at war again.

Then and Now

In 1919, President Wilson wanted to tell the American people about his plan to ensure peace after World War I. To do this, he traveled by train. He spoke to crowds of people about his plan for the League of Nations. At that time, personal appearances and newspapers were the only ways for a politician to reach a wide audience.

Now, politicians and others who need support for a cause have many choices for getting their message out. Although they still travel and talk directly to people, they also use radio and TV advertisements to spread their messages. They also understand the importance of the Internet in spreading their ideas. Many politicians now have Web sites where they spell out their views and ask for support.

Technology Connection

Rocket to the Moon

In 1920, scientist Robert H. Goddard wrote a report suggesting that a rocket could reach the moon. At the time, few people thought this would be possible. His ideas were not given much support. However, this did not stop Goddard.

He developed a rocket that used liquid fuels. His rocket weighed about 4.5 kilograms (10 pounds) and was 3.4 meters (11 feet) long. In March 1926, Goddard was ready to test his rocket. He launched the rocket at a farm in Auburn, Massachusetts. The flight lasted less than 3 seconds. The rocket soared as high as 12 meters and traveled a horizontal path of 56 meters.

Three years later, Goddard launched the first rocket that carried instruments. In this rocket were a barometer and a camera. He continued his work on rockets throughout his life and was a pioneer in rocket development. He helped set the stage for space exploration. About 50 years after Goddard's report, astronauts walked on the moon.

Word Bank

Austro-Hungarian

14 Points

League of Nations

Paris Peace Conference

Treaty of Versailles

Lesson 4 Review On a sheet of paper, write the correct word or words from the Word Bank to complete each sentence.

1. Wilson's _____ was a plan for permanent peace.

2. The _____ took place to discuss a peace treaty acceptable to all of the nations who fought in the war.

3. The _____ changed the map of Europe.

4. The _____ was part of Wilson's 14 Points.

5. The _____ Empire became Austria and Hungary.

What do you think?

Why do you think it was so important for President Wilson to find a peace plan that would last forever?

Suffragette Letter

In 1917, women picketed in front of the White House. They were picketing for women's suffrage, or right to vote. For this action some of the women were arrested and given prison sentences. Several other groups of women had also been arrested for picketing in the 1910s. The women wrote this letter from prison to the Commissioners of the District of Columbia.

As political prisoners, we, the undersigned, refuse to work while in prison. We have taken this stand as a matter of principle after careful consideration, and from it we shall not recede.

This action is a necessary protest against an unjust sentence: In reminding President Wilson of his preelection promises toward woman suffrage, we were exercising the right of peaceful petition, guaranteed by the Constitution of the United States, which declares peaceful picketing is legal in the District of Columbia. That we are unjustly sentenced has been well recognized—when President Wilson pardoned the first group of suffragists who had been given sixty days in the workhouse, and again when Judge Mullowny suspended the sentence for the last group of picketers.

We wish to point out the inconsistency and injustice of our sentences—some of us have been given sixty days, a later group, thirty days, and another group given a suspended sentence for exactly the same action.

Conscious, therefore, of having acted in accordance with the highest standards of citizenship, we ask the commissioners of the District to grant us the rights due political prisoners.

Document-Based Questions

1. What were the women refusing to do while in prison?

2. What was the reason for their refusal?

3. The women mention two people who played a part in their dilemma. Who were they?

4. What were the women asking for?

5. How convincing do you think the women's letter was?

Source: Suffragette Letter to the Commissioners of the District of Columbia, 1917.

Chapter 7 S U M M A R Y

- Woodrow Wilson succeeded in having Congress pass many reform laws. During the early part of his administration the Federal Reserve System was established and the 17th Amendment, providing for the direct election of senators, was ratified.

- In Europe, tension mounted between two groups of allied nations. Following the assassination of Archduke Francis Ferdinand in Sarajevo in 1914, war broke out in Europe. The United States remained neutral throughout the early years of the war.

- A German U-boat sank the British passenger ship *Lusitania* in 1915. Many Americans wanted the United States to become involved in the war.

- Following the publication of the Zimmermann Note, the United States declared war on Germany on April 6, 1917. President Wilson said that the war was to make the world "safe for democracy."

- American factories immediately began to manufacture military supplies, and men were drafted to become soldiers.

- By the fall of 1918 more than two million American soldiers were fighting in Europe under General John Pershing.

- The war ended on November 11, 1918. It had weakened the great European countries but had established the United States as a major world power.

- Wilson presented his 14 Points plan for a permanent peace in Europe. In this plan he called for the formation of the League of Nations.

- The Treaty of Versailles officially ended World War I and redrew the boundary lines for many of the countries of Europe.

- Many members of Congress did not like the idea of the League of Nations in the peace treaty. Wilson struggled to get the treaty approved, but Congress never approved the Treaty of Versailles. The United States did not join the League of Nations.

Chapter 7   R E V I E W

On a sheet of paper, write the correct word or words from the Word Bank to complete each sentence.

Word Bank

Allied Powers

Federal Reserve
System

Francis Ferdinand

Germany

League of Nations

submarines

Woodrow Wilson

Zimmermann
Note

1. A national banking organization called the _____ was one of President Wilson's early victories.

2. Great Britain, France, Serbia, and Russia were part of an alliance called the _____.

3. World War I began when an assassin shot Archduke _____ and his wife in Sarajevo.

4. War zones were patrolled by German _____, called U-boats, to keep supplies from reaching Great Britain.

5. _____ proposed a League of Nations as part of his plan known as the 14 Points.

6. Soon after newspapers published the _____, Congress declared war on Germany.

7. The _____ was a failure, partially because the United States refused to join.

8. _____ was not invited to attend the peace conference at the Palace of Versailles in France.

On a sheet of paper, write the letter of the answer that best answers each question.

9. When the United States entered the war, what did the government do?
   A drafted soldiers
   B lowered taxes
   C decreased factory production
   D asked the people to support the economy

10. Germany, Austria-Hungary, Bulgaria, and Turkey formed which alliance?
    A the 14 Points   **C** the Allied Powers
    B the Central Powers   **D** the League of Nations

11. What did Woodrow Wilson believe would correct the problems of an unjust peace?
  A the Treaty of Versailles
  B the Paris Peace Conference
  C the League of Nations
  D the blockade of German ports

On a sheet of paper, write the answers to the following questions. Use complete sentences.

12. What were two major events that occurred early in Woodrow Wilson's presidency?

13. What were the two European alliances and which countries belonged to each?

14. Why did sinking the *Lusitania* cause so much uproar?

15. What information was in the Zimmermann Note?

16. Why was Congress against the Treaty of Versailles?

17. What were three of the things that America did after it declared war on Germany?

18. Which four countries attended the peace conference at Versailles? Who represented each country?

Critical Thinking On a sheet of paper, write your response to each question. Use complete sentences.

19. During the early part of World War I, America remained neutral. Would it be possible for America to remain neutral today if a war broke out all over Europe? Explain.

20. World War I weakened the great powers of Europe and increased the power of the United States. In what ways was the United States' power increased?

Test-Taking Tip

Write facts and definitions on index cards. You and a partner can use them as flash cards to practice for a test.

8 The Roaring Twenties

1920–1929

With World War I over, Americans were ready to return to normal, or usual, times. As it turned out, however, the decade of the 1920s was anything but normal and restful. The "Roaring Twenties," as the decade was called, was an exciting time for many Americans. It was full of social and cultural changes. But near its end, the decade was also a time of hardship. It was the beginning of the worst depression in American history. In this chapter, you will learn about the changes and hardships America faced in the 1920s.

Goals for Learning

◆ To describe the presidencies of Warren G. Harding and Calvin Coolidge

◆ To explain some social developments of the period

◆ To describe some cultural developments during this time

◆ To identify social problems that developed during this period

◆ To explain the reasons for the 1929 stock market crash

1920
19th Amendment gives women the right to vote

1923
President Harding dies in office

1924
Congress passes Immigration Act

1929
President Hoover takes office

1920 **1921** **1923** **1924** **1926** **1929**

1921
President Harding takes office

1923
President Coolidge takes office

1929
Stock market crashes

Decade

A period of 10 years

Landslide

A majority of votes for one side

Heroics

Bravery well beyond what is needed

Solution

The answer to a problem

Import

To bring goods into a country

In 1920, the American people were tired of the tensions of reform and war. The nation had used so much energy in the last two **decades** that Americans seemed to be hoping for a rest. Average people wished the country would return to more normal times. They wanted the nation less involved in world affairs and more involved in activities at home.

What Helped Americans Return to Normal Times?

Warren G. Harding, the Republican candidate, was elected president in 1920. Harding had promised the weary voters a "return to normalcy." The word normalcy fit the feelings of the American people, and they elected him by a **landslide.** He received more than 60 percent of the vote. This was the greatest percentage of votes ever gained by a presidential candidate. For the 12 years that followed this election, the majority of Americans voted for Republican presidents.

Harding had been a senator from Ohio, while his vice president, Calvin Coolidge, was the former governor of Massachusetts. After the election, Harding announced that he was not interested in "**heroics,** but healing." He was looking for quick **solutions** for the nation's problems when he took office in 1921.

What Did Harding Do as President?

During the presidency of Warren Harding, the Emergency Quota Act was passed. The law limited immigration to the United States. A new tariff act was written, raising the tax on **imported** goods beyond the rate set under President Wilson. In 1920, Congress created the Veteran's Bureau to give different types of aid to ex-soldiers and their families. Government finances were organized as never before by the new Bureau of the Budget.

Generally, however, Harding was not an effective president. He was a poor judge of character in appointing people to government office. Several members of his administration were caught using their positions to make money for themselves.

Fraud

A lie or false act to steal money or something of value

Emotion

Feelings people express

The most serious scandal began in 1921. Two oil businessmen gave Secretary of the Interior Albert B. Fall $400,000. Fall then arranged for the men to rent, at a very low price, some government oil reserves at Teapot Dome, Wyoming, and Elk Hills, California. Fall went to prison in 1929 for his crime.

Harding did not know about the dealings of the interior secretary until the Teapot Dome Scandal became public. This embarrassment was followed by charges of **fraud** and bribery against the attorney general and the head of the Veteran's Bureau. Harding would not have allowed these scandals to happen if he had known about them.

This cartoon shows officials in President Harding's administration trying to escape being crushed by the Teapot Dome scandal.

President Harding died suddenly on August 2, 1923. Millions of people expressed their sorrow for his death. Harding had once said, "I cannot hope to be one of the great presidents, but perhaps I may be remembered as one of the most loved."

What Did Coolidge Do as President?

Vice President Calvin Coolidge became the president of the United States in 1923. Coolidge was a man of few words and showed little **emotion.** One story describes how a woman told Coolidge she had bet with a friend that she could get him to say more than two words. Coolidge answered, "You lose."

Coolidge believed that "the chief business of America is business." He was a friend and supporter of the business community. He thought that government regulations to control big business were harmful to the American economy. He rejected the reform ideas of Roosevelt and Wilson. Reformers like the Progressives still fought for more government control and regulation. That fight, though, was no longer a major force in American politics.

During the election year of 1924, Coolidge seemed calm and confident about the nation's future. The economy was strong, and many people's lives were improving. Most Americans liked what they saw and voted to "keep cool with Coolidge." Coolidge was president for the next four years.

During the 1920s, the United States became a major world power. Both Harding and Coolidge promoted economic development at home and peace abroad. Both wanted less government control of business. They wanted reduced government spending and reduced corporate taxes. Political leaders thought that the success of the United States depended on peace in the world. To create a peaceful world, nations were encouraged to destroy their weapons. In 1921, during Harding's administration, the Washington Conference was held to discuss this. In 1928, Coolidge's last year as president, the United States and 14 other nations attempted to outlaw war. They signed a treaty called the Kellogg-Briand Pact. The treaty, however, had no effective way to end warfare. Most Americans, with their economy booming, were content to ignore foreign affairs.

Word Bank

Calvin Coolidge

Emergency Quota
   Act

Teapot Dome

Veteran's Bureau

Warren G. Harding

Lesson 1 Review On a sheet of paper, write the correct word or words from the Word Bank to complete each sentence.

1. _____ promised voters a return to normal times.

2. The _____ limited immigration to the United States.

3. The most serious scandal during President Harding's term was called _____.

4. _____ became the president of the United States in 1923.

5. A(n) _____ was established to give aid to ex-soldiers and their families.

What do you think?

How do you know that Harding was not an effective president?

Mobile

Having the ability to travel

Geography Note

The rapid increase of auto ownership changed Americans' lives. Roads were improved for easier driving. People could find jobs farther from home. Suburbs and shopping malls developed to fill the needs of drivers. Today's cars continue to make life easier, but they also cause air pollution and other problems.

The 1920s in American society was a period of many social changes. Industry thrived across the nation. More Americans earned higher wages, so they could afford to spend more money on goods. If they did not have the cash, they could now buy things in monthly payments. Americans had more leisure time and more money to go out to movies or music clubs.

During the war, many American farmers had increased their production to meet a higher demand. After the war, farm prices fell and farmers had unwanted crops and expanding debts. Many of them started to consider other types of work in cities.

America became more **mobile** as a growing number of people were able to buy cars. Radios brought news and entertainment to American homes. Another invention now found in thousands of homes was the telephone. Communication by phone was helping to bring people closer.

What Was the First Widely Used Automobile?

During the 1920s, the Ford Model T automobile became the most popular way to travel. By 1916, a Model T cost about $400. Wealthy people owned most of the first automobiles. When the price of these cars dropped to about $250 by the mid-1920s, they became affordable for more Americans.

The assembly line made automobiles affordable for many families.

Assembly line

A process by which a line of workers assemble something piece by piece until it is complete

Suburb

A community built outside of a city

The Model T was the first mass-produced car. Henry Ford used an **assembly line** to make them. In an assembly line, a line of workers assembled the car piece by piece until it was complete. Every car was exactly alike. Henry Ford once commented that Americans could buy the Model T in "any color—as long as it's black." It had a canvas roof and no door for the driver. It had to be started with a hand crank in the front. Americans were proud to be seen in a "tin lizzie," as the Model T was nicknamed.

Owners found many different ways to use the Model T. Farmers, for example, used the car to pull plows, to run water pumps, and to haul hay. People made jokes about the rattling fenders and the parts that would fall out. But they kept buying the Model T until 1927 when Ford introduced the Model A.

The Model T put the nation on wheels. It became a necessary part of the lives of most Americans. The automobile gave people more choices for where they could work and live.

The federal government encouraged the building of modern highways to replace dirt roads. Suburbs, the new communities built outside of cities, grew rapidly. The automobile allowed Americans the freedom to travel from place to place.

Then and Now

If you were living in the 1920s, you might have decided to buy your first car. Although automobiles had been around for two decades, most people did not own one until the 1920s. Henry Ford's assembly line made cars affordable. Compare the features on a Model T with a modern family car.

Description	Model T	Modern Family Car
Average price	under $300	$20,000
Fastest speed	40 mph	120 mph
Speed controlled by	Lever on steering wheel	Gas pedal and cruise control
Engine	4 cylinder	4, 6, or 8 cylinder
Transmission	2 gears	3 or 4 gears
Change gears	With foot pedal	Automatic
Flat tire	Repair puncture	Change tire
Assembly	By hand	With help of computers and robots

Writing About History

Listen to a recording of an old-time radio program. Write a description of the program in your notebook. Tell how it differs from today's radio programs.

How Did Radio Change American Life?

By the mid-1920s, most middle-class Americans had a telephone, a radio, and a phonograph in their home. Silent movies had been popular since before World War I. The radio brought an unlimited source of free information and entertainment right into the home. By 1929, it was so popular that about 10 million Americans owned radios.

The first permanent commercial radio station began broadcasting in Pittsburgh in 1920. This station reported the results of the presidential election. In 1921, baseball's World Series was heard on the radio. By 1923, there were more than 500 radio stations in the United States.

Beginning in the 1920s, the radio brought information and entertainment into millions of people's homes.

What Was the 19th Amendment?

Association

A group of people joined together for a common purpose

Generation

People who live in the same time period and are about the same age

In 1869, the National Woman Suffrage **Association** had been formed. The association was led by Elizabeth Cady Stanton and Susan B. Anthony. This group wanted to amend the Constitution to give women the right to vote. Over the next 50 years, the suffrage amendment was introduced in several sessions of Congress. In August 1920, three-fourths of the states ratified the amendment. The 19th Amendment gave all American women the right to vote. The long struggle had ended in victory.

How Did Women Become More Independent?

Many young American women of the 1920s were called flappers. The name brings to mind something not tied down that flaps in the wind. These young women refused to be "tied" to the ideas, actions, and styles of an older **generation.** Flappers cut their hair short, wore skirts cut above their knees, and painted their lips bright red.

In addition to having recently won the right to vote, women gained a new independence in the 1920s. Many started to think about jobs that had been open only to men. Women began to challenge old ideas of how they should act. The changes in hair and dress styles were a clear sign that women also wanted to gain more social freedom.

Women struggled for almost 50 years to win the right to vote. They finally won that right in 1920.

Civics Connection

Women's Rights

The 19th Amendment was a great victory for women. How did votes for women change the American culture? The structure of politics did not change at all. The same political parties held the same powers. However, gradually, women's status began to change in the following ways:

• More and more women worked alongside men.

• Women formed their own political organizations.

• Women began to hold more public offices.

• More women attended college.

• More women entered professional fields.

• Women won rights to their own property and income.

• Women's health and health care improved.

• Women's earnings rose.

In 2002, women made up almost 60 percent of college graduates. U.S. women worked in larger numbers, with higher pay, and in more career fields than ever before. Yet they still did not receive equal pay for equal work.

1. Why do you think the right to vote helped women become more independent and successful?

2. Why do you think women still are not paid as well as men?

Lesson 2 Review On a sheet of paper, write the answers to the following questions. Use complete sentences.

1. Why did many farmers look for city jobs after World War I?

2. What process did Ford use to make the Model T?

3. How did radio change the American way of life?

4. What did the National Woman Suffrage Association want to do?

5. What was the purpose of the 19th Amendment?

What do you think?

Do you think radio is as important in people's lives today as it was in the 1920s? Why or why not?

Energetic

Full of energy

Improvise

To make up as you go along

Spiritual

A religious song

Composer

One who writes music

Symphony

A long, complex musical piece

Jazz in the 1920s seemed to capture the spirit of the times. The music was "hot," **energetic,** and lively. Jazz was not played just from musical notes written on paper. Jazz songs and sounds were **improvised.**

Jazz started in the South among African American musicians. These musicians used African rhythms, work songs, and **spirituals.** A spiritual is a religious song. By mixing these styles with European-style music, the artists created a truly original American sound.

Jazz had many forms. The earliest type of jazz was Dixieland of the South. However, by the 1920s, jazz bands could be found in most northern cities. Louis Armstrong played the trumpet with his small band in Chicago and New York. Duke Ellington started writing jazz music for big bands. As jazz became more popular, classical music **composers** picked up its sound. A composer is one who writes music. Composer George Gershwin used jazz in his symphony "Rhapsody in Blue" (1924) and his tone poem "An American in Paris" (1928). A **symphony** is a long, complex musical piece. A tone poem is freer in form than a symphony.

Duke Ellington directs his big band. Ellington was a major composer and developer of jazz.

New dances like "the Charleston" also became popular. While doing the Charleston, young people moved freely around the dance floor. The dancers kicked their legs into the air and waved their arms above their heads. The faster the music was played, the faster they moved. Many older Americans were concerned about the effects jazz and the new dances were having on young people. One magazine wrote that the behavior of the young people was "shocking to their grandparents." Unlike people in past generations, these young people didn't care how much they shocked others.

Which American Writers Produced Important Works?

Some of America's greatest writers produced important works during the 1920s. Writers tried to tell the story of what was happening in America. In *The Great Gatsby*, F. Scott Fitzgerald showed the unhappy life of a wealthy, popular man who was once a poor farm boy. Sinclair Lewis wrote about small-town life in America in *Main Street* and *Babbitt*. In *A Farewell to Arms*, Ernest Hemingway told the story of the impact World War I had on the life of an American man. Edith Wharton's *The Age of Innocence* told about the foolishness of New York high society of the late 1800s. In *Three Soldiers*, John Dos Passos wrote about the sadness of men after their return from the Great War.

What Was the Harlem Renaissance?

An area in New York City called Harlem became a creative center for many African Americans. The period of the 1920s to the mid-1930s is known as the Harlem Renaissance. Writers and poets like Langston Hughes and Countee Cullen, wrote about the noble past of African Americans. They also wrote of African American dreams, disappointments, and discrimination.

 History in Your Life

The Works of Langston Hughes

James Langston Hughes was one of the most productive writers of the Harlem Renaissance. Hughes brought the rhythms and styles of jazz and black speech into his poetry. In the Depression, he wrote *Not Without Laughter,* his first novel, and short stories like "The Ways of White Folks." Hughes became known as a playwright when his *Mulatto* was staged on Broadway. He founded the Harlem Suitcase Theatre in 1938. During World War II, Hughes began his weekly "Simple" column in the *Chicago Defender*. It featured an African American philosopher who talked about life, love, and race. In 1951 in his poem "Harlem," he posed a question. He asked what happens to the African American dream of equality if it continues to be put off. Would the dream, he asked, "dry up like a raisin in the sun"?

Hughes and other writers and artists of the Harlem Renaissance opened the door for many other African Americans.

Biography

Marcus Garvey: 1887–1940

Marcus Garvey was a boldly determined supporter of black nationalism. He also supported black-owned businesses. He believed blacks should have their own homeland—the entire continent of Africa. Garvey spoke out against the lynchings of blacks and urged his people to strike for freedom. In 1914, he organized the Universal Negro Improvement Association in his native Jamaica. He moved the association's headquarters to Harlem in 1916. By the 1920s, it had become the largest nonreligious association in African American history. In 1920, its first international convention brought about thousands of people from more than 20 nations. Its weekly newspaper, *Negro World,* ran for 14 years. Garvey also established a steamship line that was owned and run by African Americans. The company's ships provided transportation to Africa and helped to link black businesses worldwide.

Lesson 3 Review Choose the term in parentheses that best completes each sentence. Write your answers on a sheet of paper.

1. African Americans started the jazz movement in (Chicago, the South, Harlem).

2. Jazz music combined elements of African rhythms, work songs, and (Dixieland, European ideas, spirituals).

3. A musician who wrote jazz music for big bands was (Duke Ellington, George Gershwin, Louis Armstrong).

4. (F. Scott Fitzgerald, Ernest Hemingway, Sinclair Lewis) wrote about how World War I affected soldiers.

5. (Langston Hughes, Edith Wharton, John Dos Passos) was a voice for African Americans during the Harlem Renaissance.

What do you think?

The older generation did not understand the younger generation in the 1920s. Why do you think this happened? Does this still happen today? Why or why not?

Communist

A person who believes in a form of government that eliminates private property and shares wealth

During the 1920s, Americans became more independent and creative. They searched for fun and the good life. Still, there were problems. Many Americans were poor. The boll weevil destroyed much of southern farmers' cotton crop. Farmers in other areas still had difficulty making a living because of the low prices for crops.

What Forms of Discrimination Were Problems?

Some Americans wanted to deny equality and freedom to people who were different from them. They wanted African Americans "kept in their place." They were fearful and suspicious of immigrants. They worried about foreigners destroying American democracy. "America First" became their slogan.

A new Ku Klux Klan was formed in the South in 1915. The last time Americans had seen the Klan was during the period of Reconstruction. The new Klan feared African Americans, Jews, Catholics, and immigrants. They wanted to define an American as white, Protestant, and native born. The ideas of the Klan spread. They gained some political power and helped elect governors in two states. In 1925, Klansmen carrying American flags marched down Pennsylvania Avenue in Washington, D.C. Behind the marchers was the symbol of American democracy, the United States capitol. Fortunately, during the last years of the 1920s, the Klan's political power declined sharply.

In 1924, Congress passed the Immigration Act. This law limited the number of immigrants allowed into the United States from southern and eastern Europe. The law was passed because some felt that these immigrants were a threat to American democracy because of their political beliefs. Americans feared that the recent **Communist** revolution in Russia would spread to the United States. Communists believed in a form of government that eliminated private property and tried to share the nation's wealth equally among its citizens.

Another political group Americans feared was the anarchists. Anarchists wanted to do away with all forms of government. Some anarchists were willing to use violence to achieve their political goals. A series of bombings targeting government and business leaders in the United States in 1919 led to a "Red Scare." A red flag was the symbol of the Russian Communist revolution. When the home of the attorney general of the United States, A. Mitchell Palmer, was bombed, the federal government arrested thousands of political radicals. The "Palmer Raids" often violated people's civil rights and led to the deportation of many immigrants.

What Was Prohibition?

Crime, violence, family breakups, and child abuse were all major social problems. Reformers believed that alcohol was the root of these problems. The 18th Amendment, ratified in 1919, made it illegal to sell alcohol in the United States. The ban on making and selling of alcohol was called **Prohibition**.

Because of the ban on alcohol, the 1920s also became known as "The Dry Decade." However, it really was not all that "dry." **Bootleggers** continued to make and sell liquor illegally. The public was eager to buy it. **Speakeasies,** where illegal liquor was sold, became very popular meeting places in major cities.

Many Americans ignored the law. Organized crime made millions of dollars by making and selling liquor. Reformers may have been trying to do a good thing, but Prohibition brought a rise in crime. In 1933, the 21st Amendment to the Constitution repealed the Prohibition amendment.

Lesson 4 Review On a sheet of paper, write the correct word from the Word Bank to complete each sentence.

Word Bank

anarchists

18th

Palmer Raids

Prohibition

21st

1. The _____ led to the deportation of many immigrants.
2. Many Americans feared the _____, who wanted to do away with all forms of government.
3. The _____ Amendment made it against the law to sell alcohol in the United States.
4. _____ was the name for the ban on alcohol.
5. The _____ Amendment repealed Prohibition.

What do you think?

Do you think Prohibition would work if it was made a law today? Why or why not?

Solo

Done by one person

Stock market

A market for the buying and selling of company stock

Early in the morning of May 20, 1927, a small plane called the *Spirit of St. Louis* lifted off from New York. The pilot's name was Charles Lindbergh. He headed across the Atlantic Ocean for Paris, France. Up until this time, no one had made a nonstop, **solo** flight across the Atlantic Ocean. A $25,000 prize had been offered by a New York hotel owner to the first person who could do it. Lindbergh knew that he had to stay awake and fly the plane for more than 30 hours. Paris was 3,600 miles away.

Charles Lindbergh became the first person to fly a plane solo across the Atlantic Ocean.

Thirty-three hours later, "Lucky Lindy" touched his plane down in Paris. Lindbergh was a perfect symbol for the nation. Americans felt that the country was strong because it was made up of people like Lucky Lindy.

Who Won the Election of 1928?

People paid little attention to the fact that car sales and housing construction were decreasing by 1927. Too many good things were happening. Lindbergh had reached Paris. Babe Ruth hit 60 home runs. The **stock market** was going up. The stock market is a market for the buying and selling of company stock. People were making money by buying stocks. Business was good, and people believed it would get better.

Calvin Coolidge decided not to run for re-election in 1928. The Republican Party nominated Herbert Hoover. Although he had been poor as a child, Hoover worked his way through college to become a mining engineer. He was what Americans liked to call "self-made." Hoover had also been responsible for getting aid to European victims of the World War.

The Democrats nominated Al Smith, the governor of New York. Republican campaign posters said, "Let's keep what we've got . . . Hoover and happiness, or Smith and **soup houses.**" Soup houses were places where the poor could get food. In 1928, the voters picked Hoover for president. Hoover took office in 1929. The voters did not realize that they would soon get the soup houses anyway.

How Did the Stock Market Crash?

The stock market continued to rise through 1928 and most of 1929. Radio Corporation of America stock went from $94.50 a **share** to $505.00 in one year. People took their savings out of the bank and bought stocks. Many people even borrowed money to buy stocks. The price of many stocks was much higher than their true value. Many people did not seem to care. They were sure they could sell their stocks to someone else and make a profit.

On October 24, 1929, stock prices dropped sharply. There were more sellers than buyers. Five days later, on October 29, 1929, the stock market fell apart, or crashed. People tried to sell their stocks, but there were no buyers.

The United States was at the beginning of the worst economic depression in its history. The Roaring Twenties had come to a crashing end. The 1930s would be called the "Great Depression." It was a time of great struggle, when businesses failed and people lost their jobs.

What do you think?

How do you think the Great Depression changed people's attitudes?

Lesson 5 Review On a sheet of paper, write the answers to the following questions. Use complete sentences.

1. Why did Americans like Charles Lindbergh?

2. What is the stock market?

3. What were soup houses?

4. What caused the stock market to crash?

5. What was the Great Depression?

James Weldon Johnson

James Weldon Johnson was an African American educator, diplomat, and writer. He was a founder of the National Association for the Advancement of Colored People. In the 1920s, he was considered a primary spokesperson and interpreter of the Harlem Renaissance. This passage is from an article written in 1928 for Harper's Magazine. It is one of many magazine articles Johnson wrote at the time.

All of the Negro's folk-art creations have undergone a new evaluation. His sacred music—the spirituals; his secular music—ragtime, jazz, and the work songs; his folklore—the Uncle Remus plantation tales; and his dances have received a new and higher appreciation. I dare to say that it is now more or less acknowledged that the only things artistic that have sprung from American life, and been universally recognized as American products, are the folk creations of the Negro. . . .

But the story does not halt at this point. The Negro has done a great deal through his folk-art creations to change the national attitudes toward him; and now the efforts of the race have been reinforced and magnified by the individual Negro artist, the conscious artist. . . .

What, now, is the significance of this artistic activity on the part of the Negro and of its reactions on the American people?

I think it is twofold. In the first place, the Negro is making some distinctive contributions to our common cultural store. I do not claim it is possible for these individual artists to produce anything comparable to the folk-art in distinctive values, but I do believe they are bringing something fresh and vital into American art, something from the store of their own racial genius—warmth, color, movement, rhythm, and abandon; depth and swiftness of emotion and the beauty of sensuousness. I believe American art will be richer because of these elements in fuller quantity.

Document-Based Questions

1. In the first sentence, what does Johnson say has happened to African Americans' folk-art creations?

2. What are three specific folk-art creations from African Americans that he names?

3. In the second paragraph, what does Johnson say changed through African Americans' folk-art creations?

4. What is one thing Johnson says African Americans' contributions are bringing to American art?

5. Identify one element of our modern culture that was an African American contribution from the Harlem Renaissance.

Source: Harper's Magazine, *1928.*

- President Warren Harding faced a number of scandals during his term, including the Teapot Dome Scandal in which the secretary of the interior sold oil rights to government land.

- Calvin Coolidge became president when Harding died in office. Coolidge spoke little and showed little emotion. He was a supporter of business.

- Americans had more leisure time and earned higher wages than ever before. They were able to purchase new items such as automobiles, radios, and telephones.

- The 19th Amendment, which granted women the right to vote, was ratified in August 1920. Women gained greater independence in the 1920s. Some worked outside the home and many changed their hair and clothing styles.

- Jazz, a new style of American music, developed during this period. Louis Armstrong, Duke Ellington, and others helped make this music style popular. Along with new music came new dances like the Charleston.

- Many of America's great writers such as F. Scott Fitzgerald, Sinclair Lewis, Langston Hughes, Edith Wharton, and John Dos Passos became famous during this decade.

- There was a rebirth of pride in the African American community of Harlem in New York City. Writers, musicians, and artists were part of what became known as the Harlem Renaissance.

- African American citizens continued to face discrimination during the 1920s. Groups such as the Ku Klux Klan spread throughout the country for a brief period. Immigrants also faced discrimination.

- Prohibition, or a ban on making and selling alcoholic beverages, was in effect during this decade. There was much illegal activity because of Prohibition, including organized crime.

- In May 1927, Charles Lindbergh made the first solo transatlantic flight in his plane, the *Spirit of St. Louis*.

- After a long period of time when stock prices were overvalued, the stock market crashed on October 29, 1929. This sent the country into the Great Depression.

Chapter 8   R E V I E W

On a sheet of paper, write the correct word or words from the Word Bank to complete each sentence.

Word Bank

bootleggers

Calvin Coolidge

Charles Lindbergh

Langston Hughes

Model T

presidential
  election

radio

stock market

suffrage

Warren Harding

1. Almost everyone had a _____ in their home on which they could listen to news and entertainment.

2. President _____, who had faced several scandals, died in office.

3. _____ was a president who was known for his quiet ways and unemotional manner.

4. The great _____ crash happened in October 1929.

5. The first commercial radio broadcasts covered the _____ in 1920.

6. Women earned the right to vote, or _____, when the 19th Amendment was ratified.

7. _____ made the first solo airplane flight across the Atlantic Ocean in the *Spirit of St. Louis*.

8. One of the great writers of the Harlem Renaissance was _____.

9. People who sold illegal liquor during Prohibition were called _____.

10. For only $250 you could buy a _____ and travel the bumpy streets of America.

On a sheet of paper, write the letter of the answer that best answers each question.

11. Who was elected president just before the stock market crash of 1929?

   A Al Smith   **C** Herbert Hoover

   B Calvin Coolidge   **D** Warren Harding

12. Which of the following most helped Americans of all social levels become independent and mobile?

   A jazz   **C** affordable automobiles

   B radios   **D** suburbs

13. "America First" was the slogan of which group?

   A Ku Klux Klan   **C** flappers

   B Communists   **D** Coolidge supporters

On a sheet of paper, write the answers to the following questions. Use complete sentences.

14. Why was the decade called the "Roaring Twenties"?

15. What were some things that changed for women in the 1920s?

16. What was Prohibition and what problems did it cause?

17. What were four major cultural or social developments in the 1920s?

18. What was a major cause of the stock market crash of 1929?

Critical Thinking On a sheet of paper, write your response to each question. Use complete sentences.

19. Would you have liked to live in the "Roaring Twenties"? Why or why not?

20. In the 1920s, radio brought faraway events into the homes of millions of Americans. What would you compare this with in your lifetime? Explain your choice.

Test-Taking Tip

When you must write a paragraph to answer a question, first make a plan. Write the main idea of your paragraph. List all the supporting ideas you can think of. Then write the paragraph.

Compare and Contrast

Comparing and contrasting reveal how things are alike and how they are different. People, ideas, and events are sometimes compared and contrasted in writing. Look for words that signal comparing and contrasting when you read.

> To compare, ask: "How are these things alike?"
>
> To contrast, ask: "How are these things different?"

- To decide if things are being compared, look for words like:

> also   both   like   similar
>
> Andrew Carnegie and John D. Rockefeller were <u>both</u> industrialists.

- To decide if things are being contrasted, look for words like:

> but   however   instead
> not   only   while
>
> Andrew Carnegie's industry was steel, <u>while</u> John D. Rockefeller's industry was oil.

Decide whether each of these sentences compares or contrasts.

1. Both Theodore Roosevelt and Woodrow Wilson were U.S. presidents.

2. Roosevelt was a Progressive, while Wilson was a Democrat.

3. Roosevelt was an experienced political leader, but Wilson had been a political leader only a few years.

4. Like Roosevelt, Wilson also became a popular president.

5. Wilson, not Roosevelt, led the country through World War I.

Compare and contrast the 1910s with the 1920s. Focus on the following topics. You may write one sentence on each of the topics. Or, you may write a five-sentence paragraph on one of the topics.

6. women

7. communications

8. entertainment

9. transportation

10. international affairs

- In 1898, America and Spain had conflicts in Cuba and the Philippines.

- In 1899, America established its Open Door Policy with China.

- The Hawaiian Islands became an American territory in 1900.

- President William McKinley was assassinated in 1901. Theodore Roosevelt became president.

- The Progressive Party established political reforms.

- Congress passed laws to protect the American people.

- Roosevelt established policies for better use of natural resources. He built a strong navy for defense and to show America's strength.

- America financed the building of the Panama Canal.

- William Howard Taft became president in 1909. The 16th Amendment established an income tax.

- Woodrow Wilson became president in 1913. He got Congress to pass many reform laws.

- War began in Europe in 1914. America remained neutral at first, but declared war on Germany on April 6, 1917. The war ended on November 11, 1918. It established America as a world power.

- The Treaty of Versailles officially ended World War I and redrew European boundaries. Congress never approved the treaty.

- President Warren Harding faced a number of scandals during his term.

- Calvin Coolidge became president when Harding died in office. Coolidge supported business.

- Americans had more leisure time and earned higher wages than ever. The Ford Model T became the most popular way to travel.

- In 1920, the 19th Amendment granted women voting rights.

- Jazz developed during the 1920s.

- African American writers, musicians, and artists became part of the Harlem Renaissance.

- African Americans, immigrants, Jews, and Catholics faced discrimination in the 1920s.

- Prohibition prevented the sale of alcoholic beverages in the 1920s.

- In May 1927, Charles Lindbergh made the first solo transatlantic flight.

- On October 29, 1929, the stock market crashed. The Great Depression began.

"But with the slow menace of a glacier, depression came on. No one had any measure of its progress; no one had any plan for stopping it. Everyone tried to get out of its way."

~ *Frances Perkins, Labor Secretary, 1933–1945*

Depression and World War II

1930–1945

Have you noticed how hard times and difficulties can draw people together? That happened for Americans in the 1930s and 1940s. The sudden failure of the economy in 1929 resulted in very hard times for many Americans during the 1930s. Many were out of work and homeless. The government established economic and social programs to help them. Americans drew together to help each other. Then in the 1940s the United States entered another world war. Americans drew together at home and overseas to support the war effort.

In this unit, you will learn what Americans went through during the Great Depression. You will learn about programs that helped people through that difficult time. You will learn about events that brought about World War II. You also will learn how the United States pulled together to win that war.

Chapters in Unit 3

9 Depression and the New Deal

1930–1939

The good times of the 1920s were over when the Great Depression began. Americans spent the next decade just trying to get by. The government worked hard on plans to try to restore the country to what it had been. In this chapter, you will learn what caused the Depression, the problems and hardships people faced, and what the government did to help solve the problem.

Goals for Learning

◆ To explain the factors that contributed to the Great Depression and conditions during that time

◆ To describe Franklin Roosevelt's "New Deal" policy

◆ To explain some of the programs of the New Deal

◆ To describe some movies and well-known people of the time

1931
Sixteen percent of American workforce is unemployed

1933
Congress undergoes "Hundred Days"

1935
Congress creates Works Progress Administration

1936
President Roosevelt wins re-election

| 1930 | 1931 | 1933 | 1934 | 1935 | 1936 | 1939 |

1933
President Roosevelt takes office

1934
Federal Housing Administration is formed

1935
Congress passes Social Security Act

1939
Wizard of Oz debuts

Layoff

Letting workers go because a company cannot afford to pay them

Charity

A group that helps those in need

The stock market crash of 1929 was as big a shock to President Hoover as it was to other Americans. Before the crash, the economy seemed strong. Before 1929, less than 4 percent of American workers did not have jobs. One year later, 9 percent of the workforce was unemployed.

As sales of their products decreased, American businesses were forced into **layoffs.** A layoff occurs when a company lets workers go because it cannot afford to pay them. Layoffs are often temporary. The Ford Motor Company, for example, was forced to cut its number of workers by 44 percent. By 1931, unemployment increased to 16 percent. Eight million Americans could not find work. Many people lost their life savings.

President Hoover encouraged the American people to be patient. He believed the Depression would end with time. He said the nation had seen hard times before, and each time the economy had bounced back.

Seattle's "Hooverville" was built just south of downtown Seattle.

President Hoover did not feel the federal government should have to help the unemployed. He believed state and local governments, private groups, and **charities** should help people. A charity is a group that helps those in need. According to Hoover, America was a strong democracy because Americans took responsibility for their own lives.

Although Hoover had been president for less than a year, people blamed him for causing the Depression. Bitter "Hoover jokes" became popular. Unable to make loan payments to their banks, many people lost their homes. In many cities, homeless people built cardboard and tar paper shacks. These poorly built shelters gave some protection from bad weather. But people living in them had to do without heat, lights, or running water. These slums became known as "Hoovervilles."

What Caused the Great Depression?

Several factors caused the Depression. The stock market crash was only one of the causes. Businesses had grown rapidly in the 1920s. They had produced many products quickly and often faster than consumers could buy them. This overproduction caused big changes in many companies. As production was slowed down, workers were laid off.

When the economy was good, people spent a lot of money. The strong economy encouraged them to buy more than they could pay for. Many people had bought things on credit. Credit is the practice of buying something and paying for it later. Then, when people lost their jobs, they could not pay their debts. Banks that "held paper" on unpaid loans went out of business.

Many foreign countries still in debt from the war were unable to buy products from America. In some cases, high tariffs were placed on American goods. The American economy might have grown much stronger during the 1920s if these countries had been able to buy more U.S. goods.

How Did the Dust Bowl Affect Farm Owners, Tenants, and Sharecroppers?

After World War I, farmers struggled with great financial difficulties. Prices for their crops continued to go down. Many farmers were barely able to support their families. In an attempt to grow more crops, many farmers plowed up the grasslands of the Great Plains that stretch from Montana to Texas. In the early 1930s, these western states were hit by drought. The lack of rain dried out the soil. When the wind swept over the Plains, it created dust storms. These weather conditions turned the Plains into a "Dust Bowl" that drove many farmers from their land. It was an economic and environmental disaster.

How Did Americans Lose Confidence?

During the Depression, the American people lost confidence in themselves and in their country. People lived in fear of the future. Businesses were afraid to make new investments. Workers thought they could lose their jobs at any time. Unemployed workers had little reason to believe that they would ever find other jobs.

Families stood in **breadlines** for free food. Homeless people slept in subways, parks, and old empty warehouses. Men who once worked regularly could be seen selling apples on the street. Across the country, Americans became very concerned about the nation's future.

What Impact Did the Depression Have on African Americans and Women?

As the economy declined, many African Americans lost their jobs to unemployed white workers. African American workers, like women workers, were often "last hired, first fired." Many African Americans were sharecroppers that farmed the land in the South. Thousands of sharecroppers lost their jobs as the farm owners' income declined. Before the Depression, moving north had been a major way for Southern African Americans to find higher-paying jobs. As northern factories closed, these jobs were lost. Many married women of all races lost their jobs during the Depression. Many businesses thought that it was more important that unemployed married men be employed than married women.

Lesson 1 Review On a sheet of paper, write your answers to the following questions. Use complete sentences.

1. How did the stock market crash affect businesses?

2. Why did President Hoover not help the unemployed?

3. List three factors that helped cause the Great Depression.

4. What effects did the Depression have on the American people?

5. What were breadlines?

The weak economy did not improve as President Hoover had believed it would. He made plans to help the economy. Hoover proposed the following:

Agricultural

Having to do with raising crops or animals for food or profit

Surplus

An extra amount of something

Stabilize

To keep from changing

Insurance

A plan that protects against loss in return for regular payments

Moratorium

The legal act of delaying something

Crisis

An event that threatens people's well-being

• With the **Agricultural** Marketing Act, Congress approved $500 million to buy extra, or **surplus,** crops from farmers. Hoover hoped this act would **stabilize** farm prices. This plan was unsuccessful because the farm problem was too great. Farm prices continued to go down.

• The Reconstruction Finance Corporation was established in 1932. This corporation loaned emergency money to banks, railroads, and **insurance** companies. Insurance is a plan that protects against loss in return for regular payments.

• A federal public works program was established and $750 million was approved to create jobs. Some people went to work building dams, highways, and buildings. States and local communities were encouraged to establish similar programs.

• A **moratorium** was put on payments of war debts owed to the United States. This put off payments of debts until later. Hoover hoped to ease Europe's financial problems. Then, he believed, these countries would be able to buy more products from the United States.

How Did President Roosevelt Help the Nation Recover?

Hoover's suggestions for improving the economy were not enough for the American people. They wanted a change in the White House. In the 1932 election, Hoover was defeated in his attempt for re-election. In a landslide victory, Democrat Franklin Delano Roosevelt became the new president. Roosevelt said he had a "new deal for the American people." He promised to act quickly to put the country back on its feet.

President Roosevelt took the oath of office on March 4, 1933. In a radio message, he told the American people that the economic **crisis** would not destroy the nation. He said with confidence that "the only thing we have to fear is fear itself."

Recovery

The act of overcoming a problem

Prohibit

To prevent by law

Roosevelt promised a "New Deal" for "the forgotten man at the bottom of the economic pyramid." The plan covered three areas: relief, **recovery,** and reform. Roosevelt knew that many Americans were in need of immediate help. He had to find a way to get the economy to recover from its depression quickly. He believed that America's economic system had to be reformed. Basic changes were necessary to prevent another depression in the future.

As a young man, Roosevelt had suffered an attack of polio. He had to use a wheelchair or leg braces to walk after that. Many thought that Roosevelt's own illness made him more concerned about the problems of others.

What Actions Did Roosevelt and Congress Take?

Before he became president, Roosevelt said that he was willing to try different methods to end the Depression. "If one plan fails," he said, "admit it frankly and try another. But above all, try something."

The nation wanted action. On March 9, 1933, President Roosevelt acted boldly. He called Congress into special session. In the next 100 days, this Congress passed many important laws. Many of these early "New Deal" laws were based on ideas of progressive politicians before and during World War I. Progressives wanted more government regulation of the economy and social welfare programs. The period called the "Hundred Days" resulted in the following government actions:

- The national "bank holiday" **prohibited** people from rushing to banks and taking all of their money out. The government inspected banks before reopening them. Banks with problems could not reopen until the problems were addressed.
- The Emergency Banking Act made federal loans available to banks.
- The Federal Emergency Relief Administration loaned millions of dollars to state agencies for families who needed food, clothing, and shelter.

In 1933, Congress created the Tennessee Valley Authority (TVA) along the Tennessee River in seven southern states. The river's landscape ranges from flood plains to tall mountains. A series of dams created a chain of lakes. The valley possesses rich mineral deposits, and the TVA helped develop them.

- The Civilian Conservation Corps (CCC) hired people ages of 18 to 25 to plant trees, build roads, and work on flood control in rural areas.

- The Agricultural Adjustment Act (AAA) paid farmers for crops they destroyed. This would create a shortage of products that would in turn raise prices.

- The National Recovery Administration (NRA) was established to help businesses recover. It encouraged cooperation among business, labor, and government. It reduced the workweek, established a minimum wage, and ended child labor.

- The Truth-in-Securities Act controlled selling stocks and bonds.

- The Tennessee Valley Authority (TVA) employed thousands of people to work on environmental problems in the Tennessee River Basin. They constructed dams to control flooding and soil erosion and to generate hydroelectric power. For the first time, rural families in this area had electricity. In time, inexpensive electricity changed the area and provided stable jobs and a better home life.

Americans were hopeful that the new cooperation between businesses, labor, and the government would bring the Great Depression to an end. The Blue Eagle, the symbol for the NRA, began appearing in windows of small shops and gates of large factories. The NRA stood for the Roosevelt administration's first 100 days of efforts to end the Depression.

This eagle became the symbol of the NRA during the Great Depression.

What do you think?

Why is confidence in yourself and your country important?

Lesson 2 Review Choose the best word or name in parentheses to complete each sentence. Write your answers on a sheet of paper.

1. The (Reconstruction Finance Corporation, New Deal, Agricultural Marketing Act) allowed for $500 million to buy surplus crops from farmers.

2. President (Hoover, Roosevelt) promised the New Deal to Americans.

3. The (national bank holiday, Emergency Banking Act, National Recovery Administration) prohibited people from rushing to the banks to take their money out.

4. The (Agricultural Adjustment Act, Federal Emergency Relief Administration, Civilian Conservation Corps) loaned millions of dollars to state agencies.

5. The (Emergency Banking, Truth-in-Securities, Agricultural Adjustment) Act attempted to raise farm prices by cutting back production.

Biography

Marian Anderson: 1897–1993
Philadelphia-born Marian Anderson studied classical singing in Europe. She had a wonderful homecoming in 1935 with a concert at New York's Town Hall. Anderson was praised for her glorious voice, her beauty, and her dignity. She also became a symbol for African American resistance to injustice. In 1939, she was denied permission to sing at Constitution Hall in Washington, D.C., because of her race. The Secretary of the Interior fought the injustice by asking Anderson to perform at the Lincoln Memorial. She sang there the following Easter Sunday before 75,000 people. In 1955, Marian Anderson became the first African American to sing a role in the Metropolitan Opera. Thereafter, she toured 12 nations as a performing goodwill ambassador for the United States. After retiring, Anderson supported human rights and young performers.

Mural

An artistic painting or drawing on a wall

Restore

To give something back to its owner; to repair

During the first stage of the New Deal, the government focused on giving immediate relief to those most in need. These steps helped put the nation back on the road to economic recovery. The second stage, called the Second New Deal, tried to make economic reforms. These reforms changed the role of the federal government in the lives of Americans.

Which Reforms Changed the Government's Role?

In April 1935, Congress passed a $4.8 billion jobs program. It created the Works Progress Administration (WPA) to put every unemployed person to work. The WPA went on to build schools, hospitals, playgrounds, museums, and airports. Actors were hired to put on plays. Musicians were paid to give concerts. Artists were employed to paint **murals** on the walls of government buildings. Artists also produced hundreds of posters. They announced many new programs and encouraged people to travel. Eight million Americans found work with the WPA. The jobs helped **restore** self-respect and confidence in American workers. The restoration of the workforce helped ease the Depression. More stores opened. Factories began to hire workers as demand for their products increased.

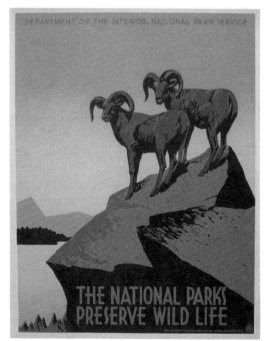

This poster from 1939 was for the National Park Service.

The Works Progress Administration (WPA) offered millions of Americans jobs working on public projects. Beginning in 1936, nearly $7 billion was spent on the program. The program did much to build and repair the nation's public resources. Workers paved or repaired 280,000 miles of roads. They built 29,000 bridges and 150 airfields. They also built 4,383 new schools and repaired or added on to 30,000 others. They constructed more than 130 hospitals. The agency closed in 1943.

Before the time of the New Deal, the federal government usually sided with business during labor disputes. However the new National Labor Relations Act, or Wagner Act, gave workers the right to form unions. Employers could not stop workers from forming a union. The National Labor Relations Board, a government agency, made sure the vote whether to join a union was fair. For the first time, the United States government encouraged unions and employers to discuss wages and working conditions. Differences could be settled peacefully in a process of **collective bargaining**. This was a way of negotiating between groups of workers and their employers.

Many unemployed laborers found work through the Works Progress Administration.

One of the most important reforms of the New Deal was the Social Security Act of 1935. Government programs took responsibility for Americans who were elderly, unemployed, or **disabled**. Someone who is disabled faces mental or physical challenges. Many of the suggestions for this law were made by Secretary of Labor Frances Perkins. She was the first woman to become a member of a president's Cabinet.

Social Security Act of 1935

Pension Benefits for the Elderly	Unemployment Compensation	Disability Benefits
Money for the pensions came from two new taxes. One tax came from the employee's pay. An equal amount came from the employer.	The employer paid an additional tax to pay unemployed workers until they found work.	Payments were made to disabled or blind Americans.

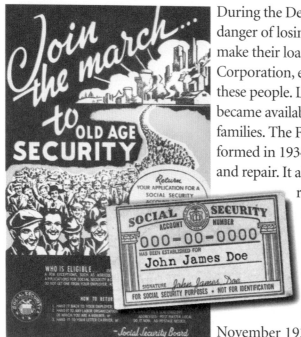

This poster from 1936 encouraged people to support Social Security programs. A Social Security card (inset) may be applied for at birth.

During the Depression, many Americans were in danger of losing their homes because they could not make their loan payments. The Home Owners Loan Corporation, established in 1933, was designed to help these people. Low-interest, long-term home loans became available to more than a million American families. The Federal Housing Administration (FHA), formed in 1934, encouraged low-cost home building and repair. It also offered banks a guarantee of repayment of loans to lower- and middle-income Americans.

Who Won the Election of 1936?

Franklin Roosevelt was elected to his second term as president in November 1936. Alf Landon, the Republican Party candidate, carried only two states—Maine and Vermont. It was a historically important election for Roosevelt and the Democratic Party. This was the first time in American history that three groups—organized labor, farmers, and African Americans—had voted in large numbers for a Democratic Party presidential candidate.

For African Americans this was a major change. Since the late 1860s, African Americans had generally voted for the Republican candidates, because they belonged to the party of Abraham Lincoln. Aid from New Deal programs convinced many African Americans to vote for Roosevelt.

How Did the Supreme Court React to Reforms?

Roosevelt and his New Deal programs ran into problems with the Supreme Court. Most of the members of the Supreme Court believed some of the New Deal legislation was unconstitutional.

The Supreme Court declared the National Recovery Act and the Agricultural Adjustment Act unconstitutional. This declaration angered President Roosevelt. He believed that the "nine old men" on the Supreme Court stood in the way of progress. Six of the justices were over 70 years old. Roosevelt decided to appoint a new justice for every justice over the age of 70.

The six new justices, Roosevelt thought, would assure that New Deal laws would not be **overturned** by the Supreme Court. Roosevelt's decision was not well accepted. Members of Congress **denounced** it as political "court-packing." Many Americans also rejected the plan.

However, as the older justices retired, Roosevelt appointed younger, more **liberal** justices. Liberals favor change. These young justices were some of the most important justices in American history—Hugo Black, William O. Douglas, and Felix Frankfurter.

How Did Labor Unions Change?

In 1881, the American Federation of Labor (AFL) had been formed. This labor union was made up of only skilled workers. Unskilled factory workers could not belong. Therefore, they had no union to represent them. The skilled workers were organized by **occupation**. Each occupation area formed its own union within the AFL. The AFL served as a governing body over all of the smaller unions.

One union leader, John L. Lewis, thought an industry-wide union was necessary. He felt that all workers, including factory workers, steelworkers, and autoworkers, should be admitted to one union.

Lewis formed a committee for industrial organizations within the AFL. However, the more **traditional** labor leaders were against this committee. Lewis broke away and established the Congress of Industrial Organizations (CIO) in 1935.

The CIO united workers from all industries into one organization. The new union used the National Labor Relations Act to increase its membership to 6 million workers by 1945. Unlike traditional unions, the CIO welcomed all workers, skilled and unskilled, including women, immigrants, and African Americans. In 1955, the American Federation of Labor and the Congress of Industrial Organizations became one organization. The new union was named the AFL-CIO.

Word Bank

American
    Federation
Industrial
    Organizations
Labor Relations
Social Security
Works Progress

Lesson 3 Review On a sheet of paper, write the correct words from the Word Bank to complete each sentence.

1. The _____ Act set up programs to help the elderly, unemployed, or disabled.

2. The National _____ Act gave workers the right to form unions.

3. The _____ Administration gave people work.

4. The _____ of Labor was made up of only skilled workers.

5. The Congress of _____ united workers from all industries.

What do you think?

Why is it important to set up programs to protect the elderly, disabled, and unemployed?

Focus on Economics

Many laws passed to ease the Great Depression are still going strong today. The Federal Deposit Insurance Corporation (1933) first insured bank deposit losses up to $2,500. Today, it insures losses up to $100,000. The Fair Labor Standards Act (1938) set a minimum wage and maximum number of hours to be worked per week. In 2004, the minimum hourly wage was $5.15, with a 40-hour work week.

The best-known program carried over from the Great Depression is the Social Security Act of 1935. Originally, it provided cash to retired industry and commerce workers. Over the years, it expanded to include widows, farm workers, and state workers. Disability insurance and Medicare were included to care for lower-income and retired workers. Today, nearly every U.S. worker is part of the system.

The Great Depression affected the life of most Americans. Many people suffered great hardships. In the hard times, though, life went on. People could escape into a theater and watch a movie for five cents. The public was eager to see a world different from its own. Hollywood provided that world through movies. The movies of the 1930s gave the American public a new world of comedy, musicals, and drama.

Ginger Rogers and Fred Astaire became America's favorite dancing couple. Child star Shirley Temple usually played an orphan with a big heart and a positive outlook. Americans laughed at the crazy comedy of the Marx brothers and their humorous adventures. A favorite film among children in 1939 was *The Wizard of Oz*. A song from this film gave viewers hope that there might be a happier life "Somewhere Over the Rainbow."

Another popular movie of 1939 was *Gone With the Wind*. It told the story of Scarlett O'Hara and the destruction of her family's Georgia plantation during the Civil War. It described the American South during another period of hard times. At the end of the movie, Scarlett's world had totally changed; yet she had survived. The message of the story seemed to be one that the nation in the hard times of the 1930s wanted to hear.

Who Were Some Heroes of the 1930s?

In 1938, Joe Louis, the heavyweight champion of the world, stepped into the boxing ring. His opponent was a German boxer named Max Schmeling. The German government published harsh words that they said came from Schmeling: "I would not take this fight if I did not believe that I, a white man, can beat a Negro." Schmeling never said these words. Joe Louis had to prove that an American could defeat a representative of Germany. Two minutes and four seconds after it began, the fight was over. Louis had won. On that night, Louis became a national hero.

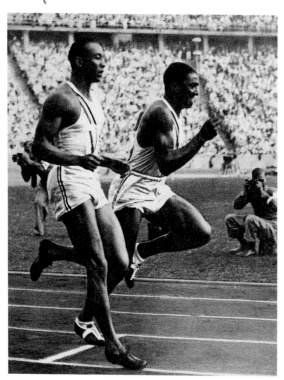

In 1936, over 5,000 athletes met in Berlin, Germany, to participate in the Olympic games. German leader Adolf Hitler hoped to prove that white German athletes were better than any other athletes. This hope was shattered by the performance of an African American athlete named Jesse Owens. Owens won four Olympic gold medals.

Jesse Owens (left) shattered Adolf Hitler's claim that white German athletes were the best in the world. Owens won four gold medals in the 1936 Olympics in Berlin, Germany.

In 1928, Amelia Earhart had become the first woman passenger and keeper of the logbook on a transatlantic flight. She flew from Newfoundland, Canada, to Wales in the United Kingdom. She went on to write a book about her experiences. Then, in 1932, Earhart became the first woman to fly alone over the Atlantic Ocean. She made the first solo flight from Hawaii to the United States in 1935. She gave talks to promote flying and to give women encouragement. In 1937, in an attempt to fly around the world, Earhart disappeared somewhere over the Pacific Ocean.

Amelia Earhart

Technology Connection

Frozen Foods

Clarence Birdseye loved cooking. He wanted to find a way to enjoy fresh food all year, not just during the summer. Birdseye worked as a biologist for the government. While he was in the Arctic, he saw how American Indians used nature to their advantage. They froze fish very quickly. Birdseye knew this process kept ice crystals from forming in the food and damaging the cells.

He experimented to find a way to freeze fresh food just as quickly. He used buckets of salt water, blocks of ice, and a fan. He packed foods into waxed cardboard boxes and then flash-froze them. Birdseye introduced his frozen foods to the public. For the first time, people could buy fresh-tasting vegetables, fruits, seafood, and meat throughout the year.

What do you think?

What themes do you think were present in entertainment in the 1930s?

Lesson 4 Review On a sheet of paper, write the answers to the following questions. Use complete sentences.

1. Why did people who lived during the Depression like watching movies or other entertainment?
2. Why did people like Gone With the Wind?
3. What did the song "Somewhere Over the Rainbow" from *The Wizard of Oz* suggest about finding a happier life?
4. What did Joe Louis do?
5. How did Jesse Owens spoil Adolf Hitler's hopes?

History in Your Life

The Development of Nylon

In the mid-1930s, Wallace H. Carothers and a team of scientists spun the first successful artificial fiber. A research chemist for Du Pont Laboratories, Carothers called the durable fiber nylon. He had experimented with fibers since the late 1920s. Using a special machine, he was able to make longer molecules than ever before. Fibers made from the compounds he used could be pulled to several times their original length. Pulling made the fibers stronger and more elastic.

Du Pont introduced the first nylon product—a toothbrush with nylon bristles—in the late 1930s. Then the first nylon stockings went on sale. Today nylon is made into powder, fibers, sheets, rods, and tubes. It is used to make parachutes, carpets, tires, clothing, fishing line, surgical thread, electrical equipment, and sporting goods. Plastic nylon panels replace steel on some automobiles. From clothes to cars, Americans enjoy the benefits of nylon every day.

Breadline

The impact of the Depression on the lives of Americans could be seen in the nation's cities. Out-of-work men gathered in breadlines to get something to eat. A few men carried signs asking for a job. This selection concerns the life of an out-of-work man in San Francisco from December 1931 to December 1933.

A wet and cold day in December, 1931, I was an active member of the breadline on Ritch Street in San Francisco. . . . I knew by bitter experience that it would be at least two hours before I could dip into a bowl of waterlogged stew. I was ravenously hungry, friendless, homeless, and far removed from the possibilities of obtaining a job.

It was four o'clock in the morning, and still pitch-dark, when our advance guard appeared and took up its position six abreast outside the municipal kitchen. . . . By six o'clock, when the actual feeding started, the line had reached as far as Folsom Street, when every moment brought its quota of semistarved, shabby, despairing men. . . .

During the daylight hours I roamed all over the city looking for work. Hatless, clad in overalls and heavy, hobnailed boots, peaked and hungry-looking, badly in need of a haircut, I must have been a sight. People didn't waste promises or interviews when I turned up. With a few exceptions they gave the cold shoulder. . . .

By the summer of 1932, I looked at least ten years older. My weight under normal conditions is about 170 pounds. After four months in the breadline I tipped the scales at 125. My ribs protruded like laths [boards], and my lusterless eyes had retreated way back into dark-ringed sockets.

I didn't beg or ransack the garbage cans; nor did I rob or steal. Instead, I walked about for hours, eyes glued to the sidewalk, looking for lost coins . . . I never found. . . .

I ate and slept in the San Francisco breadline and flophouses from the first of May to the first of December, 1933. . . . My total monthly expenses amounted to seventy cents. Thirty cents went for the purchase of a daily loaf of stale bread, at a penny a loaf, the remaining forty cents kept me in tobacco. . . .

Document-Based Questions

1. In December 1931, where did the man find himself and why was he there?

2. What did the man do during the daylight hours?

3. How did his physical appearance change?

4. By 1933, had his life improved? Why or why not?

5. By the end of 1933, what government help could this man expect?

Source: "Bread Line," The Atlantic Monthly, by Hugo Johanson, August, 1936.

Chapter 9 SUMMARY

- Following the stock market crash of 1929, the country fell into an economic slump known as the Great Depression.

- There were many reasons for the Depression. Business had expanded too rapidly. More products were made than people could buy. Businesses laid off workers. Many people bought things on credit and when they lost their jobs, they could not pay their debts. There were high tariffs placed on American products. Prices for farm products continued to decline.

- Many people were unemployed. Many were left homeless and had no way of buying food. People moved from place to place in search of work.

- President Hoover tried helping in several ways, but most of his plans and policies failed. Most of the American people blamed Hoover for the problems of the Depression.

- Franklin Delano Roosevelt became president in 1933. He set up a number of social and economic programs called the "New Deal." Among these were the Works Progress Administration (WPA), the Civilian Conservation Corps (CCC), and the Tennessee Valley Authority (TVA).

- The Social Security Act of 1935 set up the Social Security system to help the elderly and disabled.

- Frances Perkins, the first woman on a president's Cabinet, became secretary of labor under Roosevelt.

- The labor movement grew as John L. Lewis left the American Federation of Labor (AFL) and formed the Congress of Industrial Organizations (CIO).

- Roosevelt put new justices on the Supreme Court who would support his policies. Congress and the American people objected.

- The films of the period reflected the mood of the times by offering people an escape from their hardships.

- Roosevelt's plans and policies helped bring the United States out of the Great Depression.

Chapter 9 REVIEW

On a sheet of paper, write the correct word or words from the Word Bank to complete each sentence.

Word Bank

breadlines

Civilian
    Conservation
    Corps

Frances Perkins

Joe Louis

New Deal

overproduction

Social Security

Supreme Court

unemployment

Works Progress
    Administration

1. During the Depression, _____ was high because there were no jobs.

2. There were too many products and not enough people to buy them because of _____.

3. Soup kitchens and _____ helped feed people who had no money for food.

4. Roosevelt promised a "_____" for Americans.

5. _____ beat Max Schmeling in a highly publicized boxing match.

6. The _____ employed young people who planted trees, built roads, and worked on flood control.

7. The _____ Act of 1935 created programs to help the elderly, unemployed, and disabled.

8. The goal of the _____ was to put every unemployed person to work.

9. The first woman to be on a president's Cabinet was Secretary of Labor _____.

10. Roosevelt called the _____ "nine old men."

On a sheet of paper, write the letter of the answer that best completes each sentence.

11. People held Herbert Hoover responsible for _____.

    A Social Security

    B the Great Depression

    C the crash of Wall Street

    D closing charities

12. President Roosevelt felt it necessary to reform _____.

    A America's economic system

    B the Works Progress Administration

    C the Congress

    D war debts

13. By winning four Olympic gold medals in 1936, _____ defeated Hitler's plan to show German superiority.

   A Amelia Earhart   **C** Joe Louis

   B Jesse Owens   **D** Fred Astaire

On a sheet of paper, write the answer to each question. Use complete sentences.

14. What were some factors that caused the Great Depression?

15. What was life like during the Great Depression?

16. What were four programs that Roosevelt set up as part of the "New Deal?"

17. Why were the slums set up during the Depression called "Hoovervilles"?

Critical Thinking On a sheet of paper, write your response to each question. Use complete sentences.

18. Social Security was started during the Great Depression. Do you think Social Security is still important today? Explain your answer.

19. People went to the movies to escape the problems of the Depression. How does television today compare with the movies during the Depression?

20. If there were a massive depression today, do you think the government should step in and provide jobs? Why or why not?

Test-Taking Tip

When a teacher announces a test, listen carefully. Write down the topics that the teacher will include on the test. Ask if you have any questions about what the test will cover.

10 World War II
1939–1945

President Roosevelt's plans to bring the nation out of the Great Depression had helped. However, an even greater problem was on the horizon for the United States. After World War I, President Wilson had warned that the world might be in danger of another war in the future. As the 1930s ended, Europe was once again in trouble. A second world war, far more damaging than the first, began as Wilson had said. In this chapter, you will learn what caused World War II, how the war affected American life, and how the war ended.

Goals for Learning

◆ To describe events in Europe and Asia in the 1920s and 1930s and the reactions of the United States

◆ To explain the steps that led to World War II

◆ To describe how Germany came to control most of Europe, and why France and Great Britain declared war on Germany

◆ To describe the events at Pearl Harbor

◆ To describe life in the United States during the war

◆ To explain how American involvement affected the outcome of the war

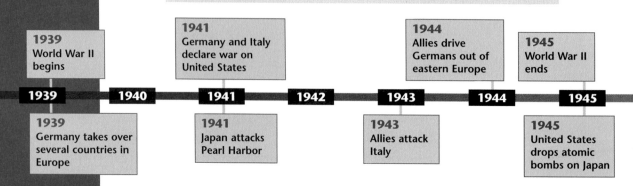

1939
World War II begins

1941
Germany and Italy declare war on United States

1944
Allies drive Germans out of eastern Europe

1945
World War II ends

1939 **1940** **1941** **1942** **1943** **1944** **1945**

1939
Germany takes over several countries in Europe

1941
Japan attacks Pearl Harbor

1943
Allies attack Italy

1945
United States drops atomic bombs on Japan

Fascist

One who believes that the state is more important than the individual

Inflation

A steady rise in prices of goods

Before and during the Great Depression in the United States, other countries around the world had depressions of their own. The social and economic problems of these different countries brought different outcomes. For example, Germany, Italy, and Japan fell under the control of dictators. The whole world would soon feel the effects of these dictators' beliefs that war might be a good solution to their nations' problems.

How Did Mussolini and Fascism Gain Support in Italy?

Benito Mussolini had controlled the Italian government since 1922. He believed that a strong leader must have full power to run the country. Under his dictatorship, other political parties were forbidden. Mussolini created the **Fascist** Party. Fascists believed the state was more important than the individual and rejected the idea of democracy. The Fascists believed military power and war were good for a nation. Italian Fascists used the slogan: "Believe! Obey! Fight!"

How Did Hitler and Nazism Gain Support in Germany?

The German people did not understand how they lost World War I. They were upset with the strict conditions of the peace settlement. When World War I ended, Germany removed its king and established a democracy. The new Republic of Germany tried to govern its troubled nation.

The economy in Germany fell apart in 1923. **Inflation** made German paper money nearly worthless. Inflation is a steady rise in prices of goods. Prices of goods doubled daily. Germans had to carry large bags of money just to buy food for one day. Many workers lost their jobs. The democratic government of Germany was criticized for being weak. The National Socialist German Workers' Party, or Nazi Party, opposed the German government. Adolf Hitler led the Nazis.

Chancellor

The chief minister in some European countries

Citizenship

The condition of belonging to a certain country

Hitler used his skills as a public speaker and organizer to increase the power of the Nazi Party. Hitler declared that democracy was weak and could not solve the nation's problems. He added that the economic crisis was not the fault of the Germans. He blamed Germany's problems on others. He told Germans that Communists and Jews were trying to destroy their government. He promised success for all Germans. He preached against democracy and for hatred of the Jews.

Adolf Hitler became the **chancellor,** or chief minister, of Germany in 1933. This happened after his Nazi Party had won a majority of seats in Germany's Parliament. Within months, Hitler became a dictator. He gave himself the title "der Führer." It meant "the leader." Hitler and the Nazi Party quickly destroyed German democracy and individual freedoms.

Hitler was successful in improving the German economy. German unemployment dropped. The standard of living for most Germans rose. Hitler continued a campaign against German Jews. He called them traitors. German Jews lost their **citizenship** and their jobs. Citizenship is the condition of belonging to a certain country.

German dictator Adolf Hitler (second from right) inspects troops.

How Did Fascism Begin in Spain?

A civil war broke out in Spain in 1936. General Francisco Franco and his forces fought against anti-Fascists. The anti-Fascists wanted Spain to have a democratic government. The Spanish Civil War became a test for the Fascist governments of Germany and Italy. Italy sent troops to fight in Spain, and German planes bombed Spanish cities.

The Communist government of the Soviet Union supported the anti-Fascists. Anti-Fascist volunteers from Great Britain, France, and the United States also fought in this war. The Americans who fought did so by their own choice, not as members of the American military. The Spanish Civil War lasted three years. The Spanish Fascist forces, supported by the governments of Italy and Germany, won in 1939. Franco became the leader of a new Fascist government.

How Did Japan Establish Control in Asia?

The worldwide depression also hurt Japan, an island nation in Asia. Japanese industries needed imported coal, oil, and iron. The depression made it difficult for nations to trade with each other. Without enough raw materials, Japan found its industries threatened.

Japan relied on imported rice to help feed its people. Unable to grow enough rice on their own, many Japanese had no food. Radical military leaders, similar to those in Germany and Italy, took control of the Japanese government. The army seized Manchuria, an area rich in coal and iron, from China. In 1937, Japan invaded China again and captured several important cities. Japan had taken its first steps to control Asia and establish a Japanese empire.

Biography

Eleanor Roosevelt: 1884–1962

Eleanor Roosevelt was a diplomat and humanitarian. She became a model for women in politics and public affairs. As First Lady when her husband Franklin D. Roosevelt was president, she had a great deal of influence. She lectured and wrote a daily newspaper column that was widely published. Active in Democratic politics, Roosevelt was a champion for the rights of women and minorities. As U.S. delegate to the United Nations, she chaired the UN's Human Rights Commission. She also took a central role in drafting the UN's Universal Declaration of Human Rights. Her uncle was President Theodore Roosevelt.

How Did America View the Problems in Europe?

Americans did not want to deal with the problems in Europe. During the 1930s, Americans had a much larger problem at home with the Great Depression. The New Deal programs took time to plan and put to use.

There was another reason Americans ignored problems in Europe. The memory of World War I was still fresh in their minds. Americans wanted no part of another foreign war. Many people felt that the United States was protected by possible attacks because of the Atlantic and Pacific oceans. Congress passed laws in 1935 and 1937 to make sure that the United States stayed neutral. These laws prevented the sale of arms or lending money to countries at war. Throughout the 1930s, Americans watched Germany, Italy, and Japan increase in military strength.

President Roosevelt was not so certain that the United States should ignore what was going on in Europe. Beginning in 1937, he tried to keep the country aware of the problems there. For that reason, some people criticized Roosevelt. They thought he wanted to start a war.

Lesson 1 Review Choose the best word or name in parentheses to complete each sentence. Write your answers on a sheet of paper.

1. (Hitler, Mussolini, Franco) started the Fascist Party in Italy.

2. (Hitler, Mussolini, Franco) became chancellor of Germany in 1933.

3. The (anti-Fascists, Fascists) in Spain wanted a democratic government.

4. The Spanish Civil War lasted (two, three, four) years.

5. Japan invaded (Italy, Spain, China) in 1937.

What do you think?

Why do you think some countries in Europe started to have dictators as leaders?

Reich

A German empire

During the years of the Spanish Civil War, Hitler moved aggressively to expand his power in Europe. His goal was to bring the German-speaking people of Austria, Czechoslovakia, and Poland under German rule. Twice before in history, the German people had built a **reich,** or empire, in Europe. Hitler wanted to create a Third Reich.

How Did European Leaders Give in to Hitler?

Hitler took the first step in creating a German empire in March 1938. German troops marched into Austria and declared it part of the German Third Reich. Although this action went against the Treaty of Versailles, the League of Nations did nothing to stop it. Hitler's next move was to bring three million Germans living in the Sudetenland into the Third Reich. The Sudetenland was an area of Czechoslovakia. Hitler threatened to use force. To avoid war, Neville Chamberlain, the prime minister of Great Britain, suggested that the major powers of Europe meet.

European leaders met in Munich, Germany, in 1938. Among those present were (from front left) Neville Chamberlain, Edouard Daladier, Adolf Hitler, and Benito Mussolini.

Appeasement

Doing something to keep peace

Synagogue

A Jewish place of worship

Chamberlain, Mussolini, Hitler, and Edouard Daladier of France met in Munich, Germany, in September 1938. Czechoslovakia was not represented. Hitler believed that the threat of war would frighten the leaders of Great Britain and France. He thought that they would give in to his demands. Chamberlain and Daladier did just that. Both leaders agreed to give Germany the Sudetenland. They felt a policy of **appeasement** was best. Appeasement is doing something to keep peace. Hitler agreed to make no more advances for territory. When Chamberlain returned to Britain, he said that the meeting in Munich had produced "peace with honor . . . peace in our time."

German soldiers gathered this group of Jewish women and children in Warsaw, Poland, in 1943.

What Was the Holocaust?

On the night of November 9, 1938, Nazis set fire to Jewish places of worship called **synagogues**. They also broke into Jewish homes, terrorized Jewish people, and destroyed Jewish businesses. This night of terror is called "Kristallnacht," or the "Night of Broken Glass." Many Jews were killed or arrested. This was only the beginning of the terror the Jews faced.

In 1939, Germany set up death camps for the Jews as a part of Hitler's "final solution." The Nazis planned to murder every Jew they could find. Jews were sent by train to the death camps. Men, women, and children were killed with gas or gunfire in these camps. Many bodies were burned in large ovens.

When it became widely known in 1945 that this **Holocaust** had occurred, the world was shocked. The government of Nazi Germany had killed nearly six million innocent European Jews. In the eyes of the Germans, the Jews were **inferior** simply because of their **ethnic heritage.** For many years after the end of World War II, Nazi war criminals were hunted and brought to justice.

Why Did Germany Attack Poland?

The Treaty of Versailles, signed at the end of World War I, had given Poland a strip of land called the Polish Corridor. On this piece of land, Poland gained access to the Baltic Sea. The Germans never liked this arrangement. The Polish Corridor isolated East Prussia and the German city of Danzig from the rest of Germany. In March 1939, Hitler demanded that Poland give back the city of Danzig in order for Germany to build a railroad through the Polish Corridor. Poland refused. Great Britain and France supported Poland. Both countries said they would go to war to defend Poland. Great Britain and France expected help from the Soviet Union in a fight against Germany.

However, Germany and the Soviet Union had signed a treaty of friendship in August 1939. The Soviet leader, Joseph Stalin, agreed not to interfere if Germany attacked Poland. In return, Germany would give the Soviet Union the eastern half of Poland. Having gained the alliance of the Soviet Union, Hitler felt confident that he could successfully seize the Polish land.

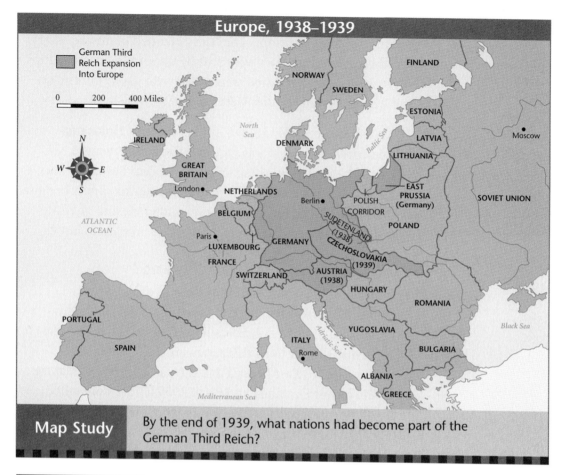

Europe, 1938–1939

German Third Reich Expansion Into Europe

0   200   400 Miles

Map Study By the end of 1939, what nations had become part of the German Third Reich?

Word Bank

France

Holocaust

Soviet Union

Sudetenland

Third Reich

What do you think?

What do you think it was like to be a Jew living during the Holocaust?

Lesson 2 Review On a sheet of paper, write the correct word or words from the Word Bank to complete each sentence.

1. Hitler's plan was to create a _____ by ruling other countries.

2. Chamberlain and Daladier agreed to give the _____ to Germany if Hitler would not seek more territory.

3. The murder of millions of Jews in Germany became known as the _____.

4. Hitler sought an agreement with the _____ in order to seize Poland.

5. Great Britain and _____ agreed to go to war to defend Poland from Germany.

German soldiers moved rapidly into Poland by trucks on September 1, 1939. They were supported with tanks and bombing attacks by the German air force. This new method of warfare was called **blitzkrieg**, or "lightning war." This simple act of German aggression was the beginning of World War II.

Blitzkrieg

"Lightning war"; a rapid military attack

Defensive

Having protection against an attack

Why Did France and Britain Declare War?

Troops of the Soviet Union also attacked Poland. Great Britain and France, attempting to aid Poland, declared war on Germany. While repeating his promise to remain neutral, President Roosevelt did not approve of the attack on Poland. He asked Congress to reverse its neutrality order so that the United States could sell weapons to France and Great Britain. After a long debate, the arms were made available.

A few weeks after the attack by the Soviet Union, Poland surrendered. Germany and the Soviet Union divided Poland between them. Through the winter of 1939 and 1940, there was little activity. Some people began to speak of a "phony war." The world watched and waited, however, for Hitler's next move. They remembered the Nazi phrase, "Today Germany, tomorrow the world!"

Suddenly, in April 1940, Germany attacked and defeated Denmark and Norway. The next month, Belgium, Luxembourg, and the Netherlands fell to the German army. Germany then attacked France. German soldiers broke through the French **defensive** line.

What Happened at Dunkirk?

More than 300,000 British, Belgian, and French soldiers were trapped between the attacking Germans and the sea. These allied troops retreated to Dunkirk, a seaport located in the north of France on the English Channel. Great Britain made a daring attempt to rescue these allied troops.

Radar

A system used to locate objects such as planes

Hundreds of ships set sail from Great Britain for Dunkirk. Most of the troops were safely rescued and were in Great Britain on June 4, 1940. Six days later, Italy sided with Germany and declared war. France surrendered and requested an armistice. Hitler agreed.

What Was the Battle of Britain?

Great Britain was left alone to fight the Nazi war machine. If Great Britain was defeated, the United States would be without an ally in Europe. Prime Minister Winston Churchill spoke to the British people on June 4, 1940. He told them, "We shall defend our island, whatever the cost may be, we shall fight on the beaches . . . we shall fight in the fields and in the streets . . . we shall never surrender."

The British waited for a German invasion of their country. The German air force began around-the-clock bombing raids on Great Britain's air force bases in August 1940. The Royal Air Force (RAF) fought back. The RAF used a new **radar** system that located incoming planes. Many German bombers were destroyed. The Germans had to change their plans to invade Great Britain.

The German air force destroyed many buildings in London.

What Happened When Hitler Attacked the Soviet Union?

Hitler attacked the Soviet Union in June 1941. He ignored their friendship treaty. This decision was a major mistake for Hitler. Great Britain, Canada, Australia, the Soviet Union, and other nations joined together to fight Germany. These countries became known as the Allies. They realized that Hitler was attempting to gain control over all of Europe.

How Did America Come Closer to War?

Most Americans still did not want the United States to enter the war. However, Americans did not try to stay neutral, as in World War I. They became concerned about America's safety.

President Roosevelt told the American people that Great Britain needed help. Great Britain needed more weapons but did not have enough money to pay for the supplies. America had to be "the arsenal of democracy." Roosevelt proposed that the United States lend Great Britain military supplies. Congress passed the Lend-Lease Act in March 1941. This policy was designed to keep America out of war in Europe.

Under the Lend-Lease Act, the United States government would provide weapons to any country considered important to American **security**. These nations could buy, lease, exchange, or borrow equipment, weapons, and supplies from the United States. During World War II, the United States provided $50 billion in lend-lease aid to the Allies.

The United States began to prepare for the chance of war. Congress approved millions of dollars to strengthen the armed forces. The Selective Training and Service Act was passed in September 1940. This was the first peacetime law that drafted men into the armed forces. The last draft had been during World War I. Men between the ages of 21 and 35 were selected by a **lottery** to serve one year in the military. The lottery was a drawing of names. Later in the war, the age was lowered to 18. Men were then called to serve by age. The oldest went first.

The United States made a trade with Great Britain and loaned it 50 small warships called destroyers. In return, Great Britain leased naval and air bases to the United States in the Western Hemisphere. These bases allowed the United States to better defend itself and to keep watch over the Panama Canal.

What do you think?

How was World War II a war for democracy?

Lesson 3 Review On a sheet of paper, write the answers to the following questions. Use complete sentences.

1. What marked the beginning of World War II?
2. Which countries did Germany capture?
3. How did the British defend themselves against German attacks?
4. What was the Lend-Lease Act?
5. What was the Selective Service Act?

Civics Connection

The Selective Training and Service Act

The Selective Training and Service Act (SSA) gave Congress the right to draft young men into the armed forces. After World War II, the U.S. government stopped using the SSA. Then from 1948 until 1973, the draft was put back into effect. Tensions with the Soviet Union and Vietnam made Americans fear they would need a reserve of soldiers. Since 1973, the law has been in "standby" status. The law requires young men to register with the Selective Service at age 18. However, the draft will not resume unless there is an emergency.

Since World War II, the nature of world conflict has changed. Problems occur more quickly. American troops usually take part in small, short conflicts. If there were a large-scale conflict, the draft might have to be used again.

Some people argue that the draft robs young people of choice. They feel military service should be voluntary. They think the military should use benefits to attract volunteers. Today, because there is no draft, all members of the U.S. military are volunteers.

1. Do you think the Selective Training and Service Act is still a useful law? Explain.
2. Do you think the government should be able to draft young men for war? Explain.

Lesson 4 — War in Asia

The Japanese government announced that it intended to rule all of Asia, including China. That type of control went against America's Open Door Policy. The United States had established the policy so that all nations would be allowed free trade with China. America protested Japan's actions. However, Japan continued its plan to create an empire. Japan joined Germany and Italy in an alliance. These three countries became known as the **Axis Powers**.

Japan invaded the French colony of Indochina in June 1941. Indochina was just south of China. The United States became concerned that Japan was gaining too much land. America decided to stop selling oil and steel to Japan. Japan desperately needed oil to continue with its plan. The United States also offered a lend-lease program to China.

When Japan invaded Indochina, Roosevelt said Japan could not use money or investments it had in the United States. This is called freezing **assets**. Japan did the same thing to the United States. Trade between the two countries stopped.

Japan's Prime Minister Fumimaro Konoye and United States Secretary of State Cordell Hull began to negotiate. The Japanese wanted to be allowed to use their assets in the United States. They also wanted to be supplied with oil. The United States wanted Japan to withdraw from China and Southeast Asia. The negotiations failed. Hideki Tojo replaced Konoye as prime minister.

Why Did Japan Attack Pearl Harbor?

Early on December 7, 1941, a Sunday morning, 353 Japanese airplanes took off from six aircraft carriers in the Pacific Ocean. Their destination was the American naval base at Pearl Harbor, Hawaii, 220 miles away. Their goal was to destroy the American naval fleet anchored there. The Japanese thought they would be better able to conquer land in Asia if these American ships were destroyed.

Infamy

Disgraceful or lacking honor

Japan bombed ships in the harbor and planes on the ground. The surprise attack occurred at 7:55 A.M. Two hours later, the United States Pacific Fleet had lost many battleships, destroyers, and planes. The attack killed more than 2,000 Americans. Roosevelt said that December 7, 1941, was "a date which will live in **infamy.**" Four days later, Germany and Italy, Japan's allies, declared war on the United States.

Japan followed up its attack on Pearl Harbor by invading the Philippine Islands and other areas in the Pacific. American and Filipino troops fought the Japanese. However, they lacked planes, tanks, and ammunition. Japan gained another victory. It now controlled the Philippine Islands.

The USS West Virginia *and the USS* Tennessee *were among the 19 American ships damaged or destroyed at Pearl Harbor.*

History in Your Life

Rosie the Riveter and the Women of World War II

When America entered World War II, most healthy young men left their jobs for the armed forces. More than 4.5 million women took their place in support of the war effort. The lively song "Rosie the Riveter" was written in 1942. The title caught on as a friendly label for all women who became manufacturing workers. The song celebrated women's contributions on the homefront. Women worked in shipyards, steel mills, foundries, lumber mills, and aircraft and ammunition plants. They learned welding, electricity, mechanics, engineering, and chemistry. Women farmed, drove buses, wrote newspaper features, and played in the country's orchestras. Americans relied on female police officers, attorneys, and doctors. Thousands of American women also served in the military. These wartime changes helped break down job discrimination against women.

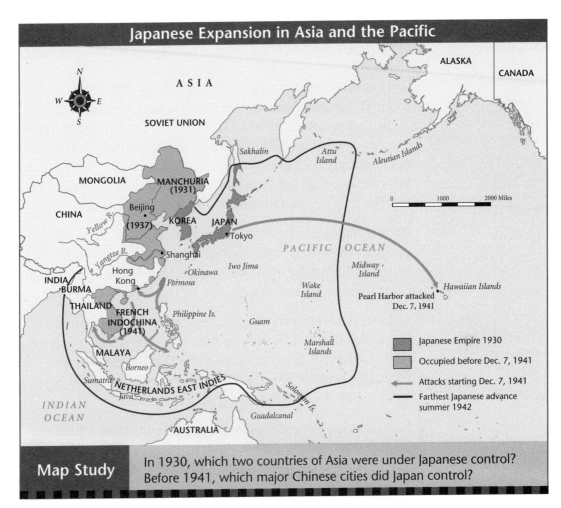

Japanese Expansion in Asia and the Pacific

ALASKA

CANADA

ASIA

SOVIET UNION

Sakhalin

Attu Island

Aleutian Islands

MONGOLIA

MANCHURIA (1931)

CHINA

Beijing (1937)

KOREA

JAPAN

Tokyo

Yellow R.

Yangtze R.

Shanghai

PACIFIC OCEAN

0   1000   2000 Miles

Hong Kong

Okinawa

Iwo Jima

Midway Island

INDIA

BURMA

Formosa

Wake Island

Hawaiian Islands

Pearl Harbor attacked Dec. 7, 1941

THAILAND

FRENCH INDOCHINA (1941)

Philippine Is.

Guam

MALAYA

Borneo

Marshall Islands

Sumatra

NETHERLANDS EAST INDIES

Java

Solomon Is.

INDIAN OCEAN

Guadalcanal

AUSTRALIA

	Japanese Empire 1930
	Occupied before Dec. 7, 1941
←	Attacks starting Dec. 7, 1941
—	Farthest Japanese advance summer 1942

Map Study In 1930, which two countries of Asia were under Japanese control? Before 1941, which major Chinese cities did Japan control?

Word Bank

assets
Axis Powers
Open Door
Pearl Harbor
Philippine Islands

Lesson 4 Review On a sheet of paper, write the word or words from the Word Bank to complete each sentence.

1. The United States opposed Japan's plan to rule Asia because it went against the American _____ policy with China.

2. Japan, Italy, and Germany were the _____.

3. When Japan attacked Indochina, the United States froze Japanese _____ and stopped selling oil and steel to Japan.

4. On December 7, 1941, the Japanese air force attacked the American fleet at _____ in Hawaii.

5. Next, the Japanese attacked and defeated the _____.

What do you think?

How do you think Japan's entering the war made things worse for the Allies?

Lesson 5 — The Home Front

Underestimate
To guess the size or importance of something as being less than it is

Patriotic
Having love for one's own country

Civilian
One who is not in the military

Ration
To use less or limit the amount of something

Combat
Battle

The United States was not prepared to fight a war in both Europe and Asia. However, Germany and Japan **underestimated** the ability of the United States to produce war supplies. The nation had a large number of workers and factories left idle by the Great Depression. For example, the American auto industry changed its plants to make tanks and planes. General Motors was able to make more war supplies than the combined output of Germany and Japan.

The war united the American people. It gave them a common purpose. **Patriotic** posters reminded Americans of their duty to "do their bit" for the war effort. American **civilians** aided the war effort in many different ways.

Millions of volunteers helped increase the supply of fresh vegetables. Parks and flower gardens were turned into "victory gardens" that produced more than one-third of the nation's vegetables by 1943. This allowed farmers to use most of their land to grow food for the armed forces.

Raw materials were needed for American industries. America became a nation of collectors. Volunteers collected tons of newspapers, tin cans, and rubber tires. Housewives collected bacon grease for use in making ammunition. Even worn nylon stockings were collected to make gunpowder bags for the navy.

Many goods were in short supply during the war. The government started to **ration** materials. This limited the amount of some goods that people could buy. Ration books contained stamps used to purchase gasoline, sugar, meat, and other products. A buyer had to pay the price for the product and a certain number of ration stamps. Shortages even changed the style of clothes. Men's pants were made without cuffs and women's dresses were shortened because extra cloth was needed for military uniforms.

Women joined the armed forces in great numbers. They served in Europe and Asia in every role except **combat.** Millions of women replaced men in the workforce. Women learned to build planes and tanks as the men left for war. They now had the opportunity to prove that they were as capable as any man.

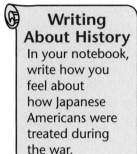

Writing About History

In your notebook, write how you feel about how Japanese Americans were treated during the war.

How Did Minorities Gain Access to Jobs During the War?

African Americans seeking jobs in the defense industry faced discrimination. A. Philip Randolph, an African American labor leader, threatened a march on Washington to protest the job discrimination. President Roosevelt responded by prohibiting racial discrimination in defense work and creating the Fair Employment Practices Committee. Because of the war emergency and worker shortages, African Americans were needed to work in the factories and at other jobs. However, the African Americans still faced discrimination. Strikes occurred at several shipyards by white workers when African Americans were hired. African American workers also successfully used strikes to protest unfair work rules and hiring practices.

How Were Japanese Americans Treated During the War?

The United States feared that Japan would invade its west coast. Some citizens thought people of Japanese ancestry living in America would aid the Japanese. President Roosevelt ordered the army to move about 110,000 of them to **detention** camps. Detention means holding people against their will. Many Japanese Americans lost their homes and businesses. Fear, the pressure of war, and prejudice caused the nation to set aside its democratic principles. Japanese American soldiers fought bravely in Europe while their government kept their parents and relatives in detention camps.

What do you think?

Did detaining Japanese Americans hurt the nation? Why or why not?

Lesson 5 Review On a sheet of paper, write the answers to the following questions. Use complete sentences.

1. How was America able to produce war supplies?

2. What were victory gardens?

3. How did Americans reuse raw materials?

4. How were women involved in the war effort?

5. Why were Japanese Americans detained?

Revenge

The act of getting back at someone for some wrongdoing

Despite the desire for **revenge** against Japan for Pearl Harbor, the United States decided that Hitler's Germany must be defeated first. The United States had strong ties to countries already defeated by Germany. Also, Germany seemed to be a greater threat to the Western Hemisphere than Japan did.

The only way to defeat Germany was through an Allied invasion of Europe. The Allies planned to hit Germany from the south through Italy and invade France from Britain. At the same time, the Soviet Union could move against the Germans from the east.

What Happened in the Invasion of Italy?

American, Canadian, and British troops invaded Italy in September 1943. They captured the island of Sicily first. As Mussolini lost the island, the Italian people, tired of war, captured and executed him. The new, rebel Italian government soon surrendered to the Allied powers.

Determined to protect Germany's southern boundary, Hitler advanced toward Italy. The Allies finally captured the city of Rome on June 4, 1944. At this time, however, the Germans occupied most of northern Italy.

Then and Now

Think how many plastic things are around you right now. You would have found far fewer plastics in 1941 than you do today. The manufacture of plastic boomed during World War II because silk and rubber were difficult to obtain. Inventors found ways to make tires, ropes, and parachutes from plastic. Electric radio cables were insulated with plastic.

Just think how many times a day plastic helps make your life easier. Today, plastic is everywhere, and its uses are growing. People predict that someday plastic will be used to build entire houses and vehicles. Medical advances with plastics are dramatic. Tiny plastic capsules one day may replace flawed or missing cells in people with progressive diseases like diabetes.

How Did the Allies Push the Germans Back?

The Nazis, who had known for some time that the United States was planning an invasion, prepared the coast of France. The beaches became death traps. The Nazis laid exploding mines in the water. They strung barbed wire all along the sandy shore.

General Dwight D. Eisenhower, commander of the Allied armies, landed his troops on the beaches of Normandy, France, on June 6, 1944. This was known as D-Day. It was a very tough battle. However, by night, the Allies occupied about 60 miles of the French coast. They could begin to move toward Germany.

By December 1944, the Allies were confident that Germany's forces were trapped. But then, suddenly, the Germans **counterattacked**. The German army pushed through the Allied line. On a map of Europe, a large bulge represented Hitler's takeover of Allied territory. Led by General George Patton, the Allies counterattacked. The Germans were pushed back. The confrontation became known as the Battle of the Bulge. It was the last offensive by the German army.

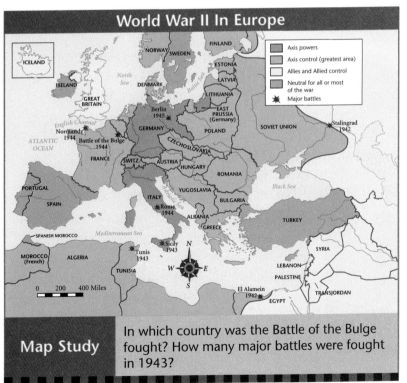

World War II In Europe

Axis powers
Axis control (greatest area)
Allies and Allied control
Neutral for all or most of the war
★ Major battles

Map Study

In which country was the Battle of the Bulge fought? How many major battles were fought in 1943?

What Was the Yalta Agreement?

President Roosevelt was re-elected for a fourth term in 1944. The strain of the war had taken its toll. He was able to cope with his polio, but he suffered from a number of other physical problems.

Bunker

An underground shelter

Atomic bomb

A bomb with great destructive powers

There was hope that the war against Germany would end early in 1945. Allied leaders met in February 1945 in Yalta, a small town on the Black Sea in the Soviet Union. Roosevelt, Churchill, and Stalin agreed on a plan to follow when Germany surrendered. The plan became known as the Yalta Agreement.

The plan had several points. First, the Soviet Union agreed to enter the war against Japan. Second, Germany would be divided into four zones, each controlled by one of the Allies. Third, the Soviet Union would hold democratic elections in eastern European countries under its control. Fourth, a world organization called the United Nations would be created. The Yalta Agreement seemed reasonable at the time. However, after the war ended, parts of the agreement caused political problems between the United States and the Soviet Union.

How Did the War End?

President Franklin Roosevelt died suddenly in April 1945. The nation was in shock. Vice President Harry S. Truman became president. On April 25, 1945, Adolf Hitler killed himself in a **bunker** in Berlin. A bunker is an underground shelter. Germany surrendered. The war in Europe was over.

The United States began to control the advance of the Japanese military. The Allies were led by American Army General Douglas MacArthur and Navy Admiral Chester Nimitz. Japan lost Guadalcanal, the Philippines, Iwo Jima, and Okinawa. Despite the losses, the Japanese refused to surrender. The Allies began to plan an invasion of Japan.

Why Were Atomic Bombs Dropped on Japan?

President Truman learned that the United States had developed a new weapon called the **atomic bomb**, or A-bomb. This bomb could end the war, but it would cause enormous loss of Japanese lives. Truman was advised that over a million American soldiers' lives would be lost if the United States invaded Japan on land. Such an invasion would also kill countless Japanese people.

Hiroshima (above) was in ruins after an American plane dropped an atomic bomb on the city. The mushroom cloud (on facing page) shows what happens when an atomic bomb goes off.

In an effort to avoid using the atomic bomb, the president gave one last warning to Japan. Japan, however, refused to surrender. Truman decided that he must approve the use of the atomic bomb on Japan.

On August 6, 1945, from a plane named *Enola Gay*, the atomic bomb was dropped on the city of Hiroshima. The weapon destroyed that major Japanese city and instantly killed or wounded 130,000 people. Three days later, a second atomic bomb was dropped on the city of Nagasaki, killing or wounding 75,000 people. On August 14, 1945, Japan asked for a **cease-fire**. They wanted to end the fighting. General MacArthur accepted the formal surrender of Japan on September 2, 1945. World War II, the worst war in history, was finally over.

Cease-fire

A call for an end to fighting

Word Bank

Battle of the Bulge

D-Day

Hiroshima

Sicily

Yalta

Lesson 6 Review On a sheet of paper, write the correct word or words from the Word Bank to complete each sentence.

1. Allied troops captured _____ in 1943.

2. The attack on Normandy was called _____.

3. The Germans were pushed back in the _____.

4. Allied leaders met at _____.

5. America dropped atomic bombs on _____ and Nagasaki.

What do you think?

World War II took millions of lives and ruined much of Europe. What do you think the world learned from the war?

Roosevelt's Four Freedoms Speech

During World War II, Americans gathered around radios to hear President Franklin Roosevelt's "fireside chats." The speeches meant much to those whose loved ones defended America overseas. Roosevelt gave this speech almost a year before America entered the war.

As men do not live by bread alone, they do not fight by armaments [weapons] alone. Those who man . . . and . . . build our defenses must have . . . an unshakable belief in the manner of life which they are defending. . . .

I have called for personal sacrifice. I am assured of the willingness of almost all Americans to respond to that call.

In the future days . . . we look forward to a world founded upon four essential human freedoms.

The first is freedom of speech and expression everywhere in the world.

The second is freedom of every person to worship God in his own way, everywhere in the world.

The third is freedom from want, which . . . means economic understandings which will secure to every nation a healthy peacetime life for all its inhabitants. . . .

The fourth is freedom from fear . . . a worldwide reduction of armaments to such a point . . . that no nation will be in a position to commit an act of physical aggression against any neighbor . . . a definite basis for a kind of world attainable in our own time. . . . That kind of world is the very antithesis of the so-called new order of tyranny which the dictators seek to create. . . .

A good society is able to face schemes of world domination and foreign revolutions alike without fear.

Since the beginning of our American history we have been engaged in . . . a perpetual, peaceful revolution . . . which goes on steadily . . . without the concentration camp . . . The world order which we seek is . . . free countries, working together in a friendly, civilized society.

Document-Based Questions

1. What was Roosevelt asking of the American people?

2. When did Roosevelt feel his ideas could be accomplished?

3. What were the four freedoms he named?

4. What is the world order Roosevelt said we sought?

5. Do you think Roosevelt expected America would enter another war? Why or why not?

Source: Four Freedoms Speech, by President Franklin Roosevelt, January 6, 1941.

- Benito Mussolini controlled the government of Italy. He created the Fascist Party.

- Francisco Franco became the leader of Spain after the Spanish Civil War.

- Adolf Hitler rose to power in Germany in the 1930s. In March 1938, Germany took over Austria and the Sudetenland. In September 1939, German forces invaded Poland. Following this act, France and Great Britain declared war on Germany.

- In 1940 Germany conquered Denmark, Norway, Belgium, the Netherlands, Luxembourg, and France. Germany continued to attack Great Britain and in June 1941 began an attack on the Soviet Union. The Allies—Australia, Canada, Great Britain, the Soviet Union, and other countries—joined to fight Germany.

- Japan began to invade portions of Indochina and formed an alliance with Germany and Italy. This group was known as the Axis Powers. On December 7, 1941, Japanese bombers launched a surprise attack on the American naval fleet anchored in Pearl Harbor in Hawaii. Four days later Japan's allies declared war on the United States.

- America focused its military to help its allies in Europe. The first thrust was in Italy, where Mussolini's government soon fell. Germany moved quickly into Italy and stopped the Allies in Rome.

- On D-Day, June 6, 1944, Allied troops landed in France and began an assault. Over the next months, Allied forces gained more ground against the Germans. By the end of April 1945, Germany surrendered and the war in Europe was over.

- During the period in which the Nazis were in power, over six million innocent European Jews were killed in concentration camps and death camps. This period, known as the Holocaust, lasted over seven years.

- President Roosevelt died in April 1945, and Harry Truman became president.

- Allied forces began to capture Japanese-controlled territory. The Japanese were forced back to Japan. Truman issued a final warning, but Japan refused to surrender. In an attempt to prevent the loss of American lives, Truman ordered the dropping of the first atomic bombs on Japan. Japan surrendered on September 2, 1945, soon after the second bomb was dropped.

Chapter 10   R E V I E W

On a sheet of paper, write the correct word or words from the Word Bank to complete each sentence.

Word Bank

Adolf Hitler

D-Day

detention camps

Dwight D.
  Eisenhower

Kristallnacht

Lend-Lease Act

Pearl Harbor

Third Reich

Winston Churchill

Yalta

1. _____ and his Nazi party attempted to make Germany the ruler of all Europe.

2. One of the early events in the Holocaust was called _____.

3. On December 7, 1941, the Japanese attacked the American fleet anchored in _____.

4. Hitler envisioned Germany as a huge empire called the _____.

5. Prime Minister _____ led Great Britain through the worst years of World War II.

6. Congress passed the _____ to help European countries fight Germany.

7. The Allied invasion of France began on June 6, 1944, which was called _____.

8. The commander of the Allied army was _____.

9. The American government forced thousands of Japanese Americans into _____.

10. Roosevelt, Stalin, and Churchill met in _____ to form an agreement for their roles after the war.

On a sheet of paper, write the letter of the choice that correctly completes each sentence.

11. _____ was the Fascist dictator of Italy from 1922 to 1943.

   A Francisco Franco   **C** Benito Mussolini

   B Neville Chamberlain   **D** Edouard Daladier

12. Germany and Japan seriously underestimated America's ability to _____.

   A produce war supplies   **C** feed itself

   B train soldiers   **D** ration goods

13. _____ was one country that had been friendly with Hitler and later joined the Allies.

   A Australia   **C** Italy

   B India   **D** The Soviet Union

On a sheet of paper, write the answers to the following questions. Use complete sentences.

14. Why was the German style of warfare called blitzkrieg, or "lightning war"?

15. What did people do at home to help the war effort?

16. What events led up to the attack on Pearl Harbor?

17. How did World War II begin in Europe?

Critical Thinking On a sheet of paper, write your response to each question. Use complete sentences.

18. At the beginning of World War II, the United States was neutral. Do you think the war would have ended sooner if America had gotten involved earlier? Explain your answer.

19. How can studying events like the Holocaust help prevent such things from happening again?

20. President Truman had the choice to drop the atomic bomb rather than invading Japan. If you had been president, what choice would you have made?

Test-Taking Tip

When studying for a test, go over the topics in the chapter. Think about the most important ideas. Then make up a practice test for yourself.

Population Growth Table

A table is an arrangement of figures or information in columns and rows. It allows you to organize information in a clear way. It also allows you to interpret information easily and quickly.

The United States takes a census, or counts the population, every 10 years. The population table below shows the figures since 1930. In addition, the table gives the percent by which the population increased.

Population of the United States: 1930–2000		
Year	**Number**	**Increase by Percent**
1930	123,202,624	16.2
1940	132,164,569	15.4
1950	151,325,798	14.5
1960	179,323,175	18.5
1970	203,302,031	13.4
1980	226,542,199	11.4
1990	248,709,873	9.8
2000	281,421,906	13.2

Use the table in the left column to answer these questions. You may need to do some math to get some of your answers.

1. What was the U.S. population in 1940?

2. What was the U.S. population in 1970?

3. By what number did the population increase from 1980 to 1990?

4. What was the percent of increase between 1980 and 1990?

5. By what number did the population increase from 1930 to 2000?

6. In what period did the U.S. population increase the most? the least?

7. Estimate the population for 1965.

8. Based on information in this table, predict what the population might be in the year 2010.

9. Why do you think the government takes a census every 10 years?

10. Write a paragraph summarizing what you learned from the table.

- The Great Depression followed the stock market crash of 1929.

- Many were unemployed and homeless. They could not buy food.

- President Hoover tried helping. Most of his plans and policies failed. Most Americans blamed Hoover for the problems of the Depression.

- Franklin Roosevelt became president in 1933. His programs helped to bring the country out of the Depression.

- The Social Security Act of 1935 set up help for the elderly and disabled.

- John L. Lewis worked to organize labor.

- Roosevelt tried to put justices on the Supreme Court who would support his policies. Congress and the American people objected.

- Films and books offered an escape from people's hardships.

- In the 1930s, Fascist Benito Mussolini ruled Italy. Francisco Franco ruled Spain's Fascist government. Nazi Adolph Hitler rose to power in Germany.

- Germany invaded Poland in 1939. France and Great Britain declared war on Germany.

- In 1940, Germany conquered Denmark, Norway, Belgium, the Netherlands, and France. It attacked Great Britain. It began attacking the Soviet Union in 1941. The Allies joined to fight Germany.

- Japan formed an alliance with Germany and Italy called the Axis Powers. On December 7, 1941, Japan bombed the U.S. naval fleet in Pearl Harbor in Hawaii. America entered World War II the next day. Four days later the Axis Powers declared war on the United States.

- America first helped the Allies in Europe. Allied forces gained ground against the Germans. By the end of April 1945, Germany surrendered. The war in Europe was over.

- The Nazis killed over six million innocent European Jews in concentration and death camps. The Holocaust lasted over seven years.

- President Roosevelt died in April 1945. Harry Truman took office.

- Allied forces began capturing Japanese-controlled territory. Japanese forces retreated to Japan. Truman ordered the first atomic bombs dropped on Japan. After the second bomb, Japan surrendered on September 2, 1945.

"We cannot seek achievement for ourselves and forget about progress and prosperity for our community. . . . Our ambitions must be broad enough to include the aspirations and needs of others, for their sakes and for our own."

~ Cesar Chavez, 1927–1993

Postwar
United States

1945–1969

Have you ever felt uneasy even when things were going well? The United States experienced both casy and uneasy times from 1945 to 1969. The nation was uneasy about Communism's grip on many parts of the world. Even though Americans enjoyed a sense of well-being in the 1950s, a time of social unrest began at home. The unrest increased during the 1960s but ended with positive civil rights laws. America cheered its successes in outer space during this time.

In this unit, you will learn about America's efforts to stop the spread of Communism. You will learn about how the nation lived through social uneasiness. You will learn about America's involvement in other wars and its place as a world leader. You will learn about its exploration of outer space.

11 A Time of Challenge and Change
1945–1959

World War II was over. The Allies had defeated the Nazis and the rest of the Axis Powers. The postwar period in America and Europe was a time of recovery. New world organizations were formed to prevent such damaging wars. At the same time, a new kind of struggle between the Soviet Union and the United States was beginning. In this chapter, you will learn about this struggle and the other changes that occurred after the war.

Goals for Learning

◆ To explain changes in the economy after World War II

◆ To describe the effects of the war, formation of the United Nations, the Fair Deal program, and the election of 1948

◆ To describe the beginnings of the cold war, the Marshall Plan, and NATO

◆ To explain America's involvement in the Korean War

◆ To describe America in the 1950s, including McCarthyism, the civil rights movement, family life, and the start of the space race

1945 United Nations is formed

1949 NATO is formed

1953 Korean War ends

1958 Americans launch *Explorer 1*

1945   1947   1949   1951   1953   1955   1957   1959

1948 President Truman is re-elected

1950 Korean War begins

1953 President Eisenhower takes office

1957 Russians launch *Sputnik*

Decline

Change to a lower level

White-collar

A name used to describe office workers and professionals

During World War II, the federal government focused the nation's economic resources on winning the war against Germany and Japan. When the war ended, the government faced serious economic problems at home.

How Did the Economy Change After the War?

The first problem was the fear of unemployment. The war effort had provided plenty of jobs for Americans at home. Now, 12 million men and women in the military would be "demobilized," or returned home to civilian life. Most of these people would be looking for work. In 1946, Congress passed the Full Employment Act. For the first time in American history, the federal government took responsibility for trying to help the economy provide jobs for the American people. As feared, when wartime production ended, the economy rapidly **declined.** However, this quickly changed. Americans wanted to buy cars, household products, and new homes. Few of these were produced during the war years.

What Was the GI Bill?

The GI Bill was an important law passed in 1944. Soldiers were called "GIs." After the war, this law provided former GIs with money to attend college and other benefits. Millions bought homes under the GI Bill. The GI Bill turned out to be a good economic investment. Americans became better educated. More people entered **white-collar** jobs. White-collar is a name used to describe office workers and professionals. Homes were now affordable for young families. Millions of new homes were built in areas surrounding cities, which were called suburbs. Large numbers of babies were born, creating a "baby boom." More children meant that more schools had to be built, creating more jobs for teachers. From 1946 into the 1960s, the United States was the strongest economy in the world. Two decades of economic prosperity led to the creation of a large American middle class.

How Did Farming Help the Economy?

After World War II, American farmers became the most productive in the world. Using science and technology, American farmers produced a surplus of food. The government bought much of this surplus and shipped it to Europe. Gas-powered tractors replaced horse and human labor. Scientific research developed grains that could resist disease. Using different machines, a single farmer could plow, plant, seed, and harvest various crops. A farm machine could dig up thousands of potatoes and put them in sacks in a matter of hours. Mechanical pickers harvested fruit. Modern irrigation systems assured that farmers would have enough water. Because of these improvements that saved time and labor, farming became a major part of the nation's growing economy.

Lesson 1 Review On a sheet of paper, write the answers to the following questions. Use complete sentences.

1. How did the U.S. government use the nation's economic resources during World War II?

2. Why was there a concern about unemployment after the war?

3. How did the government try to help provide jobs?

4. What did the GI Bill provide for former soldiers?

5. What was the baby boom?

What do you think?

Do you think it was a good idea for the federal government to help provide jobs? Why or why not?

Focus on Economics

GI Bill of Rights

President Franklin D. Roosevelt signed the "Servicemen's Readjustment Act of 1944" on June 22, 1944. This bill, known as the GI Bill of Rights, provided benefits and opportunities to attend college for veterans of World War II. Congress passed the bill because there were concerns about the country having enough jobs for returning war veterans. The bill allowed veterans to attend college rather than look for work immediately. The program for World War II veterans ended in 1956. Many feel that this bill was one of the best laws Congress ever passed. The modern GI Bill has continued to provide scholarships and other benefits to veterans.

Americans were happy that World War II had ended. Thousands celebrated in the streets of the nation's cities as their friends and loved ones returned home from the war. They waved flags, honked horns, cheered, and cried.

Germans cleared rubble from the streets of Berlin, Germany, after the war.

What Damages Did the War Cause?

The death and destruction caused by World War II was the worst in history. More than 55 million people died. The United States alone lost nearly 400,000 military men and women. Many millions more were seriously wounded. The bombings of Europe and Japan caused millions of civilian deaths.

The damage to cities in Europe cost well over $200 billion. Direct costs of fighting by all the countries combined was over a trillion dollars. Of that sum, America had spent $360 billion. For many years to come, the world would feel the effects of World War II.

How Did the War Change America's Role?

Americans knew that their role in the world had changed. The country could never again isolate itself from world problems. The United States was now one of the most powerful nations in the world. Not only did the nation have the power of the atomic bomb, but also it had new responsibilities in the world. In the months following the end of the war, Americans were uncertain how the country should move on. However, people did know that they wanted to develop a way to keep a lasting peace.

Why Was the United Nations Formed?

Delegates from 50 nations met in San Francisco, California, in April 1945. They created the United Nations (UN), a new world organization. Member countries of the General Assembly would come up with peaceful methods of settling international problems. They wanted to do a better job of preventing wars than the League of Nations had. The UN set up a Security Council. Eleven members (now 15) had the responsibility of keeping the peace. The United States, Great Britain, France, the Soviet Union, and China were made permanent members of the Security Council.

In response to the treatment of the Jews during World War II, the UN General Assembly declared **genocide** unlawful. Genocide is the killing of a group based on its race or political views. The assembly agreed that any country found guilty of this practice would be brought before an international court.

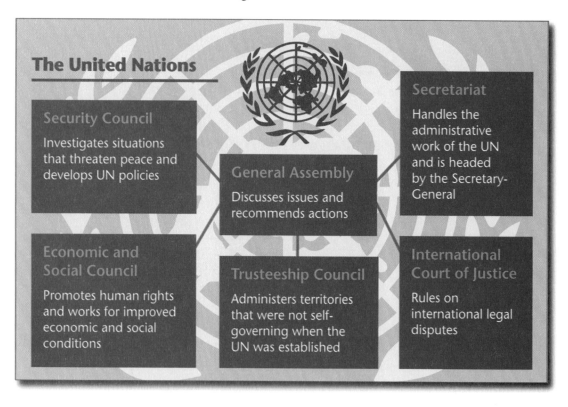

The United Nations

Security Council

Investigates situations that threaten peace and develops UN policies

General Assembly

Discusses issues and recommends actions

Secretariat

Handles the administrative work of the UN and is headed by the Secretary-General

Economic and Social Council

Promotes human rights and works for improved economic and social conditions

Trusteeship Council

Administers territories that were not self-governing when the UN was established

International Court of Justice

Rules on international legal disputes

The United Nations was soon tested with a problem in the Middle East. Palestine had been under the control of Great Britain since World War I. The Arabs and Jews who lived there wanted the British to leave. The United Nations wanted a Jewish nation and an Arab nation to be created out of Palestine. In 1948, the new nation of Israel was established. Arab nations in the Middle East objected to the creation of Israel and declared war. In 1949, the UN stopped the fighting and restored peace. The UN had passed its first test.

What Was President Truman's "Fair Deal"?

When Harry Truman became president in 1945, he had been vice president for less than three months. Although he had spent many years in the Senate, he had little experience dealing with the problems that faced the nation. Truman wanted to stabilize the country and work toward a lasting peace with other nations.

The months that followed the end of World War II were difficult for Truman. He faced many problems at home and abroad. Truman presented Congress with his own plan for improving the country. The program was called the "Fair Deal." It was based on the ideas of the New Deal. Truman wanted:

- more people included in the Social Security system;
- the minimum wage increased;
- more money for education and science; and
- public housing in cities.

The Republicans attacked the Democrats and the Fair Deal policies. They warned the American people about the power of "big government" and the growing power of labor unions. Acting on their fear, the Republican Congress ignored Truman's veto and passed the Taft-Hartley Act in 1947. This law allowed employers to hire non-union workers. Union leaders opposed this law.

Harry and Bess Truman waved from the rear platform of a train during Mr. Truman's campaign.

Who Won the 1948 Election?

Truman won his party's nomination in 1948, but few leaders believed he could win the election. The Democratic Party was split apart over civil rights for African Americans. Truman supported civil rights. As a result, southern Democrats left the party and formed a new States' Rights "Dixiecrat" party.

Truman campaigned by train, often speaking 10 times a day. The Republican Party had nominated former New York Governor Thomas E. Dewey. Union workers supported Truman. African American voters supported his stand on civil rights. Truman defeated Dewey by more than two million votes.

Lesson 2 Review Choose the word or name in parentheses that best completes each sentence. Write your answers on a sheet of paper.

1. Over (55, 65, 45) million people were killed in World War II.

2. The (League of Nations, United Nations, NATO) was set up in 1945.

3. The new nation of (Israel, Palestine) was established in 1948.

4. President Truman proposed the (Security Council, New Deal, Fair Deal).

5. (Harry Truman, Thomas E. Dewey) was elected president in 1948.

? What do you think?

If you were a representative of the United Nations today, what would you want to accomplish?

Domination

Complete control

Cold war

The disagreements between Communist and non-Communist nations over economics and politics following World War II

Descend

To come down on

Even though the United States and the Soviet Union had been allies during the final days of World War II, a struggle between the two countries began soon after the war. Since World War I, Communists had taken control of the government of the Soviet Union. These leaders promoted the spread of Communism to other countries.

What Was the Cold War?

The United States feared that the Soviet goal was world **domination** under Communism. The Soviet Union opposed UN peacekeeping efforts. Western nations, including America, started to distrust the Soviet Union. This conflict was called the **cold war.** Its weapons were mainly economics and politics. The cold war caused each nation to stay armed just in case it became an actual war.

The Soviet Union promised to hold free elections in Eastern European countries when World War II ended. This was part of the Yalta Agreement. Early in 1946, it was clear that Joseph Stalin did not plan to keep his promise. Stalin wanted the governments in Eastern Europe and Germany to be Communist. The United States was concerned about the spread of Communism in Europe. Communism was a threat to democratic governments. Most small countries would not be able to defend themselves against Communism without the help of the United States.

Winston Churchill, wartime leader of Great Britain, told an audience at a college in Missouri that "an Iron Curtain has **descended** across the continent" of Europe. He said Communist dictators controlled the people of Eastern Europe. These dictators were supported by the powerful Soviet Union. The "Iron Curtain" stood for the military weapons that the Soviet Union used to keep control of these nations. Churchill challenged the United States. He believed that the United States had the power to stop the spread of Communism before the democratic governments of Europe were threatened.

What Was the Containment Policy?

The United States believed it needed a policy to fight the spread of Communism. It developed a new policy called the Truman Doctrine. The spread of Communism was compared to water. Water flows wherever there is no **resistance** to it. The Soviet expansion was thought of in this way. Water can be contained by dams. Perhaps Communism could be contained by applying American force wherever the Soviet Union tried to gain influence.

The new policy of containment was tested in 1947. Turkey and Greece had serious political and economic problems after World War II. The Soviet Union wanted part of Turkey's territory. Civil war had broken out in Greece. Communist forces tried to gain power in each country. In March 1947, President Truman asked Congress for $400 million to help these countries. He said that "it must be the policy of the United States to support free peoples who are resisting ... outside pressures. ... If we falter in our leadership, we may endanger the peace of the world." Congress approved. Greece and Turkey were able to defeat those countries that wanted to overthrow their governments. The Truman Doctrine, now called the **containment policy,** had passed its first test.

President Truman (left) and Winston Churchill believed the spread of Communism should be stopped.

What Was the Marshall Plan?

Secretary of State George C. Marshall knew that the United States had to help Europe after the war. European cities had to be rebuilt and weak economies had to be made stronger. Marshall hoped to help Europeans avoid Communist takeovers. He asked the leaders of Europe to find out how much money they needed to rebuild their countries. A four-year, multibillion-dollar plan was proposed. Congress agreed to fund the European Recovery Program, or the Marshall Plan as it came to be known. The Soviet Union opposed the program.

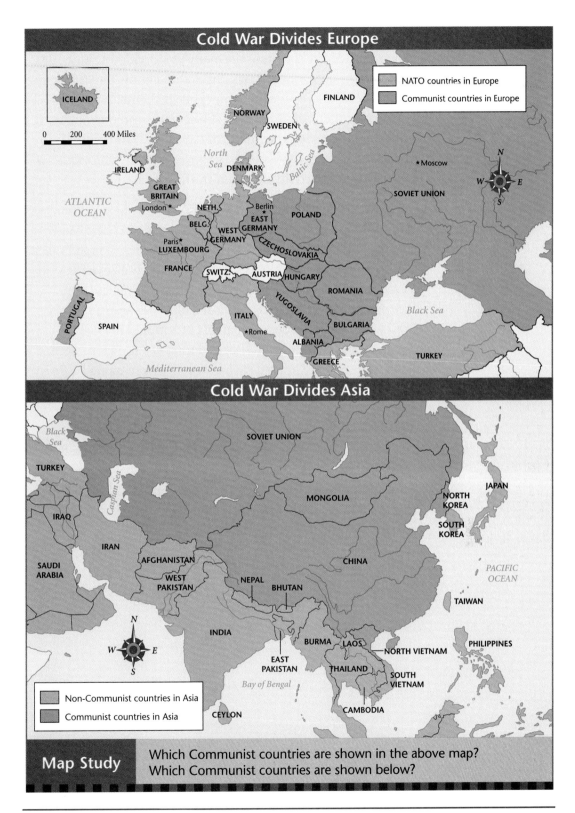

Cold War Divides Europe

NATO countries in Europe

Communist countries in Europe

ICELAND

0   200   400 Miles

FINLAND

NORWAY

SWEDEN

North Sea

DENMARK

★Moscow

IRELAND

Baltic Sea

SOVIET UNION

GREAT BRITAIN

ATLANTIC OCEAN

London ★

NETH.

Berlin ★

POLAND

BELG.

EAST GERMANY

WEST GERMANY

Paris★

LUXEMBOURG

CZECHOSLOVAKIA

FRANCE

SWITZ.

AUSTRIA

HUNGARY

ROMANIA

Black Sea

PORTUGAL

SPAIN

ITALY

YUGOSLAVIA

BULGARIA

★Rome

ALBANIA

TURKEY

Mediterranean Sea

GREECE

Cold War Divides Asia

Black Sea

SOVIET UNION

TURKEY

JAPAN

MONGOLIA

NORTH KOREA

IRAQ

Caspian Sea

SOUTH KOREA

IRAN

AFGHANISTAN

CHINA

PACIFIC OCEAN

SAUDI ARABIA

WEST PAKISTAN

NEPAL

BHUTAN

TAIWAN

INDIA

BURMA

LAOS

NORTH VIETNAM

PHILIPPINES

EAST PAKISTAN

THAILAND

SOUTH VIETNAM

Bay of Bengal

Non-Communist countries in Asia

Communist countries in Asia

CEYLON

CAMBODIA

Map Study   Which Communist countries are shown in the above map?
Which Communist countries are shown below?

What Was the Berlin Blockade and Airlift?

When World War II ended, Germany was divided among the four Allies—the United States, the Soviet Union, Great Britain, and France. France, Great Britain, and the United States agreed to combine their sections of West Germany into one nation. It was called the Federal Republic of Germany. The Soviet Union objected. To show their anger, the Soviets set up a blockade in 1948. This cut off road and train traffic into Berlin.

The German city of Berlin, capital of Germany before 1945, was located in East Germany. The Soviet Union controlled East Germany. The city of Berlin was supposed to be open to France, Great Britain, and the United States. Because the Soviet Union closed off the city, Berlin was not able to get supplies from Western Europe. Three days after the blockade was set up, President Truman ordered an **airlift** of supplies to Berlin. For more than a year, planes carried tons of supplies to Berlin. Finally, the Soviet Union gave in. West Berlin remained a free, democratic city.

Why Was NATO Formed?

The Berlin blockade made Congress think that the United States should join Canada and 10 European nations for the protection of one another. In 1949, the countries formed the North Atlantic Treaty Organization (NATO). This group's treaty said that an attack on one member would be considered an attack on all members. NATO would have its own military troops sent by the member nations. General Dwight D. Eisenhower was the first head of the NATO force. The United States volunteered 350,000 troops.

Word Bank

cold war

containment policy

Marshall Plan

NATO

Soviet Union

Lesson 3 Review On a sheet of paper, write the correct word or words from the Word Bank to complete each sentence.

1. Democratic countries tried to limit Communism during the _____.

2. _____ considers an attack on one member of its organization to be an attack on all members.

3. The _____ was a Communist country.

4. The _____ was an attempt to keep Communism from spreading in areas where there was little resistance.

5. The _____ was a plan to help Europe after the war.

What do you think?

What do you think are the dangers of a cold war?

Then and Now

Do you have a computer in your home or use one at school? The computer you use is a lot smaller than a computer was in the 1950s. One computer then filled an entire room. The room had to be kept cool and clean. People punched information onto cards and fed the cards into the computer. Only large businesses could afford a computer. Businesses used computers mainly to keep records and to print customers' bills and employees' paychecks.

Today businesses and schools have many computers. Many people have home computers. You may have learned how to use a computer in school. In the 1950s, you would have used a manual typewriter to prepare a report. Now you use a computer and maybe the Internet to do your homework. Maybe you send letters over e-mail. People with portable laptop computers carry them to the library, a business meeting, or even the park. Computer uses are endless.

Communism in Asia also presented a problem for the United States and its allies. Since the 1920s, a civil war had been waged between two Chinese political groups. Those groups were the Chinese Communist Party and the Nationalist Party, which controlled the Chinese government. During World War II, the parties joined together to fight the invading Japanese. With the defeat of Japan, these rival political groups began to fight each other again. The United States supported the Nationalist Party. In 1949, the Communist Party, led by Mao Zedong, defeated the Nationalist Party. The Truman administration opposed the new Chinese Communist government, but there was little that they could do about it. The Communist Chinese revolution caused bitter political debates in the United States over who had "lost China."

The peninsula of Korea is located between China and Japan. During World War II, the Japanese conquered Korea. After the war, the country was divided into two parts. The Soviet Union occupied the northern section. The United States controlled South Korea. In 1948, the democratic Republic of Korea was formed in the south. America withdrew its troops from the south and provided economic aid to the new country. The Soviet Union created a Communist government in North Korea called the Democratic People's Republic.

From the beginning, there was tension between North and South Korea. On June 25, 1950, North Korea invaded South Korea. Two days later, the United Nations Security Council declared that North Korea was wrong. The Security Council asked the UN to help South Korea. The Soviets had been boycotting the UN, so they were unable to veto this plan of action. With UN backing, President Truman ordered American troops to support the South Koreans.

Writing About History

Write an essay in your notebook about whether the United States should take part in foreign wars such as the Korean War.

How Did Fighting Begin?

Fifteen other nations agreed to help South Korea. Still, the defense of South Korea was mainly an American responsibility. President Truman refused to call the fighting in Korea a war. Instead, Truman called it a "police action." The goal was to force North Korean troops to return to their own territory.

Armed with many modern tanks and weapons supplied by the Soviet Union and China, North Korea captured Seoul, the South Korean capital. General Douglas MacArthur, commander of the American troops, was not prepared to fight an **offensive** war. Soon only a small area in the southeast remained under UN control.

MacArthur set up a defensive line at the southern port of Pusan. Then, with the aid of 50,000 more American troops, the UN forces were able to stop the North Koreans and take the offensive. MacArthur and his troops were able to push the North Korean army past their own capital city toward the Chinese province of Manchuria.

Communist China had warned the UN that it would become involved if troops moved any closer to Manchuria. MacArthur told Truman that China would not enter the war. However, on November 26, 1950, about 300,000 Chinese soldiers attacked the American army in North Korea. The American troops were pushed back into South Korea. Fortunately, by the following spring, they were able to set up a new defensive line there.

General MacArthur asked President Truman for permission to bomb China. Truman feared that bombing would bring the Soviet Union into the war. When Truman refused, MacArthur asked Congress for permission. This action angered Truman. General MacArthur was challenging the power of the president. Truman fired MacArthur in April 1951.

How Did the Korean War End?

Peace talks began in July 1951. The two sides disagreed on the problem of prisoner exchange. The Communists wanted all prisoners returned to their homeland. The United Nations wanted to give the prisoners a choice. The negotiations continued for two years. An agreement was reached in July 1953. Prisoners had their choice. North and South Korea became two separate nations.

North and South Korea each withdrew 1.25 miles from the final battle line. This formed a 2.5 mile neutral zone between them. The North Koreans and Chinese who opposed the Communists in North Korea were allowed to stay in South Korea. To provide protection from any future attacks, American troops stayed in South Korea. The United States also gave further economic aid.

Lesson 4 Review On a sheet of paper, write the word or words in parentheses that best complete each sentence.

1. (North Korea, The Soviet Union, Manchuria) invaded South Korea in 1950.

2. Most of the UN troops that fought in the Korean War were supplied by (the United States, Japan, Manchuria).

3. President Truman called the fighting in Korea a (war, police action, disagreement).

4. President Truman fired General MacArthur because the general (attacked Manchuria, failed to conquer North Korea, challenged the president's power).

5. After the war, the United States continued to help South Korea with troops and (tanks, economic aid, trade).

What do you think?

Do you think the United States is right to provide economic aid to poor countries? Why or why not?

Nuclear war

War that uses atomic weapons

The Republicans argued that the Democratic Party had become filled with corruption. They claimed that the Truman administration had handled the Korean War badly. "It is time for a change," the Republicans said.

General Dwight D. Eisenhower, the Republican candidate, was elected president in 1952. He won in a landslide victory over Adlai Stevenson. Known as "Ike," Eisenhower was a hero of World War II. He took office in 1953 and became a popular president.

The nation's economy was doing well during most of the years Eisenhower held office. Soldiers who had returned from fighting in World War II and Korea had started families. New home construction soared, as did the need for more and better American products. During this time, the lives of most Americans improved.

The fear of Communism and the Soviet Union still existed. The Soviet Union developed an atomic bomb. Americans were worried about a war using atomic weapons, or **nuclear war.** People built bomb shelters in their backyards. Cities set up air raid warning signals. Schoolchildren were taught to get under their desks or go to a certain place quickly when they heard air raid sirens.

This "family model" bomb shelter shows an escape opening at the top and an entrance that attached to a cellar. This kind of shelter was placed underground.

What Was McCarthyism?

Accusation

A charge of wrongdoing

Reputation

How a person is judged by others

McCarthyism

An attempt to gain power by attacking the patriotism of others

In 1947, President Truman and other political leaders feared that Communists were working within the United States government. Truman issued an order creating a loyalty-security program for federal employees. During the Truman and Eisenhower administrations, nearly 7,000 federal workers suspected of being "security risks" were either fired or forced to resign.

Americans feared Communism, and Senator Joseph McCarthy used this fear for his own political gain. He kept saying that traitors were trying to destroy the country. McCarthy became one of the most feared members of the Senate. Many American educators, journalists, and entertainers lost their jobs as a result of his **accusations.** Others had their **reputations** ruined. For a long time, few politicians were willing to challenge McCarthy.

McCarthy began to investigate army officials. The Senate held televised hearings for 36 days in 1954. When television audiences saw McCarthy as a lying bully, they demanded an investigation. A special Senate committee found that most of McCarthy's charges were untrue. With the help of television, the American people were able to take away much of McCarthy's power. The campaign he had used to make his accusations soon became known as **McCarthyism.**

How Did the Civil Rights Movement Begin?

African Americans had fought for democracy in two world wars. Yet when they returned from those wars, they were still denied basic political and social rights. In the 1950s, many African Americans decided that the members of their race could no longer be victims.

The civil rights movement was sparked by a 1954 decision of the Supreme Court, *Brown v. the Board of Education of Topeka, Kansas.* A young African American girl was denied the right to attend a white school. Her father sued the school board.

NAACP lawyers, including Thurgood Marshall, worked very hard on this case. Marshall later became the first African American appointed to the Supreme Court. In the decision, the Supreme Court ruled that separate schools for whites and African Americans were unconstitutional. In 1954, Chief Justice Earl Warren wrote that separate can never be equal. Local school boards were ordered to end school segregation.

In December 1955, Rosa Parks, a 42-year-old African American woman, got on a bus in Montgomery, Alabama. She found a seat near the middle of the bus. The bus driver asked Parks to

Rosa Parks

give up her seat to a white person. Parks would not. Police were called and she was arrested. Parks had not planned to challenge the law on that day. Parks said, "I felt it was just something that I had to do." Her decision not to move from her seat on a bus was the quiet beginning of a national civil rights movement.

History in Your Life

The Advent of Credit Cards

Credit allows a person to make purchases without cash. In America, credit plans grew quickly between 1850 and 1900. The plans allowed buyers to pay for purchases over time.

Modern credit cards began with the formation of Diners Club in 1950. Card holders used the same card to buy from many merchants. In 1951, Franklin National Bank of New York was the first bank to offer a card. By 1958, several other companies offered credit cards. In the 1980s, credit card companies had huge growth. Now nearly every American family has at least one major credit card. They use a card to buy groceries, vacations, and more.

National Guard

A state's military force

Martin Luther King Jr.

A 26-year-old minister named Martin Luther King Jr. led a boycott of the buses in Montgomery in 1956. He helped to organize car pools to help African Americans travel around the city. He was arrested for his actions. One year later the Supreme Court ruled that segregation on public transportation was unconstitutional.

King went on to become the most visible person in the civil rights movement. He urged his supporters to use non-violent protest to gain equal rights. His speeches moved many to action and drew attention to racial discrimination that affected African Americans.

A new civil rights law was passed in August 1957. This law made it illegal to use force to stop someone from voting. This was the first civil rights law since Reconstruction. Progress was continually challenged. The governor of Arkansas tried to prevent nine African American children from attending an all-white school in Little Rock. The state's **National Guard** was ordered to protect this school. A national guard is a state's military force. President Eisenhower sent federal troops to help the African American children. The governor finally backed down.

It Happened in History

Martin Luther King Jr. gave one of his most famous speeches, called "I Have a Dream," in 1963. This speech is considered to be a cornerstone of the civil rights movement. It can be found at www.stanford.edu/group/King/publications/speechesFrame.htm. (Click on A Call to Conscience: The Landmark Speeches of Martin Luther King Jr.) You can also visit The King Center Web site at www.thekingcenter.com/tkc/index.asp to learn more about Dr. King.

What Was Life Like in the 1950s?

American society experienced many changes in the 1950s. Jobs were available for most Americans. With the development of **automation,** factories employed thousands of people to produce countless new products. Advances in science and technology offered Americans better health and a higher standard of living than ever before.

The family and the home became popular symbols of American life. The image of women as "housewives" and husbands as "breadwinners" were commonly found in magazine advertising and TV commercials. In the late 1950s, many middle class families had both husbands and wives working outside the home. Most women did not hold "career" jobs like their husbands. In general, jobs held by married women were seen as temporary until children arrived. But unlike their mothers, many women thought that being a homemaker or a temporary employee was not their only choice. Women began to question the narrow role assigned to them in society. Early in the 1960s, the first steps of the women's movement were taken. The purpose of the women's movement was to seek social and economic equality for American women.

Most television programs were black and white in the 1950s.

Interstate

An action that occurs between two states

Geography Note

In 1959, Alaska and Hawaii joined the United States. They were the first states added to the nation since the admission of Arizona in 1912. Alaska was the 49th state; Hawaii was the 50th.

In 1956, the federal government started a huge program to build **interstate** highways. The highways would connect most cities with populations over 50,000. As the roads were built, suburbs attracted more home builders.

New cars had large "fins" on their rear fenders. Some young people drove hot rods, or cars that had been adjusted to go faster. Crew cuts were a common hairstyle for boys. Girls wore their hair in ponytails. Television was only black and white. Young children watched a puppet named Howdy Doody and his friend, Buffalo Bob. Rock and roll music was new, and young people loved it. The term UFO (unidentified flying object) entered the vocabulary of many Americans.

How Was Eisenhower Re-elected?

In the election of 1956, Eisenhower was elected by an even greater landslide than in the previous election. The Democrats, however, took control of Congress. Although many Republicans considered the president to be too liberal, Americans seemed to be happy with him.

Biography

Margaret Chase Smith: 1897–1995
A Republican from Maine, Margaret Chase Smith was the first woman elected to each of the houses of Congress. She completed her husband's term in the House of Representatives after his death in 1940. Then Smith was elected to four more two-year terms. She next served in the Senate for 25 years—longer than any other woman. During the early 1950s, she spoke out against the methods of Senator Joseph McCarthy. In 1964, Smith campaigned for the Republican presidential nomination. She was the first woman ever to campaign for the presidential nomination in a major party. Smith wrote the book *Gallant Women* in 1968. The book documented the lives of independent women in American public life.

An object made by humans that travels in outer space and sends signals back to Earth

How Did the Space Race Begin?

The United States was taken by surprise when the Soviet Union launched *Sputnik* on October 4, 1957. *Sputnik* was an **artificial satellite** that traveled in outer space and sent radio signals back to Earth. Everyone was concerned that a foreign country knew how to do something that the Americans did not.

The United States was developing space technology, but the Russians raced ahead. *Sputnik 2*, carrying a dog, was launched before the United States could get into space. A new battle had been added to the cold war.

On January 31, 1958, the U.S. army put the first American satellite, *Explorer 1*, into orbit. This was three months after the launch of *Sputnik 2*. The following October, the United States created the National Aeronautics and Space Administration (NASA).

Lesson 5 Review On a sheet of paper, write the answers to the following questions. Use complete sentences.

1. How did Americans prepare for a nuclear war?

2. What was McCarthyism?

3. How did Rosa Parks help begin the civil rights movement?

4. How did roads improve in the 1950s?

5. How did the Russians start the space race?

What do you think?

Do you think you would have liked living in the 1950s? Why or why not?

The Crisis at Central High School

In 1954, the Supreme Court declared school segregation unconstitutional. In 1957, Central High School in Little Rock, Arkansas, was going to admit African American students for the first time. Governor Orval Faubus said he could not maintain order if African American students tried to enter. Elizabeth Eckford was one of nine African American students who tried to integrate the school. Here are the viewpoints of Governor Faubus and Elizabeth Eckford.

The question at issue . . . is not integration versus segregation. . . . The question now is whether . . . the head of a sovereign state can exercise his constitutional powers and discretion in maintaining peace and good order within his jurisdiction, being accountable to his own conscience and to his own people. . . .

The situation in Little Rock and Arkansas grows more explosive by the hour. This is caused for the most part by the misunderstanding of our problem by a federal judge who decreed 'immediate integration' of the public schools . . . without hearing any evidence . . . as to the conditions . . . in the community. . . .

I saw a large crowd of people standing across the street from the soldiers guarding Central. As I walked on, the crowd suddenly got very quiet. Superintendent Blossom had told us to enter by the front door. . . .

When I got right in front of the school, I went up to a guard . . . he just looked straight ahead and didn't move to let me pass him. . . . I walked until I was right in front of the path to the front door.

I stood looking at the school—it looked so big! Just then the guards let some white students go through.

The crowd was quiet . . . waiting to see what was going to happen. When I was able to steady my knees, I walked up to the guard who had let the white students in. He . . . didn't move. When I tried to squeeze past him, he raised his bayonet . . . the other guards closed in and . . . raised their bayonets. . . .

I was very frightened and didn't know what to do. I turned around and the crowd came toward me. They moved closer and closer. Somebody started yelling, "Lynch her!"

Document-Based Questions

1. Why did Governor Faubus oppose admitting African American students?

2. Who did Faubus think caused the crisis?

3. What did Elizabeth Eckford see when she arrived at the school?

4. How did some white guards treat her?

5. Why do you think Elizabeth Eckford risked her safety to attend a high school?

Source: *A message from Governor Faubus to President Eisenhower, September 4, 1957.*

Source: Long Shadow of Little Rock, *by Daisy Bates, 1962.*

- Congress passed the GI Bill in 1944 and the Full Employment Act in 1946 to help Americans.

- Improvements in farming methods helped farmers produce more food.

- The United Nations was created in San Francisco, California in April 1945. The UN was established as an international organization with the responsibility of keeping peace among its member countries.

- Distrust developed between Communist and non-Communist countries. The United States did not want Communism to spread beyond the countries where it was already established. The United States fought Communism by supporting governments that were opposed to Communism.

- The Marshall Plan provided American aid to European countries that had suffered damage during the war.

- The United States, France, and Great Britain flew supplies to West Berlin during a period when the Soviet Union cut off ground transportation to the city. The Berlin airlift lasted until the Soviets reopened the railroads and highways.

- In 1950, North Korea invaded South Korea. The United States was among 16 countries that sent troops to help South Korea. After three years of fighting, the Communist North Koreans agreed to peace talks.

- General Dwight D. Eisenhower, a hero of World War II, was elected president in 1952.

- Fear of Communism was widespread. Senator Joseph McCarthy used this fear to accuse hundreds of Americans of being Communists or Communist sympathizers. Because of McCarthy, many people lost their jobs.

- The civil rights movement grew in strength in the 1950s. The Supreme Court ruled that separate schools for whites and African Americans were unconstitutional. Martin Luther King Jr. led a boycott of buses in Montgomery, Alabama. Congress passed a civil rights law in 1957.

- During the 1950s, jobs were available for most Americans. People had money to purchase such items as televisions and new cars. Because of interstate highways, people built homes in suburbs.

- America launched its first successful satellite into orbit in 1958.

Chapter 11   R E V I E W

On a sheet of paper, write the correct word or words from the Word Bank to complete each sentence.

Word Bank

General Douglas
   MacArthur

Fair Deal

Iron Curtain

Israel

Joseph Stalin

Rosa Parks

Sputnik

Taft-Hartley Act

United Nations

West Berlin

1. The United Nations established the country of _____ in the Middle East.

2. President Truman's economic plan was called the _____.

3. An international organization called the _____ was created in San Francisco in 1946.

4. Under the rules of the _____, employers could hire nonunion workers.

5. Winston Churchill used the term _____ to describe the division between Eastern and Western Europe.

6. _____ was the leader of the Soviet Union.

7. Truman helped establish an airlift to provide supplies to _____.

8. Truman fired _____ because he went to Congress and challenged the power of the president.

9. By refusing to give up her seat on the bus, _____ helped begin the civil rights movement.

10. In 1957, the Soviet Union launched _____, an artificial satellite.

On a sheet of paper, write the letter of the answer that correctly completes each sentence.

11. In 1954, the Supreme Court ruled that schools must end _____.

   A McCarthyism   **C** segregation

   B discrimination   **D** containment

12. Joseph McCarthy became powerful by playing to Americans' fear of _____.

    A Communism   **C** integration

    B nuclear war   **D** space war

13. The United States became involved in a police action when North Korea invaded _____.

    A Manchuria   **C** Japan

    B South Korea   **D** China

On a sheet of paper, write the answers to the following questions. Use complete sentences.

14. What were some of the early events of the civil rights movement?

15. What were three results of World War II?

16. What was the United States like in the 1950s?

17. How was the United States involved in the Korean War?

18. Why was America involved in the cold war?

Critical Thinking On a sheet of paper, write your response to each question. Use complete sentences.

19. Senator McCarthy used Americans' fear of Communism to accuse many people falsely. Do you think something like this could happen today? Why or why not?

20. Television had a major effect on American life in the 1950s. Do you think new Internet technology will have a major effect on life in America? Why or why not?

Test-Taking Tip

As you study for a test, look over maps, graphs, and other visuals in the chapter. Figure out how they fit in with the chapter's important ideas. Summarize the meaning of each graphic in your own words.

12 Support for Freedom
1960–1969

The 1960s was a time of protest in America. There were still many problems at home that needed to be addressed. Individual freedoms became important as never before in the nation. Yet another war—the Vietnam War—caused many of these protests. African Americans, Hispanic Americans, American Indians, and women sought to increase their rights. In this chapter, you will learn how the United States worked to gain freedom for all its citizens during the 1960s.

Goals for Learning

◆ To describe the beginning of U.S. space exploration and the election of 1960

◆ To explain the United States' involvement in world events

◆ To describe the start of the civil rights movement and the achievements and assassination of President Kennedy

◆ To describe Lyndon Johnson's presidency and the increasing U.S. involvement in Vietnam

◆ To explain the civil rights movement, the women's movement, and concerns of Hispanics and young people

◆ To describe the events of the 1968 election and the assassinations of Martin Luther King Jr. and Robert Kennedy

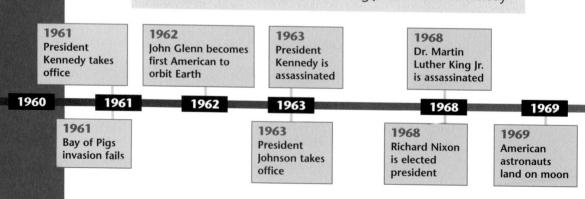

1961
President Kennedy takes office

1962
John Glenn becomes first American to orbit Earth

1963
President Kennedy is assassinated

1968
Dr. Martin Luther King Jr. is assassinated

1960　1961　1962　1963　1968　1969

1961
Bay of Pigs invasion fails

1963
President Johnson takes office

1968
Richard Nixon is elected president

1969
American astronauts land on moon

Suborbital

Not out of Earth's atmosphere

Atmosphere

The layer of gases covering Earth

The United States launched six Mercury spacecraft with people aboard between 1961 and 1963. On May 5, 1961, Alan B. Shepard Jr. piloted *Mercury-Redstone 3 (Freedom 7)* on a 15.5 minute **suborbital** flight. This means that the flight did not make it out of Earth's **atmosphere** and into orbit. John Glenn made history when he became the first American to orbit the earth. On February 20, 1962, Glenn orbited the earth three times in *Friendship 7.*

John Glenn was the first American to orbit the earth.

Project Gemini was the code name for the United States program to launch two astronauts in a spacecraft capable of orbiting for a long time. The first two-person mission of Project Gemini took place in 1965. In the years that followed, there were nine additional Gemini flights.

Technology Connection

1960s Space Exploration

The 1960s was a busy time for the space program in the United States. As the technology improved, scientists were able to gather more information from space. In addition to the missions noted above, here are some other explorations of this decade:

1962 *Ranger 4* First U.S. spacecraft to land on the moon
    Mariner 2 Flew past Venus

1964 *Ranger 7* Took close-up photos of the moon
    Mariner 4 Took close-up photos of the surface of Mars; detected a weak magnetic field on Mars

1967 *Pioneer 8* Transmitted data from a solar probe

1968 *Apollo 7* Transmitted first live television pictures from space

Who Won the 1960 Election?

The cold war briefly "thawed" in the late 1950s. Soviet Premier Nikita Khrushchev visited the United States in 1959 and invited President Eisenhower to visit the Soviet Union. However, Khrushchev quickly withdrew the invitation after the Soviets captured an American pilot flying far inside Soviet borders.

The 1960 presidential election grew in importance. The Republican Party had controlled the White House for eight years. The 22nd Amendment to the Constitution, ratified in 1951, said that a president could not serve more than two terms. Therefore, Eisenhower was **ineligible** for a third term in office. The Republicans chose Richard Nixon as their candidate. The Democrats nominated a 43-year-old senator from Massachusetts—John F. Kennedy.

Known as a tough opponent of Communist expansion, Nixon had gained experience in world affairs during his eight years as Eisenhower's vice president. Kennedy had been a member of Congress since 1946.

Kennedy and Nixon held a series of debates. For the first time, presidential debates were on national television. According to many political observers, the debates played a major role in the outcome of the election. Kennedy was young and handsome, and he remained cool under the pressure of the televised debate.

The election was very close. Kennedy narrowly won the popular vote. He was the youngest man ever to be elected president. Kennedy was also the first president who was a Roman Catholic.

Kennedy took the presidential oath of office on January 20, 1961. In his inaugural address, he called on Americans to work for the good of the nation and freedom around the world. His domestic and foreign policy goals were called the "New Frontier." The symbol of a New Frontier recalled America's past challenges. It linked them to the nation's struggles at home and the threat from Communism abroad. Kennedy's youth, confidence, and **enthusiasm** motivated many young people to help others.

Richard Nixon (left) and John F. Kennedy took part in debates on national television.

Lesson 1 Review Choose the best word or name in parentheses to complete each sentence. Write your answers on a sheet of paper.

1. (Alan B. Shepard, John Glenn) was the first American to orbit the earth.

2. (Project Gemini, *Friendship 7,* Project Mercury) was the code name for the U.S. program to launch astronauts into space for long flights.

3. The (20th, 21st, 22nd) Amendment said a president could not be elected for more than two terms.

4. The (Republicans, Democrats) chose Richard Nixon as their candidate for president.

5. (John F. Kennedy, Dwight D. Eisenhower, Richard Nixon) won the election of 1960.

What do you think?

Do you think presidential debates help determine the outcome of an election? Explain your answer.

Refugee

A person who flees his or her home country to seek protection

Geography Note

The Berlin Wall was built to stop Germans from leaving East Berlin and emigrating to West Berlin. The barrier consisted of concrete slabs, guard dogs, guard towers, trenches, barbed wire, and land mines. Eventually, about 110 miles of barriers completely surrounded West Berlin. The wall was was torn down in 1989.

The Communist government in Cuba was of major concern to the United States. Fidel Castro, the head of the Cuban government since 1959, had originally won support from the United States for leading a revolt against Cuba's dictator. Then, he surprised America by declaring that he was a Communist. He requested help from the Soviets and received it. Cuba was only 90 miles from the Florida coastline.

The Castro government seized property in Cuba owned by Americans and people from other countries. The Eisenhower administration stopped all trade with Cuba except food and medicine. It encouraged anti-Castro Cuban **refugees** to invade their homeland and overthrow the government.

When Kennedy became president, he was asked to approve an invasion plan. Kennedy approved the plan but would not allow American troops to take part. The United States did, however, train and arm the Cuban rebels.

In April 1961, American-supported Cubans invaded Cuba at the Bay of Pigs. The invaders thought that the Cuban people and the Cuban army would support them. They were wrong. The invasion was a complete failure. Within three days, most of the invaders were killed or captured. President Kennedy took full responsibility for the failure.

Why Was the Berlin Wall Built?

President Kennedy and the Soviet leader, Nikita Khrushchev, met in Vienna, Austria, in June 1961. Khrushchev believed that Kennedy was too young and inexperienced to be a strong leader. Khrushchev thought that it was time to force the United States out of West Berlin. President Kennedy said that the United States would not leave the city. The Soviet Union responded by building a wall dividing the city of Berlin. The wall was between Communist East Berlin and democratic West Berlin.

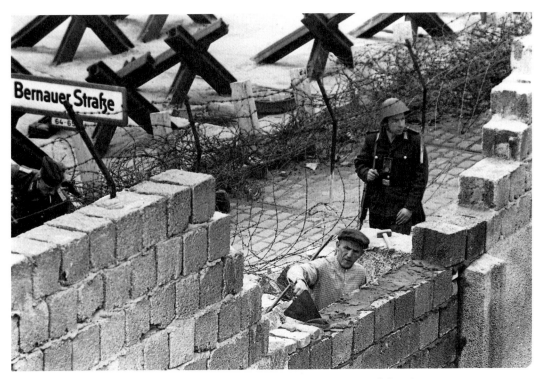
The Berlin Wall prevented East Berliners from leaving their section of the city.

What Was the Cuban Missile Crisis?

Missile

A self-driven bomb or rocket

One of the most serious events of the cold war occurred in October 1962. The Cuban **missile** crisis almost caused a war between the United States and the Soviet Union. A missile is a self-driven bomb. The United States discovered that Cuba was secretly building missile bases. Kennedy ordered the navy to stop Soviet ships from carrying missiles to Cuba. The world watched nervously as two powerful nations challenged each other to back down. Radio and television news kept the American people informed of the situation. War appeared very possible.

Suddenly, on October 26, the Soviet ships turned around. They headed back to the Soviet Union. The tension was broken. On the same day, President Kennedy received a letter from the Soviet premier. Khrushchev said that he would remove the missiles from Cuba if Kennedy would promise not to invade Cuba. The Cuban missile crisis was over. President Kennedy was praised for his tough stand.

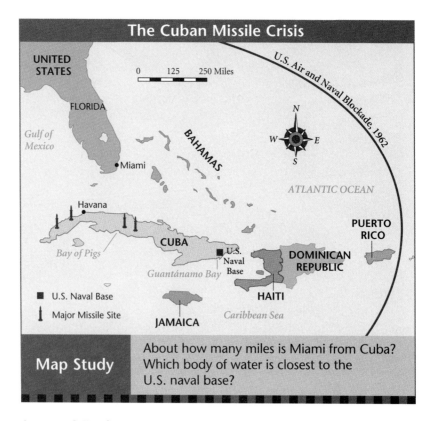

The Cuban Missile Crisis

UNITED STATES

0   125   250 Miles

U.S. Air and Naval Blockade, 1962

FLORIDA

Gulf of Mexico

BAHAMAS

•Miami

N
W   E
S

ATLANTIC OCEAN

Havana

PUERTO RICO

CUBA

U.S. Naval Base

Bay of Pigs

DOMINICAN REPUBLIC

Guantánamo Bay

■ U.S. Naval Base

HAITI

Major Missile Site

Caribbean Sea

JAMAICA

Map Study

About how many miles is Miami from Cuba? Which body of water is closest to the U.S. naval base?

Lesson 2 Review On a sheet of paper, write the answers to the following questions. Use complete sentences.

1. How far is Cuba from the United States?
2. How did Kennedy try to help the Cubans?
3. What did the Soviet Union do to Berlin?
4. How did the Cuban missile crisis almost turn into a war?
5. How did people view Kennedy after the Cuban missile crisis?

What do you think?

How would you feel if you knew there were enemy missile bases so close to the United States? Explain your answer.

Fulfill

To carry out or put into effect

Riot

A violent public disturbance

Writing About History

Research the speech Dr. Martin Luther King Jr. presented in Washington, D.C. In your notebook, write a newspaper article about it.

In the 1960s, the struggle for African American equality moved from the courts to the streets. Segregation was still the law of the land in many parts of the country. Many African Americans were denied the right to vote. Some progress had been made during the 1950s. Yet African Americans were still treated as second-class citizens in many parts of the country.

In June 1963, President Kennedy said, "The time has come for this nation to **fulfill** its promise . . . for equality. . . . Those who do nothing are inviting shame as well as violence." The federal government tried to help end inequality and segregation for African Americans.

How Did Groups Attack Segregation?

A group of African Americans and whites called "freedom riders" boarded buses and headed south. Their plan was to draw attention to segregation in the southern states. The group was led by James Farmer of the Congress of Racial Equality (CORE).

Following the example set by Martin Luther King Jr., the freedom riders believed in peaceful protests. Yet some of their buses were burned. Many people were beaten. Television cameras brought the shame of segregation into the living rooms of the American people.

During 1962 and 1963, the civil rights movement caught the attention of the nation. **Riots** broke out at the University of Mississippi. A riot is a violent public disturbance. James Meredith was not allowed to attend because he was African American. A court ordered the university to admit him. The governor of the state said that he would keep Meredith out. Meredith's life was threatened. Mobs of white people protested his admission. Local police failed to keep the peace. President Kennedy sent federal troops to the university to protect Meredith. Meredith became the first African American to attend the University of Mississippi.

How Did Violence Against Protesters Increase?

Segregation in public places was still practiced in many parts of the South. African American protesters focused their efforts on this injustice. They organized boycotts, protests, and "sit-ins." These **tactics** upset many white southerners and resulted in violence against the peaceful protesters.

It became clear that the federal government had to act. A national civil rights bill was sent to Congress by President Kennedy. It was known as the Civil Rights Act. Approved in 1964, the bill granted the federal government power to speed up school **desegregation**. It protected the voting rights of African Americans. The law also required an end to segregation of public places.

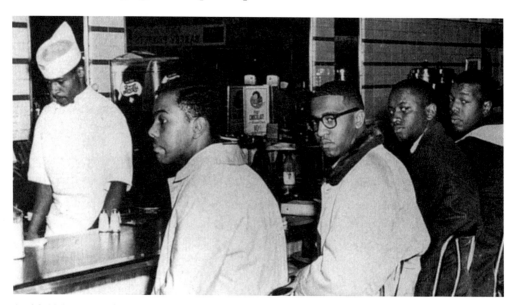

In 1960 in Greensboro, North Carolina, four college students stage a sit-in to protest their treatment at an all-white restaurant.

Citizens Seeking Change: Peaceful Protest and Riots

Americans have a long tradition of protest. Colonists used boycotts to protest their unfair treatment by England. In the Boston Tea Party, colonists ruined tons of tea, although no lives were lost.

In the mid-1900s, a civil rights movement worked to stop racist practices. Most leaders looked for peaceful ways to protest. However, protests often resulted in fights between protesters and racists. This violence helped Americans see the ugliness of racism. More and more people began to support the African Americans' cause. They pressured Congress to change the laws. The president then enforced the new laws. The violence that tried to stop the movement helped advance the cause of civil rights.

At times, riots broke out. The 1965 rioting in Watts neighborhood in Los Angeles is one example. The riots led to much damage and looting, mostly in African American communities. The riots hurt them economically. However, rioting also called attention to the anger felt by African Americans. Both protests and riots played a role in helping people see that the time for change had come.

1. Why do you think African American sit-ins and marches often resulted in violence by whites? Do you think the protesters expected this? Why or why not?

2. Which is a more effective way to get social change—peaceful protest or violent protest? Explain your opinion.

What Was the March on Washington?

On August 28, 1963, more than 200,000 people gathered peacefully at the Lincoln Memorial in Washington, D.C. The March on Washington was organized by African American leaders to show support for the passage of the civil rights bill. Participants in the march included African Americans and whites of all ages. Many waved small American flags. There were songs, prayers, and speeches. Dr. Martin Luther King Jr. spoke to the marchers of his dream for America. His speech was a challenge to the nation. It was also a message of hope.

How Was President Kennedy Assassinated?

Motorcade

A parade of cars

Developing country

A nation that is slowly improving its industry and economy

President Kennedy began to turn his thoughts toward being re-elected. He flew to Texas to begin his campaign. On Friday, November 22, 1963, President Kennedy rode through the streets of Dallas, Texas. Riding with him were his wife and Governor John Connally of Texas and Connally's wife. The **motorcade** was moving through the streets of downtown Dallas when shots were fired.

President Kennedy (rear seat to left) rode through Dallas, Texas, before he was assassinated.

Governor Connally was seriously wounded. President Kennedy, who had been shot in the head and neck, was dead. A few hours later, Vice President Johnson took the presidential oath of office. Lee Harvey Oswald was arrested and accused of killing the president. Two days later on live television, Jack Ruby shot and killed Oswald. The nation was shocked that Kennedy had been assassinated.

What Had Kennedy Achieved as President?

During President Kennedy's brief time in office, he did many things that had lasting effects. In 1961, the Peace Corps was established to work in **developing countries.** A developing country is a nation that is slowly improving its industry and economy. The first Peace Corps volunteers were sent as teachers to the African nation of Ghana. Five years later, more than 10,000 Americans were serving in 52 countries.

When Communists threatened Southeast Asia, Kennedy allowed the transport of troops and equipment to aid them. Under Kennedy, the United States, Britain, and the Soviet Union signed the Limited Test Ban Treaty. The treaty made above-ground nuclear tests illegal. One of his strongest moves was allocating $20 billion to NASA with a challenge to put an American on the moon by 1970.

The first Peace Corps volunteers provided help to nations in Africa.

What do you think?

Why do you think it is important to protest peacefully?

Lesson 3 Review Choose the term in parentheses that best completes each sentence. Write your answer on a sheet of paper.

1. The Congress of Racial Equality was led by (James Farmer, President Kennedy, Martin Luther King Jr.).

2. James Meredith's struggle drew the nation's attention to (Washington, Los Angeles, the University of Mississippi).

3. A peaceful march for civil rights was held on (June 25, 1961; August 28, 1963; November 22, 1963) in Washington, D.C.

4. The Civil Rights Act of 1964 called for an end to (segregation, sit-ins, protests).

5. President John F. Kennedy was assassinated by (John Connally, Lee Harvey Oswald, Jack Ruby).

Conservative

One who is cautious about change

President Lyndon Johnson's vision for the future of America was similar to that of John Kennedy. Johnson challenged America to wage a "War on Poverty." The country, he felt, must provide good education for every child and at least minimum health care for all Americans. Certainly it must bring an end to racial injustice. In May 1964, he gave his vision a name. He challenged the nation to build a "Great Society."

Who Won the Election of 1964?

Robert Weaver (left) was the first African American to serve in a president's Cabinet.

In 1964, the Democratic Party nominated Lyndon Johnson for president. The Republican Party nominated Senator Barry Goldwater of Arizona. There were great differences between the views of the two candidates.

Johnson felt federal programs needed to be created to improve the quality of life for every American. Goldwater, on the other hand, was very **conservative**. He felt individual states should have the final say in their policies. The federal government should not interfere.

Johnson easily won the election. He received more votes than any president before him. This election also gave the Democratic Party a stronger control of Congress.

What New Laws Did Johnson Help Pass?

President Johnson acted quickly to get Congress to pass laws to create programs for his "Great Society." A Medicare plan was passed to provide health insurance for the elderly. The Elementary and Secondary School Act provided more than $1 billion in federal funds to school districts with needy students.

Other laws attacked problems of **maintaining** clean air and water. The Housing Act encouraged the building of low-cost housing for low-income families. President Johnson appointed Robert Weaver to head the new Department of Housing and Urban Development. He was the first African American to become a member of a president's Cabinet.

For four decades, the effectiveness of these programs has been debated. Although the Great Society programs did not end poverty, the rate of poverty dropped four percent from 1965 to 1978. It was at the same level in the year 2000. Great Society programs still try to help people escape poverty. Medicare continues to provide medical care for elderly citizens. Low-cost housing is still being built. Federal funds are still provided to improve the education of elementary and secondary students from low-income families.

In 1965, President Johnson decided to expand America's role in a small country in Asia called South Vietnam. The Vietnam War became the most **divisive** conflict in the United States since the Civil War.

What Caused the Vietnam War?

After World War II, the former French colony of Vietnam was divided into two parts. North Vietnam was controlled by a Communist government. South Vietnam was non-Communist. America first became involved in this area of Southeast Asia in the 1950s.

President Johnson continued the policy set forth by previous presidents. Eisenhower had provided military weapons and economic aid to South Vietnam. Kennedy had sent military advisors. Johnson at first sent only noncombat troops to Vietnam.

Total American Troops in Vietnam by Year	
1963	15,000
1965	183,300
1967	475,000
1969	543,000

American soldiers in Vietnam had to bear harsh fighting conditions.

In August 1964, there were reports that two American ships were attacked off the coast of North Vietnam. President Johnson asked Congress for the right "to take all necessary measures" to protect American forces in the area. This vote of Congress was called the Tonkin Gulf Resolution. Congress never declared war against North Vietnam. Johnson used the Tonkin Gulf Resolution as authority to increase American involvement in South Vietnam.

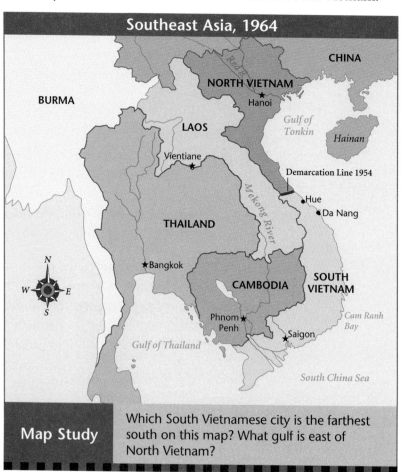

Southeast Asia, 1964

Map Study Which South Vietnamese city is the farthest south on this map? What gulf is east of North Vietnam?

Rural

Relating to places outside the city; the countryside

Replenish

To make full or complete again

Word Bank

Barry Goldwater

Housing Act

Lyndon Johnson

Medicare

Tonkin Gulf
  Resolution

What do you think?

Why is it important to have low-cost housing available?

The Communist North Vietnamese continued to hold on to **rural** sections of South Vietnam. Even though many Vietcong groups were destroyed, they were quickly **replenished** by North Vietnamese. By the start of 1968, it was clear that the United States was not winning the war.

President Johnson set up a meeting with North and South Vietnam, the United States, and the Vietcong. The 1969 meeting was held in Paris, France, just after Johnson's presidency ended. Unfortunately, this meeting had little effect on ending the fighting.

Lesson 4 Review On a sheet of paper, write the correct word or words from the Word Bank to complete each sentence.

1. _____ won the 1964 election for president.

2. The Republican Party nominated _____ for the 1964 election.

3. The _____ encouraged people to build low-cost housing.

4. The _____ Plan provided health insurance to the elderly.

5. Congress passed the _____ to protect American forces near North Vietnam.

It Happened in History

In 1900, the United States government began to protect the nation's natural environment. In that year, President William McKinley signed a law to prevent birds from being killed for their feathers. This law was the beginning of the nation's first conservation movement to protect wildlife.

Sixty years later, birds were seen dropping from the sky. In 1962, Rachel Carson published *Silent Spring.* Carson argued in her book that a chemical (DDT) created to kill insects was killing birds. Something had to be done to protect wildlife and the environment. The first Clean Air Act was passed in 1963. The National Wilderness Preservation System became law in 1964. The Endangered Species Preservation Act was passed in 1966. President John F. Kennedy wrote in 1963, "The history of America has been the story of Americans seizing, using, squandering and belatedly protecting their natural heritage."

Feminist

A person who seeks equal rights for women

Liberation

Equal social or economic rights

The 1960s was a time when many Americans were committed to changing their society. The civil rights movement started a movement for Black Power. **Feminists** called for the **liberation** of women. Hispanic Americans made their problems known to the nation. The American Indian Movement (AIM) demanded better opportunities for American Indians. College students wanted more control of what they studied. Antiwar protesters wanted to end America's involvement in the war in Vietnam. Young people challenged the basic social rules of an older generation.

Many Americans protested the Vietnam War.

Who Led the Civil Rights Movement?

Martin Luther King Jr. was awarded the Nobel Peace Prize in 1964. This award recognized the work of Dr. King in the civil rights movement. Under his leadership, progress had been made in increasing equality for African Americans. The civil rights movement tried to end segregation.

Some leaders called for a new direction for African Americans. Malcolm X, a Black Muslim, encouraged African Americans to develop their own power and separate from white Americans who treated them unequally. He believed that African Americans should start their own businesses. He wanted them to begin to control their own communities.

Stokely Carmichael, an African American leader, said African Americans needed "Black Power." He wanted them to have more than economic and political power. The Black Power movement encouraged African Americans to become interested in their history and culture. They developed a pride in their ethnic heritage.

Under the forceful leadership of President Johnson and members of Congress, the Civil Rights Act of 1964 was passed. The law prohibited discrimination in public places, such as stores, transportation facilities, and restaurants. In addition, this law prohibited those that receive federal funds from discriminating against anyone on the basis of their race, sex, religion or national origin. The Voting Rights Act of 1965 gave federal government the power to protect the right of every citizen to vote. In a few years, voter registration by African Americans in southern states increased by more than 50 percent.

What Was the Women's Movement?

In 1960, leaders of a new feminist, or women's, movement said that women should have the same social and economic rights as men. They believed women should be able to work in any job, including jobs that men usually held. Feminists wanted equal pay for equal jobs. The women's movement tried to gain full equality for women through the Equal Rights Amendment (ERA). The leaders of the movement wanted this amendment added to the Constitution. The Equal Rights Amendment was passed by many states but not enough to make it part of the Constitution.

Biography

Cesar Chavez: 1927–1993

Labor leader Cesar Chavez devoted his time to unionizing poor migrant farm workers. Chavez was born into a Mexican American family who became migrant farm laborers when he was 10 years old. As a child, Chavez worked in the fields as he moved with his family. In 1962, he established the National Farm Workers Association. Migrant farm workers lived at the mercy of their employers and without protection of federal law. He organized strikes and picket lines to gain support for their cause. Chavez also organized peaceful sit-ins and marches. His efforts included a long, bitter strike against California grape growers. One of the strategies of the strike was a nationwide refusal to buy California grapes. The strike's startling success in 1970 led to the organization of farm workers' unions in different states.

Migrant

A worker who travels from place to place to work

Baby boom

The millions of babies born after World War II

What Problems Did Hispanic Americans Face?

Americans whose parents or ancestors came from Spanish-speaking countries are called Hispanic Americans. Hispanic culture—food, music, dress, and language—had had a major influence on American life. Still, in the 1960s, many Hispanic Americans were poor and had little education. Many were discriminated against. Hispanic leaders brought these problems to the nation's attention. One such leader was Cesar Chavez. He led a movement to organize Mexican American **migrants.** These are workers who move from place to place to find work. Chavez organized the National Farm Workers Association to help Hispanic farm workers.

What Was the Youth Movement?

After World War II, millions of children were born. This was known as the **baby boom.** These children grew up during the cold war, yet they were raised in a nation with a growing economy. America held great opportunity for them.

In the 1960s, the baby boom generation reached their late teens and early 20s. Many challenged the values and views of their parents. The main challenge involved the Vietnam War. Unlike their parents who had lived through World War II, many baby boomers had trouble viewing the war as a patriotic effort.

What Was the Counterculture?

Counterculture

A culture or lifestyle that goes against the common culture

Hippie

An extreme member of the youth culture in the 1960s

In the 1960s, many young people started creating a **counterculture.** It was very different from American society at the time. Long hair, casual clothes, beads, and headbands were the accepted styles of the counterculture. Rock music became their voice. Freedom from America's social rules was one theme of the youth movement. The phrase "doing your own thing" became popular. The most extreme members of the youth culture were called **hippies.**

Many youths got very involved with their communities. They worked to clean up their environment. They became interested in politics. Many young people joined the antiwar movement. They organized protest marches to bring attention to their causes.

Then and Now

On July 20, 1969, American Astronauts Neil Armstrong and Edwin Aldrin Jr. landed their spacecraft, the *Eagle,* on the moon. This mission, called *Apollo 11,* put the first astronauts on the moon. About 6 hours after landing, Armstrong took his first steps on the moon. He said, "That's one small step for a man, one giant leap for mankind." Armstrong and Aldrin put the American flag on the moon and collected rock and soil samples.

Since that first step on the moon, our knowledge of space has grown enormously. Satellites, rovers, and space stations—as well as crews and scientists—have continued to uncover new information about the solar system. For example, in June and July 2003, twin rovers were sent to Mars. Those rovers—named *Spirit* and *Opportunity*—landed on Mars in January 2004. There they explored the rocks and craters. They found evidence that liquid water had been there in the past. An expert at NASA predicted that humans could be on Mars by the year 2030.

What Was Woodstock?

On a weekend in August 1969, a rock concert took place on a 600-acre farm in upstate New York. About 400,000 people attended the concert, which was billed as the Woodstock Music and Arts Fair. There were shortages of water and food. People shared what little they had and the crowd remained peaceful. Woodstock became national news; it was hailed for its peacefulness. Many young people hoped that Woodstock was the beginning of a new and better America.

What do you think?

How is the counterculture of the 1960s like youth today?

Lesson 5 Review On a sheet of paper, write the answers to the following questions. Use complete sentences.

1. What was the goal of feminists?

2. What did Malcolm X encourage?

3. What happened to the Equal Rights Amendment?

4. How did Cesar Chavez help Mexican American farm workers?

5. What is a counterculture?

It Happened in History

The role of the Supreme Court is to interpret the Constitution. It tells the nation what the Constitution means because it is not always clear to everyone. Interpreting the Constitution can be difficult, because it was written more than 200 years ago. For example, the First Amendment states: "Congress shall make no law respecting an establishment of religion or prohibiting the free exercise thereof. . . . "

How does Supreme Court determine what the words "respecting an establishment of religion" mean? What does the "free exercise" of religion mean? The Supreme Court looks at the "plain meaning" of the words and what the original writers of the Constitution meant. In 1963, the Supreme Court considered whether a state could require Bible reading in the public schools. The court ruled that the government must be neutral about religion. The court created a test: Laws must have a non-religious purpose that neither harms nor helps the free exercise of religious beliefs.

Ironic

The opposite of what is expected

Throughout the 1960s, the Vietnam War grew to be a major concern for Americans. Questions arose about why the United States was involved. Americans were unsure who was winning the war. One day, the United States would announce a major victory in Vietnam. The next day, news reports would announce heavy losses of American troops. The public did not know what to believe. Television brought the horrors of the war directly into American homes.

Why Did Johnson Decide Not to Run for Re-election?

President Johnson was concerned about the political election. He saw the nation becoming divided into two groups—the hawks and the doves. The hawks favored war and wanted to win at all costs. The doves did not want the United States to be involved with the war.

Johnson tried to please both sides. He increased the bombing to please the hawks. At the same time, he helped start peace talks to make the doves happy.

On March 31, 1968, President Johnson spoke to the nation on television. He began with a routine talk about the war. He announced that he was going to reduce the bombings in North Vietnam. He ended his speech with the announcement that he would not seek the Democratic nomination for president.

What Happened to Martin Luther King Jr.?

Four days later, on April 4, 1968, Martin Luther King Jr. was shot to death. He had traveled to Memphis, Tennessee, to support a strike by African American city workers. It was **ironic** that a man who had preached and practiced nonviolence died as the victim of a violent act. It was also ironic that the anger that many African Americans felt at his murder led to riots and to acts of violence. Military troops were needed to control riots in many cities.

Controversial

*Causing much debate
and disagreement*

Blue-collar

*A name used to describe
workers in jobs that
require little training*

What Happened to Robert Kennedy?

Robert Kennedy's campaign for the Democratic nomination for president had been gaining strength. On June 4, 1968, Robert Kennedy won the California primary. That night, he was shot by a young Jordanian Arab who did not like Kennedy's support for Israel. Two days after he was shot, Robert F. Kennedy died.

Who Won the Election of 1968?

The Democratic Party nominated Vice President Hubert Humphrey as its candidate for president. The Democratic convention was held in August in Chicago, Illinois. Thousands of people held antiwar protests outside of the convention site. Police broke up the protests by beating protesters with clubs. Inside the convention hall, delegates shouted angry words at each other. The Democratic Party was divided and confused. Many people felt that Humphrey would continue Johnson's **controversial** policies in Vietnam.

The Republican Party nominated Richard M. Nixon for president. Nixon's campaign theme was "Bring Us Together." He called for "law and order" and said he had a plan to end the war in Vietnam. He wanted "peace with honor."

George Wallace entered the presidential race as a candidate of the newly formed American Independent Party. He was a former Democratic governor from Alabama who had supported segregation. Wallace appealed to southern **blue-collar** workers. Many of these people had worked their way up without help from the federal government. They were not supportive of many federal programs.

The election was very close. Nixon received 31.8 million votes to Humphrey's 31.3 million votes. Wallace received almost 10 million votes. Nixon won the election, but he received less than 50 percent of the popular vote.

Word Bank

Lyndon B. Johnson

Martin Luther
King Jr.

Hubert Humphrey

Richard M. Nixon

Vietnam

What do you think?

Why do you think there was so much political violence in the 1960s?

Lesson 6 Review Choose the name in the Word Bank that best completes each sentence. Write your answers on a sheet of paper.

1. President Johnson tried to please both the hawks who wanted victory in _____ and the doves who wanted out of the war.

2. On March 31, 1968, President _____ announced that he would not run for re-election.

3. An act of violence ended the life of _____, who preached nonviolence.

4. The Democratic Party nominated _____ to run for president in 1968.

5. Republican candidate _____ won the election with less than 50 percent of the vote.

History in Your Life

Salk and the Polio Vaccine

In 1943, the most well-known person with polio was President Franklin D. Roosevelt. In 1943, polio caused 1,151 deaths. Still more people became crippled with polio that year.

A viral infection causes polio, which is short for poliomyelitis. In severe form, polio destroys nerve cells that control skeletal muscles. It paralyzes the legs, arms, or trunk. Swallowing, talking, breathing, and heart functions can be affected. Polio occurs most often in children.

In 1953, Jonas E. Salk developed a polio vaccine. After intense laboratory tests, he vaccinated Pittsburgh schoolchildren. That same year, the vaccine was tested in schools in 44 states. It was the largest field test in history. In 1956, Salk announced that before long polio would be wiped out. He was right—1969 was the first year in recorded American medical history that no one died from polio.

John F. Kennedy's Inaugural Address

On January 20, 1961, John Fitzgerald Kennedy became the 35th president of the United States. Before becoming president, Kennedy served in the House of Representatives and the Senate from Massachusetts.

As president, Kennedy wanted to gather support for his plans for the country, especially in foreign affairs. The following passages are from his inaugural address, which inspired many Americans.

We observe today not a victory of party, but a celebration of freedom—symbolizing an end, as well as a beginning—signifying renewal as well as change. . . .

Let the word go forth from this time and place, to friend and foe alike, that the torch has been passed to a new generation of Americans—born in this century, tempered by war, disciplined by a hard and bitter peace, proud of our ancient heritage—and unwilling to witness or permit the slow undoing of those human rights to which this nation has always been committed, and to which we are committed today at home and around the world.

Let every nation know, whether it wishes us well or ill, that we shall pay any price, bear any burden, meet any hardship, support any friend, oppose any foe, in order to assure the survival and success of liberty. This much we pledge—and more. . . .

Finally, to those nations who would make themselves our adversary [enemy], we offer not a pledge but a request: that both sides begin anew the quest for peace. . . .

And so, my fellow Americans: ask not what your country can do for you—ask what you can do for your country.

My fellow citizens of the world: ask not what America will do for you, but what together we can do for the freedom of man.

Finally, whether you are citizens of America or citizens of the world, ask of us here the same high standards of strength and sacrifice which we ask of you. With a good conscience our only sure reward, with history the final judge of our deeds, let us go forth to lead the land we love. . . .

Document-Based Questions

1. What did Kennedy mean when he said, "the torch has been passed to a new generation"?

2. What did Kennedy pledge Americans would do on behalf of liberty?

3. What did the president offer to enemies?

4. What did Kennedy ask Americans and world citizens to ask themselves?

5. According to Kennedy, what is the final judge of citizens?

Source: President John F. Kennedy's Inaugural Address, 1961.

- In 1961, the first of many space flights with people on board began with the Mercury and Gemini space programs.

- John F. Kennedy became president in 1961. He approved a plan developed under President Eisenhower to support an invasion of Cuba by Cuban rebels to overthrow the Castro government. The invasion at the Bay of Pigs was a complete failure.

- In 1961 the Soviets built the Berlin Wall that divided East and West Berlin.

- The Soviet Union was providing supplies for missile bases in Cuba. U.S. ships prevented Soviet ships from reaching Cuba. Later, a deal was struck between America and the Soviet Union that ended the Cuban missile crisis.

- African Americans and whites joined together to help end segregation. Hundreds of protest marches, sit-ins, and demonstrations were staged. In 1963, an immense march on Washington was held to urge passage of civil rights legislation.

- During his presidency, Kennedy had created the Peace Corps and NASA and had proposed funding to help many people in poverty. President Kennedy was assassinated in Dallas on November 22, 1963. Lyndon Johnson became president.

- President Johnson wanted to build a "Great Society." He wanted to provide education and health care for all Americans. At his urging, Congress passed legislation that created Medicare, provided federal funds for schools, and encouraged low-cost housing.

- In 1964, Congress passed the Tonkin Gulf Resolution, which allowed Johnson to send American combat troops to Vietnam.

- Among the social developments of the 1960s were the feminist movement, the Black Power movement, the antiwar movement, the organization of Hispanic migrants, and the youth movement.

- Civil rights leader Martin Luther King Jr. was assassinated on April 4, 1968.

- Richard Nixon was elected president in November 1968.

Chapter 12 REVIEW

On a sheet of paper, write the correct words from the Word Bank to complete each sentence.

Word Bank

baby boom

Cesar Chavez

Cuban missile crisis

Great Society

John F. Kennedy

Peace Corps

Robert Weaver

Tonkin Gulf
Resolution

1. President _____ ordered American ships to prevent Soviet ships from reaching Cuba.

2. The _____ was what President Johnson called his plan for the country.

3. President Kennedy started the _____, which sent American volunteers overseas to help underdeveloped nations.

4. America's population grew after World War II because of the _____.

5. _____ was the first African American to be on a president's Cabinet.

6. _____ organized a union for farm workers in California.

7. The _____ showed that President Kennedy could stand up to the Soviet Union.

8. The _____ allowed President Johnson to send combat troops to Vietnam.

On a sheet of paper, write the letter of the answer that correctly completes each sentence.

9. The Civil Rights Act passed in 1964 granted the government power to _____.

   A organize boycotts

   B increase segregation of public areas

   C use violence against peaceful protesters

   D speed up school desegregation

10. _____ were an important factor in deciding the presidential election of 1960.

    A African American votes   C Cold war fears

    B Televised debates   D Scandals

11. The _____ was a failed invasion of Cuba supported by President Kennedy.
   A Cuban missile crisis   **C** *Sputnik*
   B Bay of Pigs   **D** Berlin Wall

12. _____ was a strong leader for African American civil rights.
   A Cesar Chavez   **C** Martin Luther King Jr.
   B John Glenn   **D** Robert Weaver

On a sheet of paper, write the answers to the following questions. Use complete sentences.

13. What were three of the federal social programs that were passed during the 1960s?

14. Why were the Bay of Pigs invasion and the Cuban missile crisis major events in the Kennedy presidency?

15. What were three developments in the civil rights movement during this period?

16. Why did America become involved in Vietnam?

17. How did the Vietnam War cause a division in the American people?

18. Who were the "freedom riders" and what did they do?

Critical Thinking On a sheet of paper, write your response to each question. Use complete sentences.

19. During the 1960s, young people listened to music that spoke about their society and their concerns. Is there anything similar to this today? Explain your answer.

20. Before the space program, people had never flown in space. Today space shuttles make regular flights. Would you like to go into space? Why or why not?

Test-Taking Tip

Directions for a test may include examples. Read the examples thoroughly. Try to understand why the example is done as shown. If it is unclear to you, try reading the directions again.

Political Cartoons

Political cartoons are funny drawings about political events. The purpose of a cartoon is to make people laugh. However, cartoons also express a viewpoint about a political issue or topic. Cartoons encourage people to think about current issues. Cartoonists reveal various opinions in a drawing. They can persuade others to support their opinion through the cartoon.

Cartoons often use symbols, or objects that stand for something else. The elephant has long been a symbol of the Republican Party. The donkey is the symbol of the Democratic Party. These two animals often show up in political cartoons.

Cartoonists add labels or captions to help readers interpret the drawing. The cartoon here has three labels. They are "1964," "L.B.J.," and "Old Smoky Sauce." This cartoon was published in 1964, a presidential election year. The label "1964" is on top of a bed of hot coals. "L.B.J." is Lyndon Baines Johnson, the 36th president. LBJ was a Democrat from Texas who was campaigning for president in 1964. His opponent was Senator Barry Goldwater, a Republican from Arizona. "Old Smoky Sauce" is barbecue sauce. The cartoon shows LBJ painting Old Smoky Sauce on an elephant. He is pictured as getting ready to barbecue the Republicans in the 1964 election.

"Hang Around Till Next Fall . . . We're Planning a Big, Texas-Style Barbecue"

Study the cartoon. Then answer these questions. Use complete sentences.

1. Why is the fire labeled "1964"?
2. Why did the cartoonist dress LBJ as a cowboy?
3. What does the elephant symbolize?
4. What is the meaning of the cartoon?
5. Find a current political cartoon in your newspaper. Write what you think it means.

Unit 4   S U M M A R Y

- The United Nations was created in San Francisco, California, in April 1945.

- Distrust developed between Communist and non-Communist countries. America supported anti-Communist governments.

- The Berlin airlift lasted until the Soviets reopened railroads and highways.

- In 1950, North Korea invaded South Korea. America sent troops to South Korea. After three years, the war ended.

- World War II hero Dwight D. Eisenhower was elected president in 1952.

- Senator Joseph McCarthy used fear of Communism to accuse people of Communism or Communist sympathy.

- The civil rights movement grew in the 1950s. Congress passed the Civil Rights Law in 1957.

- During the 1950s, America was prosperous.

- America launched its first successful satellite in 1958. The first space flights with people on board began in 1961.

- John F. Kennedy became president in 1961. His plan to invade Cuba and overthrow the Castro government failed.

- The Soviets built the Berlin Wall in 1961.

- The Soviets supplied Cuban missile bases. U.S. ships kept Soviet ships from Cuba. A deal between America and the Soviets ended the crisis.

- African Americans and whites joined to help end segregation. In 1963, the March on Washington was held to urge civil rights legislation.

- President Kennedy was killed in Dallas on November 22, 1963. Lyndon Johnson became president.

- At Johnson's urging, Congress passed laws for Medicare, school funds, and low-cost housing.

- In 1964, the Tonkin Gulf Resolution allowed Johnson to send American troops to Vietnam.

- The 1960s had many social movements that changed society.

- Martin Luther King Jr. was murdered on April 4, 1968.

- Richard Nixon was elected president in 1968.

"Here on the pulse of this new day
You may have the grace to look up and out
And into your sister's eyes, and into
Your brother's face, your country
And say simply
Very simply
With hope
Good morning."

~ *Maya Angelou, "On the Pulse of Morning,"*
  read at Bill Clinton's inauguration,
  January 19, 1993

Unit 5

Contemporary United States

1970–Present

Perhaps you know how good it feels to be a peacemaker or a peacekeeper. The United States has experienced that feeling. America celebrated its 200th birthday in 1976 with the wisdom of age. Then in the 1980s and 1990s it played a role as peacemaker or peacekeeper in the troubled Middle East. America signed agreements to limit nuclear weapons. It helped other countries defend their freedom. At home, the country attempted to resolve its own social and economic struggles.

Contemporary refers to modern times. In this unit, you will learn about America's roles as an international peacemaker and peacekeeper since 1970. You will learn how the nation handled economic and social situations at home. You will learn about America's place in the world following the terrorist attacks of September 11, 2001.

13 America in a Changing World
1970–1980

The nation had been in turmoil during much of the 1960s. The Vietnam War was one of the reasons. Americans were ready to see the war end. As the nation moved into the 1970s, scandals in the presidency provided a new problem at home. International issues also challenged the nation's foreign policy. In this chapter, you will learn more about the Vietnam War, about presidential scandal, and about American involvement in international issues.

Goals for Learning

◆ To explain how the Vietnam War ended and the results of the war

◆ To describe how the United States improved relations with China and the Soviet Union

◆ To describe the events of the Watergate scandal

◆ To list the problems President Ford faced

◆ To list national and international problems President Carter faced

◆ To describe the hostage crisis and problems with the Soviet Union

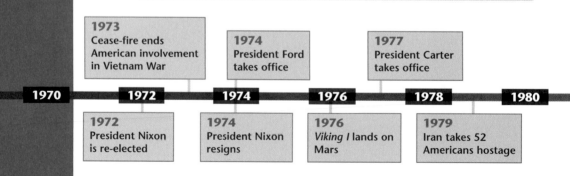

1973
Cease-fire ends American involvement in Vietnam War

1974
President Ford takes office

1977
President Carter takes office

1970   **1972**   **1974**   **1976**   **1978**   1980

1972
President Nixon is re-elected

1974
President Nixon resigns

1976
Viking I lands on Mars

1979
Iran takes 52 Americans hostage

Collapse

Breakdown or ruin

Minority

A person or group that is a smaller part of a population

Richard Nixon had promised to bring the troubled country together again. This was not a simple task. The first problem he faced when he took office in 1969 was to try to end the Vietnam War.

How Did Problems Continue in Vietnam?

Nixon announced a plan to turn the defense of South Vietnam over to the South Vietnamese during the next three years. Americans, however, had grown impatient waiting for an end to the war.

Cambodia is along the western border of South Vietnam. It tried very hard to remain neutral. However, its government could not prevent the Vietcong and the North Vietnamese from setting up bases on the South Vietnam border. The Communists used these bases to set up attacks against the Americans and South Vietnamese. In 1970, President Nixon allowed American troops to destroy the enemy supplies in Cambodia.

The North Vietnamese and Vietcong seized control of the northeastern section of Cambodia. Some Cambodians joined forces with these armies and spread out westward and southward. They were moving toward the capital of Phnom Penh. The United States wanted to prevent the complete **collapse** of the Cambodian government. It sent Cambodia large amounts of military supplies. American bombers gave air support to the Cambodian army.

What Happened at Kent State University?

The news of the American involvement in Cambodia caused large antiwar protests in cities around the country. Many protests took place at colleges. Feeling that these protesters were a small **minority,** Nixon asked for support from the "silent majority."

On May 2, 1970, a protest by students at Kent State University in Ohio ended with the burning of a school building. The governor ordered the National Guard to the university. On May 4, some students threw rocks at National Guard soldiers. The soldiers began shooting at the protesters, killing four students. This caused the Senate to end financial and military support for Cambodia.

How Did the Vietnam War End?

Nixon was re-elected president in 1972. He ran against Senator George McGovern of South Dakota. McGovern wanted to withdraw from Vietnam immediately. Many Democrats refused to support such a policy and voted for Nixon. Others voted for Nixon because he was trying to remove troops from Vietnam gradually.

In 1973 in Paris, France, North Vietnam, and the United States signed a cease-fire agreement. The Paris Peace Accords stated

that the United States would remove all troops from South Vietnam but continue to give the country military and economic aid. North Vietnam agreed to release American prisoners of war, or POWs. This agreement was only partly successful. In 1975, North Vietnam invaded South Vietnam. Without American military support, the South Vietnamese government could not survive. Their army soon fell apart. In April 1975, the army of North Vietnam captured Saigon, the capital of South Vietnam.

The Vietnam War Memorial in Washington, D.C., was designed by Maya Lin. It was built in 1982 to honor American soldiers killed or missing in Vietnam.

Helicopters from the roof of the American Embassy rescued American officials and some South Vietnamese. After a decade of fighting, the Vietnam War ended. More than one million Vietnamese on both sides died in the war. More than 50,000 American soldiers were killed.

Summary of the Vietnam War

- It was the longest war in United States history.
- About 58,000 Americans were killed; about 300,000 were wounded.
- The total cost to the United States was $150 billion.
- The war caused confusion about the nation's role in world affairs.
- The War Powers Act was passed, requiring the president to explain to Congress within 48 hours whenever American troops were to be sent into a foreign country.

Lesson 1 Review On a sheet of paper, write the answers to the following questions. Use complete sentences.

1. What was President Nixon's plan for Vietnam?
2. Why did the United States want to help Cambodia?
3. Why did violence break out at Kent State University?
4. What was the purpose of the Paris Peace Accords?
5. What became of South Vietnam once the United States stopped helping it?

What do you think?

Do you think President Nixon was right to withdraw troops from Vietnam? Why or why not?

Rival

A well-matched opponent

In the early 1950s, Chinese and American troops were enemies in the Korean War. For 20 years afterward, the relations between China and the United States had remained weak. Americans did not trade with or travel to China. The United States refused to recognize the government of the People's Republic of China. Instead, they called the Taiwan government the legal government of China.

Nixon wanted to relax the tensions of the cold war. The goal was called *détente,* a French word meaning relaxation. He hoped to improve relations with China and the Soviet Union. He waited until he thought these two countries would be open to his ideas. The Soviet Union and China were never close allies. Now their relationship was weakening, and they were becoming **rivals**. Nixon saw this as a good time for new negotiations.

What Did Nixon Do in China?

Henry Kissinger, Nixon's top foreign policy adviser, secretly went to China in 1971. He met with Chinese Premier Chou En-lai. Afterward, Chou En-lai invited Nixon to come to China. When Nixon announced to the American public that he intended to visit China, many were shocked. The Soviet Union was not pleased.

Nixon went to China in February 1972. Nixon and Chou En-lai made many efforts to settle their differences. After eight days of meetings, the two leaders announced that they agreed:

• to open up trade;

• to improve scientific and cultural relations;

• that neither country would try to dominate the Pacific;

• that the United States would recognize Taiwan as belonging to the People's Republic of China.

What Did Nixon Do in the Soviet Union?

The Soviet Union was concerned about the new relationship between the United States and China. The Soviets feared that these two countries might become allied against them. Three months after the successful meeting in China, Nixon went to Moscow. This was the first time a United States president had visited the Soviet Union in peacetime.

Nixon and Soviet President Leonid Brezhnev discussed the arms race between the two countries. They agreed to sign a treaty limiting the number of **strategic** weapons each country could have. It was called the Strategic Arms Limitation Talks (SALT). They also agreed to increase trade between the two countries and to cooperate in space exploration.

President Nixon (center, holding papers) and President Brezhnev enjoyed a light moment in Moscow. Henry Kissinger (seated) signed an agreement between the United States and the Soviet Union.

It Happened in History

Government and the Environment

During the Nixon and Ford administrations, laws were passed to clean the nation's waterways and polluted air. Laws to protect endangered species and national forests were also passed. The environment gained further protection during the Carter administration. The Clean Air Act and Clean Water Act were strengthened. More land was set aside as national parks and wilderness areas. During the Carter administration, more land came under environmental protection than under any previous president.

The Endangered Species Act passed in 1973 prohibited the federal government from changing the land if the change would harm the animals that lived there. Today there are more than 500 threatened and endangered animal species in the United States.

The Environmental Protection Agency protects against air pollution such as this.

Word Bank

China

Chou En-lai

détente

Leonid Brezhnev

trade

What do you think?

Why do you think it was important for President Nixon to meet with the Chinese and the Soviets?

Lesson 2 Review On a sheet of paper, write the correct word or words from the Word Bank to complete each sentence.

1. The word _____ was used to describe President Nixon's attempt to relax tensions of the cold war.

2. Nixon visited China and met with Chinese Premier _____.

3. Next, Nixon was asked to visit the Soviet Union and meet with its president _____.

4. The United States reached agreements with both _____ and the Soviet Union.

5. These meetings resulted in increased _____ and limited strategic weapons.

Wiretap

A device used to listen in on phone conversations

Conspiracy

A joint act of breaking the law

Guilty

Having done wrong; deserving blame

Aide

One who assists

Resign

To give up an office or position

Even though Nixon was re-elected president in 1972, he was no longer in office when the fighting in Vietnam finally stopped in 1975. The political scandal known as Watergate ended his presidency.

Former Attorney General John Mitchell was chairman of Nixon's Committee to Re-elect the President (CREEP). In March 1972, Mitchell accepted a proposal from a former FBI agent named Gordon Liddy. Liddy wanted to spy on the Democrats. On June 17, 1972, five burglars broke into the Democratic Party main office in the Watergate building in Washington, D.C. The burglars wanted to photograph documents and place devices called **wiretaps** that could be used to listen in on telephone conversations. A night watchman became suspicious and called the police, who arrested the five burglars. A White House spokesman called the break-in just a "third-rate burglary."

How Was the Watergate Scandal Exposed?

The five burglars were found guilty of **conspiracy,** burglary, and wiretapping in January 1973. A conspiracy is a joint act of breaking the law. Later, the judge received a letter from one of the men he had convicted. This man, James McCord, admitted that he lied under oath. He said that he was pressured by the Nixon administration to plead **guilty** and to remain silent about others who were involved in the spying. During the next several months, Nixon's top **aides** and advisers H. R. Haldeman and John Ehrlichman **resigned.** Another aide, John Dean, was fired.

In a televised speech on April 30, 1973, President Nixon announced the resignations of his aides and the firing of Dean. He later gave permission to Attorney General Elliot Richardson to appoint Archibald Cox as special prosecutor to investigate Watergate. Meanwhile, the Senate had formed its own committee to question members of Nixon's staff. These televised hearings lasted three months.

Subpoena

A court order

Extortion

Stealing money by using some kind of threat

Tax evasion

Failing to pay one's taxes

Evidence

Something that furnishes proof

John Dean told the Senate committee that Nixon approved paying the burglars to keep quiet. The president had committed a crime by hiding the truth. Nixon denied Dean's charges. It was one man's word against the other. During the Senate hearings, it was learned that tape recordings of White House meetings could prove whether Nixon or Dean was telling the truth. Nixon refused to give either the committee or Cox these tapes. A court order, or **subpoena,** was issued for the tapes. Nixon still refused to turn them over.

Why Did the Vice President Resign?

An unrelated scandal went on about the same time as Watergate. It involved Vice President Spiro Agnew. He was under investigation for bribery, **extortion,** and **tax evasion** during his time as Maryland governor, and while he was vice president. Extortion is stealing money by using some kind of threat. Tax evasion is failing to pay one's taxes. On October 10, 1973, Agnew resigned. Nixon nominated Congressman Gerald R. Ford of Michigan to be the new vice president.

What Happened to President Nixon?

On a Saturday, 10 days after Agnew's resignation, Nixon ordered Archibald Cox to be fired. Attorney General Richardson resigned in protest because Nixon had not kept his promise of an investigation of Watergate. Nixon later fired Richardson's deputy, William Ruckelshaus. These events became known as the "Saturday Night Massacre."

The White House was flooded with phone calls and telegrams protesting Nixon's actions, while newspapers demanded that he resign. In response, Nixon handed over the subpoenaed tapes. One tape had an 18-minute gap. Apparently, a section of the tape had been erased. Some of the tapes Nixon promised to turn over could not be found. Meanwhile, the House Judiciary Committee was gathering **evidence** that might prove that the president should be impeached. Evidence is something that furnishes proof.

Gerald Ford was sworn in as president after President Nixon resigned.

President Nixon made another important speech on television in April 1974. He calmly explained that stacks of notebooks on a table beside him contained typed pages of what was said on the missing tapes. The president hoped everyone would believe that he had nothing to hide.

Judgment

The ability a person has to decide and act on something

In May, Nixon refused when asked to turn over the disputed tapes. He knew the tapes contained evidence against him. By the end of July, the House Judiciary Committee had facts that were grounds for impeachment. In response, Nixon handed over the typed records of what was included on the tapes. These records revealed the president had been involved with the Watergate cover-up from the beginning.

The only way Nixon could avoid being impeached was to resign. On August 9, 1974, Nixon resigned from office. No president in United States history had ever resigned. While he did not admit guilt, Nixon said that some of his **judgments** were "wrong."

How Did Watergate Test the Constitution?

Several people in the Nixon administration were convicted of illegal acts in the Watergate scandal. The Constitution was tested as all three branches of government met up with a constitutional crisis. How well had the system worked? Gerald Ford said on the day he became the 38th president, "My fellow Americans, our long national nightmare is over. Our Constitution works. Our great republic is a government of laws and not of men. Here, the people rule."

Then and Now

For many years, TV viewers were limited to programs on three big television networks. Then, cable TV came along. The basic appeal of cable TV is simple. The broadcast networks must provide programs that a large general audience will watch. The cable networks, on the other hand, can offer movies without commercials, music videos, or non-stop sports 24 hours a day. The broadcast networks cannot offer such specialized programming.

During the 1970s, cable TV expanded. Along with satellite delivery systems, it allowed people to choose from dozens of entertainment and information channels. As a result, cable TV has given everyone more control over what they see and hear.

Lesson 3 Review Choose the word or name in parentheses that best completes each sentence. Write your answers on a sheet of paper.

1. Five burglars broke into the Democratic Party main office in the (Watergate, White House, Senate) building.

2. (H. R. Haldeman, John Ehrlichman, Archibald Cox) was a special prosecutor for the Watergate investigation.

3. Vice President (Spiro Agnew, John Dean, Gerald R. Ford) resigned from office.

4. President Nixon left office when he (resigned, was impeached, was put in jail).

5. (Archibald Cox, Spiro Agnew, Gerald R. Ford) replaced President Nixon.

What do you think?

You have learned about several scandals in presidencies in addition to the Watergate scandal. Why do you think there are so many scandals in presidencies?

Embargo

A government action that prevents certain goods from leaving a country

Crude oil

Oil in its natural state, before being processed

In September 1974, President Ford surprised the nation by pardoning Nixon. Ford said Nixon had suffered enough punishment. He felt the nation had to forget Watergate and move on to other matters. However, Ford was criticized for this action.

What Problems Did Ford Face?

The Ford administration was left with several problems. Inflation and unemployment were very high. People were also unhappy with the government after the Vietnam War. Ford went forward cautiously.

A new conflict broke out between Israel and its Arab neighbors in October 1973. The United States and other countries were giving aid to Israel. Because of this aid, some Arab states put an **embargo** on oil shipments to these countries. An embargo is a government action that prevents certain goods from leaving a country. This resulted in a gas shortage. People had to wait in long lines at gas stations. There was a shortage of home heating oil. Americans were shocked at how dependent they were on other countries.

The Organization of Petroleum Exporting Countries (OPEC) began to control prices. OPEC included several nations in the Middle East, Africa, and South America. OPEC countries raised the price of **crude oil**. This action drove up the price of gasoline and heating oil in the United States.

U.S. Gasoline Prices (cents per gallon)		
Year	Leaded Regular	Unleaded Regular
1973	38.8	—
1974	53.2	—
1975	56.7	—
1976	59.0	61.4
1977	62.2	65.6
1978	62.6	67.0

How Did America Celebrate Its Bicentennial?

In 1776, America declared its independence from Great Britain. The document was dated July 4, 1776. On July 4, 1976, Americans celebrated the fact that the Declaration of Independence was 200 years old. This celebration is called a **bicentennial.**

The celebration lasted for several months. More than 200 large sailing ships, called "tall ships," came from 30 nations. The ships docked in many East Coast harbors. Queen Elizabeth of Great Britain helped celebrate the independence that had been declared against King George III, her great-great-great grandfather. She presented a six-ton bell as a gift to the nation. In the nation's capital, 33 tons of fireworks lit the sky around the Washington Monument.

Although America's history was being celebrated in 1976, the nation seemed happy to forget its recent past for the moment. The nation's last 13 years had been difficult. A president and two national leaders were assassinated. A war was fought. A president and vice president resigned.

Biography

An Wang: 1920–1990

While at Harvard Computer Laboratory in 1948, physicist An Wang invented a magnetic core memory for computers. That invention was the most common early device for storing computer data. It revolutionized the computer industry before the microchip was invented. In 1951, he founded Wang Laboratories in Boston. The company produced specialty electronic devices, including desktop calculators. It was one of the largest, most successful high-tech companies in the United States in the 1970s. Wang held more than 35 patents related to computer technology. In addition, he was a board member and trustee of many institutions, including the Museum of Science of Boston. A native of Shanghai, China, Wang became a naturalized American citizen in 1954.

Fireworks celebrated America's bicentennial.

On July 4, 1976, it seemed that Americans were ready to celebrate a proud past and hope for a promising future. Two weeks later, on July 20, 1976, *Viking I* successfully landed on the surface of Mars. This was a perfect example of how far America had come in 200 years.

What do you think?

Why is it important to celebrate the nation's meaningful dates such as the bicentennial?

Lesson 4 Review On a sheet of paper, write the answers to the following questions. Use complete sentences.

1. Why did President Ford pardon Nixon?
2. What problems did President Ford face when he took office?
3. What problems did OPEC cause for America?
4. What is a bicentennial?
5. How did Americans celebrate the bicentennial?

Focus on Economics

When OPEC changes the price of crude oil, the world economy is immediately affected. The United States depends on foreign countries for more than 50 percent of its oil needs. Higher oil prices mean higher prices for gasoline and other petroleum products. When people pay more for these products, they have less to spend elsewhere. Dependence on foreign oil leaves Americans with little control over oil prices. This is one reason many Americans want to find other energy sources.

Morality

Good behavior; knowing the difference between right and wrong

July 1976 was also the month the Democratic Party held its political convention. The Democrats nominated the little-known Jimmy Carter, former governor of Georgia, for their presidential candidate. Carter campaigned very hard to get his name and ideas known to the American people. He stressed honesty, openness, trust, and **morality** in his speeches. People responded positively to his promise to restore morality in the government.

People liked Carter because he was an outsider. He was not part of the established political groups in Washington, D.C. When he accepted the nomination, he said that "1976 will not be a year of politics as usual." He said that there was a "new mood in America" in people looking for "new voices, new ideas, and new leaders." Carter promised to give the government back to the people. Senator Walter Mondale, of Minnesota, was Carter's running mate.

President Ford and Ronald Reagan, the former governor of California, ran against one another for the Republican presidential nomination. Ford won a narrow victory over Reagan at the Republican National Convention. Ford selected Senator Robert Dole, of Kansas, as his running mate.

Who Won the Election of 1976?

The 1976 presidential election focused on such issues as the economy, the reputation of the candidates, and the desire for change. The election was extremely close. Carter won a narrow victory over Ford. Ford actually carried more states than Carter, but Carter's states had more electoral votes. Carter was the first person from the Deep South to be elected president since before the Civil War.

Writing About History

List five ways you could help save energy by conserving gasoline, heating oil, or natural gas. Make a chart to keep track of your efforts.

What Changes Did President Carter Make?

Jimmy Carter wanted to bring a different style to the office of president. He wanted the American people to see him as someone like them. He wore a plain business suit to his inauguration in 1977. His goal was to restore the people's confidence in their government. He was concerned with more than just style. President Carter wanted the government to provide better service at a lower cost. He reorganized the executive branch. He added two new departments—the Department of Energy in 1977 and the Department of Education in 1979.

The United States uses large amounts of energy. In the 1970s, Americans made up six percent of the world's population but used 33 percent of the world's energy. Millions of barrels of oil were imported from the Middle East. Before Carter became president, countries in the Middle East increased the price of oil and produced less of it. President Carter said that energy was a major problem for the nation. In 1978, Congress passed an energy bill that lowered the taxes for businesses that used less energy. Automotive companies were encouraged to produce smaller cars.

The energy crisis during the 1970s caused long lines at gas stations. Energy guides (left) help consumers save energy.

Exist

To be in place or operating

Geography Note

The term *Middle East* describes an area of northeast Africa, southeast Europe, and southwest Asia. The landscape varies from mountains to deserts to seacoasts. From ancient times, the Middle East has been a crossroads of competing empires and nearly constant warfare. Islam is the major religion of the region's many ethnic groups. Oil discoveries have continued the region's importance in world politics.

President Carter wanted to improve the American economy. The energy crisis made it difficult for him to do that. In 1978, inflation became a serious problem. As prices went up, workers demanded higher wages. Higher wages increased the cost of doing business. Businesses had to raise prices to cover their costs. By 1979, inflation was just over 11 percent. Normal inflation was three to five percent per year.

What Problems Developed in Central America?

Central America became a troubled area for American foreign policy at this time. The government of Panama was not happy over American ownership of the Panama Canal. President Carter signed two treaties with the government of Panama in 1977. The treaties promised to give control of the Panama Canal to Panama in the year 2000. One treaty gave the United States the right to defend the canal against any attack. Not all Americans agreed that the United States should give up control of the Panama Canal. However, the treaties created a warmer relationship between the two countries.

Other Central American countries had problems. Civil war broke out in Nicaragua, the largest country in Central America. The dictator, Anastasio Somoza, was overthrown. An independent government was established. The United States recognized this government.

Political violence broke out in 1980 in El Salvador, a tiny country in Central America. Archbishop Oscar Romero was assassinated. Romero had been a popular figure who spoke out against the military. Later, in December, six Americans were killed. The Carter administration took away American aid to this country until an investigation was completed.

What Problems Developed with Israel?

The Middle East had had many ethnic, religious, and economic problems. The United States supported the independent state of Israel. Israel's Arab neighbors refused to recognize Israel's right to **exist.** They claimed that Israel's land belonged to the Arabs.

From left, Anwar Sadat, President Carter, and Menachem Begin shook hands after signing the peace treaty at Camp David.

Throughout the years, the Arab countries were supported by Egypt in any conflicts in which they were involved. In November 1977, Egypt's president, Anwar Sadat, attempted to make peace with Israel's government.

President Carter wanted to encourage peace between these two nations. He invited Sadat and Prime Minister Menachem Begin of Israel to Camp David, the presidential retreat in Maryland. A peace treaty was signed in March 1979. Egypt finally recognized Israel as an independent state.

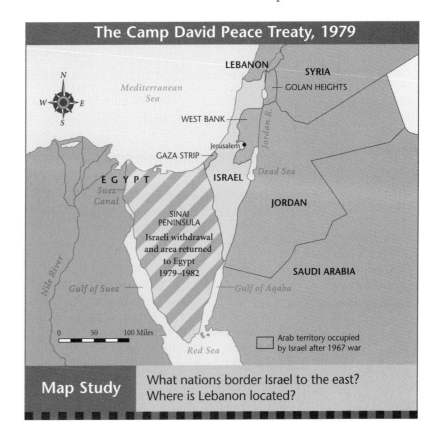

The Camp David Peace Treaty, 1979

Mediterranean Sea

LEBANON

SYRIA

GOLAN HEIGHTS

WEST BANK

Jordan R.

Jerusalem

GAZA STRIP

Dead Sea

EGYPT

ISRAEL

Suez Canal

JORDAN

SINAI PENINSULA

Israeli withdrawal and area returned to Egypt 1979–1982

Nile River

SAUDI ARABIA

Gulf of Suez

Gulf of Aqaba

0   50   100 Miles

Red Sea

Arab territory occupied by Israel after 1967 war

Map Study   What nations border Israel to the east? Where is Lebanon located?

Arab nations felt **betrayed** by Sadat. The treaty did not deal with Jerusalem or Palestine. These lands had been taken over by Israel during earlier wars. The Palestine Liberation Organization (PLO) continued **terrorist** acts against Israel. Terrorists are groups or individuals who use violence to make others give in to their demands. Lebanon, Israel's neighbor, was caught in the middle of this tension. Many members of the PLO were located in Lebanon. Israel bombed Lebanon several times. The United States continued to support Israel and worked hard to find a solution to the Palestinian problem.

Lesson 5 Review On a sheet of paper, write the correct word or words from the Word Bank to complete each sentence.

Word Bank _____

Anwar Sadat

Camp David

Israel

Jimmy Carter

PLO

1. _____ added two new departments—the Department of Energy and the Department of Education.

2. The president of Egypt was _____.

3. The prime minister of _____ was Menachem Begin.

4. Israel and Egypt signed a peace treaty at _____.

5. The _____ continued terrorist acts against Israel after the Camp David talks.

What do you think?

President Carter tried to work out disputes other countries were facing. Do you think it is America's responsibility to settle disputes?

History in Your Life

The Microwave Oven

Microwaves first caught public attention during World War II with the use of radar. Shortly after the war, scientists were able to "harness" microwaves for home cooking.

In the 1950s, manufacturers introduced microwave ovens called "radar ranges." In these ovens, an electronic vacuum tube produces bursts of microwaves. The microwaves are scattered around the oven until they enter the food. The radiation causes molecules in the food to vibrate billions of times per second. Friction among the molecules creates the heat that cooks the food. Microwave cooking produces heat directly inside the food. It greatly reduces the time needed to thaw frozen food and cook a meal. Regular ovens cook food gradually by heating the air surrounding it. In the 1970s, microwave oven sales rocketed. Today, most homes have a microwave oven.

Hostage

A person being held against his or her will by someone who wants certain demands to be met

The nation of Iran is an important oil-producing country in the Middle East. The United States depended on Iran's government to protect the flow of oil from the Middle East. The leader of Iran, Mohammad Reza Pahlavi, was called the shah. He allowed his country to adopt Western ways. As shah, he wanted Iran to be a modern nation. This went against the Islamic religious beliefs of some of his people.

In 1978, the shah began to lose his power. Public violence in the capital city of Tehran killed hundreds of people. Iranian students in the United States organized protests. The United States ordered any Americans living in Iran to leave the country.

A Muslim religious leader, the Ayatollah (meaning "reflection of God") Ruhollah Khomeini came to power in Iran. He established an Islamic republic to replace the shah in 1979.

What Was the Hostage Crisis?

In October 1979, President Carter allowed the shah to come to the United States for medical treatment. This act made some Iranians angry. On November 4, hundreds of Iranians took control of the American embassy in Iran. Sixty-six Americans were taken as **hostages.** A hostage is a person being held against his or her will by someone who wants certain demands to be met. Most of the women and all African Americans were soon released. The Iranians refused to release 52 remaining Americans until the United States returned the shah and the shah's wealth to Iran. They claimed that the shah stole money from Iran with the help of the United States.

The United States refused to return the shah. President Carter sent naval ships to the area. He ordered all oil imports from Iran stopped. Still, the Iranians refused to release the hostages. Americans paid close attention to the hostage crisis in the news.

In April 1980, President Carter sent a small group of soldiers to rescue the hostages. The mission failed. Eight soldiers died in the desert when their helicopter crashed. President Carter spent many hours trying to find a way to bring the hostages home safely. He could not find a way to do it.

Two Iranians posed with this American hostage in Tehran, Iran.

Why Did the Soviets Invade Afghanistan?

On December 27, 1979, the Middle East suffered another crisis. Soviet troop transport planes landed in Kabul, the capital of Afghanistan, in support of government groups. Two days after the invasion, President Amin of Afghanistan and his family were executed. The new president, Babrak Karmal, was friendly toward the Soviet Union.

It is believed the Soviets invaded Afghanistan because the religious unrest in the Islamic world had made its way into the Soviet Union. Invading was one way to stop this problem. President Carter protested this invasion strongly. The United States boycotted the 1980 Olympics in the Soviet Union to show disapproval of the Soviet actions. Many other countries followed the United States' decision. The United States also stopped sending wheat and corn to the Soviet Union. The protests did not stop the invasion. It took 10 years for the Soviets to end the fighting with Afghanistan.

What Was the SALT II Treaty?

Seven years after the SALT treaty was agreed to with the Soviet Union, President Carter met with Soviet Premier Leonid Brezhnev in Vienna, Austria. In 1979, they agreed to another treaty called SALT II. This treaty was never ratified by the United States Senate. Members of the Senate felt the treaty put the United States at a military disadvantage.

President Carter shook hands with Leonid Brezhnev after agreeing to the SALT II treaty.

What do you think?

Some people in the Middle East do not like Americans. Why do you think this is so?

Lesson 6 Review Choose the term in parentheses that best completes each sentence. Write your answers on a sheet of paper.

1. The shah of Iran lost power because he allowed (Islamic, Western, violent) ways.

2. Iran took American hostages to protest when (the shah, the Ayatollah, President Carter) came to the United States for medical treatment.

3. Soviet troops invaded (Iran, Afghanistan, Austria) in 1979.

4. The United States and other countries did not attend the (1980 Olympics, SALT II talks, annual trade conference) in the Soviet Union.

5. The United States also stopped sending (oil, money, grain) to the Soviet Union in protest.

This Is the America We Want

In 1976, Jimmy Carter had been nominated as the Democratic candidate for president. He was full of hope and confidence. In this part of his acceptance speech for the nomination, he describes his vision for America in 1976.

Nineteen seventy-six will not be a year of politics as usual. It can be a year of inspiration and hope, and it will be a year of concern, of quiet and sober reassessment of our nation's character and purpose . . . a year when voters have confounded the experts. And I guarantee you that it will be the year when we give the government of this country back to the people of this country.

There is a new mood in America. We have been shaken by a tragic war abroad and by scandals and broken promises at home. Our people are searching for new voices and new ideas and new leaders. . . . There is a fear that our best years are behind us. But I say to you that our nation's best is still ahead.

Our country has lived through a time of torment. It is now a time for healing. We want to have faith again. We want to be proud again. We just want the truth again. It is time for the people to run the government, and not the other way around.

It is the time to honor and strengthen our families and our neighborhoods and our diverse cultures and customs.

I have never had more faith in America than I do today. We have an America that . . . is busy being born, not busy dying. . . . I see an America on the move again, united, a diverse and vital and tolerant nation, entering our third century with pride and confidence, an America that lives up to the majesty of our Constitution and the simple decency of our people.

This is the America we want. This is the America that we will have.

Document-Based Questions

1. According to President Carter, how was 1976 different from past election years?
2. What did Carter say had shaken America?
3. What three things did Carter say that the American people wanted?
4. What kind of America did Carter say the nation could be?
5. In your opinion, has President Carter's vision of America taken place?

Source: Jimmy Carter's acceptance speech, July 15, 1976.

■ In 1969 when President Nixon took office, he announced a plan for Vietnam. This plan would end American involvement in the Vietnam War and give the South Vietnamese the responsibility of defending themselves. American forces left Vietnam in 1973. The war cost many American lives. North Vietnam took over South Vietnam by 1975.

■ President Nixon traveled to China and the Soviet Union in 1972. This improved American relations with these countries.

■ In 1974, President Nixon resigned from office to avoid being impeached because of the Watergate scandal. Evidence had been found that he had been involved in a conspiracy to spy on the Democratic party in the Watergate building.

■ President Ford was met with high inflation, unemployment, and a Middle East oil embargo when he took office in 1974.

■ America celebrated its 200th birthday, or bicentennial, in 1976.

■ President Carter took office in 1977. People liked him because he seemed to be like them. He dealt with an energy crisis and problems in the Middle East and Central America during the early years of his presidency. Iran took 52 Americans hostage in 1979. Carter was unable to find a way to get the hostages released.

■ The United States protested the Soviet Union's invasion of Afghanistan in 1979.

■ President Carter agreed to the SALT II treaty with Soviet Premier Leonid Brezhnev in Vienna, Austria, in 1979. The U.S. Senate refused to ratify the treaty.

Chapter 13 REVIEW

On a sheet of paper, write the correct word or words from the Word Bank to complete each sentence.

Word Bank

Afghanistan

bicentennial

embargo

Gerald Ford

Iran

Jimmy Carter

Richard Nixon

resigned

SALT II

Watergate

1. _____ became president in 1977.

2. _____ met with President Brezhnev of the Soviet Union in 1972.

3. The _____ scandal involved a break-in at the Democratic party's main office.

4. Richard Nixon _____ from office to avoid being impeached.

5. _____ took over as president after Nixon left office.

6. America celebrated its _____ in 1976.

7. _____ held 52 Americans hostage.

8. Some Arab states set up an oil _____ because the United States and other countries were giving aid to Israel.

9. The Soviets invaded _____ in 1979.

10. President Carter agreed to the _____ treaty with the Soviet Union in 1979.

On a sheet of paper, write the letter of the answer that correctly completes each sentence.

11. The U.S. invasion of _____ led to angry protests and four student deaths.

    A North Vietnam   **C** South Vietnam

    B Kent State   **D** Cambodia

12. The vice president who resigned over charges of wrongdoing was _____.

    A Spiro Agnew   **C** John Dean

    B John Mitchell   **D** Richard Nixon

13. Countries that belonged to _____ raised oil prices in 1973.

   A OPEC   **C** the PLO

   B the Arab-Israeli alliance   **D** Ayatollah

On a sheet of paper, write the answer to each question. Use complete sentences.

14. What were the effects of the Vietnam War on the American people?

15. How did President Nixon improve relations with the Soviet Union and China?

16. Why did President Nixon refuse at first to give tape recordings to the Senate committee?

17. How did an energy problem develop when Gerald Ford became president?

18. What problems did President Carter face with the Middle East?

Critical Thinking On a sheet of paper, write your response to each question. Use complete sentences.

19. Many Americans protested the Vietnam War. If a similar war broke out today, would you protest? Why or why not?

20. If you had been an Olympic athlete in 1980, how would you have felt about the boycott of the Olympic games?

Test-Taking Tip

When taking a true-false test, read each statement carefully. Write *true* only when the statement is totally true. Write *false* if part or all of the statement is false. After each item, ask yourself, "Is this entire item true?" If not, mark it false.

1970–1980   *America in a Changing World*   *Chapter 13*   **327**

The 1980s
1980–1989

International problems continued in the 1980s. The Reagan and Bush administrations, the next two American presidencies, faced these problems and made sweeping changes at home. During this time, the nation experienced social problems, the successes and failures of the space program, and the end of the cold war. In this chapter, you will learn about these and other important events that took place in the 1980s.

Goals for Learning

◆ To identify important national events that the Reagan administration faced

◆ To explain important foreign events facing the Reagan administration

◆ To describe events at the start of the Bush administration

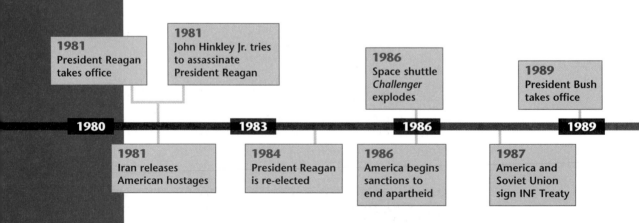

1981
President Reagan takes office

1981
John Hinkley Jr. tries to assassinate President Reagan

1986
Space shuttle *Challenger* explodes

1989
President Bush takes office

1980 — 1983 — 1986 — 1989

1981
Iran releases American hostages

1984
President Reagan is re-elected

1986
America begins sanctions to end apartheid

1987
America and Soviet Union sign INF Treaty

Surge

To rise swiftly

Dependent

Relying on others for one's needs

Budget

A plan that shows how much money is available and how the money will be spent

The Iranian hostage crisis caused the American people to question President Carter as a leader. He lost the 1980 election to Ronald Reagan. On January 20, 1981, the same day Ronald Reagan became president, Iran released the 52 American hostages.

Reagan was the oldest person ever to become president. He was 69 years old when he took office. He was well known to the American people. Reagan had been in movies and had appeared on television. He also had served as governor of California.

President Reagan wanted to return confidence to the American people. In his inaugural address, Reagan said that the country's biggest problem was inflation. He wanted to lower taxes and decrease the power of the federal government.

How Was Reagan Almost Assassinated?

President Reagan made a speech in Washington, D.C., on his 70th day in office. It was March 30, 1981. He included in his speech the remark, "Violent crime has **surged** 10 percent." Shortly thereafter, Reagan was walking toward his car when several shots were fired by a young man named John Hinkley Jr. The president, two of his aides, and a policeman were shot. Hinkley was immediately captured. President Reagan was rushed to a hospital, seriously wounded. His courage, confidence, and good humor calmed the nation. He was back in the White House full time in a month.

What Was Reagan's "New Federalism"?

President Reagan thought that many federal programs made people too **dependent** on the government. He believed that people should take responsibility for their own lives. Community problems, he said, should be solved by volunteer groups.

In 1981, Reagan announced that he wanted to cut the 1982 federal **budget** by $33 billion. He limited the amount of money spent on social programs. The only department not affected by the budget cuts was the Department of Defense. President Reagan called his plan to decrease the power of the federal government the "New Federalism."

What Was "Reaganomics"?

In an effort to get the country out of the "worst economic mess since the Great Depression," Reagan suggested tax and budget cuts. He believed these cuts would improve the economy and decrease the size of the federal government and the expansion of social programs. Congress passed the Economic Recovery Tax Act in 1981.

President Reagan's economic plan became known as "Reaganomics." This plan was based on a theory called "supply-side economics," which included these ideas: 1) When companies grow, they supply the economy with more jobs. 2) If companies spend less on paying government taxes, they will have more to invest in expanding their businesses. 3) The federal government collects too much money in taxes. 4) Paying fewer taxes and cutting government spending would eventually create more jobs.

Following this economic plan, the Reagan administration cut personal income taxes by 25 percent over a three-year period. They lowered business taxes and cut federal spending for education and the environment. Government spending on urban, social, cultural, and health problems was reduced. Critics of Reaganomics argued that cutting these programs seriously hurt the poor and middle class.

Justice Sandra Day O'Connor was the first woman to serve on the Supreme Court.

Who Did Reagan Appoint to the Supreme Court?

Reagan had promised that if a position opened on the Supreme Court, he would fill the opening with a woman. A position opened several months after Reagan took office. He appointed Sandra Day O'Connor from Arizona. She became the first woman to serve on the Supreme Court.

Reagan wanted to make the Supreme Court more conservative. Justice O'Connor was his first conservative appointment to the court. Conservatives interpret the Constitution **literally.** Conservatives have charged that liberal justices found new rights in the Constitution that were not intended when it was written.

Geraldine Ferraro: 1935–
Geraldine Ferraro is a native of New York. While she was working as a second-grade teacher, she went to school at night to earn a law degree. She practiced law and then worked as an assistant district attorney in New York. She served three terms in the House of Representatives.

She was working with the Democratic Party when Walter Mondale, who was running for president in 1984, chose her as his running mate. She was the first woman nominated to run for vice president by a major political party. Although the Mondale-Ferraro ticket lost the 1984 election, she changed ideas about women in politics. She went on to serve on the UN Human Rights Commission.

Career

A permanent job or line of work

What Did Americans Think of Reagan?

Reagan's style as a leader was criticized. He worked a normal eight-hour business day. He gave much of the responsibility of making decisions to members of his Cabinet and staff. In spite of the criticism, Reagan proved to be a popular president. He was re-elected in 1984. He defeated Walter Mondale, Carter's vice president. Mondale chose Congresswoman Geraldine Ferraro to run as his vice president.

What Happened to the Space Shuttle *Challenger*?

Before January 28, 1986, everyone thought of the space shuttle as a wonder of technology. The shuttle blasted into space and back successfully 24 times. People were confident that space travel was safe.

Much had been expected of the shuttle *Challenger.* Among the crew was a high school teacher named Christa McAuliffe. She planned to teach lessons from space and help with scientific experiments. After the flight, she would serve as a spokesperson for NASA about scientific **careers.**

Crew members of the Space Shuttle Challenger *are (left to right, front row). Michael J. Smith, Francis R. (Dick) Scobee, Ronald E. McNair; and (back row) Ellison S. Onizuka, Christa McAuliffe, Gregory Jarvis, and Judith A. Resnik.*

The *Challenger* takeoff seemed normal. However, two rubber "O-rings" failed as a result of cold temperatures. Millions of viewers across the world watched as the *Challenger* exploded into flames just 73 seconds into the flight. All seven members of the crew were killed. It was the worst disaster in 25 years of space flight. This loss and a series of rocket failures in 1986 set back the U.S. space program for two years.

Lesson 1 Review On a sheet of paper, write the correct word or words from the Word Bank to complete each sentence.

1. The first woman on the Supreme Court was _____.

2. _____ was the first woman to be nominated for vice president by a major political party.

3. President Reagan's plan to decrease the power of the federal government was known as _____.

4. _____ was President Reagan's plan to cut taxes and spending on education and the environment.

5. The crew of the space shuttle *Challenger* included _____, a high school teacher.

Word Bank

Christa McAuliffe

Geraldine Ferraro

New Federalism

Reaganomics

Sandra Day O'Connor

What do you think?

Ronald Reagan was the oldest person ever to become president. Do you think this was an advantage or a disadvantage for him? Explain your answer.

At the end of World War II, political leaders divided the world into three parts. The first group of nations were the Western democracies. The second group were Communist countries. The nations that were not part of either group were called the Third World. Today we refer to them as developing countries. Most of these countries continue to struggle. They are not industrialized and have little power in world affairs.

The United States was concerned with problems in the developing countries. The Middle East continued to be a troubled area. In Central America, Nicaragua had a Communist government. The policies of South Africa troubled many Americans.

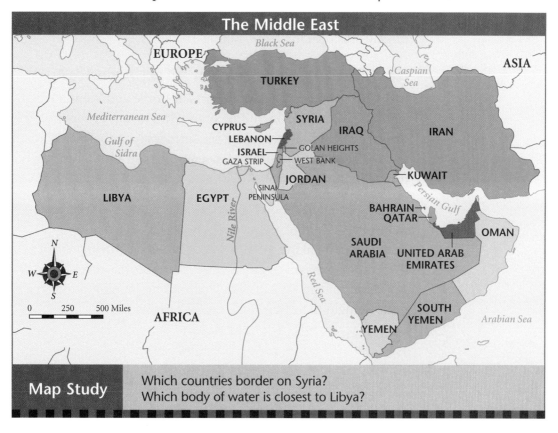

The Middle East

Map Study

Which countries border on Syria?
Which body of water is closest to Libya?

What Problems Occurred in the Middle East?

President Anwar Sadat of Egypt was assassinated in 1981. Israeli troops moved into the nation of Lebanon in 1982 to destroy the bases of the Palestine Liberation Organization (PLO). The PLO wanted a homeland for the Palestinians. The Israelis accused the PLO of being a terrorist organization.

The United States wanted a peaceful settlement and sent marines as a peacekeeping force. In October 1983, a terrorist drove a truck loaded with **explosives** into the marine base. The truck exploded. Over 200 American soldiers died. Reagan did not remove American troops from Lebanon until February 1984, but the situation was still not settled. A war between Iran and Iraq began in 1980. The United States Navy began to protect shipping lanes in the Persian Gulf. Iranians had placed mines in the water. In May 1987, an Iraqi warplane fired a missile into the USS *Stark,* killing 37 sailors.

How Did Libyan Terrorism Affect America?

In 1985, terrorist attacks at airports in Rome and Vienna killed a number of people, including many Americans. President Reagan charged Libyan leader Muammar al-Gadhafi with responsibility for the attacks. He cut off trade with Libya and froze all Libyan assets in America.

In 1986, Gadhafi's troops fired on planes flying over international waters in the Gulf of Sidra, near Libya. The United States responded by sinking two Libyan ships and destroying one of that country's missile sites. After another terrorist attack killed an American soldier, Reagan ordered bombings of Libyan military posts thought to be training areas for terrorists.

In 1980, Mount
Saint Helens
erupted violently,
leaving a huge
crater. Volcanic
ash shot 15 miles
into the sky, killing
crops and animals.
Damage from the
blast included
floods, forest fires,
and mudslides.
Sixty-two people
died. In late 2004,
the mountain
again erupted,
though less
violently than
in 1980. Scientists
were delighted at
the opportunity to
learn more about
volcanoes.

What Was the Contra Scandal?

A Communist government took power in the Central American nation of Nicaragua in 1979. The United States feared that Communists would gain power in other Central American nations. In fact, Nicaragua supplied military aid to Communist groups in other countries. The Reagan administration's policy was to fund a Nicaraguan group called the contras. The contras wanted to overthrow the Communist government of Nicaragua. Funding the contras was controversial. Members of Congress disagreed with the White House and voted to cut off funds to the contras.

In November 1986, a magazine in the Middle East reported that officials in the Reagan administration had secretly sold weapons to Iranian officials. Weapons were being exchanged for the release of American hostages. The hostages were thought to be held in Lebanon by terrorists, yet the Reagan administration had a policy of never dealing with terrorists. Later it was discovered that some of the money that paid for the weapons was sent to the contras in Nicaragua. Members of Congress were shocked at President Reagan's actions. He denied that he knew anything about it. However, several officials were charged with attempting to cheat the government.

How Did Relations Improve with the Soviet Union?

Tensions had increased between the Soviet Union and the United States during the Carter administration. The cold war appeared to be growing worse. President Reagan called the Soviet Union the "evil empire." He said the Soviets could not be trusted. The United States began the largest military buildup ever in peacetime. Critics said the United States should be trying to decrease its amount of military weapons. The Reagan administration argued that the nation had to be strong before any serious talks could take place.

President Reagan spoke with Mikhail Gorbachev in front of St. Basil's Cathedral in Moscow in 1988.

Mikhail Gorbachev became the new leader of the Soviet Union in 1985. He wanted to make changes to improve Soviet society. He spoke of a new "openness" that allowed more criticism of Soviet society. By 1987, the relations between the Soviet Union and the United States seemed to be improving.

Gorbachev and Reagan signed a treaty to decrease the amount of nuclear weapons on December 8, 1987. Both countries agreed to destroy medium-range nuclear weapons.

This new arms control agreement was called the Intermediate Nuclear Forces (INF) Treaty. Both nations agreed to allow government officials to inspect weapons factories to make sure that the terms of the treaty were being carried out. President Reagan said, "We can only hope that this history-making agreement will not be an end in itself but the beginning of a working relationship. . . ." In 1988, President Reagan visited the Soviet Union.

Apartheid

The South African policy of racial segregation

How Did America React to Apartheid?

The white government of South Africa had denied equal political and civil rights to its black population. Blacks made up over 70 percent of South Africa's population. The South African policy of racial segregation was called **apartheid.**

During the 1980s, there were protests in the United States against the policies of South Africa. Those against apartheid argued that the United States should pressure South Africa to change its policy. Others argued that the United States should not interfere in South Africa's problems.

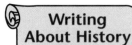

Writing About History

Choose a developing country and research it. Write a report in your notebook about the country as if you are a citizen of the country.

In an effort to end apartheid in South Africa, Congress proposed a bill imposing economic **sanctions** on the country. A sanction is an action taken to force a country to do something. Under this bill, South African imports would no longer be allowed into the United States. American exports to South Africa would be stopped. Also, Americans would no longer be able to invest in new South African businesses. The bill also canceled landing rights in America for all South African airlines.

Believing that the sanctions would do too much damage to the South African economy, President Reagan vetoed the bill. However, Congress overrode his veto. The sanctions bill became law in 1986.

How Did NASA Return to Space?

For two and a half years, NASA did not send any astronauts into space. NASA spent a lot of time making sure that the shuttle would be safe. On September 29, 1988, the space shuttle *Discovery* lifted safely into space at 11:37 a.m. It carried five astronauts and the future of America's space program. The four-day flight was, above all, a test of the shuttle itself. The shuttle worked just fine. America's first step back into space was a success.

Then and Now

You probably know that AIDS is an incurable disease caused by the virus called HIV. You probably also know that one way the virus is spread is through HIV-infected blood. The first cases to be identified as AIDS in the United States surfaced in 1981. It was 1983 before American and French researchers discovered the virus. It took until 1985 to develop the first blood test for HIV. Before 1985, one way people got AIDS was through blood transfusions. Without the test, health workers had no way to identify blood donors with HIV. There was no way to ensure the safety of blood supplied for transfusion.

If you need a transfusion today, you can be assured that the blood has been tested for HIV. People in the United States no longer get AIDS through blood transfusions. However, blood transfusions in other parts of the world are not always safe. This is one reason that AIDS has become an epidemic in poor countries throughout the world.

History in Your Life

Political Polls

Political polls are surveys of public opinion. They are especially important in election campaigns. The first political opinion poll was conducted in Pennsylvania in 1824. Early polls were simple. The person taking the poll, or pollster, went out and asked people their opinion on political issues.

Scientific polling began in the 1930s. Depending on a poll's purpose, between 500 and 2,000 people will be questioned. This small sample allows pollsters to guess accurately about a much larger population. Over time, polls have become more accurate. Still, notable failures in public opinion polls have occurred during national elections. The most famous occurred in the presidential election of 1948. Major polls predicted Thomas Dewey would defeat Harry S. Truman. Truman, however, won in a major landslide.

Some people believe polls not only record public opinion but also help shape it. For example, an exit poll may clearly show one candidate far ahead of a second. The supporters of the second candidate might decide not to vote at all if they believe their candidate will lose anyway.

What do you think?

How do you think apartheid was similar to problems African Americans have faced in America?

Lesson 2 Review Choose the best word or name in parentheses to complete each sentence. Write your answers on a sheet of paper.

1. Over 200 American soldiers died after a bombing in (Iran, Iraq, Lebanon).

2. To make sure Communism would not spread to Central American countries, the Reagan administration funded a group called the (Libyans, contras, Palestinians).

3. America bombed (Iran, Libya, Nicaragua) in 1986.

4. America and (the Soviet Union, Iran, China) signed the Intermediate Nuclear Forces (INF) Treaty in 1987.

5. Racial segregation in South Africa was called (contra, apartheid, PLO).

Deficit

Debt; spending more than what is taken in

Scourge

Widespread pain or distress

In the election of 1988, the Republican Party chose Vice President George H. W. Bush as its candidate. The Reverend Jesse Jackson was the first African American to run for president. He ran for president in the 1984 and 1988 elections. His efforts received much media attention. Massachusetts Governor Michael Dukakis eventually won the Democratic nomination in 1988, but Jackson's efforts were not forgotten.

On November 8, 1988, George H. W. Bush was elected president. Bush won 54 percent of the popular vote and 426 electoral votes. Dukakis won 112 electoral votes. On January 20, 1989, George H. W. Bush became the 41st president of the United States.

What Problems Did President Bush Face?

By January 1989, the United States had experienced six straight years of economic growth. This was the longest economic growth period in American history. Still, many problems faced the new Bush administration. The nation's banking industry was in deep trouble. The federal government had a large budget debt, or **deficit**. Many social problems challenged the United States.

What Social Problems Did Bush Face?

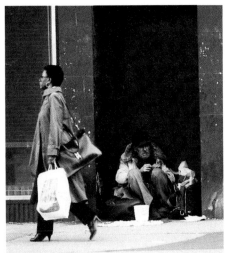

The budget was not the only problem facing the nation. The "quality of life" in America was a major concern. President Bush called the problem of crime and drug abuse a **"scourge."** Some people blamed the crime and drug problems on the fact that not all Americans were part of the 1980s economic boom. Several major American cities were in poor economic shape. Low-cost housing was in short supply throughout the nation.

Homelessness was a common sight in the 1980s.

American cities also experienced a growing problem of homelessness. People who had no homes lived in the streets and parks of many cities. Soup kitchens increased in many American cities. These places fed hundreds of hungry people daily.

How Did Women Affect the Workforce?

By the end of the 1980s, more women had entered the workforce than at any other time in American history. Because men's wages declined in the 1970s and 1980s, the two-income family became very common. Many women worked because they were the only economic support for their family. Increasing numbers of women graduated from college. Women workers became a very important part of the American economy. Working and raising a family put additional strain on most women. In 1980, about half of married women with children worked outside the home. Most married women reported that they still did more than half of the household chores. They also had more responsibility than their husband for their children.

What "Firsts" Did African Americans Achieve?

Jesse Jackson ran for president in the 1984 and 1988 elections. He was the first African American to run for president.

In 1989 and 1990, several African Americans reached positions of power never before held by an African American. General Colin Powell was appointed by President Bush to be the Chairman of the Joint Chiefs of Staff. This position made General Powell the nation's top military officer.

In Virginia, Douglas Wilder was elected the first African American governor of a state since Reconstruction. David Dinkins was elected the first African American mayor of New York City. The cities of Seattle, Washington; Durham, North Carolina; and New Haven, Connecticut, all elected their first African American mayors.

How Did Communism Begin to Fall?

In 1989, the cold war seemed to be ending. Communism was beginning to fall. During much of the 1980s, the Soviet Union had been experiencing economic problems. The Communist system had failed to provide the Soviet people with enough food. Soviet citizens demanded a more democratic voice in their government.

Communism began to show signs of falling in other parts of Europe as well. Eastern European countries under Communist rule, such as Hungary, Poland, Czechoslovakia, and East Germany, began to protest Communist rule. President Bush reacted to the situation in 1989 by saying, "The cold war began with the division of Europe. It can only end when Europe is whole."

In November 1989, the East German government announced for the first time that its citizens could leave their country if they wished. East Germany opened its borders to the west and allowed thousands of its citizens to pass through the Berlin Wall. In time, the wall was removed completely. This was only one of many changes Communist nations would see in the next few years.

Lesson 3 Review On a sheet of paper, write the answers to the following questions. Use complete sentences.

1. Why was it significant that Jesse Jackson ran for president in 1988?

2. What financial problems in America did the Bush administration face?

3. What were two social problems in America that the Bush administration faced?

4. What was happening to the Soviet Union in the 1980s?

5. What happened in East Germany in 1989?

What do you think?

What do you think should be done about the problem of homelessness?

"Women Shooting for the Stars"

Stella Guerra was the Acting Deputy Assistant Secretary of the Air Force in the 1980s. She gave this speech as a tribute and encouragement to women in the armed forces. Her comments address American women even today.

Dating back to our forebears who first stepped foot on American soil, [women] have been a part of our nation's progress. In what some have called the 'toddler years' of our country—the 1800s, we helped America take its first steps toward world prominence. We moved west, we worked in the fields tilling the soil and in the factories to produce the food and goods that our country needed to grow and prosper. . . . In the 1900s, during . . . the 'Rosie the Riveter' period, working in shipyards and steel mills, we helped our nation meet labor shortages in a time of national crisis. Afterwards, many . . . who had entered the workforce returned home—but not for long. By the midpoint of the 20th century, virtually no aspect of American society had been untouched by our eager rush into the labor force. . . .

We began to stretch, to grow, and expand our horizons. In . . . less than 50 years, our numbers in the labor force doubled. . . . In the second half of the 1970s, more of us were enrolled in college than ever before, and we began to move rapidly into business, industry, the federal sector, the teaching fields and other professions such as law and medicine. . . .

As our visions were broadened, women began to move into nontraditional areas. . . . It serves as a glistening example that in the past and in the present our hopes and dreams are interwoven into the very fiber of America. . . .

As we enter America's early adulthood we find that our hopes and dreams have been uplifted toward achievement. . . . The future holds exciting changes, challenges, and opportunities that will tax our abilities, test our skills, and require a total commitment from you and me. . . .

To meet the challenges ahead and . . . to progress, we must continue to take charge of our destinies and take responsibility for our own self-development. [No factor is more] important to our self-development . . . than self-esteem. Self-esteem comes in different doses and different degrees, and its potential is limitless.

Document-Based Questions

1. What is one contribution Guerra says women have made to America's success?

2. What years were the "toddler years"?

3. What was the "Rosie the Riveter" period?

4. What does Guerra say is most important to women's self-development?

5. How does Guerra suggest women meet the challenges ahead?

Source: "Women in America Shooting for the Stars: As We See Ourselves So Do We Act," by Stella Guerra.

Chapter 14   S U M M A R Y

- Ronald Reagan took office as president in 1981. Reagan introduced a plan to limit money to all departments except defense. Large budget and tax cuts were meant to strengthen the economy.

- Reagan appointed Sandra Day O'Connor, a conservative, as a Supreme Court justice. She was the first female justice.

- Reagan became a popular president and was re-elected in 1984.

- In January 1986, the space shuttle *Challenger* exploded, killing everyone on board. The disaster started a slump in the space program.

- Tensions eased between America and the Soviet Union when Mikhail Gorbachev and Reagan signed the INF Treaty in 1987 to reduce nuclear weapons.

- In October 1983, American marines were in Lebanon as a peacekeeping force in the Middle East conflict between Israel and the PLO. A terrorist attack killed 200 marines. The situation was unsettled when troops left in February 1984.

- Fearing the spread of Communism from Nicaragua throughout Central America, Reagan's administration funded the contras. Congress later cut off the controversial funds.

- Reagan's administration secretly sold weapons to Iran in 1986 in exchange for American hostages in Lebanon. The weapons money was used to fund the Nicaraguan contras, angering Congress after it had cut off funds.

- Several Libyan terrorist attacks killed Americans in 1985. Reagan cut off trade with Libya and froze their assets. When Libya fired on American planes and made more terrorist attacks in 1986, Reagan approved bombing Libyan military posts.

- The space program started up again in September 1988, when the space shuttle *Discovery* successfully lifted off.

- Vice President George H. W. Bush won the 1988 presidential election.

- Crime, drug abuse, and homelessness were social problems Bush faced. The Soviet Union and other Communist countries began to challenge Communism in the late 1980s.

Chapter 14 R E V I E W

On a sheet of paper, write the correct word or words from the Word Bank to complete each sentence.

Word Bank

apartheid

conservative

contras

deficit

economic

federal government

INF Treaty

Libya

sanctions

1. Reagan cut funds and limited spending to make people less dependent on the _____.

2. Reagan approved bombing military sites in _____ because of that country's terrorist attacks.

3. Mikhail Gorbachev and Reagan signed the _____ to limit nuclear weapons.

4. Sandra Day O'Connor was appointed a Supreme Court justice to make the court more _____.

5. Funds were given to the _____ because they wanted to overthrow Communism in Nicaragua.

6. The United States was against South Africa's policy of _____.

7. Congress overrode Reagan's veto of the bill to impose economic _____ on South Africa.

8. A large budget _____ faced President Bush at the start of his term.

9. Severe _____ problems in the Soviet Union led the Soviet people to begin to question Communism.

On a sheet of paper, write the letter of the answer that correctly completes each sentence.

10. An arms buildup was part of Reagan's hard line against the _____.

   A conservatives   **C** Soviet Union

   B contras   **D** Libyans

11. President Reagan's plan to decrease the power of the federal government was called _____.

   A Reaganomics   **C** apartheid

   B New Federalism   **D** the Economic Recovery Tax

12. In the election of 1988, the Republican Party chose _____ as its candidate.

    A Jesse Jackson   **C** Sandra Day O'Connor

    B Michael Dukakis   **D** George H. W. Bush

On a sheet of paper, write the answers to the following questions. Use complete sentences.

13. What were two social problems that challenged President Bush?

14. What were some "firsts" that happened for African Americans during the 1980s?

15. How did President Reagan want to solve problems with the economy?

16. What did the United States and the Soviet Union agree to do in the treaty they made in 1987?

17. What are developing countries?

18. Why did NASA wait to continue the space shuttle program after the Challenger exploded in 1986?

Critical Thinking On a sheet of paper, write your response to each question. Use complete sentences.

19. President Reagan wanted community problems to be solved by more volunteer efforts. In what ways do you think volunteers' efforts can be effective in solving community problems?

20. People demonstrated in the United States against South Africa's policies. How effective do you think demonstrations are in bringing about change? Explain.

Test-Taking Tip

If you are asked to compare and contrast things, be sure to tell how they are alike (compare) and how they are different (contrast).

The 1990s
1990–2000

World affairs continued to affect America in the 1990s. Communism in the Soviet Union ended, marking the true end of the cold war. At the same time, the Bush administration faced a new conflict in the Middle East with the nation of Iraq. This was the beginning of several conflicts America faced throughout the decade. In this chapter, you will learn about the 1990s.

Goals for Learning

◆ To explain how Communist rule in the Soviet Union ended

◆ To describe the Persian Gulf War

◆ To describe the policies and attempts at reform by the Clinton administration

◆ To explain the world conflicts involving America in the 1990s

◆ To list the problems and changes that took place in America during the 1990s

◆ To describe the beginning of the new millennium and the election of 2000

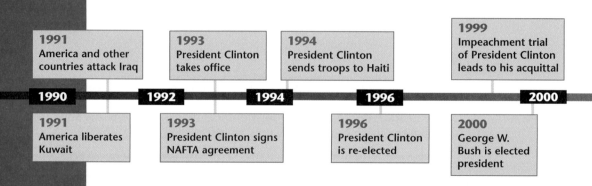

1991
America and other countries attack Iraq

1993
President Clinton takes office

1994
President Clinton sends troops to Haiti

1999
Impeachment trial of President Clinton leads to his acquittal

1990 | **1992** | **1994** | **1996** | **2000**

1991
America liberates Kuwait

1993
President Clinton signs NAFTA agreement

1996
President Clinton is re-elected

2000
George W. Bush is elected president

Reunification

Joining together as one country again

Conventional

Something that is traditional or commonly used

Summit

A meeting held between or among world leaders

In early 1990, East Germany held free elections. The new government was able to come to terms with West Germany. The four World War II nations (Australia, Canada, Great Britain, and the Soviet Union) agreed to free up their ties to either half of Berlin. After several meetings, East and West Germany agreed on **reunification.** This means they were joined into one nation again. This was made official October 3, 1990. By mid-1991, Berlin had been re-established as the capital of Germany.

What Was Done to Reduce Arms?

In the fall of 1990, the United States, the Soviet Union, and 20 other nations signed an agreement to decrease **conventional** military forces. It was known as the Conventional Forces in Europe (CFE) Treaty. The agreement set limits on military vehicles and arms in Europe.

President Bush and Soviet Premier Gorbachev held a **summit** in Moscow in 1991. A summit is a meeting held between or among world leaders. Each country agreed to reduce its store of intercontinental missiles. The Strategic Arms Reduction Treaty (START) called for 30 percent fewer missile systems within seven years of the treaty. This treaty became effective in 1994.

How Did Communism End in the Soviet Union?

Since 1949, the Soviet Union, also called the USSR, had kept economic control of many Eastern European countries. In 1991, these countries made an effort to cut their economic ties to the USSR. They looked to the West for new partnerships and financial help.

Glasnost

The Soviet policy of open discussion of political and social issues

Perestroika

The Soviet policy of economic and government reform

Commonwealth

A group of self-governing states

President Gorbachev of Russia tried to begin changes during the 1980s with his policies of **glasnost** and **perestroika.** Glasnost was open discussion of political and social issues. Perestroika was economic and government reform. However, citizens grew more and more dissatisfied. Newspapers began to run articles criticizing the government. All across the land, voters replaced many of the Communist leaders.

A group of Communists tried to overthrow Gorbachev in 1990. They held him hostage while they tried to capture Boris Yeltsin. Yeltsin was president of the Russian republic and an anti-Communist. However, thousands of citizens who assembled in Moscow in protest forced the rebels to give up. Shortly after that, Gorbachev resigned as general secretary of the Communist Party. However, he remained president of Russia.

In December 1991, three former Soviet republics—Russia, Ukraine, and Belarus—formed the Commonwealth of Independent States. A **commonwealth** is a group of self-governing states.

Russia and the Commonwealth of Independent States

Map Study How many independent states are shown on this map? Which is the largest?

Former Soviet-Influenced Countries

North Sea

IRELAND

GREAT BRITAIN

ATLANTIC OCEAN

SWEDEN
DENMARK

Baltic Sea

ESTONIA
LATVIA
LITHUANIA

NETH.

BEL.

LUX.

FRANCE

GERMANY

Former East-West German Border

POLAND

CZECH REP.

SLOVAKIA

SWITZ.

AUSTRIA

HUNGARY

SLOVENIA

ROMANIA

PORTUGAL

SPAIN

CROATIA

BOSNIA

SERBIA

BULGARIA

ITALY

MONTENEGRO

MACEDONIA

ALBANIA

GREECE

TURKEY

Mediterranean Sea

N W E S

0   200   400 Miles

Map Study

How many former Soviet-influenced countries are shown on this map?
Where is Poland located?

Vladimir Putin

The end of the USSR was made final by the resignation of Gorbachev as its president. President Yeltsin remained leader of the new Russian Federation. All but three of the former republics of the Soviet Union joined the commonwealth by 1995. These republics are Estonia, Latvia, and Lithuania. They are called the Baltic States.

Countries under Soviet control began to break away in the late 1980s and early 1990s. These included Hungary, Poland, and Czechoslovakia.

On December 31, 1999, Boris Yeltsin resigned as president of Russia. In March 2000, the Russian people elected Vladimir Putin president.

Then and Now

The Soviet Union (USSR) was founded in violence. During World War I, the Communists under Lenin staged a revolution in Russia. They overthrew and killed the tsar and other rulers. They then waged a civil war for power, executing thousands of other Russians. Over the decades, the Communists continued to use violence to add other countries to their territory.

In the early 1990s, the Soviet Union began to fall apart. Many people feared it would end as it began: violently. After the breakup of the Soviet Union in 1991, a period of violence and confusion occurred. However, in 2000 and 2004, Russia held its first free elections since the USSR began. Since then, Russia has moved more or less peacefully forward.

Word Bank

Commonwealth

glasnost

perestroika

reunification

summit

Lesson 1 Review On a sheet of paper, write the correct word from the Word Bank to complete each sentence.

1. All but three of the former Soviet republics became the _____ of Independent States.

2. German _____ was made official October 3, 1990.

3. A meeting between or among world leaders is called a _____.

4. _____ allowed open discussion of political and social issues.

5. _____ called for economic and government reform.

What do you think?

How do you think America was affected by the collapse of Communism in the Soviet Union?

In July 1990, a conflict developed in the Middle East between the nation of Iraq and its small neighbor, Kuwait. President Saddam Hussein of Iraq accused Kuwait of trying to keep oil prices low and of stealing oil from Iraq's wells.

Iraq threatened Kuwait by sending more than 100,000 troops to its border. Kuwait had only 20,000 soldiers. By the end of July, many oil-producing nations in the Persian Gulf agreed to raise the price of oil. Saddam Hussein seemed satisfied and said that he would not invade Kuwait.

What Happened When Iraq Invaded Kuwait?

On August 2, 1990, the Iraqi army invaded Kuwait. President Bush and other officials questioned whether Iraq should be allowed to conquer Kuwait. Kuwait was an independent country and member of the United Nations. In addition, they feared that Iraq might conquer oil-rich Saudi Arabia. Many nations, including the United States, were concerned about one nation controlling so much of an important natural resource.

On August 6, 1990, the United States and other members of the United Nations agreed to stop trading with Iraq in protest of the invasion. The UN said that the Iraqi army should leave Kuwait. The next day, President Bush sent American troops to protect Saudi Arabia. The military called it "Operation Desert Shield."

On November 29, the UN Security Council voted 12-2 to give Iraq until January 15, 1991, to pull out of Kuwait. If Iraq failed to meet this deadline, the United States and its UN allies could use armed force.

What Was "Operation Desert Storm"?

Diplomat

One skilled in negotiating between nations

Casualty

A person who is wounded, killed, or lost in action

Diplomats from several nations tried to get Iraq to leave Kuwait. A diplomat is a person skilled in negotiating between nations. The diplomats failed. On January 17, 1991, the United States, Great Britain, France, Saudi Arabia, Kuwait, and others launched an air attack against Iraq. "Operation Desert Shield" had become "Operation Desert Storm."

For five weeks, planes rained bombs on Iraq and Iraqi forces in Kuwait. Iraq launched missiles into Israel. Saddam Hussein wanted to draw Israel into the war. He hoped to force the Arab nations to join him in a fight with Israel. Although hit with many missiles, Israel did not enter the war.

Saddam Hussein received a final deadline to remove his army from Kuwait. When this deadline passed, the United States and its allies launched a large ground and air attack against Iraq. The ground war lasted only four days. Many Iraqi soldiers were killed; thousands surrendered to the allies. Many Iraqi civilians also died as a result of the war. The American and allied combat **casualties** during the war were about 370. A casualty is a person who is wounded, killed, or lost in action. Norman Schwarzkopf, commander of the allied forces, called it "miraculous" that there were not more allied troops killed. On February 27, 1991, President Bush announced to the nation, "Kuwait is liberated."

The United States and its allies used tanks and other vehicles to attack the Iraqi army.

During the Persian Gulf War, Arab and Western nations cooperated against a common enemy. President Bush felt that this cooperative spirit could help to bring a lasting peace to the Middle East. In March 1991, the president sent Secretary of State James Baker to the Middle East to meet with leaders. President Bush felt that the United States should help to build a "new world order" where the nations of the world seek to solve their conflicts peacefully.

Even though Saddam Hussein's army was defeated, Hussein remained in power. Problems in the Middle East remained in spite of Desert Storm.

Lesson 2 Review On a sheet of paper, write the answers to the following questions. Use complete sentences.

1. Why did Iraq invade Kuwait in 1990?
2. Why did Saddam Hussein want to draw Israel into the war?
3. Who was the commander of the allied forces?
4. Why was the United States concerned about one nation controlling so much oil?
5. Why did the UN Security Council give Iraq a deadline to pull out of Iraq?

What do you think?

The Persian Gulf War was caused in part over oil. Do you think it is necessary for America to be protective of oil? Why or why not?

Republicans backed the George H. W. Bush-Dan Quayle ticket for re-election in 1992. The Democrats chose Governor Bill Clinton of Arkansas as their presidential candidate. Senator Al Gore of Tennessee was Clinton's choice for vice president. Texas billionaire Ross Perot ran as an independent. Although the American people were pleased with the way President Bush handled the Persian Gulf War, many Americans were concerned about the economy. The unemployment rate was at an eight-year high and many families lived in poverty.

Clinton, who stressed the need for an improved economy, won the election. He took office in 1993. Perot had the best showing for a third-party candidate since Theodore Roosevelt ran for president in 1912.

The Democrats kept control of Congress, but more new people were elected to Congress in 1992 than in any year since 1948. Many longtime senators and representatives had not sought re-election. Many more women, African Americans, and

President Clinton took the oath of office in 1993. His daughter, Chelsea, (left) and his wife, Hillary Rodham Clinton, (right) were present for the ceremony.

Carol Mosely-Braun

Hispanic Americans had been elected. Carol Mosely-Braun of Illinois became the first African American woman to be elected to the Senate.

What Was NAFTA?

In December 1992, the governments of the United States, Mexico, and Canada approved the North American Free Trade Agreement (NAFTA).

Under this agreement, limits on investments, trade, and services among the three North American countries would be stopped over a 15 year period. The three countries now formed a giant market of goods and services. Mexico, a major importer of American goods and agricultural services, would stop its huge tariffs. The United States would also free Mexican imports of duties. The NAFTA agreement was signed into law by President Clinton in late 1993 and went into effect in January 1994. The NAFTA agreement led to more U.S. exports to both Canada and Mexico.

What Reforms Did President Clinton Attempt?

President Clinton proposed lowering the federal deficit by $496 billion over five years. After some changes, the bill passed in 1993. It included plans for both tax increases and budget cuts.

The Brady Bill was passed in 1993. It was named for James Brady, who was shot and permanently injured during the assassination attempt on President Reagan in 1981. This bill set a five-day waiting period for the purchase of a handgun. It also set up a national computer network to check on the criminal record and age of a person who wanted to buy a gun.

Congress passed the Omnibus Violent Crime Control and Prevention Act in 1994. The word *omnibus* means it contains many things at once. Under this act, local governments would be given power to hire 100,000 new police officers. It also called for new state prisons and crime-prevention programs. This bill also banned certain weapons and increased the number of crimes punishable by death.

Largely aided by First Lady Hillary Rodham Clinton, the president proposed huge changes in the nation's health care system to provide less expensive medical care for all Americans. Under this system, employers would have to pay most of their employees' insurance costs. After many attempts at a compromise between supporters and opponents of the plan, Congress rejected it.

Lesson 3 Review On a sheet of paper, write the answers to the following questions. Use complete sentences.

1. What was the focus of the 1992 presidential election?

2. How did the makeup of Congress change in 1992?

3. What was the NAFTA agreement?

4. What was the Brady Bill?

5. What was the Omnibus Violent Crime Control and Prevention Act?

What do you think?

Do you think the government should find a way to give all people health care? Why or why not?

During the first years of his administration, President Clinton became involved in changes affecting many other countries. Although the United States was not directly involved in many of these, it helped to promote peace or to provide aid to these other countries.

Famine

Widespread starvation

Writing About History

Find a newspaper or magazine article about a country that is experiencing famine. Write a paragraph about the hardships the people face and the reasons for the famine, if that information is available.

What Happened in Somalia?

Civil war, drought, and **famine** cost thousands of lives and threatened many more in the African nation of Somalia by 1992. America and the UN sent troops to Somalia in 1992 to bring food to Somalia's starving people. However, severe American casualties led the United States to pull out the troops by 1994. The UN pulled out its troops by 1995. While the efforts had saved millions of Somalians from starvation, the problems in that country remained.

What Middle East Peace Treaty Was Signed?

In 1993, President Clinton hosted an important summit between Israel's Prime Minister Yitzhak Rabin and Yasir Arafat of the Palestine Liberation Organization (PLO). There he witnessed the signing of a peace agreement between those two leaders that ended their 46-year war. However, tensions remain between Israel and the PLO.

What Deal Was Made with Russia and Ukraine?

President Clinton and Russian President Yeltsin met in Moscow in January 1994 to discuss further ways to curb the threat of nuclear war. They agreed that neither would aim strategic weapons at the other country. Clinton also convinced Ukraine President Kravchuk to take down that country's nuclear arsenal. Ukraine did so in exchange for $1 billion in U.S. aid and a promise of American protection in case of attack.

When Did South African Apartheid End?

Nelson Mandela

In 1994, Nelson Mandela became the first black president of South Africa. Apartheid in that country came to an end. Economic sanctions by the United States and other nations had put pressure on the South African government. Following adoption of a new constitution, the sanctions were lifted. President Clinton offered financial assistance to help strengthen the South African economy.

How Did Relations Improve with Vietnam?

Persecute

To treat someone poorly or violently because of his or her religious beliefs or ethnic background

More than 20 years after the Vietnam War, many Americans were still missing in action from the war. However, in 1995 President Clinton announced that there would be full diplomatic relations with Vietnam. Since then, Vietnam has released information about missing soldiers.

What Occurred in Bosnia-Herzegovina?

America became involved in a conflict in Bosnia-Herzegovina, part of the former Yugoslavia. Three-way fighting broke out between Croats, Bosnian Serbs, and Muslims in 1992. In 1993, America parachuted food and medicines to Muslims being **persecuted** by Serbs. Fighting continued even after a cease-fire was called in 1994. NATO began a series of air strikes against Bosnian Serbs, and UN peacekeepers were sent to the area. Bosnian Serbs took more than 350 UN peacekeepers hostage to discourage air strikes.

By 1995, the warring parties agreed to a cease-fire. A peace agreement sponsored by the United States in 1995 ended fighting by 1996. However, the war left many people homeless. In 1997, the International Criminal Tribunal tried a number of Bosnian leaders for war crimes. Human rights continue to be a big issue in this area of the world.

What Problems Developed with Haiti and Cuba?

President Clinton had met with removed Haitian President Jean-Bertrand Aristide in 1993. Clinton appealed to the UN for help in restoring Aristide to power. In September 1994, President Clinton sent out 23 warships and 20,000 troops to restore the Aristide government.

Thousands of Cubans, wanting to escape unpleasant living conditions in their homeland, fled to the United States. In the fall of 1994, after negotiations with Cuba, the United States agreed to allow 20,000 Cubans per year to enter this country. Cuban officials promised to encourage citizens to remain in their homeland.

Biography

Trevor Ferrell: 1972–

A cold December night in 1983 changed Trevor Ferrell's life forever. Trevor, who lived near Philadelphia, was only 11 years old at the time. He heard a news story about shelters for homeless people. The story shocked him. He talked his parents into driving downtown. There, the family gave blankets to the homeless. Soon the family took food and clothing downtown every night. People heard about Trevor's work and offered much support. A TV drama was made about Trevor, and President Reagan also honored him.

Trevor and his family started Trevor's Place, a homeless shelter. At age 18, Trevor left his organization, Trevor's Campaign. He did not like the public attention. Today, Trevor continues to help the less fortunate. He runs a thrift shop, and sometimes he gives speeches. "For me, it's a selfish thing. I've always enjoyed being around people, real people. It's what I've liked to do since I was 11 years old."

Lesson 4 Review Choose the best word in parentheses to complete each sentence. Write your answers on a sheet of paper.

1. America and the UN sent troops to (Bosnia, Somalia, Haiti) in 1992 to bring food to that country's starving people.

2. President Clinton met with Russian President (Rabin, Yeltsin, Aristide) in Moscow to discuss further ways to curb the threat of nuclear harm.

3. Apartheid ended in 1994 in (South Africa, Vietnam, Haiti).

4. A peace agreement sponsored by the United States ended fighting in (Haiti, Russia, Bosnia-Herzegovina) by 1996.

5. President Clinton sent 23 warships and 20,000 troops to restore the Aristide government in (Haiti, Vietnam, South Africa) in 1994.

What do you think?

Do you think it is America's responsibility to feed starving people in other countries? Why or why not?

Technology Connection

E-mail

E-mail might seem a complicated system, but it really is simple. Businesses called Internet service providers (ISPs) provide e-mail addresses. An address with an "@" symbol is needed to send or receive messages. The address acts as an address in the same way an address for regular mail does. It directs messages to the correct mailbox. ISP software lets users read, compose, and send images and attachments.

The problem of spam has grown with e-mail's popularity. Spam is annoying "junk e-mail." Spammers send these unwanted advertisements to thousands, or even millions, of people at once. Processing so many messages slows the efficiency of ISPs and frustrates e-mail users. Some countries have created laws to discourage the use of spam. Despite this problem, e-mail will most likely continue to fill an important role in daily life.

Speaker of the House

The leader of the United States House of Representatives

In 1994, the Republicans gained control of both houses of Congress for the first time since 1954. A new Republican plan called the "Contract with America" had been introduced. It was intended to balance the budget. Representative Newt Gingrich of Georgia introduced the plan. He became **Speaker of the House** in 1995.

Congress proposed a bill calling for a constitutional amendment for a balanced federal budget by the year 2002. The bill passed the House, but it was rejected by the Senate. A second bill that called for term limits for members of Congress was defeated in the House of Representatives. A third bill, however, was passed and signed into law by President Clinton. It said that the federal government could not make demands on states unless the government provided federal money for the cost of carrying out those demands.

What Was the Whitewater Affair?

Beginning in 1993, President Clinton and First Lady Hillary Rodham Clinton faced accusations in what became known as the Whitewater Affair. The Clintons were part owners of a company called the Whitewater Development Corporation in the 1970s. The company was backed by Madison Savings and Loan. A federal investigation found illegal political campaign contributions, income tax fraud, and other wrongdoings to be linked to Whitewater and Madison Savings and Loan. The Clintons denied that they took part in the illegal acts. Despite what seemed to be a scandal, Congressional hearings in 1995 found nothing to prove the Clintons took part in anything illegal.

What Terrorism Occurred on American Soil?

Buildings on American soil were targets of major acts of **terrorism** in the 1990s. In 1993, a bomb exploded in the parking garage of the World Trade Center in New York City. Six people were killed and more than 1,000 were injured. The next year four men were found guilty of charges connected with that bombing.

In 1995, a car bomb exploded next to the Murrah Federal Building in Oklahoma City, Oklahoma, killing 168 people, including 19 children. This was the worst terrorist bombing that had taken place on American soil. In 1997 Timothy McVeigh was found guilty of the bombing and executed.

In 1996, President Clinton signed antiterrorism legislation. This included stiffer penalties for terrorist actions and new methods to prevent terrorism.

A car bomb destroyed much of Oklahoma City's Murrah Federal Building in 1995.

What Was the Million Man March?

In October 1995, hundreds of thousands of African American men took part in the Million Man March in Washington, D.C. The purpose of the march was to show a sense of responsibility toward family and community. President Clinton praised the objectives of the people who participated in the rally.

Arson

The act of purposely setting fire to something

Running mate

A candidate who runs for office with a candidate who is running for another position

Incumbent

A person who currently holds a certain position or office

What Reform Legislation Was Approved?

A number of bills first introduced in Congress right after Clinton took office were passed. A welfare reform bill passed in 1996 reduced federal help to the poor. The bill gave more responsibility for dealing with poverty to the states. Under this bill, direct federal government payments to the poor were replaced by block grants to states. These grants were to be used for the poor under federal guidelines.

A health care reform bill was passed. Under this bill, an American worker could keep health insurance after leaving the company that provided it. It also became illegal for insurance companies to drop customers because of a medical condition.

Upon signing a minimum wage bill in 1996, President Clinton claimed that it would enable "10 million workers to raise stronger families." The minimum wage was raised 90 cents an hour to $5.15.

What Racial Terrorism Took Place?

In the mid-1990s, arsonists began to burn churches because of hate and racism. **Arson** is setting fire to something on purpose. Most of these church burnings took place in the southern and midwestern states. Between 1990 and January 1999, arsonists set on fire 829 churches in the United States. Of these, 376, or 45 percent, were African American churches. People in the communities, many of them white, worked together to rebuild the burnt-out churches.

Who Won the 1996 Election?

In 1996, Republicans nominated Senator Robert Dole of Kansas as their presidential candidate. Former congressman Jack Kemp was his **running mate.** Again, Ross Perot ran as the candidate of the independent Reform Party. The **incumbent** ticket of Bill Clinton and Al Gore was the Democratic Party's choice. An incumbent is a person who currently holds a certain position or office. President Clinton was re-elected by a wide margin.

On December 19, 1998, the U.S. House of Representatives approved two articles of impeachment against President Clinton. They accused him of lying under oath and of obstructing justice in an effort to conceal an extramarital affair with Monica Lewinsky. She had been an intern at the White House.

On February 12, 1999, the Senate acquitted the president. He had been only the second president to be impeached. (Andrew Johnson was the first, in 1868. He, too, was acquitted.)

Lesson 5 Review Choose the word or name in parentheses that best completes each sentence.

1. In 1994, the (Democratic, Republican, Independent Reform) Party gained control of both houses of Congress for the first time since 1952.

2. In 1997, (Timothy McVeigh, Newt Gingrich, Robert Dole) was found guilty of bombing the Federal Building in Oklahoma City, Oklahoma.

3. (Ross Perot, Jack Kemp, Bill Clinton) was elected president in 1996.

4. President Clinton was the (first, second, third) president to be impeached.

5. Ross Perot represented the (Democratic, Republican, Independent Reform) Party in the election of 1996.

What do you think?

In 1996, Ross Perot ran for president as the candidate of the Reform Party. Do you think that such "third party" candidates help or hurt the campaign and election process? Explain your answer.

Millennium

A period of 1,000 years

Geography Note

The world is more of a global village than ever before. Countries and regions are linked closely. For example, the United States imports most of the oil it needs to produce its goods. The oil comes from many foreign countries. American goods are shipped to many countries, including the countries from which the United States bought the oil to begin with.

How Did the World Celebrate the New Millennium?

As the year 2000 approached, nations around the world prepared to celebrate the ending of the second **millennium.** (A millennium represents 1,000 years.) The world began to celebrate on December 31, 1999, and continued until January 1, 2001. That date marked the beginning of the third millennium.

Some people feared that many computers had not been programmed to move from the 1900s to the year 2000. People called this problem "the Y2K Bug." (In metric measurements, *K* stands for 1,000.) Some people stockpiled food and water. They bought guns in case Y2K brought riots. However, December 31, 1999, easily turned into January 1, 2000.

One concern in the year 2000 was the rising price of gasoline. Many Americans blamed the Organization of Petroleum Exporting Countries (OPEC) for not increasing their production of oil. Around the country, people also worried about the rising price of heating oil and natural gas.

What Happened in the 2000 Election?

In 2000, Republicans nominated Texas Governor George W. Bush as their presidential candidate. He is the son of George H. W. Bush, president from 1989 to 1993. Dick Cheney, a former secretary of defense, was the Republican running mate. Pat Buchanan was the Reform Party candidate. Ralph Nader was nominated by the Green Party.

The Democrats nominated Al Gore as their presidential candidate. Gore had served as vice president during the eight years that Bill Clinton was president. Joseph Lieberman, a U.S. senator from Connecticut, was the Democratic running mate.

During the fall of 2000, the candidates for president debated their differences on the use of the budget surplus and how to handle Social Security. They argued over education and the military.

Democratic candidate Al Gore won the popular vote nationally, but did not win the presidency. The popular vote is the total number of votes cast in a presidential election. George W. Bush, the Republican candidate, won the electoral vote and the presidency. This is not the first time a presidential candidate has won the popular vote but not the electoral vote.

The Electoral College system was set up by the Constitution. It gives each state a number of electoral votes equal to the number of U.S. Senators plus the number of its U.S. Representatives. If a state has two senators and eight representatives, that state will have 10 electoral votes. There are a total of 538 electoral votes. A presidential candidate needs 270 electoral votes to win the election. Citizens vote for the president and vice president by name, but they are actually voting for an elector. The electors will vote for that president and vice president when the Electoral College meets following the election.

Florida became the deciding state in the 2000 election. The vote was too close to call. Without the Florida electoral votes, Al Gore had 266 electoral votes and George W. Bush had 246 electoral votes. Both candidates needed the 25 electoral votes from Florida to win.

George W. Bush received several hundred more votes than Al Gore. When a vote is this close, a recount is required. Many problems occurred during the recount. The United States Supreme Court ordered the recount stopped. It then heard the lawyers for both sides argue their case. On December 12, the United States Supreme Court ruled that the recount process in Florida could not continue. Al Gore conceded the election. George W. Bush became the 43rd president of the United States in January 2001.

Civics Connection

Conflicts Outside the United States

The United States Constitution protects the rights and freedoms of American citizens. It is the basis for democracy. However, not all nations are democracies. Some governments are controlled by dictators who have absolute power. They use the military to keep control. They may abuse human rights or try to take other lands by force. Conflicts result, and they can threaten an entire region.

For much of its history, the United States tried to avoid conflicts with other countries. Protecting the American people from war was important. Today, however, the United States has a more global view. Nations are connected in many ways. Conflicts in other parts of the world affect the United States. In addition, nuclear weapons have changed the security of the world. Nuclear weapons give nations the power to destroy other nations. Future wars might involve their use. This must be avoided. Therefore, it is important to solve world conflicts quickly and at a local level.

1. Do you think American soldiers should be sent to fight in other countries? Explain.

2. How do you think local governments can help solve world conflicts?

Word Bank

Al Gore

Florida

George W. Bush

oil prices

millennium

Lesson 6 Review On a sheet of paper, write the correct word or words from the Word Bank to complete each sentence.

1. The Republican presidential candidate in 2000 was _____.

2. The Democratic presidential candidate in 2000 was _____.

3. The deciding state in the 2000 election was _____.

4. The year 2001 began the third _____.

5. One of the challenges facing the United States and the world in 2000 was _____.

What do you think?

From what you know of the Electoral College, what do you think should happen for future elections?

"Favor Positive Themes"

Luis Morales is a former president of the Public Relations Society of America. In April 1996, he gave a speech entitled "Favor Positive Themes." Although he was speaking to business people, his message applies to all Americans.

"It seems to me that lost in the noise of political issues, lost in the . . . self-serving groups, is one issue that transcends everything else. . . . 'citizenship.'

Perhaps my own ethnic background makes me more conscious of this than most, but it does seem to me that the most pervasive issue facing us is the decline of America's traditional values. . . . We are rude, uncivil to one another, selfish to a fault, and uninterested or ignorant of our history. . . .

It is entirely within our field . . . to encourage respect and respectability and a sense of community. . . .

What can we do [to make change?] . . .

First, we can inform ourselves. Broaden our reading habits. Besides the major . . . periodicals, read some thoughtful books. . . .

We can expose ourselves to the thinking and ideas of others. . . . When we address the issues of diversity and multiculturalism, we will do so evenhandedly. We will become more aware and appreciative of the value and richness [of] a diverse society and workforce. . . .

We . . . can . . . promote a positive view of America. . . .

But we desperately need to recover our moral balance. . . . I urge you to join me in . . . regaining a sense of community, rebuilding our self-respect by respecting others. . . ."

Document-Based Questions

1. What is the issue that Morales says has gotten lost?

2. According to Morales, what is the largest overall issue facing Americans?

3. What is one thing he suggests people can do to make change?

4. What does Morales say we need to regain and rebuild?

5. How does Morales' view of citizenship agree or disagree with your view of it?

Source: Speech by Luis W. Morales, Vital Speeches, July 15, 1996.

Chapter 15 S U M M A R Y

■ East and West Germany were reunified in 1990.

■ In 1990, Iraq invaded Kuwait. In response, "Operation Desert Shield" sent American troops to protect Saudi Arabia from the Iraqi army. In 1991, America and its allies liberated Kuwait and caused severe casualties to the Iraqi army.

■ Communism collapsed in the Soviet Union in 1991. All but three of the former Soviet republics joined to form the Commonwealth of Independent States by 1995.

■ President Clinton took office in 1993. He signed the NAFTA agreement in 1993 to reduce restrictions on trade with Canada and Mexico.

■ President Clinton sent a number of proposals to Congress and proposed huge changes to the health care system. Congress rejected Clinton's initial health care plans.

■ Beginning in 1992, America experienced much foreign involvement. America improved relations with Russia, the Ukraine, South Africa, and Vietnam, and worked with Israeli and Arab leaders to form a peace agreement. It was also involved militarily in Somalia, Bosnia-Herzegovina, and Haiti.

■ Beginning in 1993, the Clintons were investigated for wrongdoings in what became known as the Whitewater Affair.

■ In 1994, Republicans gained control of Congress and implemented their plan called the "Contract with America." Among the ideas of this plan was to balance the federal budget by 2002.

■ Terrorism began to occur on American soil in 1993.

■ Welfare reform and minimum wage bills were passed in 1996.

■ In 1995, the Million Man March took place in Washington, D.C. It focused on the responsibilities of African American men toward family and community.

■ In 1998, the U.S. House of Representatives approved two articles of impeachment against President Clinton. In early 1999, the U.S. Senate held an impeachment trial. The Senate acquitted President Clinton.

■ George W. Bush, governor of Texas, became president in January 2001.

Chapter 15   R E V I E W

On a sheet of paper, write the word or words from the Word Bank to complete each sentence.

Word Bank

Al Gore

Boris Yeltsin

Brady Bill

Commonwealth of Independent States

Desert Storm

Bill Clinton

Kuwait

millennium

Million Man March

NAFTA

Newt Gingrich

Saddam Hussein

1. All but three of the Soviet republics formed the _____.

2. _____ was the president of Russia in 1994.

3. Iraq attacked _____ in 1990.

4. The American ground attack on Iraq was called Operation _____.

5. The _____ agreement reduced limits on trade among Canada, America, and Mexico.

6. The leader of Iraq during the Persian Gulf War was _____.

7. The _____ focused on the responsibilities of African American men.

8. _____ took office as president in 1993.

9. The _____ put more controls on guns in America.

10. _____ and the Republican Congress proposed the "Contract with America."

11. During the year 2000, people celebrated the start of the third _____, which began on January 1, 2001.

12. The Democratic candidate in the 2000 election was _____.

On a sheet of paper, write the letter of the answer that correctly completes each sentence.

13. The organization that decides how much oil to produce is called _____.

    A NAFTA   **C** OPEC

    B Desert Shield   **D** the Electoral College

14. The Strategic Arms Reduction Treaty called for 30 percent fewer _____ within seven years.

   A political parties   **C** petroleum exports

   B missile systems   **D** candidates

15. In 1995, America sponsored a peace agreement to end fighting in _____.

   A Bosnia-Herzegovina   **C** South Africa

   B Somalia   **D** Cuba

On a sheet of paper, write the answer to each question. Use complete sentences.

16. What became of the Soviet Union?

17. What was the purpose of the Contract with America?

18. There were many changes throughout the world in the 1990s. What were two of them?

Critical Thinking On a sheet of paper, write your response to each question. Use complete sentences.

19. Are events such as the Million Man March helpful in making positive changes in the United States? Explain your answer.

20. Do you think it is the responsibility of the United States to help developing countries? Explain your answer.

Test-Taking Tip

Avoid waiting until the night before a test to study. Plan your time so that you can get a good night's sleep the night before a test.

The 21st Century Begins
2001–Present

As the 21st century began, the people and leaders of America had many fears. Some were concerned about the economy and health care. Others were troubled by global issues like war, poverty, and the environment.

Sadly, the new century began with tragedy. On September 11, 2001, terrorists attacked the United States. These attacks killed many Americans and others from around the world. The attacks also changed the lives of all American citizens. In this chapter, you will learn about these attacks and the events that followed. You will also learn about other political, social, and scientific concerns of this time.

Goals for Learning

◆ To define terrorism and describe the terrorist attacks of September 11, 2001

◆ To describe the wars in Afghanistan and Iraq

◆ To list the events following the war in Iraq

◆ To describe the presidential election of 2004

◆ To describe life in the United States at the beginning of the 21st century

September 2001
Terrorists attack New York City and Washington, D.C.

October 2001
Patriot Act is signed into law

November 2002
Department of Homeland Security is created

May 2003
President Bush declares that major fighting is over in Iraq

November 2004
President George W. Bush is re-elected

2001   **2002**   **2003**   **2004**

October 2001
United States and Great Britain attack Afghanistan

March 2003
United States and Great Britain invade Iraq

December 2003
Saddam Hussein is captured

Al Qaeda

The terrorist group that attacked New York City and Washington, D.C., on September 11, 2001

9/11

The shortened name for the terrorist attacks on September 11, 2001

Who Are Terrorists?

Terrorists use violence to frighten people and leaders. They hope this fear will allow their demands to be met. There are many kinds of terrorists. National terrorists want to change the government or create their own nation on land controlled by someone else. Religious terrorists want to force people to follow their religious beliefs. Environmental terrorists want to bring attention to the destruction of the natural environment.

What Terrorism Took Place in 2001?

In January 2001, George W. Bush became president of the United States. As the former governor of Texas, he had little experience with world problems. President Bush was more concerned with solving problems at home. The president and American citizens were not prepared for terrorism. Americans had experienced terrorism before, but nothing like what happened on September 11, 2001. On that day, terrorists attacked New York City and Washington, D.C.

A terrorist group headed by a man named Osama bin Laden planned these attacks. The terrorist group is called **Al Qaeda.** On that day in September, 19 Al Qaeda terrorists, in three groups, crashed airplanes into buildings in New York City and Washington, D.C. For Americans, the day came to be known simply as **9/11.**

On September 11, 2001, terrorists flew an airplane into each of the twin towers of the World Trade Center in New York City.

Both World Trade Center towers fell to the ground after the terrorist attacks.

Hijack

To steal an occupied vehicle by use of force

The first attack struck the two towers of the World Trade Center in New York City. Terrorists **hijacked** two passenger planes, meaning they took over the planes by use of force. The terrorists flew a plane into each of the World Trade Center's twin buildings. The jet fuel in the crashing planes started a huge fire. Hundreds of people were trapped inside each tower.

The fire soon weakened the buildings, and they came crashing to the ground. Almost 2,800 people died. Hundreds more were injured.

The second attack was aimed at the Pentagon building outside Washington, D.C. The Pentagon is the huge, five-sided headquarters for the U.S. Department of Defense. As they did with the Trade Center, the terrorists crashed a passenger plane into the Pentagon. At the Pentagon, 189 people were killed and many were injured.

The terrorists wanted to attack a third target. This target was thought to be the White House or the Capitol building in Washington, D.C. These buildings were never attacked because the fourth hijacked plane crashed in a field in Pennsylvania.

The passengers and crew decided to fight the hijackers and take control of the plane. Some of the passengers had learned about the attacks on New York City and Washington, D.C., by using their cell phones. Their heroic actions prevented another terrorist attack. Unfortunately, the crash killed all 40 people on board.

How Did the American People and Government React to the Terrorist Attacks?

The terrorist attacks on the United States shocked Americans. But in spite of this horrible event, thousands of Americans acted very bravely. **Patriotism,** or pride in one's own country, increased. Suddenly American flags were flying everywhere. Patriotic songs were playing on radio and television and sung at public gatherings.

In New York City, hundreds of firefighters and police officers died trying to save people trapped in the World Trade Center towers before their collapse. The attacks created many heroes. Rudy Giuliani, the mayor of New York City, was widely praised for the way he handled the crisis in his city.

President Bush announced that the "war on terrorism . . . will be the focus of my administration from now on." To protect the nation from future terrorist attacks, the president created the Department of Homeland Security. Congress passed a new law called the Patriot Act in October 2001.

Many Americans gathered together to remember those killed in the terrorist attacks.

What Is the Purpose of the Patriot Act?

The Patriot Act gave the government new powers to fight terrorism. It allowed the government to get court approval to secretly search the homes and businesses of suspected terrorists without showing a search warrant. It also allowed the government to use a court order to get information about e-mail and Internet usage of suspected terrorists. Business, medical, library, and bookstore records of suspected terrorists could also be seized, if there was court approval. Some people believed the Patriot Act gave too much power to the executive branch of government. They feared that the constitutional rights of American citizens would be violated.

What Is the Department of Homeland Security?

President Bush created the new Office of Homeland Security in October 2001. It became the Department of Homeland Security in November 2002. It is responsible for seeing that more than 22 federal agencies work together to protect American citizens. State law enforcement agencies are also involved in homeland security. The federal government took more control over airport and seaport security.

Why Was the United States Attacked?

The buildings that were attacked are well-known symbols of American economic and political power. The World Trade Center was a symbol of America's economic power. The Pentagon is a symbol of America's military power. The White House and the Capitol building are symbols of America's democracy.

Osama bin Laden hated the United States for many reasons. He did not like that the United States supported the country of Israel. He wanted the United States to remove its troops from the Middle East. He believed that American economic and political power were changing traditional ways of life in the Middle East.

Osama bin Laden wanted to show that the United States could be a successful target of terrorism. He wanted to prove that his terrorist group could destroy important symbols of American power. By doing this he hoped to get other terrorists to attack Americans at home and abroad.

What do you think?

Do you think the Patriot Act restricts the rights of Americans? Do you think it was necessary? Explain.

Lesson 1 Review On a sheet of paper, write the answers to the following questions. Use complete sentences.

1. What is terrorism?

2. What terrorism occurred on September 11, 2001?

3. Why were the World Trade Center and the Pentagon buildings attacked?

4. What is the purpose of the Patriot Act?

5. What is the purpose of the Department of Homeland Security?

Biography

Colin Powell: (1937–)
Colin Powell was born April 5, 1937, in New York City. His parents emigrated from Jamaica, an island country southeast of the United States. After graduating from the City College of New York, Powell attended military school. Beginning as an army lieutenant, Powell rose through the ranks. He served in Vietnam starting in 1962, then again from 1968 to 1969. At his retirement, Powell was a general in the U.S. Army. He earned a master of business administration degree, held several government posts, and directed the first Gulf War in 1991. Beginning in 2001, Powell served as the secretary of state to George W. Bush. He has received many awards for his military and nonmilitary service. Powell is widely admired around the world.

Taliban

The group that controlled the government of Afghanistan

Al Qaeda had headquarters in Afghanistan. Because of this, the war on terror started there in October 2001. President Bush called America's response to 9/11 "the war on terror."

How Did the War on Terror Begin?

A group called the **Taliban** controlled the government of Afghanistan. Under Taliban rule, females could not go to school or work outside the home. Television was banned. Harsh punishment was given to anyone who disobeyed their rules. Osama bin Laden and Al Qaeda were allowed to train in Afghanistan. The United States and the United Nations warned the Taliban to turn over Osama bin Laden and other terrorists or face war.

After repeated warnings, the United States and Great Britain began bombing Afghanistan on October 7, 2001. Some Afghan soldiers had been fighting the Taliban for years. With the help of these troops and bombings, the Taliban soon fell apart, but Osama bin Laden was not found.

The people of Afghanistan were very poor before the war started. After the war, the United States and other nations helped Afghanistan rebuild. In June 2002, Hamid Karzai became the president of Afghanistan. A new government was formed with the goal of creating a democracy.

The Afghanistan war destroyed most of the training camps and headquarters of Al Qaeda. It also removed the Taliban from power. More than three years after the attacks on the United States, Osama bin Laden still had not been captured. Many Al Qaeda leaders had not been found. Al Qaeda appeared to still be active.

Weapons of mass destruction

Weapons that cause death on a large scale

Geography Note

Iraq borders the Persian Gulf between the countries of Iran, Turkey, Syria, Jordan, Saudi Arabia, and Kuwait. Most of the land is desert, but there are mountains in northern Iraq. The country is about twice the size of the state of Idaho and is home to about 25 million people. Desertification, or the destruction of good soil to form a desert, is a major problem, and there is a shortage of water.

Why Did the United States Believe Saddam Hussein Was a Threat?

In the fall of 2002, the United States turned its attention to Iraq and its leader, Saddam Hussein. The United States thought that Hussein was a threat to them and to other nations of the world.

In 1991, the United States had led a military force that defeated the Iraqi army. This followed Hussein's invasion of Kuwait, a neighboring country. After this war, called the Persian Gulf War, it was thought that Hussein was hiding **weapons of mass destruction.** These are weapons that cause death on a large scale. Hussein was told to destroy these weapons in 1991. By 2000, some believed that he was trying to create nuclear weapons. They believed he would give them to terrorist groups.

What Caused the Invasion of Iraq?

By fall 2002, United States leaders believed that it did not matter whether Iraq and Al Qaeda were linked. President Bush said, "You can't distinguish between Al Qaeda and Saddam when you talk about the war on terror."

The United Nations Security Council warned Iraq that it would face "serious consequences" if it did not cooperate with the United Nations inspectors searching for weapons of mass destruction. France, Germany, and other countries in the United Nations argued that Iraq should be given more time to cooperate. The United States and Great Britain disagreed. On March 19, 2003, the United States and Great Britain invaded Iraq.

How Long Did the Iraq War Last?

American and British troops moved quickly into the country from the south. In three weeks, the capital city of Baghdad was under the control of the United States and Great Britain. On April 15, President Bush said that the government of Saddam Hussein no longer existed. In early May 2003, Bush declared that the war was over. However, American soldiers continued to die.

History in Your Life

The Life-Changing Attacks of September 11
Many people have said that the attacks of September 11, 2001, changed life in the United States. Short-term changes included stopping all U.S. air traffic for a brief period, a shutdown of the stock markets, and other measures.

Long-term changes will be felt for many years to come. Several government agencies responsible for the safety of the United States were combined into the Department of Homeland Security. Airports and public buildings saw increased security. Economically, the U.S. had been in a recession, and the attacks sharply increased the effects. Unemployment climbed. Several major airlines suffered financial problems because travelers were afraid to travel on airplanes.

Lesson 2 Review On a sheet of paper, write the answers to the following questions. Use complete sentences.

1. Why did the war on terror begin in Afghanistan?

2. What was the Taliban?

3. What freedoms did the Taliban deny its people?

4. What was it believed that Saddam Hussein was hiding?

5. Why did President Bush say in May 2003 that the war in Iraq was over?

What do you think?

Do you think the United States and Great Britain had the right to attack Afghanistan? Explain your answer.

Saddam Hussein

After the main fighting ended in Iraq, the United States and allied forces remained there. Soldiers searched for weapons of mass destruction. They also wanted to find Saddam Hussein and to change Iraq into a new democratic nation.

Were Weapons of Mass Destruction Found?

By the end of 2003, no weapons of mass destruction had been found. But the graves of thousands of people murdered by Hussein's government were found. On December 13, 2003, Saddam Hussein was captured by American soldiers. President Bush said Hussein would face justice.

What Was Iraq Like After the War?

Nearly 130,000 American and British soldiers remained in Iraq. The United States and Great Britain wanted to create a new democratic Iraq. That was not an easy goal. In the 1980s, Iraq had fought a long war with Iran. This had left Iraq a poor country. Hussein's government had done little to improve the lives of its citizens.

The Iraqi economy had to be rebuilt. After the invasion, Iraq had no army. It had no police force. Looting and robbery increased. Water and electrical systems had been damaged. The United States and Great Britain hoped that Iraq's huge supply of oil would help pay for its reconstruction. However, Iraq's oil wells needed many costly repairs.

At first the American government said that it did not need support from the United Nations to remain in Iraq. But that changed after American soldiers began dying in terrorist attacks. It was hoped that soldiers from other countries would help American and British troops. The cost of rebuilding Iraq would be billions of dollars. By September 2003, the United States and Great Britain sought more military and financial help for Iraq from United Nations members. President Bush asked Congress for $87 billion to pay for the reconstruction of Iraq and Afghanistan.

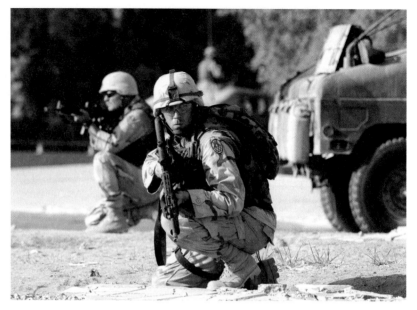

American forces remained in Iraq after President Bush said the war had ended.

Some believe that the United States and other countries will have to stay in Iraq for many years. How long it will take to make Iraq a democratic country controlled by its own people is unknown. However, there are plans in place for elections to be held in 2005. Between March 2003 and the end of November 2004, the number of U.S. service members killed was 1,256.

Lesson 3 Review On a sheet of paper, write the answers to the following questions. Use complete sentences.

1. Why did U.S. military forces remain in Iraq?

2. What happened to Saddam Hussein?

3. What problems did Iraq have after the war?

4. How did the United States and Great Britain hope to pay for rebuilding Iraq?

5. Why did the United States ask the United Nations for help?

President George W. Bush campaigned for a second term as president.

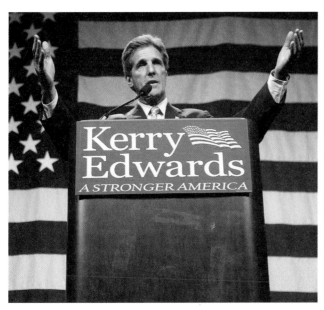

Massachusetts Senator John Kerry was the Democratic candidate for president.

As the presidential election of 2004 approached, people were considering many issues. Terrorism, the war in Iraq, education, healthcare, prescription drug costs, the environment, and the economy were all concerns.

Republican George W. Bush hoped to win a second term in the White House. Bush's running mate was Vice President Dick Cheney. His challenger, Democratic Senator John Kerry from Massachusetts, thought he could do a better job as president. Kerry's running mate was Senator John Edwards of North Carolina. Four debates on TV between the candidates made their positions clearer. But few people said they changed their minds because of the debates.

The war in Iraq proved to be an issue that divided people. President Bush thought that the war was going in the right direction and that Iraq would soon have democratic elections. Kerry wanted to fight the war differently and bring home troops sooner. He thought that the United States should have allowed more time for UN sanctions to work before attacking Iraq.

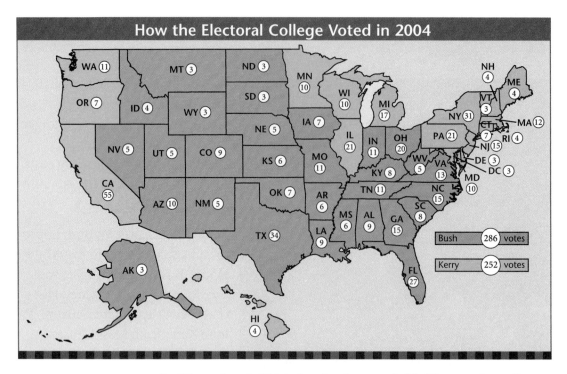

How the Electoral College Voted in 2004

WA ⑪
OR ⑦
ID ④
MT ③
WY ③
ND ③
SD ③
MN ⑩
WI ⑩
MI ⑰
NH ④
ME ④
VT ③
NY ㉛
MA ⑫
CT ⑦
RI ④
NJ ⑮
DE ③
DC ③
MD
NV ⑤
UT ⑤
CO ⑨
NE ⑤
IA ⑦
IL ㉑
IN ⑪
OH ⑳
PA ㉑
WV ⑤
VA ⑬
CA ㊺
AZ ⑩
NM ⑤
KS ⑥
MO ⑪
KY ⑧
TN ⑪
NC ⑮
SC ⑧
OK ⑦
AR ⑥
MS ⑥
AL ⑨
GA ⑮
TX ㉞
LA ⑨
AK ③
Bush ㉛ 286 votes
Kerry 252 votes
FL ㉗
HI ④

On November 2, 2004, the election was held. The number of electoral votes needed to win the presidency is 270. Bush ended up with 286 electoral votes and Kerry with 252 electoral votes. The map above shows how the Electoral College voted. California, with 55, has the most electoral votes. Alaska, Montana, North Dakota, South Dakota, Delaware, Vermont, Washington, D.C., and Wyoming have three votes each. Bush won 31 states and 51 percent of the popular vote. Kerry won 19 states plus the District of Columbia, and 48 percent of the popular vote. George W. Bush began his second term in January 2005.

What do you think?

What do you think was the most important issue in the election of 2004? Why?

Lesson 4 Review On a sheet of paper, answer each of the following questions. Use complete sentences.

1. Who was George W. Bush's running mate?

2. Who was John Kerry's running mate?

3. Why do you think that the debates did not make many people change their minds?

4. Why do you think that people had strong opinions about the war in Iraq?

5. How many electoral votes are needed to win the presidency?

How Has Space Exploration Continued?

The United States has experienced both disaster and success in the opening years of the century. On the morning of Saturday, February 1, 2003, the space shuttle *Columbia* exploded shortly before it was scheduled to land. All seven members of the crew were killed. The crew included two women and five men, one of whom was Israel's first astronaut.

A piece of foam came off the shuttle during takeoff and hit the left wing. The damage to the wing was thought to be the cause of the disaster. Flights of space shuttles came to a halt while NASA continued to investigate the tragedy. *Columbia,* which was on its 28th mission, was the oldest of the shuttles at NASA.

The International Space Station

The International Space Station celebrated its fourth year in existence in November 2004. Russian cosmonauts and American astronauts at the space station maintain the craft and conduct experiments. When the space station is completed, possibly in 2010, it will be the third-brightest object in the night sky. Only the moon and the planet Venus will be brighter.

Can New Technology Help or Harm Us?

In the early part of the 20th century, people predicted that technology would solve many of the world's problems. Electricity would provide the energy for many labor-saving machines. People would work only a few hours a week. Everyone would have an automobile. Airplanes would fill the sky.

Telecommuni-cations

The transfer of information over long distances using such things as telephone lines, radio waves, or satellites

Today, people around the world share ideas, art, music, and different ways of living. Technology has helped to create global connections. What happens in one country affects every other country. Satellites, computers, and **telecommunications** have led to a higher living standard in industrialized nations like the United States.

New technology has been behind many advances in medicine. Doctors are now able to remove a person's heart and fix it. They replace livers and hips. They sew fingers, arms, and legs onto a person who has lost them in an accident. Technology makes all this possible.

However, some people think that we are losing our freedom. Every time we use a credit card, a computer files the information away. Computers also contain information about medicines we take. The government collects information about us and stores it on computers. This leads to a loss of privacy.

But who will decide how to use all this information? How can we control what people know about us? If technology can cause harm, should we limit its development? Who will decide what that limit is? These important questions have no easy answers.

What Are Some Concerns About the Environment?

In the 1960s, astronauts went into space. They took pictures that showed Earth as a beautiful, blue planet. But today, satellite pictures show polluted air and water.

Air pollution affects our health, and it may change our climate. The burning of coal, oil, and natural gas causes most air pollution. We also have water pollution. Farming and industry have poisoned lakes and rivers.

Farmers around the world use fertilizers to make crops grow and pesticides to kill bugs. Rain makes these chemicals run off into rivers, lakes, and oceans. Then they end up in the bodies of fish and other animals. People who eat these animals or drink the water get sick. The problem is most serious in developing countries where many people cannot get clean water.

Since the 1980s, scientists have warned us about **global warming.** They believe that gases from cars and factories are heating up the earth. Burning wood, coal, oil, or natural gas releases carbon monoxide. Trees remove this gas from the air and release oxygen into the air for us to breathe. But overpopulated countries are now cutting down forests and jungles to provide farmland and firewood.

Many people fear that this will increase the carbon dioxide in the air and raise the earth's temperature. This might change rainfall patterns around the world. Too much rain would cause floods; too little rain would cause droughts and famine. Scientists also believe that the polar ice caps are melting. This will raise the sea levels and flood cities like New York, which are on the coast. If this happens, two billion people around the world would have to move inland.

Do All People Receive Equal Treatment?

Generally, women's organizations shared several important goals over the last three decades. These include equal opportunity for women in higher education, equal access to professional careers, and equal pay for equal work. Although equal opportunity for women in education and professions is a reality, the "pay gap" continues. Women now earn 77 cents for every dollar a man earns.

As the nation enters the 21st century, racial and ethnic minorities still have real concerns about protection of their rights. In a poll taken in 2000, more than 40 percent of African Americans felt that police stopped them because of the color of their skin. This is called **racial profiling.** More than 80 percent of African Americans polled felt that racial profiling was widespread. Just over 50 percent of white Americans agreed. In a democracy there will always be differences of opinion. With the Constitution as a foundation, the nation has addressed the concerns of minorities and expanded the Constitutional rights and protections to all the citizens of the United States.

Where Do We Live?

Beginning in the 1960s, America's older industrial cities in the Northeast and Midwest began to grow slowly or lose population. These cities, such as Philadelphia, Baltimore, Cleveland, and Detroit, were named the "Rust Belt." Suburbs surrounding these cities gained population. Also, many people moved from the colder climates in the North to the warmer climates of southwestern states. These warmer states were named the "Sun Belt."

What Other Changes Are Happening?

By 2000, globalization, or the knitting together of all the world's economies, had changed the world. Like many other nations, the United States has begun to trade without barriers between countries.

What Does the "Aging of America" Mean?

During the 1960s, 17 million Americans were 65 years or older. By 2003 that number had more than doubled. Older Americans now make up almost 13 percent of the population. Many of them will live past age 80. Many plan to continue to work, even if only part-time. Others look forward to volunteering in their communities. As the first of the "baby boomers" become senior citizens, their skills, experience, and energy will be a new resource for the nation.

What Is the United States Population?

In 1900, the United States population was around 76 million. In 1990, the total U.S. population was around 249 million. The 2000 U.S. Census results, released in January 2001, showed the population at 281,421,906. Thirteen percent of United States citizens are African Americans, and 12 percent are Hispanics. Four percent of the U.S. population are Asian or from the Pacific Islands. Around 1 percent are American Indian or Alaskan Inuit. Over 70 percent of the population are non-Hispanic caucasians. Around 92 percent of the population were born in the United States, and 8 percent were born in other countries.

In the last 100 years, nearly 40 million people have emigrated to the United States. The largest number of immigrants today are from Cuba, Mexico, and other Latin American countries. Within 50 years, it is predicted that Hispanics will make up 20 percent of the United States population.

Then and Now

Do you realize how rapidly the world's population is growing? The number of people living on Earth is exploding. Some scientists blame overpopulation for problems like pollution, famine, and global warming. The world's population is expected to increase by one billion people every 12 years. Many people think overcrowding will be the major problem in the future. They are concerned with being able to feed so many people. Look at the world population figures and estimates in the chart at the right.

Year	Approximate Number of People
1800	1 billion
1930	2 billion
1968	3.5 billion
1990	5.3 billion
2002	6.3 billion
2014	7.1 billion

Lesson 5 Review On a sheet of paper, write the answers to the following questions. Use complete sentences.

1. What was the cause of the space shuttle *Columbia* disaster?

2. What are some ways that technology helps us? What are some concerns about technology?

3. Which environmental problem do you think is most important? Why?

4. In what part of the country is the Rust Belt? the Sun Belt?

5. What is the "aging of America"?

What do you think?

What do you think will be the most difficult problem facing the United States in the future? Why?

George W. Bush's Speech on Terrorism

On September 20, 2001, President George W. Bush addressed the U.S. Congress. He thanked the world for its support, and then outlined his war on terror. In the following paragraphs, President Bush describes Al Qaeda and the Taliban, who ruled Afghanistan until October 2001.

[Al Qaeda] and its leader—a person named Osama bin Laden—are linked to many other organizations in different countries. . . .They are recruited from their own nations and neighborhoods and brought to camps in places like Afghanistan, where they are trained in the tactics of terror. They are sent back to their homes or sent to hide in countries around the world to plot evil and destruction.

The leadership of Al Qaeda has great influence in Afghanistan and supports the Taliban regime in controlling most of that country. In Afghanistan, we see Al Qaeda's vision for the world.

Afghanistan's people have been brutalized—many are starving and many have fled. Women are not allowed to attend school. You can be jailed for owning a television. Religion can be practiced only as their leaders dictate. A man can be jailed in Afghanistan if his beard is not long enough. . . .

And tonight, the United States of America makes the following demands on the Taliban: Deliver to United States authorities all the leaders of Al Qaeda who hide in your land. Release all foreign nationals, including American citizens, you have unjustly imprisoned. Protect foreign journalists, diplomats and aid workers in your country. Close immediately and permanently every terrorist training camp in Afghanistan, and hand over every terrorist, and every person in their support structure, to appropriate authorities. Give the United States full access to terrorist training camps, so we can make sure they are no longer operating.

These demands are not open to negotiation or discussion. The Taliban must act, and act immediately. They will hand over the terrorists, or they will share in their fate. . . .

Document-Based Questions

1. What does President Bush say is Al Qaeda's goal?

2. According to President Bush, who is Al Qaeda's leader?

3. Why does the president say Al Qaeda's vision can be seen in Afghanistan?

4. What does President Bush mean when he says the Taliban might share the terrorists' fate?

5. Why do you think the president says Al Qaeda plots "evil and destruction"?

Source: "Address to a Joint Session of Congress and the American People," The White House, http://www.whitehouse.gov/news/releases/2001/09/20010920-8.html.

Chapter 16 S U M M A R Y

- Terrorism is planned violence by individuals or groups against civilians for political reasons. Terrorists hope to frighten people in order to get what they want.

- On September 11, 2001, a terrorist group named Al Qaeda attacked the United States. The leader of Al Qaeda is Osama bin Laden. Terrorists crashed two passenger planes into the World Trade Center and one into the Pentagon. Another attack with a passenger plane, planned for either the White House or the Capitol building, failed.

- Americans were shocked by the terrorist attacks. Many Americans acted bravely. Patriotism increased.

- The American government responded to the attacks by passing the Patriot Act. Signed in October 2001, it gave government officials new powers to prevent terrorism. The Department of Homeland Security was made official in November 2002. It combines the efforts of more than 22 federal agencies to protect American citizens.

- The war on terrorism began in Afghanistan. Al Qaeda headquarters were based there. The Taliban controlled the government of Afghanistan.

- The United States and Great Britain attacked Afghanistan in October 2001. The Taliban government fell apart in November 2001. Osama bin Laden was not found. The United States and many other nations gave money to help rebuild Afghanistan.

- By the fall of 2002, the United States focused on Iraq and Saddam Hussein. Some feared that he had weapons of mass destruction. When Hussein would not cooperate with weapons inspectors, American and British troops invaded Iraq in March 2003. President Bush said in May 2003 that the fighting was over.

- After the main fighting ended in Iraq, American and allied forces remained. Their task was to search for weapons of mass destruction, find Saddam Hussein and other Iraqi leaders, help rebuild the economy, and help Iraq become a democracy. No weapons of mass destruction were found in Iraq.

- Saddam Hussein was captured in December 2003.

- George W. Bush won a second term as president on November 2, 2004. He beat his Democratic challenger, John Kerry.

- Terrorism, the economy, the environment, and healthcare were concerns of many people in the first years of the 21st century.

Chapter 16   R E V I E W

On a sheet of paper, write the correct word or words from the Word Bank to complete each sentence.

Word Bank

9/11

Afghanistan

Al Qaeda

George W. Bush

hijacked

Iraq

Osama bin Laden

Saddam Hussein

Taliban

terrorism

weapons of mass destruction

1. Planned violence by individuals or groups against civilians for political reasons is called _____.

2. _____ became president of the U.S. in January 2001.

3. The terrorist group that attacked the United States on September 11, 2001, is called _____.

4. The leader of the terrorist group that attacked the United States is named _____.

5. Terrorists _____ passenger planes and crashed them into buildings in Washington, D.C., and New York City.

6. The attacks on September 11, 2001, are known as _____.

7. The _____ controlled the government of Afghanistan.

8. The war on terror began in the nation of _____.

9. The leader of Iraq was _____.

10. Some people believed that Saddam Hussein had _____.

11. American and British forces invaded _____ on March 19, 2003.

On a sheet of paper, write the letter of the answer that correctly completes each sentence.

12. Cities in the Northeast and Midwest, such as Philadelphia and Detroit, are called the _____.
    A Sun Belt **C** Population Belt
    B Rust Belt **D** Technology Belt

13. The state of _____, with 55, has the most electoral votes.
    A Vermont **B** Alaska **C** California **D** New York

14. The number of _____ votes needed to win the presidency is 270.
    A Democratic **C** popular
    B Republican **D** electoral

15. Cities in the southwestern states are called the _____.

   A Sun Belt   **C** Population Belt

   B Rust Belt   **D** Technology Belt

16. Every state in the United States has at least _____ electoral votes.

   A 3   **B** 13   **C** 30   **D** 300

17. The knitting together of all the world's economies is called _____.

   A global warming   **C** the aging of America

   B racial profiling   **D** globalization

On a sheet of paper, write the answers to the following questions. Use complete sentences.

18. How did the United States respond to the terrorist attacks?

19. What is the Patriot Act?

20. What does the Department of Homeland Security do?

21. Why did American and British forces attack Afghanistan?

22. Why did American and British forces invade Iraq?

23. What happened after President Bush said the war had ended in Iraq?

Critical Thinking On a sheet of paper, write your response to each question. Use complete sentences.

24. Do you think the United States took the correct course of action after the September 11 attacks? Why or why not?

25. Do you think that the United States should have stopped exploring space after the *Columbia* space shuttle tragedy? Explain your answer.

Test-Taking Tip

Decide which questions you will do first and last. Limit your time on each question accordingly.

Voting

As U.S. citizens, we vote to elect leaders and decide certain issues. As voters, we can do several things to inform ourselves about different candidates and issues. We can read newspapers and listen to political debates on radio and TV. We can read articles about candidates in news magazines. We can become informed by reading flyers delivered to our door. We may attend political rallies at which candidates speak. We can get information from the political party of our choice. Studying a voting record on issues can show the positions of a candidate already holding office.

Voter Registration Application
For U.S. Citizens

Qualified voters 18 and older must first register at a city or county clerk's office. In some states they also can register at the polls on election day. The polls are usually open from 7 a.m. to 8 p.m. Each voter is assigned a polling place in his or her district. The local newspaper usually tells people where to vote. Voters also can call the city or county clerk's office to learn their polling place. Voters who will be out of town on election day can request an absentee ballot in person or by mail. They can mark and turn in the absentee ballot ahead of the election.

At the polls, voters fill out a ballot. Election judges instruct voters on how to fill out the ballot. Different districts use various methods. Voters might have to mark Xs or complete arrows with a pen, punch holes, or pull a lever. To ensure privacy, voters make their selections in a private booth.

Election judges at each polling place count the votes at the end of election day. They deliver the count to the city or county clerk's office. Television, radio, and newspapers give election results. When all votes are counted, a winner is declared.

Before you can vote, you need to know several things. Find out the answers to these questions.

1. How long must I live in my state and district before I can vote?
2. Where do I register to vote?
3. How do I register to vote?
4. Where do I vote?
5. Where do I get an absentee ballot?
6. How do I decide who to vote for?
7. How do I fill out the ballot?
8. How are the votes counted?
9. Why do you think it is important to vote in elections?
10. Identify the day, month, and year when you can vote in a national election for the first time.

- In 1973, signing of the Paris Peace Accords ended U.S. involvement in the Vietnam War.
- President Nixon resigned in 1974, and Gerald Ford became president.
- America celebrated its 200th birthday in 1976.
- Jimmy Carter became president in 1977. He signed the SALT II treaty with Leonid Brezhnev in 1979.
- Ronald Reagan became president in 1981. He wanted to make people less dependent on the government.
- Sandra Day O'Connor became the first female Supreme Court justice.
- Reagan was re-elected in 1984.
- In 1986, the space shuttle *Challenger* exploded.
- Mikhail Gorbachev and Reagan signed the INF Treaty in 1987.
- In October 1983, a terrorist attack killed 200 U.S. marines in Lebanon.
- Libya made terrorist attacks in 1985 and 1986. U.S. planes bombed Libyan military posts.
- The space program started again in September 1988.
- George H.W. Bush became president in 1989. A growing budget deficit, crime, drug abuse, and homeless people were problems he faced.
- East and West Germany were reunified in 1990.

- In 1990, Iraq invaded Kuwait. U.S. and UN forces freed Kuwait and caused severe Iraqi casualties.
- Communism fell in the Soviet Union in 1991.
- Bill Clinton became president in 1993. He was re-elected in 1996.
- In 1993, the NAFTA agreement opened trade with Canada and Mexico. In 2000, the Senate passed a bill to open more trading with China.
- In April 2000, Israeli Prime Minister Barak asked the United States to help negotiate peace talks between the Israelis and the Palestinians.
- In 2000, George W. Bush was elected to the presidency. The election was so close that the outcome was not announced until five weeks after the election.
- Given current immigration, Hispanics will represent one in five Americans within 50 years.
- The 21st century offers many challenges to the United States. One of the most pressing is global warming.
- The worst terrorist attacks ever on American soil occurred on September 11, 2001, in New York City and Washington, D.C.
- George W. Bush won a second term as president in November 2004.

The Declaration of Independence

Adopted in Congress July 4, 1776
The Unanimous Declaration of the
Thirteen United States of America

When, in the course of human events, it becomes necessary for one people to dissolve the political bands which have connected them with another, and to assume among the powers of the earth, the separate and equal station to which the laws of nature and of nature's God entitle them, a decent respect to the opinions of mankind requires that they should declare the causes which impel them to the separation.

We hold these truths to be self-evident, that all men are created equal, that they are endowed by their Creator with certain unalienable rights, that among these are life, liberty, and the pursuit of happiness. That to secure these rights, governments are instituted among men, deriving their just powers from the consent of the governed. That whenever any form of government becomes destructive of these ends, it is the right of the people to alter or to abolish it, and to institute new government, laying its foundation on such principles and organizing its powers in such form, as to them shall seem most likely to effect their safety and happiness. Prudence, indeed, will dictate that governments long established should not be changed for light and transient causes;

and accordingly all experience hath shown that mankind are more disposed to suffer, while evils are sufferable, than to right themselves by abolishing the forms to which they are accustomed. But when a long train of abuses and usurpations, pursuing invariably the same object evinces a design to reduce them under absolute despotism, it is their right, it is their duty, to throw off such government, and to provide new guards for their future security.

Such has been the patient sufferance of these colonies; and such is now the necessity which constrains them to alter their former systems of government. The history of the present King of Great Britain is a history of repeated injuries and usurpations, all having in direct object the establishment of an absolute tyranny over these states. To prove this, let facts be submitted to a candid world.

He has refused his assent to laws, the most wholesome and necessary for the public good.

He has forbidden his governors to pass laws of immediate and pressing importance, unless suspended in their operation till his assent should be obtained; and when so suspended, he has utterly neglected to attend to them.

He has refused to pass other laws for the accommodation of large districts of people, unless those people would relinquish the right of representation in the legislature, a right inestimable to them and formidable to tyrants only.

He has called together legislative bodies at places unusual, uncomfortable, and distant from the depository of their public records, for the sole purpose of fatiguing them into compliance with his measures.

He has dissolved representative houses repeatedly, for opposing with manly firmness his invasions on the rights of the people.

He has refused for a long time, after such dissolutions, to cause others to be elected; whereby the legislative powers, incapable of annihilation, have returned to the people at large for their exercise; the state remaining in the mean time exposed to all the dangers of invasion from without, and convulsions within.

He has endeavored to prevent the population of these states; for that purpose obstructing the laws for naturalization of foreigners; refusing to pass others to encourage their migrations hither, and raising the conditions of new appropriations of lands.

He has obstructed the administration of justice, by refusing his assent to laws for establishing judiciary powers.

He has made judges dependent on his will alone, for the tenure of their offices, and the amount and payment of their salaries.

He has erected a multitude of new offices, and sent hither swarms of officers to harass our people, and eat out their substance.

He has kept among us, in times of peace, standing armies without the consent of our legislatures.

He has affected to render the military independent of and superior to the civil power.

He has combined with others to subject us to a jurisdiction foreign to our constitution, and unacknowledged by our laws; giving his assent to their acts of pretended legislation:

For quartering large bodies of armed troops among us:

For protecting them, by a mock trial, from punishment for any murders which they should commit on the inhabitants of these states:

For cutting off our trade with all parts of the world:

For imposing taxes on us without our consent:

For depriving us in many cases, of the benefits of trial by jury:

For transporting us beyond seas to be tried for pretended offenses:

For abolishing the free system of English laws in a neighboring province, establishing therein an arbitrary government, and enlarging its boundaries so as to render it at once an example and fit instrument for introducing the same absolute rule into these colonies:

For taking away our charters, abolishing our most valuable laws, and altering fundamentally the forms of our governments:

For suspending our own legislatures, and declaring themselves invested with power to legislate for us in all cases whatsoever.

He has abdicated government here, by declaring us out of his protection and waging war against us.

He has plundered our seas, ravaged our coasts, burned our towns, and destroyed the lives of our people.

He is at this time transporting large armies of foreign mercenaries to complete the works of death, desolation and tyranny, already begun with circumstances of cruelty and perfidy scarcely paralleled in the most barbarous ages, and totally unworthy the head of a civilized nation.

He has constrained our fellow citizens taken captive on the high seas to bear arms against their country, to become the executioners of their friends and brethren, or to fall themselves by their hands.

He has excited domestic insurrections amongst us, and has endeavored to bring on the inhabitants of our frontiers, the merciless Indian savages, whose known rule of warfare, is an undistinguished destruction of all ages, sexes, and conditions.

In every stage of these oppressions we have petitioned for redress in the most humble terms: our repeated petitions have been answered only by repeated injury. A prince, whose character is thus marked by every act which may define a tyrant, is unfit to be the ruler of a free people.

Nor have we been wanting in attentions to our British brethren. We have warned them from time to time of attempts by their legislature to extend an unwarrantable jurisdiction over us. We have reminded them of the circumstances of our emigration and settlement here. We have appealed to their native justice and magnanimity, and we have conjured them by the ties of our common kindred to disavow these usurpations, which would inevitably interrupt our connections and correspondence. They too have been deaf to the voice of justice and of consanguinity. We must, therefore, acquiesce in the necessity, which denounces our separation, and hold them, as we hold the rest of mankind, enemies in war, in peace friends.

We, therefore, the representatives of the United States of America, in General Congress, assembled, appealing to the Supreme Judge of the world for the rectitude of our intentions, do, in the name, and by authority of the good people of these colonies, solemnly publish and declare, that these united colonies are, and of right ought to be free and independent states; that they are absolved from all allegiance to the British Crown, and that all political connection between them and the state of Great Britain, is and ought to be totally dissolved; and that as free and independent states, they have full power to levy war, conclude peace, contract alliances, establish commerce, and to do all other acts and things which independent states may of right do. And for the support of this declaration, with a firm reliance on the protection of Divine Providence, we mutually pledge to each other our lives, our fortunes, and our sacred honor.

Signed by John Hancock of Massachusetts as President of the Congress and by the fifty-five other Representatives of the thirteen United States of America:

New Hampshire
Josiah Bartlett
William Whipple
Matthew Thornton

Connecticut
Roger Sherman
Samuel Huntington
William Williams
Oliver Wolcott

Massachusetts Bay
Samuel Adams
John Adams
Robert Treat Paine
Elbridge Gerry

Rhode Island
Stephen Hopkins
William Ellery

Pennsylvania
Robert Morris
Benjamin Rush
Benjamin Franklin
John Morton
George Clymer
James Smith
George Taylor
James Wilson
George Ross

Delaware
Caesar Rodney
George Read
Thomas M'Kean

New York
William Floyd
Philip Livingston
Francis Lewis
Lewis Morris

Virginia
George Wythe
Richard Henry Lee
Thomas Jefferson
Benjamin Harrison
Thomas Nelson, Jr.
Francis Lightfoot Lee
Carter Braxton

North Carolina
William Hooper
Joseph Hewes
John Penn

South Carolina
Edward Rutledge
Thomas Heyward, Jr.
Thomas Lynch, Jr.
Arthur Middleton

Georgia
Button Gwinnett
Lyman Hall
George Walton

Maryland
Samuel Chase
William Paca
Thomas Stone
Charles Carroll of
    Carrollton

New Jersey
Richard Stockton
John Witherspoon
Francis Hopkinson
John Hart
Abraham Clark

Appendix B

The Constitution of the United States

Preamble

We the people of the United States, in order to form a more perfect Union, establish justice, insure domestic tranquility, provide for the common defense, promote the general welfare, and secure the blessings of liberty to ourselves and our posterity, do ordain and establish this Constitution for the United States of America.

Article I
The Legislative Branch*

Congress

Section 1 All legislative powers herein granted shall be vested in a Congress of the United States, which shall consist of a Senate and House of Representatives.

The House of Representatives

Section 2 (1) The House of Representatives shall be composed of members chosen every second year by the people of the several states, and the electors in each state shall have the qualifications requisite for electors of the most numerous branch of the state legislature.

(2) No person shall be a representative who shall not have attained to the age of twenty-five years, and been seven years

a citizen of the United States, and who shall not, when elected, be an inhabitant of that state in which he shall be chosen.

(3) Representatives and direct taxes shall be apportioned among the several states which may be included within this Union, according to their respective numbers, [which shall be determined by adding to the whole number of free persons, including those bound to service for a term of years, and excluding Indians not taxed, three-fifths of all other persons]. The actual enumeration shall be made within three years after the first meeting of the Congress of the United States, and within every subsequent term of ten years, in such manner as they shall by law direct. The number of representatives shall not exceed one for every thirty thousand, but each state shall have at least one representative; [and until such enumeration shall be made, the state of New Hampshire shall be entitled to choose 3, Massachusetts 8, Rhode Island and Providence Plantations 1, Connecticut 5, New York 6, New Jersey 4, Pennsylvania 8, Delaware 1, Maryland 6, Virginia 10, North Carolina 5, South Carolina 5, and Georgia 3].

* Headings and paragraph numbers have been added to help the reader. The original Constitution has only the article and section numbers.

(4) When vacancies happen in the representation from any state, the executive authority thereof shall issue writs of election to fill such vacancies.

(5) The House of Representatives shall choose their speaker and other officers; and shall have the sole power of impeachment.

The Senate

Section 3 (1) The Senate of the United States shall be composed of two senators from each state, [chosen by the legislature thereof,] for six years; and each senator shall have one vote.

(2) Immediately after they shall be assembled in consequence of the first election, they shall be divided as equally as may be into three classes. The seats of the senators of the first class shall be vacated at the expiration of the second year, of the second class at the expiration of the fourth year, and of the third class at the expiration of the sixth year, so that one-third may be chosen every second year; [and if vacancies happen by resignation, or otherwise, during the recess of the legislature of any state, the executive thereof may make temporary appoint-ments until the next meeting of the legislature, which shall then fill such vacancies].

(3) No person shall be a senator who shall not have attained to the age of thirty years, and been nine years a citizen of the United States, and who shall not, when elected, be an inhabitant of that state for which he shall be chosen.

(4) The Vice President of the United States shall be president of the Senate, but shall have no vote, unless they be equally divided.

(5) The Senate shall choose their other officers, and also a president pro tempore, in the absence of the Vice President, or when he shall exercise the office of President of the United States.

(6) The Senate shall have the sole power to try all impeachments. When sitting for that purpose, they shall be on oath or affirmation. When the President of the United States is tried, the Chief Justice shall preside: and no person shall be convicted without the concurrence of two-thirds of the members present.

(7) Judgment in cases of impeachment shall not extend further than to removal from office, and disqualification to hold and enjoy any office of honor, trust, or profit under the United States: but the party convicted shall nevertheless be liable and subject to indictment, trial, judgment, and punishment, according to law.

Organization of Congress

Section 4 (1) The times, places, and manner of holding elections for senators and representatives, shall be prescribed in each state by the legislature thereof; but the Congress may at any time by law make or alter such regulations, [except as to the places of choosing senators].

(2) The Congress shall assemble at least once in every year, [and such meeting shall be on the first Monday in December,] unless they shall by law appoint a different day.

Rules and Procedures
Section 5 (1) Each house shall be the judge of the elections, returns and qualifications of its own members, and a majority of each shall constitute a quorum to do business; but a smaller number may adjourn from day to day, and may be authorized to compel the attendance of absent members, in such manner, and under such penalties as each house may provide.

(2) Each house may determine the rules of its proceedings, punish its members for disorderly behavior, and, with the concurrence of two-thirds, expel a member.

(3) Each house shall keep a journal of its proceedings, and from time to time publish the same, excepting such parts as may in their judgment require secrecy; and the yeas and nays of the members of either house on any question shall, at the desire of one-fifth of those present, be entered on the journal.

(4) Neither house, during the session of Congress, shall, without the consent of the other, adjourn for more than three days, nor to any other place than that in which the two houses shall be sitting.

Payment and Privileges
Section 6 (1) The senators and representatives shall receive a compensation for their services, to be ascertained by law, and paid out of the treasury of the United States. They shall in all cases, except treason, felony, and breach of the peace, be privileged from arrest during their attendance at the session of their respective houses, and in going to and returning from the same; and for any speech or debate in either house, they shall not be questioned in any other place.

(2) No senator or representative shall, during the time for which he was elected, be appointed to any civil office under the authority of the United States, which shall have been created, or the emoluments whereof shall have been increased during such time; and no person holding any office under the United States, shall be a member of either house during his continuance in office.

How a Bill Becomes a Law
Section 7 (1) All bills for raising revenue shall originate in the House of Representatives; but the Senate may propose or concur with amendments as on other bills.

(2) Every bill which shall have passed the House of Representatives and the Senate, shall, before it becomes a law, be presented to the President of the United States; if he approve he shall sign it, but if not he shall return it, with his

objections to that house in which it shall have originated, who shall enter the objections at large on their journal, and proceed to reconsider it. If after such reconsideration two-thirds of that house shall agree to pass the bill, it shall be sent, together with the objections, to the other house, by which it shall likewise be reconsidered, and if approved by two-thirds of that house, it shall become a law. But in all such cases the votes of both houses shall be determined by yeas and nays, and the names of the persons voting for and against the bill shall be entered on the journal of each house, respectively. If any bill shall not be returned by the President within ten days (Sundays excepted) after it shall have been presented to him, the same shall be a law, in like manner as if he had signed it, unless the Congress by their adjournment prevent its return, in which case it shall not be a law.

(3) Every order, resolution, or vote to which the concurrence of the Senate and House of Representatives may be necessary (except on a question of adjournment) shall be presented to the President of the United States; and before the same shall take effect, shall be approved by him, or being disapproved by him, shall be repassed by two-thirds of the Senate and House of Representatives, according to the rules and limitations prescribed in the case of a bill.

Powers Granted to Congress

Section 8 The Congress shall have power:

(1) To lay and collect taxes, duties, imposts, and excises, to pay the debts and provide for the common defense and general welfare of the United States; but all duties, imposts, and excises shall be uniform throughout the United States;

(2) To borrow money on the credit of the United States;

(3) To regulate commerce with foreign nations, and among the several states, and with the Indian tribes;

(4) To establish a uniform rule of naturalization, and uniform laws on the subject of bankruptcies throughout the United States;

(5) To coin money, regulate the value thereof, and of foreign coin, and fix the standard of weights and measures;

(6) To provide for the punishment of counterfeiting the securities and current coin of the United States;

(7) To establish post offices and post roads;

(8) To promote the progress of science and useful arts, by securing for limited times to authors and inventors the exclusive right to their respective writings and discoveries;

(9) To constitute tribunals inferior to the Supreme Court;

(10) To define and punish piracies and felonies committed on the high seas, and offenses against the law of nations;

(11) To declare war, grant letters of marque and reprisal, and make rules concerning captures on land and water;

(12) To raise and support armies, but no appropriation of money to that use shall be for a longer term than two years;

(13) To provide and maintain a navy;

(14) To make rules for the government and regulation of the land and naval forces;

(15) To provide for calling forth the militia to execute the laws of the Union, suppress insurrections and repel invasions;

(16) To provide for organizing, arming, and disciplining, the militia, and for governing such part of them as may be employed in the service of the United States, reserving to the states respectively, the appointment of the officers, and the authority of training the militia according to the discipline prescribed by Congress;

(17) To exercise exclusive legislation in all cases whatsoever, over such district (not exceeding ten miles square) as may, by cession of particular states, and the acceptance of Congress, become the seat of the government of the United States, and to exercise like authority over all places purchased by the consent of the legislature of the state in which the same shall be, for the erection of forts, magazines, arsenals, dockyards, and other needful buildings; —And

(18) To make all laws which shall be necessary and proper for carrying into execution the foregoing powers, and all other powers vested by this Constitution in the government of the United States, or in any department or officer thereof.

Powers Denied Congress

Section 9 (1) The migration or importation of such persons as any of the states now existing shall think proper to admit, shall not be prohibited by the Congress prior to the year one thousand eight hundred and eight, but a tax or duty may be imposed on such importation, not exceeding ten dollars for each person.

(2) The privilege of the writ of habeas corpus shall not be suspended, unless when in cases of rebellion or invasion the public safety may require it.

(3) No bill of attainder or ex post facto law shall be passed.

(4) No capitation, [or other direct,] tax shall be laid, unless in proportion to the census or enumeration herein before directed to be taken.

(5) No tax or duty shall be laid on articles exported from any state.

(6) No preference shall be given by any regulation of commerce or revenue to the ports of one state over those of another: nor shall vessels bound to, or from, one state, be obliged to enter, clear, or pay duties in another.

(7) No money shall be drawn from the treasury, but in consequence of appropriations made by law; and a regular statement and account of the receipts and expenditures of all public money shall be published from time to time.

(8) No title of nobility shall be granted by the United States: And no person holding any office of profit or trust under them, shall, without the consent of the Congress, accept of any present, emolument, office, or title, of any kind whatever, from any king, prince, or foreign state.

Powers Denied the States
Section 10 **(1)** No state shall enter into any treaty, alliance, or confederation; grant letters of marque and reprisal; coin money; emit bills of credit; make anything but gold and silver coin a tender in payment of debts; pass any bill of attainder, ex post facto law, or law impairing the obligation of contracts, or grant any title of nobility.

(2) No state shall, without the consent of the Congress, lay any imposts or duties on imports or exports, except what may be absolutely necessary for executing its inspection laws: and the net produce of all duties and imposts, laid by any state on imports or exports, shall be for the use of the treasury of the United States; and all such laws shall be subject to the revision and control of the Congress.

(3) No state shall, without the consent of Congress, lay any duty of tonnage, keep troops, or ships of war in time of peace, enter into any agreement or compact with another state, or with a foreign power, or engage in war, unless actually invaded, or in such imminent danger as will not admit of delay.

ARTICLE II
The Executive Branch

The President
Section 1 **(1)** The executive power shall be vested in a President of the United States of America. He shall hold his office during the term of four years, and, together with the Vice President, chosen for the same term, be elected, as follows:

(2) Each state shall appoint, in such manner as the legislature thereof may direct, a number of electors, equal to the whole number of senators and representatives to which the state may be entitled in the Congress: but no senator or representative, or person holding an office of trust or profit under the United States, shall be appointed an elector.

[The electors shall meet in their respective states, and vote by ballot for two persons, of whom one at least shall not be an inhabitant of the same state with themselves. And they shall make a list of all the persons voted for, and of the number of votes for each; which list they shall sign and certify, and transmit sealed to the seat of the government of the United States, directed to the president of the Senate. The president of the Senate shall, in the presence of the Senate and House of Representatives, open all the certificates, and the votes shall then be counted. The person having the greatest number of votes shall be the President, if such number be a majority of the whole number of electors appointed; and if there be more than one who have such majority, and have an equal number of votes, then the House of Representatives shall immediately choose by ballot one of them for President; and if no person have a majority, then from the five highest on the list the said House shall in like manner choose the President. But in choosing the President, the votes shall be taken by states, the representation from each state having one vote; a quorum for this purpose shall consist of a member or members from two-thirds of the states, and a majority of all the states shall be necessary to a choice. In every case, after the choice of the President, the person having the greatest number of votes of the electors shall be the Vice President. But if there should remain two or more who have equal votes, the Senate shall choose from them by ballot the Vice President.]

(3) The Congress may determine the time of choosing the electors, and the day on which they shall give their votes; which day shall be the same throughout the United States.

(4) No person except a natural-born citizen, or a citizen of the United States at the time of the adoption of this Constitution, shall be eligible to the office of President; neither shall any person be eligible to that office who shall not have attained to the age of thirty-five years, and been fourteen years a resident within the United States.

(5) In case of the removal of the President from office, or of his death, resignation, or inability to discharge the powers and duties of the said office, the same shall devolve on the Vice President, and the Congress may by law provide for the case of removal, death, or resignation or inability, both of the President and Vice President, declaring what officer shall then act as President, and such officer shall act accordingly, until the disability be removed, or a President shall be elected.

(6) The President shall, at stated times, receive for his services, a compensation, which shall neither be increased or diminished during the period for which he shall have been elected, and he shall not receive within that period any other emolument from the United States, or any of them.

(7) Before he enter on the execution of his office, he shall take the following oath or affirmation: —"I do solemnly swear (or affirm) that I will faithfully execute the office of President of the United States, and will to the best of my ability, preserve, protect, and defend the Constitution of the United States."

Powers of the President

Section 2 (1) The President shall be commander in chief of the Army and Navy of the United States, and of the militia of the several states, when called into the actual service of the United States; he may require the opinion, in writing, of the principal officer in each of the executive departments, upon any subject relating to the duties of their respective offices, and he shall have power to grant reprieves and pardons for offenses against the United States, except in cases of impeachment.

(2) He shall have power, by and with the advice and consent of the Senate, to make treaties, provided two-thirds of the senators present concur; and he shall nominate, and by and with the advice and consent of the Senate, shall appoint ambassadors, other public ministers and consuls, judges of the Supreme Court, and all other officers of the United States, whose appointments are not herein otherwise provided for, and which shall be established by law: but the Congress may by law vest the appointment of such inferior officers, as they think proper, in the President alone, in the courts of law, or in the heads of departments.

(3) The President shall have power to fill up all vacancies that may happen during the recess of the Senate, by granting commissions which shall expire at the end of their next session.

Duties of the President

Section 3 He shall from time to time give to the Congress information of the state of the Union, and recommend to their consideration such measures as he shall judge necessary and expedient; he may, on extraordinary occasions, convene both houses, or either of them, and in case of disagreement between them, with respect to the time of adjournment, he may adjourn them to such time as he shall think proper; he shall receive ambassadors and other public ministers; he shall take care that the laws be faithfully executed, and shall commission all the officers of the United States.

Impeachment

Section 4 The President, Vice President, and all civil officers of the United States, shall be removed from office on impeachment for, and conviction of, treason, bribery, or other high crimes and misdemeanors.

ARTICLE III
The Judicial Branch

Federal Courts and Judges
Section 1 The judicial power of the United States, shall be vested in one Supreme Court, and in such inferior courts as the Congress may from time to time ordain and establish. The judges, both of the Supreme and inferior courts, shall hold their offices during good behavior, and shall, at stated times, receive for their services, a compensation, which shall not be diminished during their continuance in office.

Jurisdiction of United States Courts
Section 2 (1) The judicial power shall extend to all cases, in law and equity, arising under this Constitution, the laws of the United States, and treaties made, or which shall be made, under their authority; — to all cases affecting ambassadors, other public ministers and consuls; — to all cases of admiralty and maritime jurisdiction; — to controversies to which the United States shall be a party; — to controversies between two or more states; — [between a state and citizens of another state;] — between citizens of different states; — between citizens of the same state claiming lands under grants of different states, and between a state, or the citizens thereof, and foreign states, [citizens or subjects].

(2) In all cases affecting ambassadors, other public ministers and consuls, and those in which a state shall be party, the Supreme Court shall have original jurisdiction. In all the other cases before mentioned, the Supreme Court shall have appellate jurisdiction, both as to law and fact, with such exceptions, and under such regulations as the Congress shall make.

(3) The trial of all crimes, except in cases of impeachment, shall be by jury; and such trial shall be held in the state where the said crimes shall have been committed; but when not committed within any state, the trial shall be at such place or places as the Congress may by law have directed.

Treason
Section 3 (1) Treason against the United States, shall consist only in levying war against them, or in adhering to their enemies, giving them aid and comfort. No person shall be convicted of treason unless on the testimony of two witnesses to the same overt act, or on confession in open court.

(2) The Congress shall have power to declare the punishment of treason, but no attainder of treason shall work corruption of blood, or forfeiture except during the life of the person attainted.

ARTICLE IV
The States and the Federal Government

State Acts and Records

Section 1 Full faith and credit shall be given in each state to the public acts, records, and judicial proceedings of every other state. And the Congress may by general laws prescribe the manner in which such acts, records, and proceedings shall be proved, and the effect thereof.

Rights of Citizens

Section 2 (1) The citizens of each state shall be entitled to all privileges and immunities of citizens in the several states.

(2) A person charged in any state with treason, felony, or other crime, who shall flee from justice, and be found in another state, shall on demand of the executive authority of the state from which he fled, be delivered up, to be removed to the state having jurisdiction of the crime.

(3) [No person held to service or labor in one state, under the laws thereof, escaping into another, shall, in consequence of any law or regulation therein, be discharged from such service or labor, but shall be delivered up on claim of the party to whom such service or labor may be due.]

New States and Territories

Section 3 (1) New states may be admitted by the Congress into this Union; but no new state shall be formed or erected within the jurisdiction of any other state; nor any state be formed by the junction of two or more states, or parts of states, without the consent of the legislatures of the states concerned as well as of the Congress.

(2) The Congress shall have power to dispose of and make all needful rules and regulations respecting the territory or other property belonging to the United States; and nothing in this Constitution shall be so construed as to prejudice any claims of the United States, or of any particular state.

Protection of States Guaranteed

Section 4 The United States shall guarantee to every state in this Union a republican form of government, and shall protect each of them against invasion; and on application of the legislature, or of the executive (when the legislature cannot be convened) against domestic violence.

ARTICLE V
Amending the Constitution

The Congress, whenever two-thirds of both houses shall deem it necessary, shall propose amendments to this Constitution, or, on the application of the legislatures of two-thirds of the several states, shall call a convention for proposing amendments, which, in either case, shall be valid to all intents and purposes, as part of this Constitution, when ratified by the legislatures of three-fourths of the several states, or by conventions in three-fourths thereof, as the one or the other mode of ratification may be proposed by the Congress; provided [that no amendment which may be made prior to the year one thousand eight hundred and eight shall in any manner affect the first and fourth clauses in the ninth section of the first article; and] that no state, without its consent, shall be deprived of its equal suffrage in the Senate.

ARTICLE VI
General Provisions

(1) All debts contracted and engagements entered into, before the adoption of this Constitution, shall be as valid against the United States under this Constitution, as under the Confederation.

(2) This Constitution, and the laws of the United States which shall be made in pursuance thereof; and all treaties made, or which shall be made, under the authority of the United States, shall be the supreme law of the land; and the judges in every state shall be bound thereby, anything in the constitution or laws of any state to the contrary notwithstanding.

(3) The senators and representatives before mentioned, and the members of the several state legislatures, and all executive and judicial officers, both of the United States and of the several states, shall be bound by oath or affirmation, to support this Constitution; but no religious test shall ever be required as a qualification to any office or public trust under the United States.

ARTICLE VII
Ratifying the Constitution

The ratification of the conventions of nine states shall be sufficient for the establishment of this Constitution between the states so ratifying the same.

Done in convention by the unanimous consent of the states present the seventeenth day of September in the year of our Lord one thousand seven hundred and eighty-seven and of the independence of the United States of America the twelfth. In witness thereof we have hereunto subscribed our names.

George Washington —
President and deputy from Virginia

Delaware
George Read
Gunning Bedford, Jr.
John Dickinson
Richard Bassett
Jacob Broom

Maryland
James McHenry
Dan of St. Thomas Jenifer
Daniel Carroll

Virginia
John Blair
James Madison, Jr.

North Carolina
William Blount
Richard Dobbs Spaight
Hugh Williamson

South Carolina
John Rutledge
Charles Cotesworth
    Pinckney
Charles Pinckney
Pierce Butler

Georgia
William Few
Abraham Baldwin

New Hampshire
John Langdon
Nicholas Gilman

Massachusetts
Nathaniel Gorham
Rufus King

Connecticut
William Samuel Johnson
Roger Sherman

New York
Alexander Hamilton

New Jersey
William Livingston
David Brearley
William Paterson
Jonathan Dayton

Pennsylvania
Benjamin Franklin
Thomas Mifflin
Robert Morris
George Clymer
Thomas FitzSimons
Jared Ingersoll
James Wilson
Gouverneur Morris

Attest:
William Jackson, Secretary

Amendments to the Constitution

The Bill of Rights
(Amendments 1–10)

AMENDMENT 1
Religious and Political Freedoms (1791)

Congress shall make no law respecting an establishment of religion, or prohibiting the free exercise thereof; or abridging the freedom of speech, or of the press; or the right of the people peaceably to assemble, and to petition the government for a redress of grievances.

AMENDMENT 2
Right to Bear Arms (1791)

A well-regulated militia, being necessary to the security of a free state, the right of the people to keep and bear arms shall not be infringed.

AMENDMENT 3
Housing of Soldiers (1791)

No soldier shall, in time of peace be quartered in any house, without the consent of the owner, nor in time of war, but in a manner to be prescribed by law.

AMENDMENT 4
Search and Arrest Warrants (1791)

The right of the people to be secure in their persons, houses, papers, and effects, against unreasonable searches and seizures, shall not be violated, and no warrants shall issue, but upon probable cause, supported by oath or affirmation, and particularly describing the place to be searched, and the persons or things to be seized.

AMENDMENT 5
Rights in Criminal Cases (1791)

No person shall be held to answer for a capital, or otherwise infamous crime, unless on a presentment or indictment of a grand jury, except in cases arising in the land or naval forces, or in the militia, when in actual service in time of war or public danger; nor shall any person be subject for the same offense to be twice put in jeopardy of life or limb; nor shall be compelled in any criminal case to be a witness against himself, nor be deprived of life, liberty, or property, without due process of law; nor shall private property be taken for public use, without just compensation.

AMENDMENT 6
Rights to a Fair Trial (1791)

In all criminal prosecutions, the accused shall enjoy the right to a speedy and public trial, by an impartial jury of the state and district wherein the crime shall have been committed, which district shall have been previously ascertained by law, and to be informed of the nature and cause of the accusation; to be confronted with the witnesses against him; to have compulsory process for obtaining witnesses in his favor, and to have the assistance of counsel for his defense.

AMENDMENT 7
Rights in Civil Cases (1791)

In suits at common law, where the value in controversy shall exceed twenty dollars, the right of trial by jury shall be preserved, and no fact tried by a jury, shall be otherwise re-examined in any court of the United States, than according to the rules of the common law.

AMENDMENT 8
Bails, Fines, and Punishments (1791)

Excessive bail shall not be required, nor excessive fines imposed, nor cruel and unusual punishments inflicted.

AMENDMENT 9
Rights Retained by the People (1791)

The enumeration in the Constitution, of certain rights, shall not be construed to deny or disparage others retained by the people.

AMENDMENT 10
Powers Retained by the States and the People (1791)

The powers not delegated to the United States by the Constitution, nor prohibited by it to the states, are reserved to the states respectively, or to the people.

AMENDMENT 11
Lawsuits Against States (1795)

The judicial power of the United States shall not be construed to extend to any suit in law or equity, commenced or prosecuted against one of the United States by citizens of another state, or by citizens or subjects of any foreign state.

AMENDMENT 12
Election of the President and Vice President (1804)

The electors shall meet in their respective states and vote by ballot for President and Vice President, one of whom, at least, shall not be an inhabitant of the same state with themselves; they shall name in their ballots the person voted for as President, and in distinct ballots the person voted for as Vice President, and they shall make distinct lists of all persons voted for as President, and of all persons voted for as Vice President, and of the number of votes for each, which lists they shall sign and certify, and transmit sealed to the seat of the government of the United States, directed to the president of the Senate; — the president of the Senate shall, in the presence of the Senate and House of Representatives, open all the certificates and the votes shall then be counted; — the person having the greatest number of votes for President, shall be the President, if such number be a majority of the whole number of electors appointed; and if no person have such majority, then from the persons having the highest numbers not exceeding three on the list of those voted for as President, the House of Representatives shall choose immediately, by ballot, the President. But in choosing the President, the votes shall be taken by states, the representation from each state having one vote; a quorum for this purpose shall consist of a member or members from two-thirds of the states, and a majority of all the states shall be necessary to a choice. And if the House of Representatives shall not choose a President whenever the right of choice shall devolve upon them, [before the fourth day of March next following,] then the Vice President shall act as President, as in the case of the death or other constitutional disability of the President.

The person having the greatest number of votes as Vice President, shall be the Vice President, if such number be a majority of the whole number of electors appointed, and if no person have a majority, then from the two highest numbers on the list, the Senate shall choose the Vice President; a quorum for the purpose shall consist of two-thirds of the whole number of senators, and a majority of the whole number shall be necessary to a choice. But no person constitutionally ineligible to the office of President shall be eligible to that of Vice President of the United States.

AMENDMENT 13
Abolition of Slavery (1865)

Section 1 Neither slavery nor involuntary servitude, except as a punishment for crime whereof the party shall have been duly convicted, shall exist within the United States, or any place subject to their jurisdiction.

Section 2 Congress shall have power to enforce this article by appropriate legislation.

AMENDMENT 14
Civil Rights (1868)

Section 1 All persons born or naturalized in the United States, and subject to the jurisdiction thereof, are citizens of the United States and of the state wherein they reside. No state shall make or enforce any law which shall abridge the privileges or immunities of citizens of the United States; nor shall any state deprive any person of life, liberty, or property, without due process of law; nor deny to any person within its jurisdiction the equal protection of the laws.

Section 2 Representatives shall be apportioned among the several states according to their respective numbers, counting the whole number of persons in each state, [excluding Indians not taxed]. But when the right to vote at any election for the choice of electors for President and Vice President of the United States, representatives in Congress, the executive and judicial officers of a state, or the members of the legislature thereof, is denied to any of the male inhabitants of such state, being twenty-one years of age, and citizens of the United States, or in any way abridged, except for participation in rebellion, or other crime, the basis of representation therein shall be reduced in the proportion which the number of such male citizens shall bear to the whole number of male citizens twenty-one years of age in such state.

Section 3 No person shall be a senator or representative in Congress, or elector of President and Vice President, or hold any office, civil or military, under the United States, or under any state, who, having previously taken an oath, as a member of Congress, or as an officer of the United States, or as a member of any state legislature, or as an executive or judicial officer of any state, to support the Constitution of the United States, shall have engaged in insurrection or rebellion against the same, or given aid or comfort to the enemies thereof. But Congress may by a vote of two-thirds of each House, remove such disability.

Section 4 The validity of the public debt of the United States, authorized by law, including debts incurred for payment of pensions and bounties for services in suppressing insurrection or rebellion, shall not be questioned. But neither the United States nor any state shall assume or pay any debt or obligation incurred in aid of insurrection or rebellion against the United States, or any claim for the loss or emancipation of any slave; but all such debts, obligations, and claims shall be held illegal and void.

Section 5 The Congress shall have power to enforce, by appropriate legislation, the provisions of this article.

AMENDMENT 15
Right to Vote (1870)

Section 1 The right of citizens of the United States to vote shall not be denied or abridged by the United States or by any state on account of race, color, or previous condition of servitude.

Section 2 The Congress shall have power to enforce this article by appropriate legislation.

AMENDMENT 16
Income Taxes (1913)

The Congress shall have power to lay and collect taxes on incomes, from whatever source derived, without apportionment among the several states, and without regard to any census or enumeration.

AMENDMENT 17
Direct Election of Senators (1913)

(1) The Senate of the United States shall be composed of two senators from each state, elected by the people thereof for six years; and each senator shall have one vote. The electors in each state shall have the qualifications requisite for electors of the most numerous branch of the state legislatures.

(2) When vacancies happen in the representation of any state in the Senate, the executive authority of such state shall issue writs of election to fill such vacancies: provided, that the legislature of any state may empower the executive thereof to make temporary appointments until the people fill the vacancies by election as the legislature may direct.

(3) This amendment shall not be so construed as to affect the election or term of any senator chosen before it becomes valid as part of the Constitution.

AMENDMENT 18
Prohibition of Liquor (1919)

Section 1 After one year from the ratification of this article the manufacture, sale, or transportation of intoxicating liquors within, the importation thereof into, or the exportation thereof from the United States and all territory subject to the jurisdiction thereof for beverage purposes is hereby prohibited.

Section 2 The Congress and the several states shall have concurrent power to enforce this article by appropriate legislation.

Section 3 This article shall be inoperative unless it shall have been ratified as an amendment to the Constitution by the legislatures of the several states, as provided in the Constitution, within seven years from the date of the submission hereof to the states by the Congress.

AMENDMENT 19
Women's Suffrage (1920)

Section 1 The right of citizens of the United States to vote shall not be denied or abridged by the United States or by any state on account of sex.

Section 2 Congress shall have power to enforce this article by appropriate legislation.

AMENDMENT 20
Terms of the President and Congress (1933)

Section 1 The terms of the President and Vice President shall end at noon on the 20th day of January, and the terms of senators and representatives at noon on the third day of January, of the years in which such terms would have ended if this article had not been ratified; and the terms of their successors shall then begin.

Section 2 The Congress shall assemble at least once in every year, and such meeting shall begin at noon on the third day of January, unless they shall by law appoint a different day.

Section 3 If, at the time fixed for the beginning of the term of the President, the President elect shall have died, the Vice President elect shall become President. If a President shall not have been chosen before the time fixed for the beginning of his term, of if the President elect shall have failed to qualify, then the Vice President elect shall act as President until a President shall have qualified; and the Congress may by law provide for the case wherein neither a President elect nor a Vice President elect shall have qualified, declaring who shall then act as President, or the manner in which one who is to act shall be selected, and such person shall act accordingly until a President or Vice President shall have qualified.

Section 4 The Congress may by law provide for the case of the death of any of the persons from whom the House of Representatives may choose a President whenever the right of choice shall have devolved upon them, and for the case of the death of any of the persons from whom the Senate may choose a Vice President whenever the right of choice shall have devolved upon them.

Section 5 Sections 1 and 2 shall take effect on the 15th day of October following the ratification of this article.

Section 6 This article shall be inoperative unless it shall have been ratified as an amendment to the Constitution by the legislatures of three-fourths of the several states within seven years from the date of its submission.

AMENDMENT 21
Repeal of Prohibition (1933)

Section 1 The eighteenth article of amendment to the Constitution of the United States is hereby repealed.

Section 2 The transportation or importation into any state, territory, or possession of the United States for delivery or use therein of intoxicating liquors, in violation of the laws thereof, is hereby prohibited.

Section 3 This article shall be inoperative unless it shall have been ratified as an amendment to the Constitution by conventions in the several states, as provided in the Constitution, within seven years from the date of the submission hereof to the states by the Congress.

AMENDMENT 22
Limitation on Presidential Terms (1951)

Section 1 No person shall be elected to the office of the President more than twice, and no person who has held the office of President, or acted as President, for more than two years of a term to which some other person was elected President shall be elected to the office of the President more than once. But this article shall not apply to any person holding the office of President when this article was proposed by the Congress, and shall not prevent any person who may be holding the office of President, or acting as President, during the term within which this article becomes operative from holding the office of President or acting as President during the remainder of such term.

Section 2 This article shall be inoperative unless it shall have been ratified as an amendment to the Constitution by the legislatures of three-fourths of the several states within seven years from the date of its submission to the states by the Congress.

AMENDMENT 23
Suffrage in the District of Columbia (1961)

Section 1 The district constituting the seat of government of the United States shall appoint in such manner as the Congress may direct: A number of electors of President and Vice President equal to the whole number of senators and representatives in Congress to which the district would be entitled if it were a state, but in no event more than the least populous state; they shall be in addition to those appointed by the states, but they shall be considered, for the purposes of the election of President and Vice President, to be electors appointed by a state; and they shall meet in the district and perform such duties as provided by the twelfth article of amendment.

Section 2 The Congress shall have power to enforce this article by appropriate legislation.

AMENDMENT 24
Poll Taxes (1964)

Section 1 The right of citizens of the United States to vote in any primary or other election for President or Vice President, for electors for President or Vice President, or for senator or representative in Congress, shall not be denied or abridged by the United States or any state by reason of failure to pay any poll tax or other tax.

Section 2 The Congress shall have power to enforce this article by appropriate legislation.

AMENDMENT 25
Presidential Disability and Succession (1967)

Section 1 In case of the removal of the President from office or of his death

or resignation, the Vice President shall become President.

Section 2 Whenever there is a vacancy in the office of the Vice President, the President shall nominate a Vice President who shall take office upon confirmation by a majority vote of both houses of Congress.

Section 3 Whenever the President transmits to the president *pro tempore* of the Senate and the Speaker of the House of Representatives his written declaration that he is unable to discharge the powers and duties of his office, and until he transmits to them a written declaration to the contrary, such powers and duties shall be discharged by the Vice President as acting President.

Section 4 Whenever the Vice President and a majority of either the principal officers of the executive departments or of such other body as Congress may by law provide, transmit to the president pro tempore of the Senate and the Speaker of the House of Representatives their written declaration that the President is unable to discharge the powers and duties of his office, the Vice President shall immediately assume the powers and duties of the office as acting President.

Thereafter, when the President transmits to the president pro tempore of the Senate and the speaker of the House of Representatives his written declaration that no inability exists, he shall resume the powers and duties of his office unless the Vice President and a majority of either the principal officers of the executive department or of such other body as Congress may by law provide, transmit within four days to the president pro tempore of the Senate and the Speaker of the House of Representatives their written declaration that the President is unable to discharge the powers and duties of his office. Thereupon Congress shall decide the issue, assembling within forty-eight hours for that purpose if not in session. If the Congress, within twenty-one days after receipt of the latter written declaration, or, if Congress is not in session, within twenty-one days after Congress is required to assemble, determines by two-thirds vote of both houses that the President is unable to discharge the powers and duties of his office, the Vice President shall continue to discharge the same as acting President; otherwise, the President shall resume the powers and duties of his office.

AMENDMENT 26
Suffrage for 18-Year-Olds (1971)

Section 1 The right of citizens of the United States, who are eighteen years of age or older, to vote shall not be denied or abridged by the United States or by any state on account of age.

Section 2 The Congress shall have power to enforce this article by appropriate legislation.

AMENDMENT 27
Congressional Pay (1992)

No law, varying the compensation for the services of the senators and representatives, shall take effect, until an election of representatives shall have intervened.

Presidents of the United States

1. George Washington
Term of Office: 1789–1797
Elected From: Virginia
Party: None
Born: 1732   Died: 1799

2. John Adams
Term of Office: 1797–1801
Elected From: Massachusetts
Party: Federalist
Born: 1735   Died: 1826

3. Thomas Jefferson
Term of Office: 1801–1809
Elected From: Virginia
Party: Democratic-Republican
Born: 1743   Died: 1826

4. James Madison
Term of Office: 1809–1817
Elected From: Virginia
Party: Democratic-Republican
Born: 1751   Died: 1836

5. James Monroe
Term of Office: 1817–1825
Elected From: Virginia
Party: Democratic-Republican
Born: 1758   Died: 1831

6. John Quincy Adams
Term of Office: 1825–1829
Elected From: Massachusetts
Party: None
Born: 1767   Died: 1848

7. Andrew Jackson
Term of Office: 1829–1837
Elected From: Tennessee
Party: Democratic
Born: 1767   Died: 1845

8. Martin Van Buren
Term of Office: 1837–1841
Elected From: New York
Party: Democratic
Born: 1782   Died: 1862

9. William H. Harrison
Term of Office: 1841
Elected From: Virginia
Party: Whig
Born: 1773   Died: 1841

10. John Tyler

Term of Office: 1841–1845
Elected From: Virginia
Party: Whig
Born: 1790   Died: 1862

11. James K. Polk

Term of Office: 1845–1849
Elected From: Tennessee
Party: Democratic
Born: 1795   Died: 1849

12. Zachary Taylor

Term of Office: 1849–1850
Elected From: Virginia
Party: Whig
Born: 1784   Died: 1850

13. Millard Fillmore

Term of Office: 1850–1853
Elected From: New York
Party: Whig
Born: 1800   Died: 1874

14. Franklin Pierce

Term of Office: 1853–1857
Elected From: New Hampshire
Party: Democratic
Born: 1804   Died: 1869

15. James Buchanan

Term of Office: 1857–1861
Elected From: Pennsylvania
Party: Democratic
Born: 1791   Died: 1868

16. Abraham Lincoln

Term of Office: 1861–1865
Elected From: Illinois
Party: Republican
Born: 1809   Died: 1865

17. Andrew Johnson

Term of Office: 1865–1869
Elected From: Tennessee
Party: Republican
Born: 1808   Died: 1875

18. Ulysses S. Grant

Term of Office: 1869–1877
Elected From: Ohio
Party: Republican
Born: 1822   Died: 1885

19. Rutherford B. Hayes
Term of Office: 1877–1881
Elected From: Ohio
Party: Republican
Born: 1822   Died: 1893

20. James A. Garfield
Term of Office: 1881
Elected From: Ohio
Party: Republican
Born: 1831   Died: 1881

21. Chester A. Arthur
Term of Office: 1881–1885
Elected From: New York
Party: Republican
Born: 1830   Died: 1886

22., 24. Grover Cleveland
Term of Office: 1885–1889,
   1893–1897
Elected From: New York
Party: Democratic
Born: 1837   Died: 1908

23. Benjamin Harrison
Term of Office: 1889–1893
Elected From: Indiana
Party: Republican
Born: 1833   Died: 1901

25. William McKinley
Term of Office: 1897–1901
Elected From: Ohio
Party: Republican
Born: 1843   Died: 1901

26. Theodore Roosevelt
Term of Office: 1901–1909
Elected From: New York
Party: Republican
Born: 1858   Died: 1919

27. William H. Taft
Term of Office: 1909–1913
Elected From: Ohio
Party: Republican
Born: 1857   Died: 1930

28. Woodrow Wilson
Term of Office: 1913–1921
Elected From: New Jersey
Party: Democratic
Born: 1856   Died: 1924

29. Warren G. Harding
Term of Office: 1921–1923
Elected From: Ohio
Party: Republican
Born: 1865   Died: 1923

30. Calvin Coolidge
Term of Office: 1923–1929
Elected From: Massachusetts
Party: Republican
Born: 1872   Died: 1933

31. Herbert Hoover
Term of Office: 1929–1933
Elected From: California
Party: Republican
Born: 1874   Died: 1964

32. Franklin D. Roosevelt
Term of Office: 1933–1945
Elected From: New York
Party: Democratic
Born: 1882   Died: 1945

33. Harry S. Truman
Term of Office: 1945–1953
Elected From: Missouri
Party: Democratic
Born: 1884   Died: 1972

34. Dwight D. Eisenhower
Term of Office: 1953–1961
Elected From: Kansas
Party: Republican
Born: 1890   Died: 1969

35. John F. Kennedy
Term of Office: 1961–1963
Elected From: Massachusetts
Party: Democratic
Born: 1917   Died: 1963

36. Lyndon B. Johnson
Term of Office: 1963–1969
Elected From: Texas
Party: Democratic
Born: 1908   Died: 1973

37. Richard M. Nixon
Term of Office: 1969–1974
Elected From: California
Party: Republican
Born: 1913   Died: 1994

38. Gerald R. Ford

Term of Office: 1974–1977
Elected From: Michigan
Party: Republican
Born: 1913

39. James E. Carter

Term of Office: 1977–1981
Elected From: Georgia
Party: Democratic
Born: 1924

40. Ronald W. Reagan

Term of Office: 1981–1989
Elected From: California
Party: Republican
Born: 1911   Died: 2004

41. George H.W. Bush

Term of Office: 1989–1993
Elected From: Texas
Party: Republican
Born: 1924

42. William J. Clinton

Term of Office: 1993–2001
Elected From: Arkansas
Party: Democratic
Born: 1946

43. George W. Bush

Term of Office: 2001–2009
Elected From: Texas
Party: Republican
Born: 1946

Articles of the 1999 Presidential Impeachment

On December 19, 1998, the U.S. House of Representatives approved two articles of impeachment. These accused President Bill Clinton of obstruction of justice and perjury in connection with his relationship to Monica Lewinsky. Lewinsky was a White House intern during Clinton's presidency. The U.S. Constitution required that the Senate try the president on the two articles of impeachment.

The last time the Senate had conducted a presidential impeachment trial was in 1867. The House impeached Andrew Johnson for firing his secretary of war against the wishes of Congress. However, after a two-month trial, the Senate failed to remove him from office by one vote.

The impeachment trial of President Clinton began on January 7, 1999. As chief justice of the United States, William Rehnquist presided over the proceedings. He administered an oath to the 100 senators who served as the jury in the trial.

The House Judiciary Committee acted as the prosecutors. Henry Hyde, Republican representative from Illinois, served as the committee chairman. In addition to Hyde, twelve other House Republican members served on the committee.

The Senate first heard opening arguments from the House prosecutors and from President Clinton's lawyers. Then they questioned the two sides. After that the senators subpoenaed three witnesses. These witnesses responded with a closed-door, videotaped deposition.

While the impeachment trial was proceeding, the senators discussed three ways of dealing with the alleged conduct of the president. Some wanted to censure, or condemn, him and impose a fine. Many, however, questioned whether that was constitutional.

Others wanted to adopt a "finding of fact." That option would punish the president without removing him from office. However, many senators maintained that only one constitutional option was open to them. They could acquit the president or convict him and remove him from office.

On February 12, 1999, in an open Senate session, the 100 senators voted on each of the two articles of impeachment. Conviction required a two-thirds majority vote of all the senators present. All 100 were present on that day, so conviction meant 67 guilty votes. With a strong partisan vote, the Senate acquitted the president of perjury and obstruction of justice.

The senators rejected Article 1, the charge of perjury, by a vote of 55-45. They voted 50-50 on Article 2, the charge of obstruction of justice. One hundred senators, 45 Democrats and 55 Republicans, voted. All the Democrats voted not guilty on both articles. Of the 55 Republicans, 45 voted guilty on both articles; 5 voted not guilty on both articles; and 5 voted not guilty on Article 1. The same five Republicans voted guilty on Article 2.

The 50 United States

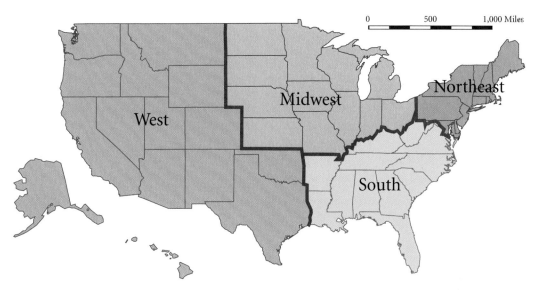

State population ranks are from 2003 population figures.

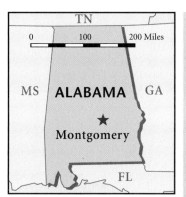

Alabama

Capital: Montgomery
Organized as a territory: March 3, 1817
Entered Union: December 14, 1819
Order of entry: 22nd state
Motto: We dare defend our rights.
Geographic region: South
Nicknames: Yellowhammer State, The Heart of Dixie
Origin of name Alabama: May come from a Choctaw word, meaning "thicket clearers" or "vegetation gatherers"
State flower: Camellia
State bird: Yellowhammer
Largest city: Birmingham
Land area: 50,750 square miles
Land area rank: 28th largest state
Population: 4,500,752
Population rank: 23rd largest state
Postal abbreviation: AL

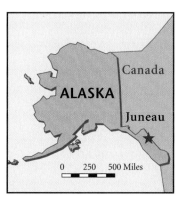

Alaska

Capital: Juneau
Organized as a territory: 1912
Entered Union: January 3, 1959
Order of entry: 49th state
Motto: North to the future.
Geographic region: West
Nicknames: The Last Frontier, Land of the Midnight Sun
Origin of name Alaska: Misinterpreted Aleut word, meaning "great land" or "that which the sea breaks against"
State flower: Forget-me-not
State bird: Willow ptarmigan
Largest city: Anchorage
Land area: 570,374 square miles
Land area rank: Largest state
Population: 648,818
Population rank: 47th largest state
Postal abbreviation: AK

Arizona

Capital: Phoenix
Organized as a territory: February 24, 1863
Entered Union: February 14, 1912
Order of entry: 48th state
Motto: God enriches.
Geographic region: West
Nickname: Grand Canyon State
Origin of name Arizona: From the Indian word Arizonac, meaning "little spring" or "young spring"

State flower: Saguaro cactus flower
State bird: Cactus wren
Largest city: Phoenix
Land area: 114,000 square miles
Land area rank: 6th largest state
Population: 5,580,811
Population rank: 18th largest state
Postal abbreviation: AZ

Arkansas

Capital: Little Rock
Organized as a territory: March 2, 1819
Entered Union: June 15, 1836
Order of entry: 25th state
Motto: The people rule.
Geographic region: South
Nickname: Land of Opportunity
Origin of name Arkansas: From the Quapaw Indians

State flower: Apple blossom
State bird: Mockingbird
Largest city: Little Rock
Land area: 52,075 square miles
Land area rank: 27th largest state
Population: 2,725,714
Population rank: 32nd largest state
Postal abbreviation: AR

California

Capital: Sacramento
Organized as a territory: 1847
Entered Union: September 9, 1850
Order of entry: 31st state
Motto: I have found it.
Geographic region: West
Nickname: Golden State
Origin of name California: From a book, *Las Sergas de Esplandián,* by Garcia Ordóñez de Montalvo, written about 1500

State flower: Golden poppy
State bird: California valley quail
Largest city: Los Angeles
Land area: 155,973 square miles
Land area rank: 3rd largest state
Population: 35,484,453
Population rank: Largest state
Postal abbreviation: CA

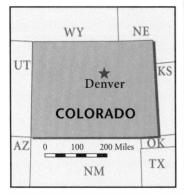

Colorado

Capital: Denver
Organized as a territory: February 28, 1861
Entered Union: August 1, 1876
Order of entry: 38th state
Motto: Nothing without Providence.
Geographic region: West
Nickname: Centennial State
Origin of name Colorado: From Spanish, meaning "ruddy" or "red"

State flower: Rocky Mountain columbine
State bird: Lark bunting
Largest city: Denver
Land area: 103,730 square miles
Land area rank: 8th largest state
Population: 4,550,688
Population rank: 22nd largest state
Postal abbreviation: CO

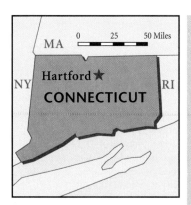

Connecticut

Capital: Hartford
Became a colony: 1662
Entered Union: January 9, 1788
Order of entry: 5th state
Motto: He who transplanted still sustains.
Geographic region: Northeast
Nicknames: Nutmeg State, Constitution State

Origin of name Connecticut: From the Indian word *Quinnehtukqut,* meaning "beside the long tidal river"
State flower: Mountain laurel
State bird: American robin
Largest city: Bridgeport
Land area: 4,845 square miles
Land area rank: 48th largest state
Population: 3,483,372
Population rank: 29th largest state
Postal abbreviation: CT

Delaware

Capital: Dover
Became a colony: 1682
Entered Union: December 7, 1787
Order of entry: First state
Motto: Liberty and independence.
Geographic region: Northeast
Nicknames: Diamond State, First State, Small Wonder
Origin of name Delaware: From Delaware River and Bay, which were

named for Sir Thomas West, Lord De La Warr
State flower: Peach blossom
State bird: Blue hen chicken
Largest city: Wilmington
Land area: 1,982 square miles
Land area rank: 49th largest state
Population: 817,491
Population rank: 45th largest state
Postal abbreviation: DE

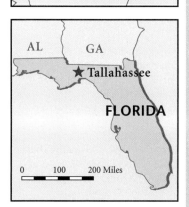

Florida

Capital: Tallahassee
Organized as a territory: March 20, 1822
Entered Union: March 3, 1845
Order of entry: 27th state
Motto: In God we trust.
Geographic region: South
Nickname: Sunshine State
Origin of name Florida: From the Spanish, meaning "feast of flowers"

State flower: Orange blossom
State bird: Mockingbird
Largest city: Jacksonville
Land area: 53,997 square miles
Land area rank: 26th largest state
Population: 17,019,068
Population rank: 4th largest state
Postal abbreviation: FL

Georgia

Capital: Atlanta
Became a colony: 1733
Entered Union: January 2, 1788
Order of entry: 4th state
Motto: Wisdom, justice, and moderation.
Geographic region: South
Nicknames: Peach State, Empire State of the South

Origin of name Georgia: In honor of King George II of England
State flower: Cherokee rose
State bird: Brown thrasher
Largest city: Atlanta
Land area: 57,919 square miles
Land area rank: 21st largest state
Population: 8,684,715
Population rank: 9th largest state
Postal abbreviation: GA

Hawaii

Capital: Honolulu
Organized as a territory: 1900
Entered Union: August 21, 1959
Order of entry: 50th state
Motto: The life of the land is perpetuated in righteousness.
Geographic region: West
Nickname: Aloha State
Origin of name Hawaii: Islands may have been named by Hawaii Loa, their traditional discoverer; may have been named after Hawaii or Hawaiki, the traditional home of the Polynesians
State flower: Yellow hibiscus
State bird: Nene (hawaiian goose)
Largest city: Honolulu
Land area: 6,423.4 square miles
Land area rank: 47th largest state
Population: 1,257,608
Population rank: 42nd largest state
Postal abbreviation: HI

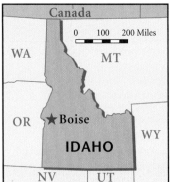

Idaho

Capital: Boise
Organized as a territory: March 3, 1863
Entered Union: July 3, 1890
Order of entry: 43rd state
Motto: It is forever.
Geographic region: West
Nicknames: Gem State, Spud State, Panhandle State
Origin of name Idaho: An invented name of unknown meaning
State flower: Syringa
State bird: Mountain bluebird
Largest city: Boise
Land area: 82,751 square miles
Land area rank: 11th largest state
Population: 1,366,332
Population rank: 39th largest state
Postal abbreviation: ID

Illinois

Capital: Springfield
Organized as a territory: February 3, 1809
Entered Union: December 3, 1818
Order of entry: 21st state
Motto: State sovereignty, national union.
Geographic region: Midwest
Nickname: Prairie State
Origin of name Illinois: From an Indian word and French suffix, meaning "tribe of superior men"
State flower: Violet
State bird: Cardinal
Largest city: Chicago
Land area: 55,593 square miles
Land area rank: 24th largest state
Population: 12,653,544
Population rank: 5th largest state
Postal abbreviation: IL

Indiana

Capital: Indianapolis
Organized as a territory: May 7, 1800
Entered Union: December 11, 1816
Order of entry: 19th state
Motto: The crossroads of America.
Geographic region: Midwest
Nickname: Hoosier State
Origin of name Indiana: Meaning "land of Indians"
State flower: Peony
State bird: Cardinal
Largest city: Indianapolis
Land area: 35,870 square miles
Land area rank: 38th largest state
Population: 6,195,643
Population rank: 14th largest state
Postal abbreviation: IN

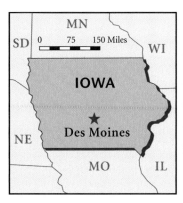

Iowa

Capital: Des Moines
Organized as a territory: June 12, 1838
Entered Union: December 28, 1846
Order of entry: 29th state
Motto: Our liberties we prize and our rights we will maintain.
Geographic region: Midwest
Nickname: Hawkeye State
Origin of name Iowa: Probably from an Indian word meaning "I-o-wa, this is the place," or "the beautiful land"
State flower: Wild rose
State bird: Eastern goldfinch
Largest city: Des Moines
Land area: 55,875 square miles
Land area rank: 23rd largest state
Population: 2,944,062
Population rank: 30th largest state
Postal abbreviation: IA

Kansas

Capital: Topeka
Organized as a territory: May 30, 1854
Entered Union: January 29, 1861
Order of entry: 34th state
Motto: To the stars through difficulties.
Geographic region: Midwest
Nicknames: Sunflower State, Jayhawk State
Origin of name Kansas: From a Sioux word, meaning "people of the south wind"
State flower: Sunflower
State bird: Western meadowlark
Largest city: Wichita
Land area: 81,823 square miles
Land area rank: 13th largest state
Population: 2,723,507
Population rank: 33rd state
Postal abbreviation: KS

Kentucky

Capital: Frankfort
Became a colony: 1607, as part of Virginia
Entered Union: June 1, 1792
Order of entry: 15th state
Motto: United we stand, divided we fall.
Geographic region: South
Nickname: Bluegrass State
Origin of name Kentucky: From the Iroquoian word *Ken-tah-ten,* meaning "land of tomorrow"
State flower: Goldenrod
State bird: Kentucky cardinal
Largest city: Louisville
Land area: 39,732 square miles
Land area rank: 36th largest state
Population: 4,117,827
Population rank: 26th largest state
Postal abbreviation: KY

Louisiana

Capital: Baton Rouge
Organized as a territory: March 26, 1804
Entered Union: April 30, 1812
Order of entry: 18th state
Motto: Union, justice, and confidence.
Geographic region: South
Nicknames: Pelican State, Sportsman's Paradise, Creole State, Sugar State
Origin of name Louisiana: In honor of King Louis XIV of France
State flower: Magnolia
State bird: Pelican
Largest city: New Orleans
Land area: 43,566 square miles
Land area rank: 33rd largest state
Population: 4,496,334
Population rank: 24th largest state
Postal abbreviation: LA

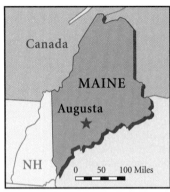

Maine

Capital: Augusta
Became a colony:
1620, as part of Massachusetts
Entered Union: March 15, 1820
Order of entry: 23rd state
Motto: I lead.
Geographic region: Northeast
Nickname: Pine Tree State
Origin of name Maine: It has been considered a compliment to Henrietta Maria, wife of King Charles I of England, who was said to have owned the province of Mayne in France.
State flower: White pine cone and tassel
State bird: Chickadee
Largest city: Portland
Land area: 30,865 square miles
Land area rank: 39th largest state
Population: 1,305,728
Population rank: 40th largest state
Postal abbreviation: ME

Maryland

Capital: Annapolis
Became a colony: 1632
Entered Union: April 28, 1788
Order of entry: 7th state
Motto: Manly deeds, womanly words.
Geographic region: Northeast
Nicknames: Free State, Old Line State
Origin of name Maryland: In honor of Henrietta Maria, wife of King Charles I of England
State flower: Black-eyed susan
State bird: Baltimore oriole
Largest city: Baltimore
Land area: 9,775 square miles
Land area rank: 42nd largest state
Population: 5,508,909
Population rank: 19th largest state
Postal abbreviation: MD

Massachusetts

Capital: Boston
Became a colony: 1620
Entered Union: February 6, 1788
Order of entry: 6th state
Motto: By the sword we seek peace, but peace only under liberty.
Geographic region: Northeast
Nicknames: Bay State, Old Colony State
Origin of name Massachusetts: From two Indian words, meaning "great mountain place"
State flower: Mayflower
State bird: Chickadee
Largest city: Boston
Land area: 7,838 square miles
Land area rank: 45th largest state
Population: 6,433,422
Population rank: 13th largest state
Postal abbreviation: MA

Michigan

Capital: Lansing
Organized as a territory:
January 11, 1805
Entered Union: January 26, 1837
Order of entry: 26th state
Motto: If you seek a pleasant peninsula, look around you.
Geographic region: Midwest
Nickname: Wolverine State
Origin of name Michigan: From Indian word *Michigana*, meaning "great or large lake"
State flower: Apple blossom
State bird: Robin
Largest city: Detroit
Land area: 56,809.2 square miles
Land area rank: 22nd largest state
Population: 10,079,985
Population rank: 8th largest state
Postal abbreviation: MI

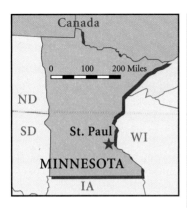

Minnesota

Capital: St. Paul
Organized as a territory: March 3, 1849
Entered Union: May 11, 1858
Order of entry: 32nd state
Motto: The North Star.
Geographic region: Midwest
Nicknames: North Star State, Gopher State, Land of 10,000 Lakes
Origin of name Minnesota: From a Dakota Indian word, meaning "sky-tinted water"
State flower: Showy lady slipper
State bird: Common loon
Largest city: Minneapolis
Land area: 79,617 square miles
Land area rank: 14th largest state
Population: 5,059,375
Population rank: 21st largest state
Postal abbreviation: MN

Mississippi

Capital: Jackson
Organized as a territory: April 7, 1798
Entered Union: December 10, 1817
Order of entry: 20th state
Motto: By valor and arms.
Geographic region: South
Nickname: Magnolia State
Origin of name Mississippi: From an Indian word, meaning "Father of Waters"
State flower: Flower of the magnolia or evergreen magnolia
State bird: Mockingbird
Largest city: Jackson
Land area: 46,914 square miles
Land area rank: 31st largest state
Population: 2,881,281
Population rank: 31st largest state
Postal abbreviation: MS

Missouri

Capital: Jefferson City
Organized as a territory: June 4, 1812
Entered Union: August 10, 1821
Order of entry: 24th state
Motto: The welfare of the people shall be the supreme law.
Geographic region: Midwest
Nickname: Show-Me State
Origin of name Missouri: Named after Missouri Indians; *Missouri* means "town of the large canoes"
State flower: Hawthorn
State bird: Bluebird
Largest city: Kansas City
Land area: 68,945 square miles
Land area rank: 18th largest state
Population: 5,704,484
Population rank: 17th largest state
Postal abbreviation: MO

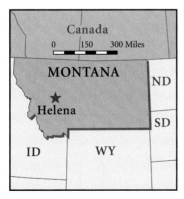

Montana

Capital: Helena
Organized as a territory: May 26, 1864
Entered Union: November 8, 1889
Order of entry: 41st state
Motto: Gold and silver.
Geographic region: West
Nickname: Treasure State
Origin of name Montana: Latinized Spanish word, meaning "mountainous"
State flower: Bitterroot
State bird: Western meadowlark
Largest city: Billings
Land area: 145,556 square miles
Land area rank: 4th largest state
Population: 917,621
Population rank: 44th largest state
Postal abbreviation: MT

Nebraska

Capital: Lincoln
Organized as a territory: May 30, 1854
Entered Union: March 1, 1867
Order of entry: 37th state
Motto: Equality before the law.
Geographic region: Midwest
Nicknames: Cornhusker State, Beef State, Tree Planter State

Origin of name Nebraska: From an Oto Indian word, meaning "flat water"
State flower: Goldenrod
State bird: Western meadowlark
Largest city: Omaha
Land area: 76,878 square miles
Land area rank: 15th largest state
Population: 1,739,291
Population rank: 38th largest state
Postal abbreviation: NE

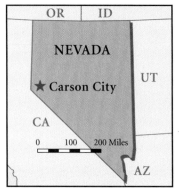

Nevada

Capital: Carson City
Organized as a territory: March 2, 1861
Entered Union: October 31, 1864
Order of entry: 36th state
Motto: All for our country.
Geographic region: West
Nicknames: Sagebrush State, Silver State, Battle Born State
Origin of name Nevada: Spanish word, meaning "snowcapped"

State flower: Sagebrush
State bird: Mountain bluebird
Largest city: Las Vegas
Land area: 109,806 square miles
Land area rank: 7th largest state
Population: 2,241,154
Population rank: 35th largest state
Postal abbreviation: NV

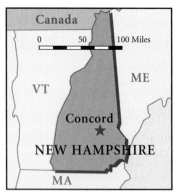

New Hampshire

Capital: Concord
Became a colony: 1623
Entered Union: June 21, 1788
Order of entry: 9th state
Motto: Live free or die.
Geographic region: Northeast
Nickname: Granite State
Origin of name New Hampshire: From the English county of Hampshire

State flower: Purple lilac
State bird: Purple finch
Largest city: Manchester
Land area: 8,969 square miles
Land area rank: 44th largest state
Population: 1,287,687
Population rank: 41st largest state
Postal abbreviation: NH

New Jersey

Capital: Trenton
Became a colony: 1702
Entered Union: December 18, 1787
Order of entry: 3rd state
Motto: Liberty and prosperity.
Geographic region: Northeast
Nickname: Garden State
Origin of name New Jersey: From the Channel Isle of Jersey

State flower: Purple violet
State bird: Eastern goldfinch
Largest city: Newark
Land area: 7,419 square miles
Land area rank: 46th largest state
Population: 8,638,396
Population rank: 10th largest state
Postal abbreviation: NJ

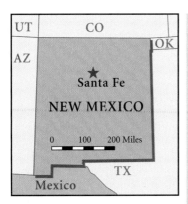

New Mexico

Capital: Santa Fe
Organized as a territory: September 9, 1850
Entered Union: January 6, 1912
Order of entry: 47th state
Motto: It grows as it goes.
Geographic region: West
Nicknames: Land of Enchantment, Sunshine State

Origin of name New Mexico: From the country of Mexico
State flower: Yucca
State bird: Roadrunner
Largest city: Albuquerque
Land area: 121,635 square miles
Land area rank: 5th largest state
Population: 1,874,614
Population rank: 36th largest state
Postal abbreviation: NM

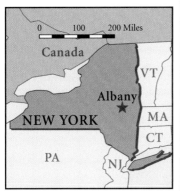

New York

Capital: Albany
Became a colony: 1609 as a Dutch colony, 1664 as an English colony
Entered Union: July 26, 1788
Order of entry: 11th state
Motto: Ever upward.
Geographic region: Northeast
Nickname: Empire State
Origin of name New York: In honor of the English Duke of York

State flower: Rose
State bird: Bluebird
Largest city: New York City
Land area: 47,224 square miles
Land area rank: 30th largest state
Population: 19,190,115
Population rank: 3rd largest state
Postal abbreviation: NY

North Carolina

Capital: Raleigh
Became a colony: 1663
Entered Union: November 21, 1789
Order of entry: 12th state
Motto: To be rather than to seem.
Geographic region: South
Nickname: Tar Heel State
Origin of name Carolina: In honor of King Charles I of England

State flower: Dogwood
State bird: Cardinal
Largest city: Charlotte
Land area: 48,718 square miles
Land area rank: 29th largest state
Population: 8,407,248
Population rank: 11th largest state
Postal abbreviation: NC

North Dakota

Capital: Bismarck
Organized as a territory: March 2, 1861
Entered Union: November 2, 1889
Order of entry: 39th state
Motto: Liberty and union, now and forever, one and inseparable.
Geographic region: Midwest
Nicknames: Sioux State, Flickertail State, Peace Garden State

Origin of name Dakota: From the Sioux tribe, meaning "allies"
State flower: Wild prairie rose
State bird: Western meadowlark
Largest city: Fargo
Land area: 68,994 square miles
Land area rank: 17th largest state
Population: 633,837
Population rank: 48th largest state
Postal abbreviation: ND

Ohio

Capital: Columbus
Organized as a territory: 1783
Entered Union: March 1, 1803
Order of entry: 17th state
Motto: With God, all things are possible.
Geographic region: Midwest
Nickname: Buckeye State
Origin of name Ohio: From an Iroquoian word, meaning "great river"

State flower: Scarlet carnation
State bird: Cardinal
Largest city: Columbus
Land area: 40,953 square miles
Land area rank: 35th largest state
Population: 11,435,798
Population rank: 7th largest state
Postal abbreviation: OH

Oklahoma

Capital: Oklahoma City
Organized as a territory: May 2, 1890
Entered Union: November 16, 1907
Order of entry: 46th state
Motto: Labor conquers all things.
Geographic region: West
Nickname: Sooner State
Origin of name Oklahoma: From two Choctaw Indian words, meaning "red people"

State flower: Mistletoe
State bird: Scissor-tailed flycatcher
Largest city: Oklahoma City
Land area: 68,679 square miles
Land area rank: 19th largest state
Population: 3,511,532
Population rank: 28th largest state
Postal abbreviation: OK

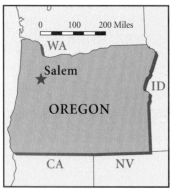

Oregon

Capital: Salem
Organized as a territory: August 14, 1848
Entered Union: February 14, 1859
Order of entry: 33rd state
Motto: She flies with her own wings.
Geographic region: West
Nickname: Beaver State
Origin of name Oregon: Unknown, but generally accepted to have been taken from the writings of Major Robert Rogers, an English army officer
State flower: Oregon grape
State bird: Western meadowlark
Largest city: Portland
Land area: 96,003 square miles
Land area rank: 10th largest state
Population: 3,559,596
Population rank: 27th largest state
Postal abbreviation: OR

Pennsylvania

Capital: Harrisburg
Became a colony: 1681
Entered Union: December 12, 1787
Order of entry: 2nd state
Motto: Virtue, liberty, and independence.
Geographic region: Northeast
Nickname: Keystone State
Origin of name Pennsylvania: In honor of Admiral Sir William Penn, father of William Penn, meaning "Penn's woodland"
State flower: Mountain laurel
State bird: Ruffed grouse
Largest city: Philadelphia
Land area: 44,820 square miles
Land area rank: 32nd largest state
Population: 12,365,455
Population rank: 6th largest state
Postal abbreviation: PA

Rhode Island

Capital: Providence
Became a colony: 1636
Entered Union: May 29, 1790
Order of entry: 13th state
Motto: Hope.
Geographic region: Northeast
Nickname: The Ocean State
Origin of name Rhode Island:
From the Greek island of Rhodes

State flower: Violet
State bird: Rhode Island Red
Largest city: Providence
Land area: 1,045 square miles
Land area rank: Smallest state
Population: 1,076,164
Population rank: 43rd largest state
Postal abbreviation: RI

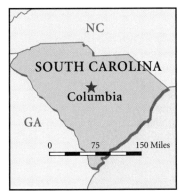

South Carolina

Capital: Columbia
Became a colony: 1663
Entered Union: May 23, 1788
Order of entry: 8th state
Mottoes: Prepared in mind and resources. While I breathe, I hope.
Geographic region: South
Nickname: Palmetto State
Origin of name Carolina:
In honor of King Charles I of England

State flower: Carolina yellow jessamine
State bird: Carolina wren
Largest city: Columbia
Land area: 30,111 square miles
Land area rank: 40th largest state
Population: 4,147,152
Population rank: 25th largest state
Postal abbreviation: SC

South Dakota

Capital: Pierre
Organized as a territory: March 2, 1861
Entered Union: November 2, 1889
Order of entry: 40th state
Motto: Under God the people rule.
Geographic region: Midwest
Nicknames: Mount Rushmore State, Coyote State
Origin of name Dakota: From the Sioux Indians, meaning "allies"

State flower: American pasqueflower
State bird: Ring-necked pheasant
Largest city: Sioux Falls
Land area: 75,898 square miles
Land area rank: 16th largest state
Population: 764,309
Population rank: 46th largest state
Postal abbreviation: SD

Tennessee

Capital: Nashville
Organized as a territory: 1790
Entered Union: June 1, 1796
Order of entry: 16th state
Motto: Agriculture and commerce.
Geographic region: South
Nickname: Volunteer State
Origin of name Tennessee:
Cherokee word of unknown meaning

State flower: Iris
State bird: Mockingbird
Largest city: Memphis
Land area: 41,220 square miles
Land area rank: 34th largest state
Population: 5,841,748
Population rank: 16th largest state
Postal abbreviation: TN

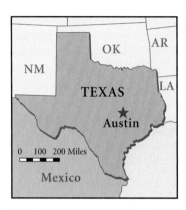

Texas

Capital: Austin
Became an independent republic: 1836
Entered Union: December 29, 1845
Order of entry: 28th state
Motto: Friendship.
Geographic region: West
Nickname: Lone Star State
Origin of name Texas: From an Indian word, meaning "friends"

State flower: Bluebonnet
State bird: Mockingbird
Largest city: Houston
Land area: 261,914 square miles
Land area rank: 2nd largest state
Population: 22,118,509
Population rank: 2nd largest state
Postal abbreviation: TX

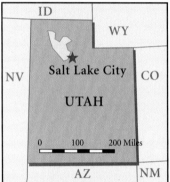

Utah

Capital: Salt Lake City
Organized as a territory: September 9, 1850
Entered Union: January 4, 1896
Order of entry: 45th state
Motto: Industry.
Geographic region: West
Nickname: Beehive State
Origin of name Utah: From the Ute Indians, meaning "people of the mountains"

State flower: Sego lily
State bird: California gull
Largest city: Salt Lake City
Land area: 82,168 square miles
Land area rank: 12th largest state
Population: 2,351,467
Population rank: 34th largest state
Postal abbreviation: UT

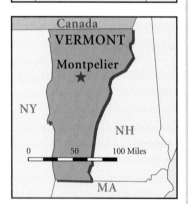

Vermont

Capital: Montpelier
Became a colony: 1623, as part of New Hampshire
Entered Union: March 4, 1791
Order of entry: 14th state
Motto: Vermont, freedom, and unity.
Geographic region: Northeast
Nickname: Green Mountain State
Origin of name Vermont: From the French words *vert mont,* meaning "green mountain"

State flower: Red clover
State bird: Hermit thrush
Largest city: Burlington
Land area: 9,249 square miles
Land area rank: 43rd largest state
Population: 619,107
Population rank: 49th largest state
Postal abbreviation: VT

Virginia

Capital: Richmond
Became a colony: 1607
Entered Union: June 25, 1788
Order of entry: 10th state
Motto: Thus always to tyrants.
Geographic region: South
Nicknames: The Old Dominion, Mother of Presidents
Origin of name Virginia: In honor of Elizabeth I, "Virgin Queen" of England

State flower: American dogwood
State bird: Cardinal
Largest city: Virginia Beach
Land area: 39,598 square miles
Land area rank: 37th largest state
Population: 7,386,330
Population rank: 12th largest state
Postal abbreviation: VA

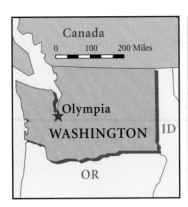

Washington

Capital: Olympia
Organized as a territory: March 2, 1853
Entered Union: November 11, 1889
Order of entry: 42nd state
Motto: Al-Ki (Indian word, meaning "by and by").
Geographic region: West
Nicknames: Evergreen State, Chinook State

Origin of name Washington: In honor of George Washington.
State flower: Coast rhododendron
State bird: Willow goldfinch
Largest city: Seattle
Land area: 66,582 square miles
Land area rank: 20th largest state
Population: 6,131,445
Population rank: 15th largest state
Postal abbreviation: WA

West Virginia

Capital: Charleston
Became a colony: 1607, as part of Virginia colony
Entered Union: June 20, 1863
Order of entry: 35th state
Motto: Mountaineers are always free.
Geographic region: South
Nickname: Mountain State
Origin of name Virginia: In honor

of Elizabeth I, "Virgin Queen" of England
State flower: Rhododendron
State bird: Cardinal
Largest city: Charleston
Land area: 24,087 square miles
Land area rank: 41st largest state
Population: 1,810,354
Population rank: 37th largest state
Postal abbreviation: WV

Wisconsin

Capital: Madison
Organized as a territory: July 4, 1836
Entered Union: May 29, 1848
Order of entry: 30th state
Motto: Forward.
Geographic region: Midwest
Nickname: Badger State
Origin of name Wisconsin: French misinterpretation of an Indian word whose meaning is disputed

State flower: Wood violet
State bird: Robin
Largest city: Milwaukee
Land area: 54,314 square miles
Land area rank: 25th largest state
Population: 5,472,299
Population rank: 20th largest state
Postal abbreviation: WI

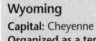

Wyoming

Capital: Cheyenne
Organized as a territory: May 19, 1869
Entered Union: July 10, 1890
Order of entry: 44th state
Motto: Equal rights.
Geographic region: West
Nickname: Equality State
Origin of name Wyoming: From the Delaware Indian word, meaning "mountains and valleys alternating"

State flower: Indian paintbrush
State bird: Meadowlark
Largest city: Cheyenne
Land area: 97,105 square miles
Land area rank: 9th largest state
Population: 501,242
Population rank: Smallest state
Postal abbreviation: WY

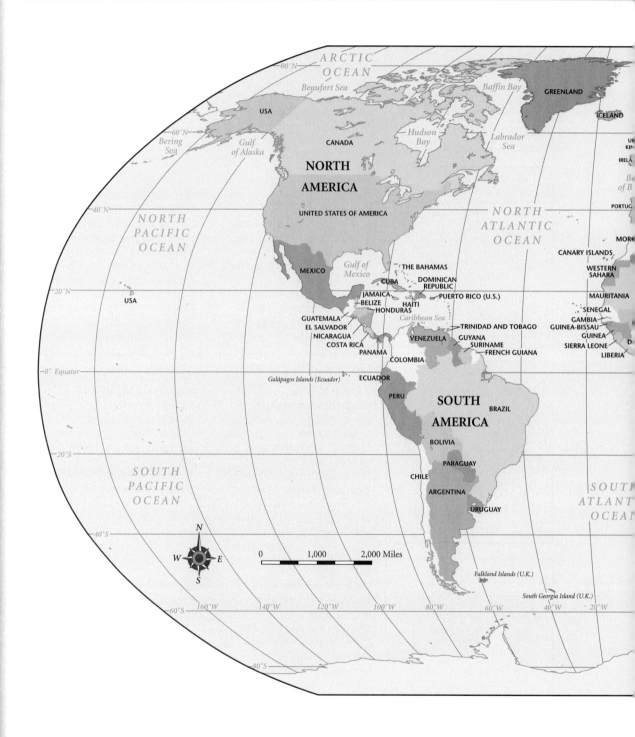

ARCTIC OCEAN

Beaufort Sea

Baffin Bay

GREENLAND

ICELAND

USA

Gulf of Alaska

CANADA

Hudson Bay

Labrador Sea

UNITED KIN

IRELA

NORTH AMERICA

B of B

PORTUG

UNITED STATES OF AMERICA

NORTH ATLANTIC OCEAN

NORTH PACIFIC OCEAN

CANARY ISLANDS

MEXICO

Gulf of Mexico

THE BAHAMAS

CUBA

DOMINICAN REPUBLIC

MOR

WESTERN SAHARA

USA

JAMAICA

BELIZE

HAITI

PUERTO RICO (U.S.)

MAURITANIA

HONDURAS

SENEGAL

GUATEMALA

EL SALVADOR

Caribbean Sea

TRINIDAD AND TOBAGO

GAMBIA

GUINEA-BISSAU

NICARAGUA

VENEZUELA

GUYANA

GUINEA

COSTA RICA

SURINAME

SIERRA LEONE

D

PANAMA

FRENCH GUIANA

LIBERIA

COLOMBIA

Galápagos Islands (Ecuador)

ECUADOR

Equator

PERU

SOUTH AMERICA

BRAZIL

BOLIVIA

SOUTH PACIFIC OCEAN

PARAGUAY

SOUT ATLANT OCEAN

CHILE

ARGENTINA

URUGUAY

N
W   E
S

0   1,000   2,000 Miles

Falkland Islands (U.K.)

South Georgia Island (U.K.)

160°W   140°W   120°W   100°W   80°W   60°W   40°W   20°W

80°N   60°N   40°N   20°N   0°   20°S   40°S   60°S   80°S

ARCTIC OCEAN

80°N

SWEDEN
NORWAY
FINLAND

RUSSIA

ASIA

60°N

DENMARK
ESTONIA
LATVIA
LITHUANIA
POLAND BELARUS

Sea of
Okhotsk

GERMANY
LUX. CZECH
AUST. HUNG.
SLOVAK.
SLOV.
ITALY
CROATIA
BOS. & HERZ.
ALB.
MAC.
GREECE

EUROPE
SLOVAK.
MOLDOVA
UKRAINE
SERB.
& MONT.
BULG.

Black Sea

KAZAKHSTAN

MONGOLIA

GEORGIA

UZBEKISTAN

KYRGYZSTAN

NORTH
KOREA

Sea of
Japan

40°N

TUNISIA

TURKEY
ARMENIA
SYRIA AZERBAIJAN
IRAQ
LEBANON
ISRAEL
JORDAN

Caspian Sea

TURKMENISTAN

IRAN

AFGHANISTAN

TAJIKISTAN

CHINA

SOUTH
KOREA

JAPAN

NORTH
PACIFIC
OCEAN

Mediterranean Sea

KUWAIT

LIBYA

EGYPT

SAUDI
ARABIA

QATAR
U.A.E.

PAKISTAN

NEPAL

BHUTAN

INDIA

East
China
Sea

TAIWAN

20°N

AFRICA

Red Sea

OMAN

Arabian Sea

INDIA

MYANMAR

South
China
Sea

Philippine
Sea

NIGER

CHAD

SUDAN

ERITREA
DJIBOUTI

YEMEN

Gulf of Aden

BANGLADESH

LAOS

THAILAND

CAMBODIA

PHILIPPINES

NIGERIA

CENTRAL AFRICAN
REPUBLIC

ETHIOPIA

VIETNAM

BRUNEI

CAMEROON

GABON

UGANDA

SOMALIA

SRI LANKA

MALAYSIA

RWANDA
DEM. REP.
OF THE
CONGO

KENYA

SINGAPORE

0° Equator

(RWANDA
ANGOLA)

BURUNDI
TANZANIA

Java Sea

INDONESIA

PAPUA
NEW GUINEA

CONGO

Arafura Sea

ANGOLA

ZAMBIA

MALAWI

INDIAN
OCEAN

Timor Sea

Coral Sea

ZIMBABWE

MADAGASCAR

FIJI

NAMIBIA

BOTSWANA

20°S

NEW
CALEDONIA

MOZAMBIQUE

AUSTRALIA

SOUTH
AFRICA

SWAZILAND

LESOTHO

Great
Australian
Bight

Tasman Sea

40°S

NEW ZEALAND

20°E 40°E 60°E 80°E 100°E 120°E 140°E 160°E

60°S

80°S

ANTARCTICA

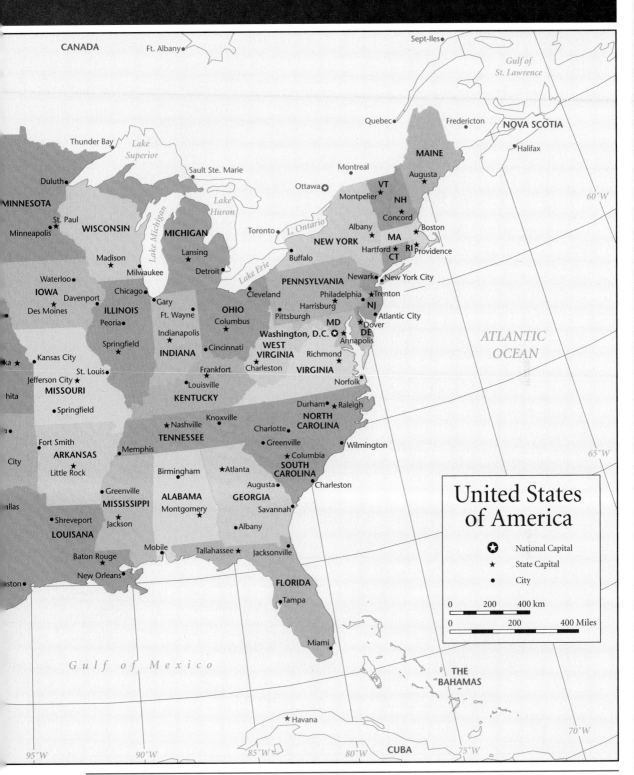

United States of America

CANADA
Ft. Albany
Sept-Iles
Gulf of St. Lawrence

Quebec • Fredericton
NOVA SCOTIA
• Halifax

Thunder Bay
Lake Superior
Montreal
MAINE
Augusta ★

Duluth
Sault Ste. Marie
Ottawa ✪
VT
Montpelier ★
NH
Concord ★

MINNESOTA
Lake Huron
Toronto •
L. Ontario
Albany ★
MA
Boston ★

St. Paul
WISCONSIN
MICHIGAN
Lake Michigan
Lansing
Buffalo
NEW YORK
Hartford ★ RI ★ Providence
CT

Minneapolis
Madison ★
Milwaukee
Detroit
Lake Erie
Cleveland •
PENNSYLVANIA
Newark • New York City

Waterloo •
IOWA
Chicago •
Gary •
Ft. Wayne
OHIO
Pittsburgh •
Harrisburg ★
Philadelphia •
NJ
Trenton ★
Atlantic City

Davenport
ILLINOIS
Peoria •
Columbus ★
Indianapolis ★
Cincinnati •
Dover ★

Des Moines
Springfield ★
INDIANA
Washington, D.C. ✪ ★
MD
DE
Annapolis ★

a ★
Kansas City
St. Louis •
Frankfort ★
WEST VIRGINIA
Richmond ★

Jefferson City ★
MISSOURI
Louisville •
Charleston •
VIRGINIA
Norfolk •

hita •
Springfield •
KENTUCKY
Durham •
Raleigh ★

Knoxville •
NORTH CAROLINA

a •
Fort Smith •
★ Nashville
Charlotte •
Greenville •
Wilmington •

City •
ARKANSAS
TENNESSEE
Memphis •
Columbia ★
SOUTH CAROLINA

Little Rock ★
Birmingham •
★ Atlanta
Charleston •

Greenville •
Augusta •

allas •
MISSISSIPPI
ALABAMA
GEORGIA
Savannah •

Shreveport •
Jackson ★
Montgomery ★
Albany •

LOUISIANA
Mobile •
Tallahassee ★
Jacksonville •

ston •
Baton Rouge ★
New Orleans •
FLORIDA
Tampa •

ATLANTIC OCEAN

THE BAHAMAS

Gulf of Mexico
★ Havana
Miami •

CUBA

United States of America

✪ National Capital
★ State Capital
• City

0   200   400 km
0   200   400 Miles

60°W
65°W
70°W

95°W   90°W   85°W   80°W   75°W

North America

Caribbean Sea

Managua ★

San José ★

Panama

Barranquilla ●

Cúcuta ●

Medellín ●

Bogotá ★

COLOMBIA

Mitú ●

10°N

Valencia ●

Caracas ★

VENEZUELA

TRINIDAD AND TOBAGO

Georgetown ★

Paramaribo

GUYANA

SURINAME

Cayenne ●

FRENCH GUIANA

Quito ★

ECUADOR

Guayaquil ●

0°

Galápagos
Islands
(Ecuador)

Talara ●

PERU

Trujillo ●

Huánuco ●

Lima ★

Ica ●

Cuzco ●

10°S

Manaus ●

Belém ●

Fortaleza ●

Pôrto Velho ●

Recife ●

BRAZIL

Salvador ●

BOLIVIA

La Paz ★

Santa Cruz ●

Sucre ★

Brásilia ★

Goiânia ●

Iquique ●

20°S

Antofagasta ●

PARAGUAY

Asunción ★

Rio de Janeiro ●

São Paulo ●

PACIFIC OCEAN

CHILE

30°S

Córdoba ●

Rosario ●

Santiago ★

Buenos Aires ★

URUGUAY

Montevideo ●

Concepción ●

ARGENTINA

ATLANTIC OCEAN

Valdivia ●

40°S

Puerto Montt ●

N
W   E
S

Comodoro Rivadavia ●

50°S

Falkland Islands
(U.K.)

South Georgia Island
(U.K.)

0   250   500 Miles

90°W   80°W   70°W   60°W   50°W   40°W

Time Zones of the United States

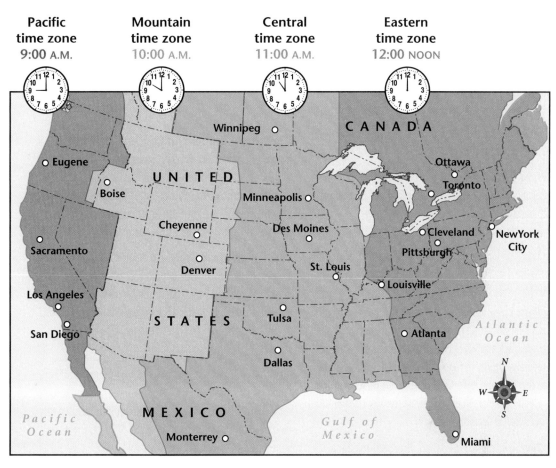

**Pacific
time zone
9:00 A.M.**

**Mountain
time zone
10:00 A.M.**

**Central
time zone
11:00 A.M.**

**Eastern
time zone
12:00 NOON**

CANADA

Winnipeg

UNITED

Eugene

Boise

Minneapolis

Cheyenne

Des Moines

Ottawa

Toronto

Cleveland

NewYork
City

Sacramento

Denver

St. Louis

Pittsburgh

Louisville

Los Angeles

STATES

Tulsa

Atlanta

*Atlantic
Ocean*

San Diego

Dallas

*Pacific
Ocean*

MEXICO

Monterrey

*Gulf of
Mexico*

Miami

N
W   E
S

**Hawaii-Aleutian
time zone
7:00 A.M.**

Honolulu

**Alaska
time zone
8:00 A.M.**

Juneau

Selected Landmark Decisions of the U.S. Supreme Court

1803: *Marbury v. Madison.* The Court ruled that Congress exceeded its power in the Judiciary Act of 1789; the Court thus established its power to review acts of Congress and declare invalid those it found in conflict with the Constitution.

1819: *McCulloch v. Maryland.* The Court ruled that Congress had the authority to charter a national bank, under the Constitution's granting of the power to enact all laws "necessary and proper" to responsibilities of government.

1857: *Dred Scott v. Sanford.* The Court declared unconstitutional the already-repealed Missouri Compromise of 1820 because it deprived a person of his or her property—a slave—without due process of law. The Court also ruled that slaves were not citizens of any state nor of the U.S. (The latter part of the decision was overturned by ratification of the 14th Amendment in 1868.)

1896: *Plessy v. Ferguson.* The Court ruled that a state law requiring federal railroad trains to provide separate but equal facilities for black and white passengers neither infringed upon federal authority to regulate interstate commerce nor violated the 13th and 14th Amendments. (The "separate but equal" doctrine remained effective until the 1954 *Brown v. Board of Education* decision.)

1904: *Northern Securities Co. v. U.S.* The Court ruled that a holding company formed solely to eliminate competition between two railroad lines was a combination in restraint of trade, violating the federal antitrust act.

1908: *Muller v. Oregon.* The Court upheld a state law limiting the working hours of women. (Instead of presenting legal arguments, Louis D. Brandeis, counsel for the state, brought forth evidence from social workers, physicians, and factory inspectors that the number of hours women worked affected their health and morals.)

1911: *Standard Oil Co. of New Jersey et al. v. U.S.* The Court ruled that the Standard Oil Trust must be dissolved because of its unreasonable restraint of trade.

1919: *Schenck v. U.S.* The Court sustained the Espionage Act of 1917, maintaining that freedom of speech and press could be constrained if "the words used . . . create a clear and present danger. . ."

1925: *Gitlow v. New York.* The Court ruled that the First Amendment prohibition against government abridgment of the freedom of speech applied to the states as well as to the federal government. The decision was the first of a number of rulings holding that the 14th Amendment extended the guarantees of the Bill of Rights to state action.

1935: *Schechter Poultry Corp. v. U.S.* The Court ruled that Congress exceeded its authority to delegate legislative powers and to regulate interstate commerce when it enacted the National Industrial Recovery Act, which afforded the U.S. president too much discretionary power.

1951: *Dennis et al. v. U.S.* The Court upheld convictions under the Smith Act of 1940 for invoking Communist theory that advocated the forcible overthrow of the government. (In the *1957 Yates v. U.S.* decision, the Court moderated this ruling by allowing such advocacy in the abstract, if not connected to action to achieve the goal.)

1954: *Brown v. Board of Education of Topeka.* The Court ruled that separate public schools for black and white students were inherently unequal, so that state-sanctioned segregation in public schools violated the equal protection guarantee of the 14th Amendment. And in *Bolling v. Sharpe* the Court ruled that the congressionally mandated segregated public school system in the District of Columbia violated the 5th Amendment's due process guarantee of personal liberty. (The *Brown* ruling also led to abolition of state-sponsored segregation in other public facilities.)

1961: *Mapp v. Ohio.* The Court ruled that evidence obtained in violation of the 4th Amendment guarantee against unreasonable search and seizure must be excluded from use at state as well as federal trials.

1962: *Engel v. Vitale.* The Court held that public schools could not require pupils to recite a state-composed prayer, even if nondenominational and voluntary, because this would be an unconstitutional attempt to establish religion.

1962: *Baker v. Carr.* The Court held that the constitutional challenges to the unequal distribution of voters among legislative districts could be resolved by federal courts, rejecting its own *1946* precedent.

1963: *Gideon v. Wainwright.* The Court ruled that state and federal defendants charged with serious crimes must have access to an attorney, at state expense if necessary.

1964: *New York Times Co. v. Sullivan.* The Court ruled that the First Amendment guarantee of freedom of the press protected the press from libel suits for defamatory reports on public officials unless it was proved that the reports were made from malice, i.e., "with knowledge that [the defamatory statement] was false or with reckless disregard of whether it was false or not."

1966: *Miranda v. Arizona.* The Court ruled that, under the guarantee of due process, suspects in custody, before being questioned, must be informed that they have the right to remain silent, that anything they say may be used against them, and that they have the right to counsel.

1974: *U.S. v. Nixon.* The Court ruled that neither the separation of powers nor the need to preserve the confidentiality of presidential communications could alone justify an absolute executive privilege of immunity from judicial demands for evidence to be used in a criminal trial.

1976: *Gregg v. Georgia, Profitt v. Fla., Jurek v. Texas.* The Court held that death, as a punishment for persons convicted of first degree murder, was not in and of itself cruel and unusual punishment in violation of the 8th Amendment. But the Court ruled that the sentencing judge and jury must consider the individual character of the offender and the circumstances of the particular crime.

1978: *Regents of Univ. of Calif. v. Bakke.* The Court ruled that a special admissions program for a state medical school, under which a set number of places were reserved for minorities, violated the 1964 Civil Rights Act, which forbids excluding anyone, because of race, from a federally funded program. However, the Court ruled that race could be considered as one of a complex of factors.

1995: *Adarand Constructors v. Peña.* The Court held that federal programs that classify people by race, unless "narrowly tailored" to accomplish a "compelling governmental interest," may violate the right to equal protection.

1995: *U.S. Term Limits Inc. v. Thornton.* The Court ruled that neither states nor Congress could limit terms of members of Congress, since the Constitution reserves to the people the right to choose federal lawmakers.

1998: *Clinton v. City of New York.* The Court struck down the Line-Item Veto Act (1996), holding that it unconstitutionally gave the president "the unilateral power to change the text of duly enacted statutes."

2000: *Bush v. Gore.* The Court ruled that manual recounts of presidential ballots in the Nov. 2000 election could not proceed because inconsistent evaluation standards in different counties violated the equal protection clause. In effect, the ruling meant existing official results leaving George W. Bush as narrow winner of the election would prevail.

2003: *Ewing v. California* and *Lockyer v. Andrade.* The court, in two 5-4 rulings, held that California's "three-strikes" law, which dramatically increased penalties for those convicted of a third felony offense, did not constitute cruel and unusual punishment.

2003: *Georgia v. Ashcroft.* The justices ruled, 5-4, that the 1965 Voting Rights Act allowed Southern states to redraw legislative districts to reduce the number of districts in which blacks and other minorities formed large voting majorities, as long as the intent was to widen their political influence, not dilute it.

The Emancipation Proclamation

January 1, 1863

Abraham Lincoln

Whereas, on the twenty-second day of September, in the year of our Lord one thousand eight hundred and sixty-two, a proclamation was issued by the President of the United States, containing, among other things, the following, to wit:

"That on the first day of January, in the year of our Lord one thousand eight hundred and sixty-three, all persons held as slaves within any State or designated part of a State, the people whereof shall then be in rebellion against the United States, shall be then, thenceforward, and forever free; and the Executive Government of the United States, including the military and naval authority thereof, will recognize and maintain the freedom of such persons, and will do no act or acts to repress such persons, or any of them, in any efforts they may make for their actual freedom. . . .

Now, therefore I, Abraham Lincoln, President of the United States . . . order and designate as the States and parts of States wherein the people thereof respectively, are this day in rebellion against the United States, the following, to wit: Arkansas, Texas, Louisiana . . . Mississippi, Alabama, Florida, Georgia, South Carolina, North Carolina, and Virginia. . . .

And by virtue of the power, and for the purpose aforesaid, I do order and declare that all persons held as slaves within said designated States, and parts of States, are, and henceforward shall be free; and that the Executive government of the United States, including the military and naval authorities thereof, will recognize and maintain the freedom of said persons."

For the full text of this document, go to the following Web site and click on "Transcript of the Proclamation"
www.archives.gov/exhibit_hall/featured_documents/emancipation_proclamation/

"Common Sense"

Author Thomas Paine met Benjamin Franklin in London in 1774. At Franklin's encouragement, Paine traveled to America where he began writing and publishing. His writings helped to move the colonists toward declaring independence from Britain. Here is a selection from Paine's pamphlet called "Common Sense."

"It is repugnant to reason . . . that this continent can longer remain subject to any external power. . . . The utmost stretch of human wisdom cannot, at this time, compass a plan short of separation, which can promise the continent even a year's security. Reconciliation is now a fallacious dream.

As to government matters, it is not in the power of Britain to do this continent justice: The business of it will soon be too weighty, and intricate, to be managed with any tolerable degree of convenience by a power so distant from us, and so very ignorant of us; for if they cannot conquer us, they cannot govern us. To be always running three or four thousand miles with a tale or a petition, waiting four or five months for an answer, which when obtained requires five or six more to explain it in, will in a few years be looked upon as folly and childishness—There was a time when it was proper, and there is a proper time for it to cease. . . .

To talk of friendship with those in whom our reason forbids us to have faith . . . is madness and folly. Every day wears out the little remains of a kindred between us and them, and can there be any reason to hope, that as the relationship expires, the affection will increase, or that we shall agree better, when we have ten times more and greater concerns to quarrel over than ever? . . .

O ye that love mankind! Ye that dare oppose, not only the tyranny but the tyrant, stand forth! Every spot of the old world is overrun with oppression. Freedom hath been hunted round the globe. Asia and Africa have long expelled her—Europe regards her like a stranger, and England hath given her warning to depart. O! Receive the fugitive, and prepare in time an asylum for mankind."

Source: "Common Sense," 1776, by Thomas Paine.

Glossary

A

Abolish (ab ə lish´) To get rid of something (p. 18)

Abroad (ə bròd´) Throughout the world (p. 132)

Accusation (ak yə zā´ shən) A charge of wrongdoing (p. 260)

Administration (ad min ə strā´ shən) The period of time a president is in office (p. 39)

Advertise (ad´ vər tīz) To announce publicly (p. 89)

Agency (ā´ jən sē) An organization set up by the federal government (p. 28)

Aggressive (ə gres´ iv) Forceful (p. 159)

Agreement (ə grē´ mənt) An arrangement between people or countries as to the course of action (p. 129)

Agricultural (ag´ rə kul chər əl) Having to do with raising crops or animals for food or profit (p. 198)

Aide (ād) One who assists (p. 309)

Airlift (âr´ lift) Using planes to deliver food and supplies (p. 254)

Alien (ā´ lyən) Someone who lives in a country but is not a citizen of that country (p. 10)

Alliance (ə lī´ əns) An agreement that joins groups of people or countries together (p. 5)

Allied Powers(ə līd´ pou´ ərz) A group of allied nations that included Great Britain, France, Serbia, Belgium, and Russia (p. 151)

Al Qaeda (al kī´ dəh) The terrorist group that attacked New York City and Washington, D.C., on September 11, 2001 (p. 373)

Amendment (ə mend´ mənt) A change (p. 9)

Ammunition (am yə nish´ ən) Bullets, gunpowder, and other things used with guns or other weapons (p. 19)

Amnesty (am´ nə stē) A pardon granted by the government (p. 25)

Anarchist (an´ ər kist) A person or group against all forms of government (p. 110)

Anthem (an´thəm) A song or hymn of praise or gladness (p. 13)

Apartheid (ə pärt´ hāt) The South African policy of racial segregation (p. 336)

Appeasement (ə pēz´ mənt) Doing something to keep peace (p. 220)

Appoint (ə point´) To name or choose a person to do something (p. 9)

Armistice (är´ mə stis) A break in a war to talk peace (p. 127)

Arsenal (är´ sə nəl) A place used to make or store military weapons (p. 19)

Arson (är ´sən) The act of purposely setting fire to something (p. 362)

Artificial satellite (är tə fish´ əl sat´ l īt) An object made by humans that travels in outer space and sends signals back to Earth (p. 265)

Assassination (ə sas´ ən ā shən) The killing of a politically important person (p. 25)

Assembly line (ə sem´ blē līn) A process by which a line of workers assemble something piece by piece until it is complete (p. 173)

Asset (as´ et) Something of worth that someone owns (p. 227)

Association (ə sō sē ā´ shən) A group of people joined together for a common purpose (p. 175)

Atmosphere (at´ mə sfir) The layer of gases covering Earth (p. 271)

Atomic bomb (ə tom´ ik bom) A bomb with great destructive powers (p. 234)

Automation (ò tə mā´ shən) The use of machines to do work (p. 263)

Axis Powers (ak´ sis pou´ərz) The alliance of Japan, Italy, and Germany in World War II (p. 227)

B

Baby boom (bā´ bē büm) The millions of babies born after World War II (p. 288)

Betray (bi trā´) To go against someone's trust (p. 320)

Bicentennial (bī sən ten´ ē əl) A 200th year celebration (p. 314)

Black Codes (blak kōds) Laws that prevented African Americans from owning certain land, voting, and working certain skilled jobs (p. 277)

Blitzkrieg (blitz' krēg) "Lightning war"; a rapid military attack (p. 223)

Blockade (blo kād') Something that prevents goods or people from entering a country (p. 20)

Blue-collar (blü kol' ər) A name used to describe workers in jobs that require little training (p. 292)

Bootlegger (büt' leg ər) Someone who made or sold alcohol illegally during Prohibition (p. 180)

Boundary (boun' dər ē) A real or imaginary marker that shows what land a person owns (p. 8)

Boycott (boi' kot) To refuse to have dealings with a person, country, or group (p. 6)

Breadline (bred līn) A place where people could get free food (p. 197)

Bribe (brīb) A payment to someone to make a person act in a certain way (p. 105)

Budget (buj' it) A plan that shows how much money is available and how the money will be spent (p. 329)

Bunker (bung' kər) An underground shelter (p. 234)

By-product (bī' prod əkt) Something produced in the process of making something else (p. 75)

C

Cabinet (kab' ə nit) A group of advisers to the president (p. 9)

Campaign (kam pān') A group of activities connected to getting elected to office (p. 15)

Canal (kə nal') A waterway made by humans (p. 1)

Candidate (kan' də dāt) A person who has been selected to run for a political office (p. 10)

Capable (kā' pə bəl) Having the ability for a task (p. 15)

Capital (kap' ə təl) Money used for investments (p. 73)

Career (kə rir') A permanent job or line of work (p. 331)

Carpetbagger (kär' pit bag ər) A Northerner elected to political office in the South who took advantage of people; carried belongings in carpetbags (p. 33)

Casualty (kazh' ü əl tē) A person who is wounded, killed, or lost in action (p. 352)

Cease-fire (sēs fīr') A call for an end to fighting (p. 234)

Centennial (sen ten' ē əl) A 100th-year celebration (p. 40)

Central Powers (sen' trəl pou' ərz) A group of allied nations that included Germany, Austria-Hungary, and later Turkey and Bulgaria (p. 151)

Chain reaction (chān rē ak' shən) A series of events linked to one another (p. 151)

Chancellor (chan' sə lər) The chief minister in some European countries (p. 216)

Charity (châr' ə tē) A group that helps those in need (p. 195)

Charter (chär' tər) A written agreement granting power in the name of a state or country (p. 3)

Citizenship (sit' ə zən ship) The condition of belonging to a certain country (p. 216)

Civics (siv' iks) The study of the duties, rights, and privileges of citizens

Civilian (sə vil' yən) One who is not in the military (p. 230)

Civilization (siv ə lə zā' shən) A high level of cultural development (p. xxiv)

Civil rights (siv' əl rīts) Basic human rights belonging to all people (p. 29)

Civil service (siv' əl sėr' vis) A system in which government employees are hired according to their qualifications (p. 105)

Civil war (siv' əl wôr) A war between groups within the same country (p. 20)

Cold war (kōld wôr) The disagreements between Communist and non-Communist nations over economics and politics that caused tensions following World War II (p. 251)

a	hat	e	let	ī	ice	ô	order	ù	put	sh	she		a	in about
ā	age	ē	equal	o	hot	oi	oil	ü	rule	th	thin		e	in taken
ä	far	ėr	term	ō	open	ou	out	ch	child	ẞ	then	ə	i	in pencil
â	care	i	it	ȯ	saw	u	cup	ng	long	zh	measure		o	in lemon
													u	in circus

Collapse (kə laps´) Breakdown or ruin (p. 303)

Collective bargaining (kə lek´ tiv bär´ gən ing) A way of negotiating between groups of workers and employers (p. 203)

Colony (kol´ ə nē) A group of people living in a new area under rule of their native land (p. 3)

Combat (kəm´ bat) Battle (p. 230)

Commander (kə man´ dər) Someone who controls an army or some other military group (p. 6)

Commercial (kə mèr´ shəl) Something linked to business or buying and selling (p. 137)

Commonwealth (kom´ən welth) A group of self-governing states (p. 348)

Communication (kə myü nə kā´ shən) The act of sending and receiving information (p. 17)

Communist (kom´ yə nist) A person who believes in a form of government that eliminates private property and shares wealth(p. 180)

Compete (kəm pēt´) To try to win or gain something (p. 125)

Composer (kəm pō´ zər) One who writes music (p. 177)

Compromise (kom´ prə mīz) A settlement of differences in which each side gives up some of its demands (p. 8)

Confederacy (kən fed´ ər ə sē) A group that has formed an alliance; the Confederate States of America (p. 20)

Conference (kon´ fər əns) A meeting among a large group of people (p. 161)

Conflict (kon´ flikt) A fight, battle, or war (p. 12)

Congress (kong´ gris) The body of government that makes laws, consisting of the House of Representatives and the Senate (p. 6)

Conquer (kong´ kər) To gain something by force; defeat (p. 3)

Conservation (kon sər vā´ shən) The act of protecting or limiting the use of natural resources (p. 78)

Conservative (kən sər´ və tiv) One who is cautious about change (p. 282)

Conspiracy (kən spir´ ə sē) A joint act of breaking the law (p. 309)

Constitutional (kon stə tü´ shə nəl) Something that follows the ideas set forth in the Constitution (p. 30)

Consumer goods (kən sü´ mər güdz) Objects or things the average person buys and uses (p. 157)

Containment policy (kən tān´ mənt pol´ ə sē) The policy of using strength or threat of force to prevent the spread of Communism (p. 252)

Continent (kon´ tə nənt) A large land mass on Earth; for example, North America or Africa (p. 2)

Contract (kon´ trakt) A work agreement between at least two groups (p. 103)

Controversial (kon trə vèr´ shəl) Causing much debate and disagreement (p. 292)

Convention (kən ven´ shən) A formal meeting called for a special purpose (p. 6)

Conventional (kən ven´ shə nəl) Something that is traditional or commonly used (p. 347)

Corporation (kôr pə rā´ shən) A large, organized company owned by stockholders (p. 72)

Corruption (kə rup´ shən) Using wrong or unlawful ways for financial gain (p. 33)

Counterattack (koun´ tər ə tak) To fight back following an attack (p. 233)

Counterculture (koun´ tər kul´ chər) A culture or lifestyle that goes against the common culture (p. 289)

Cowhand (kou´ hand) A person who tends cattle (p. 50)

Crisis (krī´ sis) An event that threatens people's well-being (p. 198)

Criticize (krit´ ə sīz) To show disapproval (p. 72)

Crude oil (krüd oil) Oil in its natural state, before being processed (p. 313)

Culture (kul´ chər) The values, attitudes, and customs of a group (p. xxiv)

D

Debate (di bāt´) An argument or discussion among persons or a group (p. 128)

Decade (dek´ ād) A period of 10 years (p. 169)

Decline (di klīn´) Change to a lower level (p. 245)

Defensive (di fen´ siv) Having protection against attack (p. 223)

Deficit (def´ ə sit) Debt; spending more than what is taken in (p. 339)

Delegate (del´ ə git) A person elected to serve in government (p. 6)

Democracy (di mok´ rə sē) A government in which the power is held by the people (p. 113)

Denounce (di nouns´) To reject or show disapproval (p. 205)

Dependent (di pen´dənt) Relying on others for one's needs (p. 329)

Depression (di presh´ən) A period of financial difficulties experienced by an entire country (p. 16)

Descend (di send´) To come down on (p. 251)

Desegregation (dē seg rə gā´ shən) Acts to remove segregation in public places (p. 278)

Detention (di ten´ shən) The act of holding someone against his or her will (p. 231)

Developing country (di vel´ ə ping kun´ trē) A nation that is slowly improving its industry and economy (p. 280)

Dictator (dik´ tā tər) A person ruling a country with total control (p. 16)

Diplomat (dip´ lə mat) One skilled in negotiating between nations (p. 352)

Disabled (dis ā´ bəld) Having mental or physical challenges (p. 203)

Discrimination (dis krim ə nā´ shən) Treating people unfairly because of their race, sex, religion, or age (p. 89)

Dispute (dis pyüt´) A quarrel between people or groups (p. 136)

Divisive (də vi´ siv) Dividing or separating in a damaging way (p. 283)

Doctrine (dok´ trən) A statement of a certain government policy (p. 15)

Domination (dom ə nā´ shən) Complete control (p. 251)

Draft (draft) The practice of selecting people to serve in the armed forces (p. 158)

Due process (dü pros´es) The formal process of justice carried out in a court of law (p. 28)

Dweller (dwel´ er) A person who lives in a place (p. 85)

E

Economics (ē kə nom´ iks) The study of how people and countries use their resources

Economy (ē kon´ ə mē) A system of producing, using, and distributing wealth (p. 135)

Effective (ə fek´ tiv) Able to cause a desired result (p. 154)

Elector (i lek´ tər) A person who is chosen to vote for the president and vice president (p. 11)

Electoral college (i lek´ tər əl kol´ ij) A group of people chosen to elect the president and vice president (p. 10)

Electoral vote (i lek´ tər əl vōt) A ballot cast by a person who is chosen to vote for the president and vice president (p. 364)

Embargo (em bär´ gō) A government action that prevents certain goods from leaving a country (p. 313)

Emotion (i mō´ shən) Feelings people express (p. 170)

Emperor (em´ pər ər) The male ruler of an empire (p. 149)

Empire (em´ pīr) A large amount of territory under one ruler (p. 1)

Employer (em ploi´ ər) A person or company that pays workers for their services (p. 86)

Energetic (en ər jet´ ik) Full of energy (p. 177)

Enforce (en fôrs´) To make sure something is done according to a law (p. 5)

Engineering (en jə nir´ ing) Using science and math to design and construct buildings or other objects (p. 68)

Enthusiasm (en thü´ zē as əm) A strong feeling of excitement (p. 272)

Entrepreneur (än trə prə nėr´) A person who starts and organizes a business (p. 67)

Environmental (en vi rən men´ tl) Having to do with the surroundings that affect the growth and development of living things (p. 78)

Equality (i kwol´ ə tē) Having the same rights as others (p. 4)

Ethnic heritage (eth´ nik her´ ə tij) One's background or race (p. 221)

Evidence (ev´ ə dəns) Something that furnishes proof (p. 310)

Execute (ek´ sə kyüt) To put to death (p. 15); to complete or carry out an order or task

a	hat	e	let	ī	ice	ȯ	order	ù	put	sh	she		ə	a	in about
ā	age	ē	equal	o	hot	oi	oil	ü	rule	th	thin			e	in taken
ä	far	ėr	term	ō	open	ou	out	ch	child	ᴛʜ	then			i	in pencil
â	care	i	it	ȯ	saw	u	cup	ng	long	zh	measure			o	in lemon
														u	in circus

Executive (eg zek´ yə tiv) The branch of government that works to enforce laws (p. 8)

Exist (eg zist´) To be in a place or operating (p. 318)

Expedition (ek spə dish´ ən) A journey made by a person or group for a certain purpose (p. 3)

Explosive (ek splō´ siv) A device that explodes, such as a bomb (p. 334)

Extortion (ek stôr´ shən) Stealing money by using some kind of threat (p. 310)

F

Famine (fam´ ən) Widespread starvation (p. 357)

Fascist (fash´ ist) One who believes that the state is more important than the individual (p. 215)

Federal government (fed´ ər əl guv´ ərn mənt) A government that is divided between central and state governments (p. 8)

Feminist (fem´ ə nist) A person who seeks equal rights for women (p. 286)

Financial (fə nan´ shəl) Having to do with money (p. 9)

Fixed price (fikst prīs) A set cost for a product or service (p. 94)

Flexible (flek´ sə bəl) Able to move or twist easily (p. 67)

Foreign policy (fôr´ ən pol´ ə sē) The plan a government follows when dealing with other nations (p. 136)

Fraud (frȯd) A lie or false act to steal money or something of value (p. 170)

Free state (frē stāt) A state that did not allow the practice of slavery (p. 14)

Freedmen (frēd´ mən) Former slaves (p. 27)

Frontier (frun tir´) A region with little population (p. 5)

Fugitive (fyü´ jə tiv) One who is fleeing from danger or from being kept against one's will (p. 18)

Fulfill (fül fil´) To carry out or put into effect (p. 277)

G

General assembly (jen´ ər əl ə sem´ blē) A group that makes laws for a larger group (p. 4)

Generation (jen ə rā´ shən) People who live in the same time period and are about the same age (p. 175)

Genocide (jen´ ə sīd) The killing of a group based on its race or political views (p. 248)

Gilded (gil´did) Covered with a thin coating of gold (p. 103)

Glasnost (glaz´ nost) The Soviet policy of open discussion of political and social issues (p. 348)

Global warming (glō´ bəl wôrm´ ing) A rise in the earth's temperature (p. 387)

Gold standard (gōld stan´ dərd) A system in which a basic unit of currency is equal to a certain weight of gold (p. 114)

Governor (guv´ ər nər) A person chosen to lead a group of people within a given area, such as a colony or a state (p. 4)

Grandfather clause (grand´ fä thər klȯz) A clause that stated that any adult African American male could vote if his grandfather was a registered voter on January 1, 1867 (p. 38)

Guilty (gil´ tē) Having done wrong; deserving blame (p. 309)

H

Heroics (hi rō´ iks) Bravery well beyond what is needed (p. 169)

Hijack (hī´ jak) To steal an occupied vehicle by use of force (p. 374)

Hippie (hip´ ē) An extreme member of the youth culture in the 1960s (p. 289)

Holocaust (hol´ ə kȯst) The mass murder of European Jews during World War II (p. 221)

Homeland (hōm´ land) Land that a person or group came from originally (p. 16)

Homesteader (hōm´ sted ər) A pioneer who owned land under the Homestead Act (p. 53)

Horizontal combination (hōr ə zon´ tl kom bə nā´ shən) A kind of business organization that joins two or more businesses that are in the same industry (p. 73)

Hostage (hos´ tij) A person being held against his or her will by someone who wants certain demands to be met (p. 321)

I

Immigrant (im´ ə grənt) A person who comes to live in a new country (p. 10)

Impeach (im pēch´) To charge a president with misconduct (p. 31)

Imperialism (im pir´ ē ə liz əm) The practice of taking over land to become a stronger nation (p. 132)

Import (im´ pôrt) A good brought in from a foreign country (p. 169)

Improvise (im´ prə vīz) To make up as you go along (p. 177)

Inaugural address (in ò´ gyər əl ə dres´) A speech a president gives to accept the presidency (p. 25)

Income (in´ kum) Money earned (p. 94)

Income tax (in´ kum taks) Tax placed on money people earn (p. 141)

Incumbent (in kum´ bənt) A person who currently holds a certain position or office (p. 363)

Independence (in di pen´ dəns) Ability to take care of oneself (p. 7)

Industry (in´ də strē) Related to business and manufacturing (p. 35)

Ineligible (in el´ ə jə bəl) Not able to do something because it is against rules (p. 272)

Infamy (in´ fə mē) Disgraceful or lacking honor (p. 228)

Inferior (in fir´ ē ər) Less advanced or lower in position (p. 221)

Inflation (in flā´ shən) A steady rise in prices of goods (p. 215)

Initiative (i nish´ ə tiv) The power citizens have to suggest new laws (p. 134)

Insurance (in shùr´ əns) A plan that protects against loss in return for regular payments (p. 198)

Interfere (in tər fir´) To enter into or take part in other people's business (p. 6)

Interpret (in tèr´ prit) To explain or tell the meaning of something (p. 8)

Interstate (in´ tər stāt) An action that occurs between two states, such as trade (p. 264)

Invade (in vād´) To attack or take over something (p. 7)

Investigate (in ves´ tə gāt) To look into something to solve a problem or to answer a question (p. 104)

Ironic (ī ron´ ik) The opposite of what is expected (p. 291)

Isolate (ī´ sə lāt) To set apart from others (p. 7)

J

Jim Crow Laws (jim krō´ lòz) Laws that separated African Americans and whites in public places (p. 92)

Judgment (juj´ mənt) The ability a person has to decide and act on something (p. 311)

Judicial (jü dish´ əl) The branch of government that interprets laws (p. 8)

K

Kerosene (ker´ ə sēn) A fuel used in lamps (p. 72)

Ku Klux Klan (kü´ kluks klan´) A secret group against people who were not white (p. 39)

L

Landslide (land´ slīd) A majority of votes for one side (p. 169)

Lawsuit (lò´ süt) A case brought before a court of law (p. 28)

Layoff (lā´ òf) Letting workers go because a company cannot afford to pay them (p. 195)

Legal (lē´ gəl) Having to do with law (p. 6)

Legislative (lej´ ə slā tiv) The branch of government that makes laws (p. 8)

Leisure (lē´ zhər) Something that is done for amusement (p. 93)

Liability (lī ə bil´ ə tē) A risk (p. 73)

Liberal (lib´ ər əl) One who favors change (p. 205)

Liberation (lib ə rā´ shən) Equal social or economic rights (p. 286)

Literally (lit´ ər ə lē) Taken exactly as something is stated, written, or directed (p. 330)

Lottery (lot´ ər ē) Drawing names to decide who is drafted into the military (p. 225)

Loyalist (loi´ ə list) An American who supported the king of Great Britain (p. 7)

M

Maintain (mān tān´) To keep in good condition (p. 283)

Majority (mə jòr´ ə tē) A number greater than half of the total (p. 4)

a	hat	e	let	ī	ice	ò	order	ù	put	sh	she	a in about
ā	age	ē	equal	o	hot	oi	oil	ü	rule	th	thin	e in taken
ä	far	èr	term	ō	open	ou	out	ch	child	ŦH	then	ə i in pencil
â	care	i	it	ò	saw	u	cup	ng	long	zh	measure	o in lemon
												u in circus

Manifest Destiny (man´ ə fest des´ tə nē) A belief something is meant to happen, especially that America would own land from coast to coast (p. 17)

Mass-produce (mas prə düs´) To make great amounts of product very fast (p. 15)

McCarthyism (mə kär´ thē iz əm) An attempt to gain power by attacking the patriotism of others (p. 260)

Melting pot (melt´ ing pot) A nation where several groups of people belonging to different races or cultures live together (p. 15)

Merchant (mėr´ chənt) A buyer and seller of goods (p. 2)

Method (meth´ əd) A way of doing something (p. 67)

Migrant (mī´ grənt) A worker who travels from place to place to work (p. 288)

Military (mil´ ə ter ē) Having to do with armed forces (p. 1)

Millennium (məl len´ ē um) A period of 1,000 years (p. 365

Mine (mīn) A bomb that explodes when touched (p. 159)

Minimum wage (min´ ə mem wāj) The smallest amount a person can be paid to do a job (p. 142)

Minority (mə nôr´ ə tē) A group of people that is a smaller part of a population (p. 303)

Minutemen (min´ it men) A group of men trained to be soldiers and who agreed to gather at a minute's notice (p. 6)

Misconduct (mis kon´ dukt) Wrongdoing by someone holding a political or business position (p. 31)

Misunderstanding (mis un dər stan´ ding) Failure to understand (p. 58)

Mobile (mō´ bəl) Having the ability to travel (p. 172)

Monopoly (mə nop´ ə lē) A corporation that has little competition (p. 72)

Morality (mə ral´ə tē) Good behavior; knowing the difference between right and wrong (p. 316)

Moratorium (môr ə tôr´ ē əm) The legal act of delaying something (p. 198)

Motorcade (mō´ tər kād) A parade of cars (p. 280)

Movement (müv´ mənt) A series of actions carried out to work toward a certain goal (p. 14)

Muckraker (muk´ rā kər) A person who wrote articles and books describing corruption and problems (p. 134)

Mugwump (mug´ wump) A reform group that wanted to replace the spoils system with civil service (p. 105)

Mural (myůr´ əl) An artistic painting or drawing on a wall (p. 202)

N

National Guard (nash´ ə nəl gärd) A state's military force (p. 262)

Natural resources (nach´ ər əl ri sors´ ez) Raw materials from nature, such as water and soil (p. 78)

Negotiate (ni gō´ shē āt) To work out a deal (p. 10)

Neutral (nü´ trəl) Not siding with any particular person or group (p. 10)

9/11 (nīn i lev´ ən) The shortened name for the terrorist attacks on September 11, 2001 (p. 373)

Nomads (nō´ madz) People who do not live in one place (p. 1)

Nominate (nom´ ə nāt) To choose someone to do something, such as run for office (p. 107)

Nuclear war (nü´ klē ər wôr) War that uses atomic weapons (p. 259)

O

Oath (ōth) A pledge that promises loyalty to a government or other cause (p. 25)

Occupation (ok yə pā´shən) A person's job or line of work (p. 205)

Offensive (ə fen´ siv) Attacking rather than defending (p. 257)

Organize (ôr´ gə nīz) To put together in some kind of order (p. 9)

Overproduction (ō vər prə duk´ shən) Producing too many goods (p. 196)

Override (ō vər rīd´) To reject or not accept (p. 30)

Overturn (ō vər tėrn´) To reverse (p. 205)

P

Patriotic (pā trē ot´ ik) Having love for one's country (p. 230)

Patriotism (pā′ trē ə tiz əm) Pride in one's country (p. 375)

Perestroika (per ə stroi′ kə) The Soviet policy of economic and government reform (p. 348)

Permanent (pėr′ mə nənt) Meant to last for a long time (p. 9)

Persecute (pėr′ sə kyüt) To treat someone poorly or violently because of his or her religious beliefs or ethnic background (p. 358)

Petroleum (pə trō′ lē əm) A liquid that can be made into fuel (p. 67)

Phonograph (fō′ nə graf) A machine used to reproduce sound (p. 76)

Pioneer (pī ə nir′) One of the first persons to settle in a territory (p. 8)

Plantation (plan tā′ shən) A large farm that grows huge amounts of a certain crop (p. 14)

Policy (pol′ ə sē) A set of rules or an action plan set forth by a person or group (p. 12)

Political boss (pə lit′ ə kəl bȯs) A professional politician who controls the actions of a political party (p. 105)

Political party (pə lit′ ə kəl pär′ tē) A group that represents a certain political belief (p. 9)

Pollution (pə lü′ shən) Anything added to the environment that is harmful to living things (p. 78)

Prejudice (prej′ə dis) A belief or action against someone because of race, sex, religion, or age (p. 90)

Primary election (prī′ mer ē i lek′ shən) An election in which the people choose candidates (p. 134)

Proclamation (prok lə mā′ shən) An official public announcement (p. 21)

Profitable (prof′ ə tə bəl) Able to bring in money above operating costs (p. 14)

Progressives (prə gres′ ivz) People who believed that America should pass laws to correct America's social and political problems (p. 133)

Prohibit (prō hib′ it) To prevent by law (p. 199)

Prohibition (prō ə bish′ ən) The ban on making or selling alcohol (p. 180)

Prosecute (pros′ ə kyüt) To charge with a crime (p. 112)

Prospector (pros′pek tər) A person who searches an area for gold, silver, or other minerals (p. 50)

Publish (pub′ lish) To print something, such as a book, newspaper, or magazine (p. 2)

Purify (pyür′ ə fī) To make something pure (p. 67)

R

Racial profiling (rā′ shəl prō′ fīl ing) The practice of stopping and searching cars based only on the race of the driver (p. 387)

Radar (rā′ där) A system used to locate objects such as planes (p. 224)

Radical (rad′ ə kəl) Very great; more than usual (p. 30)

Ratify (rat′ ə fī) To approve something (p. 9)

Ration (rash′ ən) To use less or limit the amount of something (p. 230)

Rebellion (ri bel′ yən) A group fighting another group that is in power (p. 8)

Rebuild (rē bild′) To build something again (p. 21)

Recall (ri kȯl′) The act of voting someone who has performed poorly out of office (p. 134)

Reconstruction (rē kən struk′ shən) Rebuilding of the South after the Civil War (p. 26)

Recovery (ri kuv′ ər ē) The act of overcoming a problem (p. 199)

Referendum (ref ə ren′dem) The practice of giving voters the right to approve or not approve bills (p. 134)

Refinery (ri fī′ nər ē) A place where a good is made pure or made into other products (p. 71)

Reform (ri fȯrm′) A change intended to make something better (p. 103)

Refugee (ref yə jē′) A person who flees his or her home country to seek protection (p. 274)

Reich (rīk) A German empire (p. 219)

Reject (ri jekt′) To refuse to accept (p. 134)

Religious (ri lij′ əs) Relating to a belief in a higher being (p. 3)

Repeal (ri pēl′) To remove something, especially a law (p. 6)

a	hat	e	let	ī	ice	ȯ	order	u̇	put	sh	she	ə	a	in about
ā	age	ē	equal	o	hot	oi	oil	ü	rule	th	thin		e	in taken
ä	far	ėr	term	ō	open	ou	out	ch	child	ᵺ	then		i	in pencil
â	care	i	it	ȯ	saw	u	cup	ng	long	zh	measure		o	in lemon
													u	in circus

Replenish (ri plen´ish) To make full or complete again (p. 285)

Representative (rep ri zen´ tə tiv) A person who is given power to act for others; a government with officials elected by the people (p. 4)

Reproduce (rē prə düs´) To copy or duplicate (p. 76)

Republic (ri pub´ lik) A government in which citizens elect people to speak and act for them (p. 129)

Reputation (rep yə tā´ shən) How a person is judged by others (p. 260)

Reservation (rez ər vā´ shən) Land set aside by the government for the American Indians (p. 56)

Resign (ri zīn´) To give up an office or job (p. 309)

Resistance (re zis´ təns) An act of opposing something (p. 252)

Resolution (rez ə lü´ shən) An expression of opinion or intent voted on by a group (p. 10)

Resource (ri sôrs´) A thing of value, often found in nature, that can be used to do or make something (p. 10)

Restore (ri stôr´) To put something back or give something back to its owner (p. 202)

Retail (rē´ tāl) Relating to the buying and selling of goods (p. 93)

Reunification (rē yü nə fə kā´ shən) Joining together as one country again (p. 347)

Revenge (ri venj´) The act of getting back at someone for some wrongdoing (p. 232)

Revise (ri vīz´) To make changes, especially to a document (p. 139)

Revolt (ri vōlt´) A rebellion (p. 15)

Revolution (rev ə lü´ shən) The act of overthrowing and replacing a government (p. 6)

Riot (rī´ ət) A violent public disturbance (p. 277)

Rival (rī´ vəl) A well-matched opponent (p. 306)

Ruling (rü´ ling) A decision of a court case (p. 19)

Running mate (run´ing māt) A candidate who runs for office with a candidate who is running for another position (p. 363)

Rural (rür´ əl) Relating to places well outside of cities; in the country (p. 285)

S

Saloon (sə lün´) A public building where people gathered to drink or gamble (p. 52)

Sanction (sangk´ shən) An action taken to force a country to do something (p. 337)

Sanitation (san ə tā´ shən) The act of disposing of waste and keeping areas clean (p. 95)

Scalawag (skal´ ə wag) A white Southerner who controlled the new politicians who had little government knowledge (p. 33)

Scandal (skan´ dl) A disgraceful event (p. 39)

Scourge (skėrj) Widespread pain or distress (p. 339)

Security (si kyùr´ ə tē) Safety (p. 225)

Segregate (seg´ rə gāt) To separate by race (p. 36)

Settlement (set´ l mənt) A place or region newly settled (p. xxiv)

Share (shâr) A certificate bought from a stock company that represents a certain part of ownership of the company (p. 183)

Sharecropper (shâr´ krop ər) A farmer who pays some of his or her crops to a landowner as rent (p. 34)

Skyscraper (skī´ skrā pər) A tall building (p. 68)

Slaughter (slò´ tər) To kill animals for food and other products (p. 75)

Slavery (slā´ vər ē) Forcing a person or group to work without pay or rights (p. 3)

Slave state (slāv stāt) A state that could practice slavery (p. 14)

Slum (slum) A run-down urban area often without electricity or indoor plumbing (p. 95)

Sod (sod) Thickly matted grass and roots (p. 53)

Solo (sō´ lō) Done by one person (p. 182)

Solution (sə lü´ shən) The answer to a problem (p. 169)

Soup house (süp hous) A place where the poor could get food (p. 183)

Speakeasy (spēk´ ē zē) A place where liquor was sold illegally during Prohibition (p. 180)

Speaker of the House (spē´ kər ov thə hous) Leader of House of Representatives (p. 361)

Specialize (spesh´ ə līz) To make and sell goods or services in one or two areas of business (p. 85)

Spectator (spek´ tā tər) One who watches an event (p. 94)

Spiritual (spir´ ə chü əl) A religious song (p. 177)

Spoils system (spoilz sis´ təm) The practice of giving government jobs to loyal supporters (p. 15)

Stabilize (stā´ bə līz) To keep from changing (p. 198)

Stagecoach (stāj′ kōch) A horse-drawn coach that was used for transporting people or mail (p. 47)

Stampede (stam pēd′) A wild rush of animals (p. 52)

Standstill (stand′ stil) Something that is not changing or improving (p. 156)

Steerage (stir′ ij) A part of a ship for passengers paying the lowest fare (p. 88)

Stock market (stok mär′ kit) A market for the buying and selling of company stock (p. 182)

Strategic (strə tē′ jik) Important or helpful in carrying out a plan (p. 307)

Streetcar (strēt′ kär) A horse-drawn or electric carriage that rides on rails and is used for transportation (p. 93)

Strike (strīk) The act of stopping work to get better pay and working conditions (p. 109)

Strikebreaker (strīk′ brā kər) A worker used to replace a striking union worker (p. 110)

Stronghold (strȯng′ hōld) A place, such as a military base, that is well-protected from attack (p. 5)

Submarine (sub′ mə rēn) A ship that can travel underwater (p. 153)

Suborbital (sub ȯr′ bə təl) Not out of Earth's atmosphere (p. 271)

Subpoena (sə pē nə) A court order (p. 310)

Suburb (sub′ ėrb) A community built outside of a city (p. 173)

Suffrage (suf′ rij) The right to vote (p. 35)

Summit (sum′it) A meeting held between or among world leaders (p. 347)

Supreme (sə prēm′) To the highest degree (p. 9)

Surge (sėrj) To rise swiftly (p. 329)

Surplus (sėr′ pləs) An extra amount of something (p. 198)

Suspension bridge (sə spen′ shən brij) A large bridge supported by wires or chains attached to tall towers (p. 68)

Symphony (sim′ fə nē) A long, complex musical piece (p. 177)

Synagogue (sin′ ə gȯg) A Jewish place of worship (p. 220)

T

Tactic (tak′ tik) A method of doing something (p. 278)

Taliban (tal′ i ban) The group that controlled the government of Afghanistan (p. 378)

Tariff (tar′ if) A tax on goods leaving or entering some place (p. 15)

Tax evasion (taks i vā′ zhən) Failing to pay one's taxes (p. 310)

Technology (tek nol′ ə jē) The use of science to create new machines or other advances

Telecommunications (tel′ ə kə myü nə kā′ shən) The transfer of information over long distances using such things as telephone lines, radio waves, or satellites (p. 386)

Telegraph (tel′ ə graf) A device that uses coded signals to send communications over a wire (p. 17)

Tenant farmer (ten′ ənt fär′ mər) A farmer who pays rent to a landowner for use of the land (p. 34)

Tenement (ten′ ə mənt) A cheaply made building divided into apartments (p. 95)

Tension (ten′ shən) Uncomfortable feelings toward another person or group (p. 18)

Territory (ter′ ə tȯr ē) Land belonging to a country or government (p. 10)

Terrorism (ter′ ə riz əm) Planned violence by individuals or groups against civilians for political reasons; people who commit terrorism are called terrorists (p. 362)

Terrorist (ter′ ər ist) A group or individual who uses violence to make others give in to its demands (p. 320)

Tobacco (tə bak′ ō) A plant that some people smoke or chew (p. 35)

Torpedo (tȯr pē′ dō) A self-powered bomb that is shot from a tube of a submarine or other ship (p. 153)

Traditional (trə dish′ ə nəl) The usual way of doing things (p. 205)

Traitor (trā′ tər) Someone who turns against his or her own country (p. 7)

a	hat	e	let	ī	ice	ȯ	order	ú	put	sh	she		a	in about
ā	age	ē	equal	o	hot	oi	oil	ü	rule	th	thin	ə	e	in taken
ä	far	ėr	term	ō	open	ou	out	ŦH	then		i	in pencil
â	care	i	it	ȯ	saw	u	cup	ng	long	zh	measure		o	in lemon
													u	in circus

Transcontinental (tran skon tə nen′ tl) Extending across a continent (p. 47)

Treaty (trē′ tē) An agreement to end fighting (p. 5)

Trolley (trol′ ē) A carriage that rides on rails and is used for transportation (p. 93)

Trust company (trust kum′ pə nē) A large, powerful company that often is a monopoly (p. 74)

Typesetting (tīp′ set ing) The methods used to prepare type to be printed (p. 76)

U

Underestimate (un dər es′ tə māt) To guess the size or importance of something as being less than it is (p. 230)

Unemployment (un em ploi′ mənt) The state of not having work (p. 16)

Urban (ėr′ bən) Related to the city (p. 85)

V

Ventilation (ven′ tl ā′ shən) The process of circulating fresh air in an enclosed area (p. 96)

Vertical combination (vėr′ tə kəl kom bi nā′ shən) A kind of business organization that controls each step in making something (p. 73)

Veto (vē′ tō) The power given to the president to turn down a bill (p. 28)

Violence (vī′ ə l) Rough or harmful action (p. 39)

Voyage (voi′ ij) A trip, especially by sea (p. 2)

W

Wagon train (wag′ ən trān) A large number of wagons traveling together (p. 47)

Weapons of mass destruction (wep′ əns ov mas di struk′ shən) Weapons that cause death on a large scale (p. 379)

Western Hemisphere (wes′ tərn hem′ ə sfir) The land and oceans around North and South America (p. 15)

White-collar (wīt kol′ ər) A name used to describe office workers and professionals (p. 245)

Windmill (wind′ mil) A wind-powered device used to pump water from a well (p. 54)

Wiretap (wīr′ tap) A device used to listen in on phone conversations (p. 309)

Index

Clinton, Hillary Rodham, 356, 361
Clinton, William, 31, 346, 354–65, 369–70
Coal, 67, 82
    miners, 133
Cochise, 58
Cochrane, Elizabeth Jane, 97
Cody, William F., 55
Cold war, 251, 244, 251–55, 265, 269, 306, 308,
    335, 340–41
    defined, 251
Colfax, Schuyler, 104
Collapse defined, 303
Collective bargaining, 203
    defined, 203
Colony defined, 3
Colorado, 50, 63
Colored Farmers Alliance, 112
Columbia, 137–38
    space shuttle, 385, 389
Comanche, 55, 57
Combat defined, 230
Commander defined, 6
Commercial defined, 137
Committee to Re-elect the President (CREEP), 309
Commonwealth defined, 348
Commonwealth of Independent States, 348–50,
    369–70
Communication defined, 17; *See also* Telegraph;
    Telephone
Communism, 182–83, 216–17, 251–55, 259–60,
    272, 281, 299, 338, 340–41, 346–50, 369
    in Asia, 251–52, 256, 258–60, 267, 269, 283–85
Communist defined, 180
Compete defined, 125
Composers, 177, 179
    defined, 177
Compromise defined, 8
Computers, 255, 314, 386
Concentration camps, 221, 237, 241
Confederacy defined, 20
Conference defined, 161
Conflict defined, 12
Congress defined, 6
Congress of Industrial Organizations (CIO),
    205–06, 211
Congress of Racial Equality (CORE), 277, 281
Connally, John, 280
Connecticut, 55, 59, 62, 65–66, 87, 146, 247
Conquer defined, 3
Conservation
    defined, 78
    programs, 78, 136, 141, 142, 145, 146, 285
Conservative defined, 282

Conspiracy defined, 309
Constitutional defined, 30
Consumer goods defined, 157
Containment Policy, 252, 255
    defined, 252
Continent defined, 2
Contract defined, 103
Contract With America, 361, 369–70
Contra Scandal, 335, 344
Controversial defined, 292
Convention defined, 6
Conventional Forces in Europe Treaty (CFE), 347
Conventional defined, 347
Coolidge, Calvin, 170–73, 184, 187–88, 191
Corporation, 72–74, 81–83, 113, 121
    defined, 72
Corruption, 33, 39, 41, 43. *See also* Political
    corruption
    defined, 33
Cotton,
    importance of, 35–36
Counterattack defined, 233
Counterculture, 289–90
    defined, 289
Cowhand, 50, 52, 54, 63, 121
    defined, 50
Cox, Archibald, 309–10, 312
Crazy Horse, 57
Credit, 196, 211, 261
Credit cards, 386
Crédit Mobilier Company, 104
Crédit Mobilier Scandal, 103–04, 117–18
Crime, 183, 187, 339, 343
Crisis defined, 198
Criticize defined, 72
Crook, George, 58
Crude oil defined, 313
Cuba, 125–29, 132, 145, 146, 191, 359, 389
Missile Crisis, 275–76, 295–96, 299
Cullen, Countee, 180
Culture, xxiv, 179–81, 186, 189
    defined, xxiv
Custer, George Armstrong, 57–58, 63–64
Custer's Last Stand, 57–70
Czechoslovakia, 161, 219–20, 341, 349

D

Daladier, Edouard, 220, 222
Dallas (Texas), 280, 299
Dams, 136, 200
Dance, 179, 187
Danzig (Germany), 221

North Pole, 140
North Vietnam, 303–05, 325
Norway and Norwegians, 223, 237, 241
    immigrants, 88
Nuclear war, 259, 265
    defined, 259
Nuclear weapons, 336, 343, 379
Nylon, 209

O

Oath defined, 25
O'Connor, Sandra Day, 330, 332, 343–44
Offensive defined, 257
Office of Homeland Security, 376
Oglala Sioux, 58
Oil, 71–74, 81–83, 85, 100, 121, 351, 353
Oil Creek, 71
Okinawa, 234
Oklahoma, 29
Oklahoma City (Oklahoma), 362, 364
Old immigrants, 88
Olympic Games, 151, 208, 213
Omaha (Nebraska), 25, 49
Omnibus Violent Crime Control and Prevention
    Act, 355–56
Open Door Policy, 130, 131, 137, 145, 191, 227,
    229
Oregon, 25
Organization of Petroleum Exporting Countries
    (OPEC), 313, 315, 327, 365
Organize defined, 9
Orlando, Vittorio, 161
Oswald, Lee Harvey, 280–81
Otis, Elisha G., 77
Overpopulation, 389
Overproduction defined, 196
Override defined, 30
Overturn defined, 205
Owens, Jesse, 208–09

P

Pahlavi, Shah Mohammad Reza, 321
Palace of Versailles, 161, 168
Palestine, 249, 320
Palestine Liberation Organization (PLO), 320, 334,
    357
Palmer, A. Mitchell, 183
Palmer Raids, 183
Panama Canal, 137–38, 145, 146, 147, 191, 226,
    318
Panama (Republic of Columbia), 137–38

Paris Peace
    Accords, 304–05
    Conference, 161, 165, 168
Parks, Rosa, 261, 265, 268
Patriot Act, 375–77, 391
Patriotic defined, 230
Patriotism, 375, 391
    dcfined, 375
Patton, George, 233
Peace Corps, 280, 295–96
Pearl Harbor, 214, 227–29, 237–39, 241
Peary, Robert E., 140
Pennsylvania, 133
Pentagon building, 374, 376–77, 391
People's Party. *See* Populist Party
People's Republic of China, 306
Perestroika, 348, 350
    defined, 348
Perkins, Frances, 203, 211–12
Permanent defined, 9
Perot, Ross, 354, 363–64
Persecute defined, 358
Pershing, John J., 158–59, 167
Persian Gulf War, 334, 346, 351–53, 370, 379
Pesticides, 386
Petroleum, 66–67, 71–72, 81–83, 121
    defined, 67
Philadelphia (Pennsylvania), 95, 157, 388
Philippine Islands, 125–30, 132, 145, 146, 191,
    228–30, 234
Phnom Penh, 303
Phonographs, 76, 81–82
    defined, 76
Pinchback, Pinckney B. S., 36
Pinchot, Gifford, 136
Pioneer defined, 8
Pittsburgh (Pennsylvania), 71, 85, 87, 94
Plains Indians, 29, 55–58, 63–65
Plantation, 14, 33–35
    defined, 14
Plastics, 232
Plessy, Homer, 92
Plessy v. Ferguson, 92, 101
Poe, Edgar Allan, 249, 253
Poland and Polish, 161, 163, 341, 349
    immigrants, 88, 99, 121
    World War II and, 219, 221–23, 237, 241
Policy defined, 12
Polio, 199, 233, 293
Polish Corridor, 221
Political,
    cartoons, 105, 117–19, 121, 298
    corruption, 102–09, 117, 121, 134

Resolution defined, 10
Resource defined, 10
Retail defined, 93
Reunification defined, 39
Revenge defined, 232
Revise defined, 139
Revolt, 15, 137–38
    defined, 15
Revolution defined, 6
Rice, 35, 217
Rich, Adrienne, 115
Richardson, Elliot, 309–10
Riis, Jacob, 96
Riots, 157, 277, 279, 291, 365
    defined, 277
Rival defined, 306
Roads, 36
Roaring Twenties, 170–91
Rockefeller, John D., 67, 72–74, 81–83, 121, 134
Rockets, 165
Rocky Mountains, 25, 50, 63–65
Roebling, Emily and John, 69
Rome (Italy), 232, 237, 334
Romero, Oscar, Archbishop, 318
Roosevelt Corollary, 137
Roosevelt, Eleanor, 217
Roosevelt, Franklin Delano, 194, 198–201, 204–05,
    211–13, 214, 217–18, 223, 225, 227–28, 231,
    233–34, 236–38, 241, 246, 293
Roosevelt, Theodore, 78, 122, 134, 135, 137,
    132–43, 145–47, 154, 172, 191
"Rosie the Riveter," 228
Rough Riders, 137, 138
Rovers, 289
Royal Air Force (RAF), 224
Ruby, Jack, 280
Ruckelshaus, William, 310
Ruling defined, 19
Running mate defined, 363
Rural defined, 285
Russia and Russians, 137, 265, 348–50, 357, 360,
    369–70. *See also* Soviet Union
    Communism and, 182–83
    immigrants, 88, 99, 121
    World War I and, 149, 151, 168
Russian Federation, 349
Rust Belt, 388–89
Ruth, Babe, 184

S

Sacramento (California), 25, 49
Sadat, Anwar, 319–20, 334

Saigon (South Vietnam), 304–05
St. Louis (Missouri), 25
Salk, Jonas E., 293
Salt Lake City (Utah), 85
Salvation Army, 96, 99
Sampson, William, 137
San Antonio (Texas), 64
Sanction defined, 337
San Francisco (California), 85, 138, 210, 248,
    267–68, 299
Sanitation, 95, 99–100
    defined, 95
San Juan Hill, 137, 145
Santiago harbor, 137
Santo Domingo, 137
Sarajevo, 149–50, 167, 168
Satellites, 312, 265, 267–68, 289, 299, 386
Saturday Night Massacre, 310
Saudi Arabia, 351–52, 369
Sauk and Fox, 151
Scalawag, 33, 37, 39, 43
    defined, 33
Scandal, 39, 172, 187–88, 191. *See also* Contra
    Scandal; Crédit Mobilier Scandal; Teapot Dome;
    Watergate Scandal; Whiskey Ring Scandal
    defined, 39
Schmeling, Max, 207, 212
Schwarzkopf, Norman, 352
Scourge defined, 339
Sears, Richard W., 70
Second Great Removal, 29
Second New Deal, 202–06
Security Council, 248
Security defined, 225
Segregate defined, 36
Segregation, 36–37, 90–92, 260–62, 267, 277–78,
    299. *See also* Apartheid
Selective Service, 158
Selective Training and Service Act, 225–26
Senate, 31, 98, 113, 163, 167
Seoul (South Korea), 257
Serbia, 149–52, 161, 168
Servicemen's Readjustment Act, 246
Settlement defined, xxiv
Settlement houses, 111
Seward, William, 28
17th Amendment, 149, 152, 167
Seventh Cavalry, 60–61, 63–64
Seymour, Horatio, 32, 43
Share defined, 183
Sharecroppers, 34, 37, 197
    defined, 34
Shawnees, 29

Acknowledgements

Acknowledgment is made for permission to reprint and record the following copyrighted material.

Page 62: Excerpt from *China Men* by Maxine Hong Kingston. Copyright © 1977, 1978, 1979, 1980 by Maxine Hong Kingston. Reprinted by permission of Alfred A. Knopf, a division of Random House, Inc.

Page 186: Excerpt from article by James Weldon Johnson in *Harper's Magazine,* 1928. Used by permission by the Estate of James Weldon Johnson.

Page 210: Excerpt from "Bread Lines," by Hugo Johanson, *The Atlantic Monthly,* 1936. Reproduced with permission of *The Atlantic Monthly*.

Page 242: Quote reprinted with permission of Cesar E. Chavez Foundation.

Page 266: Excerpt from *The Long Shadow of Little Rock* by Daisy Bates. Reprinted by permission of The University of Arkansas Press. Copyright © 1987 by Daisy Bates.

Page 300: From poem "On the Pulse of Morning" by Maya Angelou, copyright © 1993 by Maya Angelou. Used by permission of Random House, Inc.

Page 342: Excerpt from *Vital Speeches of the Day,* "Women in America Shooting for the Stars: As We See Ourselves So Do We Act" by Stella Guerra, September 15, 1986.

Page 368: Excerpt from *Vital Speeches of the Day,* "Favor Positive Themes" by Luis W. Morales, July 15, 1996.

Other Acknowledgments

Page 42: Excerpt from W. E. B. DuBois letter to student, 1905, as appeared in *A Documentary History of the Negro People in the United States,* by Herbert Aptheker. (Public Domain)

Page 80: Excerpt from *History of the Later Years of the Hawaiian Monarchy,* by W. D. Alexander, 1896. (Public Domain)

Pages 450–451: From *The World Almanac and Book of Facts 2005,* pages 43, 571–572; © 2005 World Almanac Education Group, a WRC Media Inc. company.

Image Credits

Front Matter

Page 1, © Nancy Carter/North Wind Pictures Archives; Page 2, © The Granger Collection, New York; Page 5, © White House Historical Association; Pages 7, 9, 11, 12, © The Granger Collection, New York; Page 13 © Bettman/Corbis; Page 14 © Corbis; Pages 19, 21, © The Granger Collection, New York

Unit 1 Opener

© The Granger Collection, New York

Chapter 1

Page 25, © Bettmann/Corbis; Pages 26, 30, © The Granger Collection, New York; Page 33, © Bettmann/Corbis; Page 36, © Underwood Photo Archives; Page 37, © J.C. Coovert/Library of Congress; Page 38, © Library of Congress; Page 39, © The Granger Collection, New York; Page 42, © Brown Brothers

Chapter 2

Page 47, © Underwood & Underwood/Corbis; Page 48, © Union Pacific Historical Collection; Page 51, © Brown Brothers; Page 55, © The Granger Collection, New York; Pages 57, 59, © Bettmann/Corbis; Page 60 (both), © The Granger Collection, New York

Chapter 3

Pages 67, 69, © Brown Brothers; Pages 71, 72, © Bettmann/Corbis; Pages 75, 76, © Culver Pictures; Page 77, © The Granger Collection, New York; Pages 79, 80, © The Granger Collection, New York

Chapter 4

Page 86, © Brown Brothers; Page 87, © Bettmann/ Corbis; Page 88, © Culver Pictures; Page 89, © Bettmann/Corbis; Page 93, © Brown Brothers; Pages 95, 97, © Bettmann/Corbis; Page 98, Corbis

Chapter 5

Page 103, © Culver Pictures; Page 106, © The Granger Collection, New York; Page 108, © PHOTODISC; Page 109, © Bettmann/ Corbis; Pages 110, 111, 114, © The Granger Collection, New York

Unit 2 Opener

© Corbis

Chapter 6

Page 126, © The Granger Collection, New York; Page 128, © Corbis; Pages 133, 138, © Brown Brothers; Page 140, © The Granger Collection, New York; Page 142, © Culver Pictures; Page 144, © Brown Brothers

Chapter 7

Page 150, © Bettmann/Corbis; Page 151, © Culver Pictures; Pages 154, 157, © Bettmann/ Corbis; Page 158, © The Granger Collection, New York; Page 163, © Bettmann/Corbis; Page 164, © Stock Montage

Chapter 8

Page 172, © The Granger Collection, New York; Page 174, © Culver Pictures; Page 176, © Brown Brothers; Page 177, © Bettman/Corbis; Page 179, © Brown Brothers; Page 181, © Bettmann/ Corbis; Page 184, © Culver Pictures; Page 186, © Corbis

Unit 3 Opener

© Hulton Archive/Getty Images

Chapter 9

Page 195, © Seattle Post-Intelligencer Collection; Museum of History & Industry/Corbis; Page 200, © Corbis; Page 201, © Culver Pictures; Page 202, © Library of Congress, Prints & Photographs Division, WPA Poster Collection, [reproduction number LC-USZC2-5639]; Pages 202, 203, © AP/ Wide World Photos; Page 208 (both) © Bettmann/Corbis

Chapter 10

Page 216, © Stock Photo; Page 217, © The Granger Collection, New York; Page 219, © AP/ Wide World Photos; Page 220, © Corbis; Page 224, © AP/Wide World Photos; Page 228, © Bettmann/Corbis; Pages 234, © Owen/ Blackstar; Page 235, © Bettmann/Corbis

Unit 4 Opener

© Wally McNamee/Corbis

Chapter 11

Page 247, © Bettmann/Corbis; Pages 250, 252, 259, © AP/Wide World Photos; Page 261, © Stock Photo; Page 262 © Flip Schulke/ CORBIS; Pages 263, 264, © Bettmann/Corbis

Chapter 12

Page 271, © Stock Photo; Page 273, © Bettmann/ Corbis; Page 275, © AP/Wide World Photos; Page 278, © The Granger Collection, New York; Page 280, © Bettmann/ Corbis; Page 281, © Jim Pickerell/Black Star; Page 282, © Bettmann/ Corbis; Page 284, © Stock Photo; Page 286, © The Granger Collection, New York; Page 294, © Bettman/Corbis

Unit 5 Opener

© Brand X Pictures

Chapter 13

Page 304, © Bettmann/Corbis; Page 307, © AP/ Wide World Photos; Page 308, © Peter Dejong/ AP/Wide World Photos; Page 311, © AP/Wide World Photos; Page 314, © UPI/Corbis; Page 315, © SuperStock; Page 317, © AP/Wide World Photos; Page 319, © Stock Photo; Pages 322, 323, © AP/Wide World Photos

Chapter 14

Page 330, © AP/Wide World Photos; Page 331, © Stock Photo; Page 332, © Bettmann/Corbis; Page 336, © Ira Schwartz/AP/Wide World Photos; Pages 339, 340, © Stock Photo

Chapter 15

Pages 349, 352, © AP/Wide World Photos; Page 355, © Stock Photo; Page 358, © Bettmann/ Corbis; Page 362, © Eric Draper/AP/Wide World Photos; Page 368, © PHOTODISC

Chapter 16

Page 373, © Masatomo Kuriya/Corbis; Page 374, © Neville Elder/Corbis/Sygma; Page 375, © Time Life Pictures/Getty Images Editorial; Page 377, © Reuters/Corbis; Page 381, © Time Life Pictures/Getty Images Editorial; Page 382, © Lynsey Addario/Corbis; Page 383 (top), © Kevin Lamarque/Reuters/Corbis; Page 383 (bottom), © Justin Sullivan/Getty Images Editorial; Page 385, © NASA; 390, © Reuters/ Corbis; Pages 421-425, © White House Historical Association, except Kennedy © Bettmann/ Corbis, George W. Bush © Rick Patrick/Rick Patrick Photography